COGNITIVE THEORY

Volume 2

COGNITIVE THEORY
Volume 2

edited by

[N. John Castellan, Jr.
David B. Pisoni
George R. Potts]

 LAWRENCE ERLBAUM ASSOCIATES, PUBLISHERS

1977   Hillsdale, New Jersey

DISTRIBUTED BY THE HALSTED PRESS DIVISION OF

JOHN WILEY & SONS

New York   Toronto   London   Sydney

Copyright © 1977 by Lawrence Erlbaum Associates, Inc.
All rights reserved. No part of this book may be reproduced in
any form, by photostat, microform, retrieval system, or any other
means, without the prior written permission of the publisher.

Lawrence Erlbaum Associates, Inc., Publishers
62 Maria Drive
Hillsdale, New Jersey 07642

Distributed solely by Halsted Press Division
John Wiley & Sons, Inc., New York

Library of Congress Cataloging in Publication Data

Main entry under title:

Cognitive theory.

    Includes bibliographical references and indexes.
    1. Cognition.   2. Speech perception.
3. Judgment.   4. Memory.   I. Castellan, N. John.
II. Pisoni, David B.   III. Potts, George.
BF311.C553   153.4   74-14293
ISBN 0-470-99025-2

Printed in the United States of America

Contents

Preface

This book contains chapters based on papers presented as part of the Eighth Annual Indiana Cognitive/Mathematical Psychology Conference held at Indiana University in April, 1975. As noted in the Preface to Volume 1, the content of these annual conferences has changed over the years, reflecting, we hope, the dynamic nature of modern cognitive–mathematical–theoretical psychology. For the psychologist, the middle years of the 1970s are exciting: some recent developments have led to the discard of some conceptions of the last generation, and the rediscovery and embracing of even older conceptions. At the same time, we see the purview of psychology increasing and the applications and implications of research and theory expanding at a high rate. It is this spirit of change and growth that we have tried to capture in the chapters of this volume.

The contributors to the Conference were requested to emphasize the relatively broad theoretical significance of their work, to incorporate the work of others, and—if they were willing—to speculate about future developments. With one exception, each of the contributions to this book was presented at the Conference, and the authors were able to incorporate the collective feedback from all participants into the final drafts. (The exception is the contribution by Newport, who was not able to participate in person.)

As editors, we had the main responsibility of organizing the Conference and encouraging the authors in their efforts. In this work we had support from the faculty of the Psychology Department at Indiana University. Frank Restle, Harold Lindman, and Richard Shiffrin, who have been involved in most of the earlier Conferences, continued to play a major role in the success of the Annual Meeting. We also benefited from the counsel of Charles Kalme, who, along with George Potts, spent the year as a Fellow in the Cognitive Institute at Indiana University. Karlene Ball and Judy Hupp were responsible for attending to the multitude of small but absolutely essential details in organizing and running the Conference. Finally, we wish to thank Lawrence Erlbaum, whose encouragement and gentle prodding ensured completion of the book.

Part I

PROBLEM SOLVING

One of the classic questions in the study of cognitive processes concerns the form in which information is stored in memory. Frequently, especially in the psycholinguistic literature, specification of the structure of stored information is viewed as an end in itself. It should be clear, however, that the nature of the stored representation of information will have important effects on what people can and will do with such information. The chapters in this section focus on the nature of the internal representation of a problem and the effect that this representation has on the process of problem solving.

In the first two chapters of this section it is strongly suggested that a person's interpretation or representation of a problem is not dictated by the formal problem structure. Reed observed a surprising lack of transfer between two problems (the missionary–cannibal and jealous husbands- problems) which are very similar in formal structure; prior solution of one problem did not significantly affect the solution of the other. In order for transfer to be observed, it was necessary to point out explicitly the similarity between the two problems and to suggest that people make use of their original solution in solving the second problem. A reasonable interpretation of this result is that, although the two problems were formally very similar, the internal representations of the two problems were quite different and hence the formal relation between the problems was not recognized.

Using a set of "monster problems," Hayes and Simon go a step farther by showing that, even among formally identical (isomorphic) problems, changes in wording of the task lead to substantial differences in the notation people use spontaneously to describe their solutions. In addition, such changes in wording were found to alter the difficulty of the problem by a factor or two.

In both of these chapters the problem-solving situation is described in terms of an initial situation or initial internal representation, a goal, and a set of operations that enable one to alter the initial situation. Solution of a problem consists of finding a sequence of operators that will transform the initial situation into the goal. One has solved the problem when one successfully reaches the goal state. This characterization of problem solving is typical of most current approaches. In the final chapter of the section, Greeno argues that this characterization is not sufficient because it ignores the question of what it means to "understand" a problem.

The question of what it means to "understand," ignored for so long in the experimental literature, has come to play a key role in the "new cognitive psychology." Drawing heavily on recent work in the area of psycholinguistics and text processing, Greeno contends that the key to understanding in problem solving lies in the nature of the internal representation of the problem. He presents three criteria by which one may judge the degree to which good understanding of a problem has been achieved, and then describes in detail a model of how students attack the problem of proving theorems in geometry. Greeno concludes by evaluating the model in terms of his three criteria for good understanding. Regardless of whether one agrees with Greeno's model or his specific three criteria for good understanding, one should consider seriously the implications of his distinction between simply reaching a goal state and solving a problem with understanding.

1

Facilitation of Problem Solving

Stephen K. Reed

Case Western Reserve University

My interests in problem solving are primarily concerned with the facilitation of problem solving. I am interested in learning what kind of information is useful in helping a person solve a problem. I am particularly interested in how the structure of the task environment may determine the potential usefulness of information.

The term "task environment" is often associated with the work of Newell and Simon and my own research has been within the framework of their theoretical approach (Newell & Simon, 1972). This approach views the problem solver as progressing from the initial state of a problem to a goal state by applying a sequence of operators. For example, a logic problem might consist of the statement $(\sim P \cdot Q) \, v \, (P \cdot \sim P)$ as the initial state and the statement Q as the goal state. The problem would be solved by finding a sequence of operators that would transform the initial statement into the goal statement. The operators in this case consist of rules of logic which can be used to transform logical statements. The problem states are all the possible logical statements that can be derived by applying sequences of rules to the initial statement.

I will use the term "task environment" to refer to the space of legal problem states. The task environment should therefore show all the operators which legally apply to each problem state and the new problem states which result from the application of the operators. The task environment has an important role in Newell and Simon's (1972) theory because it is a major determinant of the problem space through which a subject searches in attempting to solve a problem. Although a task environment can be very large, I have chosen to study a problem with a reasonably small number of problem states. The problem is the missionary–cannibal task which can be stated as follows:

> Three missionaries and three cannibals having to cross a river at a ferry, find a boat but the boat is so small that is can contain no more than two persons. If the missionaries on

either bank of the river, or in the boat, are outnumbered at any time by cannibals, the cannibals will eat the missionaries. Find the simplest schedule of crossings that will permit all the missionaries and cannibals to cross the river safely. It is assumed that all passengers on the boat unboard before the next trip and at least one person has to be in the boat for each crossing.

Figure 1 shows the space of legal moves for this problem, each state being described by four numbers. The first number is the number of missionaries on the left (initial) bank; the second number, the number of cannibals on the left bank; the third number, the number of missionaries on the right bank; and the fourth number, the number of cannibals on the right bank. The pairs of numbers connecting the problem states show how many missionaries (first number) and how many cannibals (second number) are transferred in the boat. The asterisk shows the location of the boat. State B is the initial state in which all missionaries, cannibals, and the boat are on the left bank and state O is the goal state in which all missionaries, cannibals, and the boat are on the right bank. As can be seen in Fig. 1, there are very few legal moves available at each problem state.

We have used the missionary–cannibal task to study the usefulness of analogy and subgoals in problem solving. The first section of this chapter summarizes my research with Ernst and Banerji on analogy, which explored the amount of transfer between the missionary–cannibal problem and the jealous husbands problem. We were interested in whether the similarity of the two task environments would facilitate transfer from one problem to the other. The second section considers the effectiveness of subgoals as it relates to various characteristics of the task environment, such as the size of the task environment or the distance of a subgoal from the initial state. The third section discusses a computer simulation model which Professor Herbert Simon and I have recently developed in an attempt to predict how subjects progress through a problem space in solving a more complicated version of the missionary–cannibal task. One of the issues raised here is how does the task environment and a subject's strategies combine to determine the problem space in which a subject searches for a solution. The fourth section presents an overview of the current status of this research.

ANALOGY

One source of useful information in solving a problem is analogy—using the previously attained solution of a similar problem (Newell & Simon, 1972). Since most tests in mathematics courses contain problems that are similar, but not identical to homework problems, a student's score should be partially determined by how well he or she can make use of analogy. Although it seems intuitively reasonable that we often use analogy in solving problems, we know

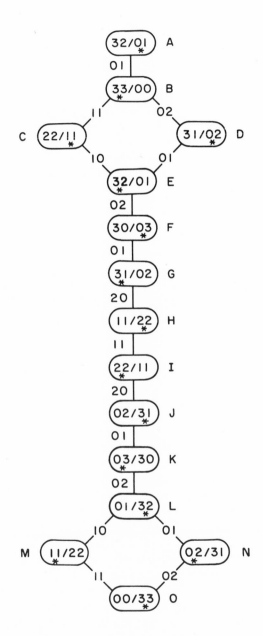

FIG. 1 Problem space of legal moves for the three missionary–three cannibal problem.

very little about the conditions that determine whether it can be successfully used.

A prerequisite for studying the degree of transfer between two problems is to show how the problems are similar. The missionary—cannibal problem and the jealous husbands problem satisfy this criterion because their similarity can be formally defined. The jealous husbands problem can be stated as follows:

> Three jealous husbands and their wives having to cross a river at a ferry find a boat but the boat is so small that it can contain no more than two persons. Find the simplest schedule for crossings that will permit all six people to cross the river so that none of the women shall be left in the company with any of the men, unless her husband is present. It is assumed that all passengers on the boat unboard before the next trip, and at least one person has to be in the boat for each crossing.

The problem space for the jealous husbands problem is identical to the problem space for the missionary—cannibal problem if (1) husbands are substituted for missionaries, (2) wives are sustituted for cannibals, and (3) husbands and wives are paired as couples. If only the first two constraints applied, the two problems would be isomorphic, as discussed by Hayes and Simon for a different set of problems (this volume). However, the third constraint makes the relationship between the two problem spaces a homomorphic one, defined by a many-to-one mapping from the jealous husbands problem to the missionary—cannibal problem. Thus, moving two particular husbands implies a unique move in the missionary—cannibal problem (moving two missionaries), but moving two missionaries does not imply a unique move because only certain husbands may be moveable in order to preserve the pairing between husbands and wives. Although all missionaries are equivalent and all cannibals are equivalent, husbands and wives have their separate identities.

In order to study whether there would be significant transfer between the two problems, we asked our subjects to solve both problems (Reed, Ernst, & Banerji, 1974). Pennies were used to represent cannibals, dimes were used to represent missionaries, and three different-colored wooden figures were used to represent the three couples. Subjects (college students) moved the markers across a table and we recorded their legal moves, illegal moves, and solution time.

The first experiment tested whether the prior solution of one of the problems would help subjects solve the other problem when they were not told that the two problems were related. Half of the subjects solved the missionary—cannibal problem first and half of the subjects solved the jealous husbands problem first. Table 1 shows the total time, the total number of moves, and amount of transfer when subjects solved the missionary—cannibal problem (MC) and jealous husbands problem (JH). The results indicated that there was no significant transfer between the two problems, since the prior solution of one problem did not greatly help subjects in solving the other problem. These findings were somewhat surprising since we thought the close similarity of the two problems would result in some transfer, even if subjects were not told there was a relationship.

TABLE 1

Degree of Improvement: Analogy and Subgoals

A. Analogy Experiment

Experiment	Problem	Total time (sec)			Total moves		
		Trial 1	Trial 2	Improvement (%)	Trial 1	Trial 2	Improvement (%)
Relation not specified	MC	252	230	8	18.3	17.3	5
	JH	355	317	11	19.6	19.8	0
Learning	MC	246	184	25	18.0	16.5	8
	JH	403	222	45**	19.1	15.8	17
Relation specified	MC	283	162	43**	17.8	15.5	13
	JH	304	301	1	17.3	16.5	5

B. Subgoal Experiment

Experiment	Problem	Time	Improvement (%)	Legal moves	Improvement (%)	Illegal moves	Improvement (%)
5MC	No subgoal	883	–	27.6	–	5.5	–
	Subgoal L	437	51**	20.3	36**	3.7	33*
3MC	No subgoal	361	–	20.0	–	4.1	–
	Subgoal F	297	18	18.8	6	3.5	15
	Subgoal K	329	9	20.2	0	4.1	0

*significant at the $p < .05$ level.
**significant at the $p < .01$ level.

An obvious follow-up experiment would be to test whether transfer would occur if subjects were informed of the relation between the two problems. However, we first wanted to make sure that transfer would occur between two identical problems, that is, that subjects would show a significant improvement in resolving the same problem. There were two groups of subjects in the learning experiment. One group solved the missionary–cannibal problem twice and one group solved the jealous husbands problem twice. There was a 25% reduction in solution time for the missionary–cannibal problem and a 45% reduction for the jealous husbands problem when solving the problem for the second time.

Our third experiment examined whether transfer would occur between two similar problems if subjects were told the correspondence between the two problems and were encouraged to make use of their solution to the first problem. Informing subjects about the relationship between the two problems resulted in asymmetrical transfer: Solving the jealous husbands problem helped subjects solve the missionary–cannibal problem, but solving the missionary–cannibal problem first did not help subjects solve the jealous husbands problem (see Table 1).

The results of the three experiments suggest that analogy is not used as readily as we may have believed. A high degree of similarity between two task environments is not a sufficient condition for transfer between two problems. Perhaps this is not surprising if we consider possible conditions for analogy to be useful. First, subjects must recognize that the current problem is analogous to a previously solved problem. Second, they must be able to remember something about how they solved the analogous problem. Third, they must be able to translate the previous solution into operations that apply to the current problem. Fourth, the translation must either define a unique operation or reduce the number of operations that would otherwise have to be considered. And finally, the total time to retrieve, translate, and use analogous information to find an operator should be less than the total time to find the same operator without using information from a previous problem.

Two aspects of this research are consistent with the asymmetrical transfer found in Experiment III. The results of Experiment II revealed that subjects showed more transfer in their second attempt at the jealous husbands problem than in their second attempt at the missionary–cannibal problem. If subjects have a better memory for the solution of the jealous husbands problem, transfer should be best from the jealous husbands problem to the missionary–cannibal problem as found in Experiment III. However, the translation between the two problems is also consistent with these results. The solution of the jealous husbands problem defines a unique solution for the missionary–cannibal problem, but the solution of the missionary–cannibal problem does not define a unique solution to the jealous husbands problem because of the one-to-many mapping between the two task environments.

Although further research on analogy might resolve the reasons for the asymmetrical transfer, further study of analogy might be easier if we first learned about more fundamental issues in problem solving, such as memory for problem solutions and the effectiveness of subgoals. If subjects have only a limited memory for how they solved a problem (as suggested by verbal reports collected in Experiment III), then transfer effects that do occur may depend on memory for a few important subgoals. Our next project sought to learn more about how the structure of the task environment might influence the effectiveness of a subgoal.

SUBGOALS

I will use the word "subgoal" to refer to a problem state that subjects are told they must reach in order to solve the problem. The advantage of giving subjects an intermediate problem state is that it can theoretically reduce the size of the problem space in which subjects search for a solution (cf. Newell & Simon, 1972; Wickelgren, 1974). Knowing a problem state is on a correct solution path might prevent subjects from making a sequence of moves that would lead to a very inefficient solution or perhaps no solution at all. This analysis suggests that the size of the task environment should influence the effectiveness of a subgoal. If the task environment is already small and legal moves are constrained to occur on the solution path, as is shown in Fig. 1, a subgoal might not be very useful.

Let us, therefore, consider a different version of the missionary–cannibal task in which there are five missionaries (instead of three), five cannibals, and a boat which can hold three people. We will refer to this version as the 5MC problem and to the previous version as the 3MC problem. The problem space for the 5MC problem is shown in Fig. 2 (the symbols are interpreted the same as in Fig. 1). Both problems can be solved in eleven moves and there are some similarities in the two solutions. However, the problem space for the 5MC problem is larger and includes blind alleys such as States J and K. Giving subjects a subgoal for the 5MC problem might prevent them from entering a blind alley or repeating a sequence of legal moves that does not bring them closer to the goal.

In order to test the hypothesis that a subgoal would be more effective for the 5MC problem than for the 3MC problem we used four groups of subjects in Experiment I (Reed & Abramson, 1976). The groups were differentiated by which problem they were given and whether they received a subgoal. State G (two cannibals across the river without the boat) was the subgoal for the 3MC problem and State L (three cannibals across the river without the boat) was the subgoal for the 5MC problem. Both subgoals can be reached in four moves.

The results indicated that the specification of a subgoal did not significantly improve total performance for either of the two problems. The only improvement that did occur was that subjects solving the 3MC problem reached the subgoal state significantly faster and in significantly fewer legal moves when they were given a subgoal. The lack of a subgoal effect for the 5MC problem contradicted our hypothesis, but was likely the result of a methodological

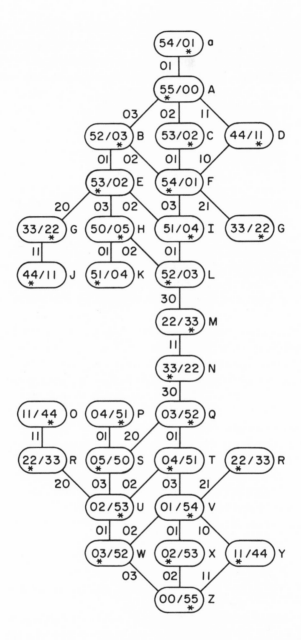

FIG. 2. Problem space of legal moves for the five missionary–five cannibal problem.

weakness which was corrected in Experiment II. Although there were 25 subjects in each group, only 10 solved the 5MC problem in the no-subgoal condition and only 13 solved the problem in the subgoal condition. The large number of nonsolvers, and the different number of nonsolvers in the two subgoal conditions, made it necessary to modify the procedure.

Experiment II repeated the two subgoal conditions for the 5MC problem but allowed subjects more time to solve the problem. The experimenter also encouraged a subject to think of a new move whenever he entered a problem state that he had previously reached. This change of procedure was successful, since all 50 subjects solved the problem within a 30-min time limit. The results clearly showed the usefulness of a subgoal. Not only did subjects reach the subgoal state faster when given a subgoal, but they significantly reduced the number of their legal moves, illegal moves, and solution time in solving the entire problem. Table 1 shows these results.

Another variable that we thought would influence the effectiveness of a subgoal is the distance of the subgoal from the initial problem state. We hypothesized that a subgoal relatively close to the initial state would be effective, but a subgoal farther away would likely not be effective. In order to investigate the effect of subgoal distance, we tested three groups of subjects in Experiment III. All groups solved the 3MC problem. One group was given State F (three cannibals across the river by themselves) as a subgoal and one group was given State K (three missionaries across the river by themselves) as a subgoal. State F can be reached in three moves from the starting point, whereas State K required eight moves (see Fig. 1). A control group was not given a subgoal. The results for State F replicated the results of Experiment I which used State G as a subgoal. The subgoal did not significantly affect total performance (see Table 1), but did significantly reduce the number of legal moves and the time to reach the subgoal state. In contrast, subgoal State K was ineffective in changing either total performance or performance prior to reaching the subgoal state.

The results of the three experiments suggest that both the size of the problem space and the distance of a subgoal can influence the effectiveness of a subgoal. Experiment II showed that giving subjects a subgoal significantly improved their total performance on the 5MC problem. Experiments I and III showed that giving subjects a subgoal in the 3MC problem only significantly improved their performance prior to the subgoal and this only occurred when the subgoal could be reached in three or four moves.

How do these findings relate to the transfer discussed in the previous section on analogy? The fact that the specification of a subgoal did not improve total performance on the 3MC problem makes it doubtful that memory for a single subgoal could account for positive transfer. However, the finding that subjects did improve their performance prior to the subgoal state when given a subgoal suggests that memory for two subgoals would likely result in a significant improvement in total performance. This could be tested by giving subjects States

F and *K* as subgoals, but we have not yet done the experiment. Subjects would, of course, have to know the order   of the subgoals—that it is necessary to isolate three cannibals across the river before isolating three missionaries across the river. The distinction between ordered and unordered subgoals is discussed by Wickelgren (1974).

The results reported in this section leave unanswered the question of exactly how a subgoal exerts its influence. In order to try to answer this question, Herbert Simon and I have taken a close look at the moves subjects make in solving the 5MC problem. We have attempted to simulate the average number of moves made by subjects between any two problem states and account for how their moves change when they are given a subgoal.

COMPUTER SIMULATION

Table 2 shows the average number of moves made by subjects between any two problem states for the 5MC problem (Reed & Abramson, Experiment 2, 1976). Forward moves are moves toward the goal (such as moving from *B* to *C*), whereas backward moves are moves away from the goal (such as moving from *C* to *B*). Our objective was to construct a simulation model that would make the same average number of moves between problem states as were made by subjects (Simon & Reed, 1976).

One of the key theoretical concepts used to guide problem solving is *means–end analysis* (Newell & Simon, 1972). Using a means–end strategy, a problem solver should make the move that brings him as close to the goal as possible. Since the goal of the missionary-cannibal problem is to move all missionaries and cannibals across the river, a means–end analysis would suggest taking as many people across the river as possible on each move and bringing back as few as possible. Would simulation of such a strategy predict human performance on the 5MC problem? We found that, although predictions based on this strategy were generally successful, there were several notable violations where subjects appeared to be using an alternative strategy.

The first violation of the means–end strategy occurs on the very first move and is particularly evident for subjects not given a subgoal. There was an average of 1.1 moves taking a missionary and a cannibal across initially, 0.4 moves taking three cannibals across, and 0.1 moves taking two cannibals across. The violation occurs because the most popular move was taking two people across even though subjects could take three people across. The violation was not as frequent for the subjects given a subgoal (0.5 moves, 0.5 moves, and 0.1 moves, respectively). Another violation of the means–end strategy occurs at State *E*. Subjects who had not been given a subgoal averaged 1.0 moves taking two missionaries across and 0.5 moves taking three cannibals across. The violations, however, seemed to reveal a pattern because the result of a violation was usually the creation of a problem state in which there was an equal number of missionaries and cannibals

TABLE 2
Simulation of Moves between Legal States for the
Subgoal Experiment

| | Forward moves | | | | Backward moves | | | |
| | Subgoal | | Control | | Subgoal | | Control | |
States	Subjects	Model	Subjects	Model	Subjects	Model	Subjects	Model
AB	0.5	0.3	0.4	0.2	0.1	0	0.3	0.1
AC	0.2	0.2	0.1	0.2	0	0	0.1	0.1
AD	0.5	0.6	1.1	1.2	0.1	0.1	0.3	0.3
BE	0.7	0.5	0.8	0.4	0.2	0.1	0.7	0.3
BF	0.1	0	0.2	0.2	0.1	0.2	0.2	0.2
CF	0.2	0.2	0.2	0.2	0	0	0.1	0.2
DF	0.5	0.6	1.2	1.0	0	0	0.3	0.2
EG	0.5	0.2	1.0	0.5	0.8	0.8	1.7	1.4
EH	0.2	0.1	0.5	0.2	0	0.1	0.4	0.3
EI	0.7	1.1	0.9	1.3	0	0.1	0.2	0.2
FG	0.8	0.8	1.7	1.6	0.5	0.2	1.0	0.7
FI	0.2	0.2	0.2	0.2	0	0.2	0.2	0.3
GJ	0.8	0.3	2.0	2.0	0.8	0.3	2.0	2.0
HK	0.2	0.2	0.7	0.9	0.2	0.2	0.7	0.9
HL	0.3	0.1	0.5	0.3	0.2	0.1	0.2	0.4
IL	0.9	1.4	1.0	1.5	0	0.3	0.3	0.4
LM	1.6	1.6	1.4	1.7	0.6	0.6	0.4	0.7
MN	1.8	1.9	1.7	2.0	0.8	0.9	0.7	1.0
NQ	1.0	1.0	1.0	1.1	0	0.1	0	0.1
OR	0	0	0	0	0	0	0	0
PS	0	0	0	0	0	0	0	0
QS	0.1	0.1	0.1	0.1	0	0	0	0
QT	0.9	0.9	0.9	1.0	0	0	0	0
RU	0	0	0	0	0	0	0	0
RV	0	0	0	0	0	0	0	0
SU	0.1	0.2	0.1	0.1	0	0	0	0
TU	0.2	0.1	0.1	0	0	0	0	0
TV	0.8	0.8	0.8	1.0	0	0	0	0
UW	0.2	0.2	0.2	0.1	0	0	0	0
VW	0	0	0	0.1	0.1	0.1	0.1	0
VX	0.9	0.9	0.8	0.9	0	0	0	0
VY	0	0	0	0	0	0	0	0
WZ	0.1	0.2	0.1	0.1	–	–	–	–
XZ	0.9	0.8	0.8	0.8	–	–	–	–
YZ	0	0	0	0	–	–	–	–

13

across the river. Thus, the violation at State A resulted in one missionary and one cannibal across the river and the violation of State E resulted in two missionaries and two cannibals across the river. We will refer to a strategy that attempts to equalize the number of missionaries and cannibals across the river as a *balance* strategy.

Four moves that occur in the first half of the problem space result in balanced states: moves *AD, EG, FG,* and *GJ.* It should be noted that the latter three moves bring subjects into a blind alley (Fig. 2) and subjects using a balance strategy will therefore be at a disadvantage. The data, in fact, suggest that many subjects do use a balance strategy and that these subjects do more poorly in reaching the subgoal.

Our computer simulation program has three parameters, which we estimated to predict the subject data presented in Table 2. The program always begins with a balance strategy, and the first parameter determines how soon it switches to a means–end strategy. We assume that subjects switch to a means–end strategy with probability p_1 prior to making each move. The balance strategy is identical to a means–end strategy (taking as many people across as possible and bringing back as few as possible) except in attempting to equalize the number of missionaries and cannibals across the river by making moves *AD* instead of *AB*, *EG* instead of *EH*, *FG* instead of *FI*, and *GJ* instead of *GE*. Moves *FG* and *FI*, and moves *GJ* and *GE*, are also both consistent with a means–end strategy, but the balance strategy resolves the choice in favor of creating a balanced state.

The improvement in problem solving that results from having a subgoal is represented in our model by the speed at which subjects switch from a balance strategy to the more efficient means–end strategy. Our estimate of the probability (per move) of switching is .07 for the control group and .25 for the subgoal group. Thus, subjects given a subgoal are less likely to enter a blind alley that can result from the use of a balance strategy. The data support this aspect of the simulation since the control group averaged 2.0 moves into State J (the end of a blind alley) compared to 0.8 moves for the subgoal group.

The second parameter in the simulation represents the probability of following a strategy, as opposed to choosing a move at random. The model assumes that subjects select a move consistent with their strategy with probability p_2 and select a move at random with probability $1 - p_2$. The probability of following a strategy begins at 0.5 and increases according to a specified formula (Simon & Reed, 1976). The third parameter represents the probability of not reversing the previous move and also allows for learning. The model assumes that the probability of rejecting an immediate back-up (taking back the previous move) begins at .5 and increases slightly after each move. The values of the second and third parameters are identical for the simulation of the subgoal and control groups, so the performance difference between the two groups is accounted for solely by the difference in probability of switching strategies.

Table 3 shows the mean and standard deviation of the number of legal moves made by the subjects and the strategy shift model. The correlation for the move

TABLE 3
Simulation of Subjects' Performance on Problem 5MC

Problem solver	Average moves	SD	Correlation	Variance (%)
Control group	30.6[a]	17.1	–	–
Strategy shift model	30.7	13.7	0.95	90
Undirected search model	133.0	126.0	0.64	41
Subgoal group	20.3	6.7	–	–
Strategy shift model	20.2	7.7	0.94	88
Undirected search model	133.0	126.0	0.40	16

[a]The mean of 27.6 reported in Table 1 did not include one subject who solved the problem in 103 moves. All 25 subjects were used for this analysis.

frequencies between problem states is .95 for the model and the control group, and .94 for the model and the subgoal group. The last column of Table 3 shows the percentage of variance accounted for by the model, which equals the square of the correlation coefficient. The average number of moves between problem states for the subjects and the strategy shift model is shown in Table 2. There are, however, two exceptions to the means–end strategy that were included in the model: Move EI is preferred to move EH, and Move NM is preferred to Move NQ, which is consistent with the balance strategy. We cannot give a convincing explanation of these preferences, but their exclusion from the simulation reduces the goodness of fit.

In order to investigate how much the task environment contributed to the predictions of the strategy shift model, Simon and I tested an undirected search model that randomly selected a legal move at each point in solving the problem. Table 3 shows the results. As expected, the high mean (133 moves) and standard deviation (126 moves) of the undirected search model indicates that it is a poor model of subjects' performance. However, the correlation of .64 between the average number of moves between problem states taken by the control group and the model shows that the number of moves are somewhat proportional. The undirected search model accounts for 41% of the control group's performance, a sizable contribution but much less than the 90% of the variance accounted for by the strategy shift model.

Subjects who are better informed are less influenced by the structure of the task environment. As might be expected, giving subjects a subgoal made their search more directed toward the goal and less predictable by the undirected search model. The correlation with the subgoal group was 0.40, accounting for only 16% of the variance, compared to 88% for the strategy shift model. The results suggest that the structure of the task environment contributes to the predictions of subjects' performance, but that strategies must be considered in order to make accurate predictions. This is particularly true when the search for the solution becomes more efficient, as demonstrated by the performance of the subgoal group.

One characteristic of the model which should be mentioned is that it is formulated at a general rather than at a specific level. The subgoal state is not explicitly a part of the model; hence, reaching the subgoal has no direct effect on the model's performance. The effect of the subgoal is represented indirectly, since the more rapid switch to a means–end strategy tends to guide the simulation toward the subgoal and away from blind alleys. The advantage of a more general approach is that one can apply the model to other experiments that are not concerned with subgoals. Simon and I plan, for example, to test the model's performance on learning data to see how it might account for improved performance when a subject solves a problem for the second time. The disadvantage of a more general approach is that it may not be sensitive enough to the specific nature of the subgoal. The subgoal given in this experiment (three cannibals across the river by themselves) is an unbalanced state, so it seems reasonable that it could cause subjects to abandon a balance strategy. However, if one gives subjects a balanced state as a subgoal, the model would lose some face validity if the subgoal group continued to perform better than the control group, since a balanced subgoal might encourage subjects to use a balance strategy. More applications of the model are therefore necessary to determine whether its level of generality is appropriate.

OVERVIEW

In this final section I would like to review the results reported in the previous sections, considering their possible implications for a theory of problem solving. I would like to emphasize, however, that the interpretation of these results must be considered quite speculative at this time. We simply don't have enough experimental data on problem solving to allow us to reach firm conclusions regarding the issues considered here.

The principle question raised in this chapter is: How does the task environment influence the facilitation of problem solving? I first considered this question by exploring whether transfer would occur between two problems that had very similar task environments (Reed, Ernst, & Banerji, 1974). The similarity of the two task environments was not a sufficient condition for significant transfer between the two problems. This occurred only when the subjects were informed of the relation between the two problems and the jealous husbands problem was given first. The asymmetrical transfer is predictable from the many-to-one mapping that relates the two task environments, but may be the result of other variables unrelated to the task environment. Hayes and Simon (Chapter 2 of this volume), for example, found asymmetrical transfer between problems that were related by a one-to-one mapping between moves. As these authors point out, the fact that two problems are exact isomorphs—have formally identical task environments—does not guarantee that they are of equal difficulty for human subjects. Alternative explanations of asymmetrical transfer may be based on the information processing capabilities of problem solvers, such as the extent to which they can remember the correct solution for different problems.

The size of the task environment is another variable that we investigated in order to determine whether it would influence the effectiveness of a subgoal (Reed & Abramson, 1976). Our results suggest that the effectiveness of a subgoal is more useful in a larger problem space in which subjects have a greater chance of making moves that do not bring them closer to the goal. In an attempt to understand how providing a subgoal facilitated performance, Herbert Simon and I tested a strategy shift model that successfully predicted the average number of moves between problem states. However, the structure of the task environment also influences the average number of moves between problem states, in addition to subjects' strategies. A model that randomly selected legal moves, and was therefore constrained only by the structure of the task environment, accounted for a moderate amount of subjects' performance when they did not receive a subgoal, but only a small amount of subjects' performance when they did receive a subgoal. These results show how the task environment can contribute to the predictions of a simulation model, but becomes a less important determinant of performance when subjects receive information about the correct solution path, enabling them to explore a problem space which is smaller than the space of all legal problem states.

In addition to the size of the problem space, Abramson and I considered the effect of subgoal distance on the usefulness of a subgoal, arguing that a subgoal may not facilitate problem solving if there are too many intervening problem states between the initial state and the subgoal state. One factor which may limit the generality of these results is that the complexity of problem solving tasks makes it difficult to vary an independent variable (such as "subgoal distance") without changing other variables at the same time. In changing the distance of a subgoal from the initial state, we are also changing the problem state which constitutes the subgoal. As mentioned in the previous section, subgoal State L (an unbalanced problem state) and subgoal State M (a balanced problem state) may have a differential effect on performance on the 5MC problem even though they are approximately the same distance from the initial state. This would occur if subjects would more likely use a balance strategy when given State M as a subgoal. One might also argue that subgoal State K was not as effective as States F or G for the 3MC problem because it specified all missionaries across the river by themselves, a state which cannot be reached until all cannibals are across the river by themselves.

However, subgoal distance is one of the few variables which psychologists have found some consistent results regarding its effect on problem solving. It is particularly impressive that these results have been found in a number of different tasks. Hayes (1966) had subjects memorize a communications network and then gave them tasks such as getting a message from Bob (initial state) to Bill (goal state) through Joe (subgoal state). He found that subjects' memory retrievals become increasingly faster as they approached the subgoal state. Egan and Greeno (1974) asked their subjects to solve the Tower of Hanoi, a problem that requires transferring disks from one peg to another peg without placing a larger disk on a smaller disk. Subjects could generate their own subgoals in this task and their errors showed a uniform decline as they approached the subgoal. The 8 puzzle is another problem in which subjects can generate their own subgoals (Ericsson, 1974). It consists of placing 8 numbers in numerical order in a 3×3 array. Ericsson found a fairly uniform decline in latencies as subjects approached the subgoal of arranging the first row in numerical order. These results are encouraging because they give some generality to the concept of subgoal distance as a useful variable.

Another possible limitation in extending the generality of results in problem solving is that some problems have more convenient problem spaces than others. The problem space of the missionary–cannibal task has several convenient properties which makes it an attractive problem for research purposes. First, the homomorphism between the missionary–cannibal task and the jealous husbands task made it possible to formally define the similarity between the two problems when investigating transfer. Other problems may not have readily available homomorphisms or isomorphisms, but it may be possible to create isomorphisms following the example of Hayes and Simon (Chapter 2, this volume). Second, the problem spaces for both the 3MC and 5MC problems contain problem states which subjects must enter in order to solve the problem. I found in a pilot study that giving subjects a subgoal which they did not have to enter (such as State H in Fig. 2) could create confusion when solving the problem. Third, the size of the problem space could be varied without changing the minimal number of steps needed to solve the problem. For example, one can vary the size of the problem space in the Tower of Hanoi task by changing the number of disks but this also changes the number of moves needed to solve the problem. The size of the problem space is also a critical factor when one attempts a simulation such as reported in the previous section. The 3MC problem has too small a problem space to attempt a simulation because there is very little choice at each problem state. Other problems, such as chess, have too large a problem space to make this kind of simulation practical.

In conclusion, I hope the research reported in this chapter shows ways in which the task environment can influence problem solving—through transfer between similar task environments, the effect of the size of the task environment and subgoal distance on subgoal facilitation, and the extent to which the structure of the task environment contributes to predicting the relative number of legal moves between problem states. The purpose of this chapter was not to emphasize the role of the task environment as the sole determinant of problem-solving behavior, but to attempt to understand its relative importance in different problem-solving situations.

SUMMARY

The research presented here attempted to investigate how the structure of the task environment—the arrangement of legal problem states—influences problem solving. Emphasis was placed on studying how analogy and subgoals could facilitate problem solving. The many-to-one mapping from the jealous husbands problem to the missionary—cannibal problem allowed us to study whether analogy could be used in transfer from one problem to the other. Significant transfer occurred only when subjects were informed of the relationship between the two problems and solved the jealous husbands problem first. The results are discussed within the framework of a possible set of prerequisites for analogy to be useful.

The specification of a subgoal for the missionary—cannibal problem significantly improved total performance only for a version of the problem having the larger problem space. A subgoal in the smaller problem space improved performance only in reaching the subgoal and this occurred only when the subgoal was within four moves of the initial state. A computer simulation model, in which the effect of the subgoal is represented by a more rapid shift to an efficient strategy, was proposed to account for the subjects' performance. The model accurately predicted the average number of moves between problem states, although further applications are necessary to determine whether its level of generality is appropriate. The model was contrasted with an undirected search model in which the choice of moves was constrained only by the structure of the task environment.

The final section reviewed the extent to which the task environment influenced problem solving in the different experiments and discussed the generality of the findings.

ACKNOWLEDGMENTS

This research was supported by NIMH Grant MH-23297. I am grateful to Herbert Simon and George Potts for their comments on the manuscript, which was written while the author held a visiting position at Carnegie-Mellon University.

REFERENCES

Egan, D., & Greeno, J. Theory of rule induction: Knowledge acquired in concept learning, serial pattern learning, and problem solving. In L. W. Gregg (Ed.), *Knowledge and cognition.* Hillsdale, N.J.: Lawrence Erlbaum Assoc., 1974.

Ericsson, K. A. Problem-solving behavior with the 8-puzzle III: Process in terms of latencies. Unpublished manuscript, University of Stockholm, 1974.

Hayes, J. R. Memory, goals, and problem solving. In B. Kleinmuntz (Ed.), *Problem solving: Research, method and theory.* New York: Wiley, 1966.

Newell, A., & Simon, H. A. *Human problem solving*. Englewood Cliffs, N.J.: Prentice-Hall, 1972.

Reed, S. K., & Abramson, A. Effect of the problem space on subgoal facilitation. *Journal of Educational Psychology*, 1976, 68, 243–246.

Reed, S. K., Ernst, G. W., & Banerji, R. The role of analogy in transfer between similar problem states. *Cognitive Psychology*, 1974, 6, 436–450.

Simon, H. A., & Reed, S. K. Modeling strategy shifts in a problem solving task. *Cognitive Psychology*, 1976, 8, 86–97.

Wickelgren, W. A. *How to solve problems*. San Francisco, California: W. H. Freeman, 1974.

2
Psychological Differences among Problem Isomorphs

J. R. Hayes
H. A. Simon

Carnegie-Mellon University

The fact that two problems are exact isomorphs—that legal moves can be mapped between them in one-to-one fashion—does not guarantee that they are of equal difficulty for human subjects. On the contrary, we will show in this chapter that changing the written problem instructions, without disturbing the isomorphism between problem forms, can affect by a factor of two the times required by subjects to solve a problem. This effect is produced because different problem instructions cause subjects to adopt different problem representations, even when the problems are formally isomorphic.

To understand a written problem text, a person must do two things. First, he must read the sentences of the text and extract information from them by grammatical and semantic analysis. Second, he must construct from the newly extracted information a representation of the problem that is adequate for its solution. This representation must include the initial conditions of the problem, its goal, and the operators for reaching the goal from the initial state.

In earlier papers (Hayes & Simon 1974; Simon & Hayes, 1976), the authors presented protocol analyses of subjects' attempts to understand Tower of Hanoi-like puzzles and described the UNDERSTAND program—a simulation model of the process by which humans come to understand problem texts. The model, while imperfect, matched the gross structure of the subject's behavior, quite well.

The structure of the UNDERSTAND program implies that certain changes in the form of the problem text that do not change its meaning will lead to changes in the representation adopted for the problem. Thus, the sentence, "The monster stood on the globe," would be represented as a monster having a globe as an attribute, while the sentence, "The globe supported the monster," would be represented as a globe having a monster as an attribute. Since it is known that changes in the *representation* of a problem can change the solution process significantly (Newell & Simon 1972), it is possible that changes in the *problem statement* can also have important effects on the solution process.

PROBLEM MATERIALS

The purpose of this study is to explore the influence of changes in the form of the problem text on the representation of problems, and consequently upon the process of solution of problems, by humans. To do this, we have employed sets of problem isomorphs. Two problems are isomorphic if they are essentially the same problem disguised in different words. More formally, two problems are isomorphs if any solution path of one may be translated step by step into a solution path of the other and vice versa. Problem isomorphs are of interest because they allow one to control such formal properties of a problem as the number of steps required for solution, or the number of blind alleys, while varying the way in which the problem is presented. Systematic differences among isomorphs can provide especially good clues, unconfounded with differences in formal properties, to determinants of problem difficulty, transfer of training, and manner of problem formulation.

The materials to be used here are eight "monster" problems, all of which are variants of the Tower of Hanoi puzzle. All of the monster problems concern a set of objects that are transformed from one set of permissible states to another. The problems differ, however, in two systematic ways. First, in Problems TA and TP, which will be called *transfer* problems, the transformation is a movement of something from one location to another. In Problems CA and CP, which will be called *change* problems, the transformation is a change in property rather than a movement.

The second systematic difference among the problems involves agent–patient relations. In Problem TA and CA, which will be called *agent* problems, the monsters are agents but not patients of the transformations. In Problems TP and CP, which will be called *patient* problems, the monsters are both agents and patients of the transformations. The key difference for the agent–patient variable, then, is whether the monsters transfer or change the globes or whether they transfer or change themselves.

The differences that have been incorporated into the problem set reflect our hypotheses about the kinds of changes in problem text that are likely to influence the internal representations of problems and the ways they are solved. Suppose that some underlying problem feature is represented in the text of one problem isomorph by element A and in the text of a second, by element B. Elements A and B will both be subjected to grammatical and semantic analysis early in the subject's attempt to understand the problems. If A and B are similar for example, both are nouns designating animals, we would expect them to receive very similar analyses (and the UNDERSTAND program does so predict). However, if they are dissimilar, for example, if A is a verb and B, a concrete noun, they would receive very different analyses. We hypothesize that if A and B receive similar grammatical and semantic analyses, then the two isomorphs will be represented and solved in similar ways and transfer of training between the isomorphs will be large. However, if A and B receive very different analyses, then the two isomorphs are likely to be represented and solved in disimilar ways and transfer of training will be small. In particular, we hypothesize that elements that are classified into different cases by a case grammar analysis such as Fillmore's (1968) will yield isomorphs (1) that are represented and solved differently and (2) that will consequently exhibit little mutual transfer of training.

EXPERIMENT 1

Experiment 1 employed eight monster problems. Monster problems TA, TP, CA, and CP are shown in *Table 1*. Problems TA$'$, TP$'$, CA$'$, and CP$'$ were identical, respectively, to Problems TA, TP, CA, and CP except for Sentence 3. In the unprimed problems, Sentence 3 matches the medium-sized monster with the

TABLE 1
Four Monster Problems

a. Monster problem TA

Three five-handed extraterrestrial monsters were holding three crystal globes. Because of the quantum-mechanical peculiarities of their neighborhood, both monsters and globes come in exactly three sizes with no others permitted: small, medium, and large. The medium-sized monster was holding the small globe; the small monster was holding the large globe; and the large monster was holding the medium-sized globe. Since this situation offended their keenly developed sense of symmetry, they proceeded to transfer globes from one monster to another so that each monster would have a globe proportionate to its own size.

Monster etiquette complicated the solution of the problem since it requires that:

1. only one globe may be transferred at a time;
2. if a monster is holding two globes, only the larger of the two may be transferred;
3. a globe may not be transferred to a monster who is holding a larger globe.

By what sequence of transfers could the monsters have solved this problem?

b. Monster problem TP

Three five-handed extraterrestrial monsters were standing on three crystal globes. Because of the quantum-mechanical peculiarities of their neighborhood, both monsters and

(Continued)

TABLE 1 *(Continued)*

globes come in exactly three sizes with no others permitted: small, medium, and large. The medium-sized monster was standing on the small globe; the small monster was standing on the large globe; and the large monster was standing on the medium-sized globe. Since this situation offended their keenly developed sense of symmetry, they proceeded to transfer themselves from one globe to another so that each monster would have a globe proportionate to its own size.

Monster etiquette complicated the solution of the problem since it requires that:

1. only one monster may be transferred at a time;
2. if two monsters are standing on the same globe, only the larger of the two may be transferred;
3. a monster may not be transferred to a globe on which a larger monster is standing.

By what sequence of transfers could the monsters have solved this problem?

c. Monster problem CA

Three five-handed extraterrestrial monsters were holding three crystal globes. Because of the quantum-mechanical peculiarities of their neighborhood, both monsters and globes come in exactly three sizes with no others permitted: small, medium, and large. The medium-sized monster was holding the small globe; the small monster was holding the large globe; and the large monster was holding the medium-sized globe. Since this situation offended their keenly developed sense of symmetry, they proceeded to shrink and expand globes so that each monster would have a globe proportionate to its own size.

Monster etiquette complicated the solution of the problem since it requires that:

1. only one globe may be changed at a time;
2. if two globes have the same size, only the globe held by the larger monster may be changed;
3. a globe may not be changed to the same size as the globe of a larger monster.

By what sequence of changes could the monsters have solved this problem?

d. Monster problem CP

Three five-handed extraterrestrial monsters were holding three crystal globes. Because of the quantum-mechanical peculiarities of their neighborhood, both monsters and globes come in exactly three sizes with no others permitted: small, medium, and large. The medium-sized monster was holding the small globe; the small monster was holding the large globe; and the large monster was holding the medium-sized globe. Since this situation offended their keenly developed sense of symmetry, they proceeded to shrink and expand themselves so that each monster would have a globe proportionate to its own size.

Monster etiquette complicated the solution of the problem since it requires that:

1. only one monster may be changed at a time;
2. if two monsters have the same size, only the monster holding the large globe may be changed;
3. a monster may not be changed to the same size as a monster holding a larger globe.

By what sequence of changes could the monsters have solved this problem?

small globe, the small monster with the large globe, and the large monster with the medium-sized globe. In the primed problems, Sentence 3 matches the medium-sized monster with the large globe, the large monster with the small globe; and the small monster with the medium-sized globe.

We have included the primed as well as the unprimed problems in the experiment because there are slight differences in the solution paths for Problems TA, TP', CA', and CP, on the one hand, and problems TA', TP, CA, and CP', on the other. Thus, the four problems in the first set are isomorphs of each other, as are the four problems in the second set. The two sets, however, are not isomorphic. Each of the sets is isomorphic to a Tower of Hanoi puzzle, but the two Tower of Hanoi puzzles do not have the same starting place. (See Nilsson, 1971, for a discussion of solution paths in the Tower of Hanoi puzzle.)

Procedure

In Experiment 1, each subject was asked to solve two problems—one was a transfer problem (Problem TA or TP) and the other a change problem (Problem CA or CP). Four pairs of problems, involving one transfer and one change problem each, were employed. These pairs were Problems TA and CA, Problems TA' and CA', Problem TP and CP, and Problems TP' and CP'. In half of the cases, the transfer problem was solved before the change problem, and in the other half, the solution order was reversed.

Each problem was presented to the subject typed on a single sheet of paper. The subject was asked to solve the problem, to write his solution on the problem sheet in any notation he desired, and to bring it to the experimenter to be checked for correctness. If his solution was correct, the subject was given the next problem. If incorrect, he was told the location of his error, for example "step 3 is not correct:," and asked to try again. The solution times shown below are the sums of all the intervals during which the subject worked on the problem. They do not include the times required for the experimenter to check the solutions.

Results

Solution time. Table 2 shows the mean solution time for each of the eight monster problems, both when the problem was solved first and when it was solved second. To provide a clear differentiation of the initial difficulty of the problems from transfer-of-training effects, a separate analysis was performed on the data for problems solved first.

An unequal-n three-factor analysis of variance (transfer—change $\times$ agent—patient $\times$ primed—unprimed) of the log transformed solution times for the problems solved first revealed that the main effect for transfer versus change was significant ($p < .00001$) but that no other main effects or interactions

TABLE 2 EXPERIMENT 1:
Mean Solution Times (min)

	Problem for which solution time is given							
Order in pair	TA	TA′	TP	TP′	CA	CA′	CP	CP′
First Solution time	13.78	19.00	15.50	13.11	35.00	25.75	28.67	25.33
Number of subjects	9	10	10	9	8	8	9	6
Pair in which problem occured	TA–CA	TA–CA′	TP–CP	TP′–CP′	CA–TA	CA′–TA′	CP–TP	CP′–TP′
Second Solution time	19.13	11.625	13.78	5.83	15.00	14.60	19.90	25.22
Number of subjects	8	8	9	6	9	10	10	9
Pair in which problem occurred	CA–TA	CA′–TA′	CP–TP	CP′–TP′	TA–CA	TA′–CA′	TP–CP	TP′–CP′

approached significance even at the .05 level. The transfer problems required an average of 15.45 min for solution, whereas the change problems required an average of 28.90 min or nearly twice as long. Thus, the nature of the transformation made a very large difference in solution time, while the agent–patient variation did not have a significant effect.

Errors. Thirteen subjects failed to solve the first problem presented to them within the 60-min time limit and two subjects failed to solve the second problem after having successfully solved the first. The analysis of solution times presented above and the analyses of notation presented below include no data from subjects who failed to solve either problem. The 13 failures to solve the first problem were distributed as follows: for TA problems there were no failures among 19 subjects; for TP problems, two failures among 21 subjects; for CA problems, eight failures among 24 subjects; and for CP problems, three failures among 18 subjects. A chi-square test revealed a significant difference in error frequency between transfer and change problems ($\chi^2 = 1.7$, $df = 1$).

Transfer of training. In interpreting the transfer results presented below, one should notice the different roles played by the agent–patient and transfer–change variations in each of the first two experiments. In Experiment 1, transfer of training was always from a change to a transfer problem or from a transfer to a change problem with the agent–patient relation held constant. In Experiment 2, transfer of training was always from an agent problem to a patient problem or from a patient problem to an agent problem with the transfer change relation held constant.

An analysis of variance was performed on the log transformed data for all 16 conditions represented in Table 2. Significant main effects were found for order of presentation ($p < .00001$) reflecting strong transfer-of-training effects and for transfer versus change ($p < .00001$) confirming the result found in the analysis of problems solved first.

The analysis also revealed a significant interaction between transfer versus change and agent versus patient ($p < .01$) which was not found in the analysis of the solution times of problems solved first.

In the agent condition, transfer-of-training between transfer and change problems was quite asymmetric. Transfer from TA to CA problems was 51% on the average while transfer from CA to TA problems was only 6%. In the patient condition, the asymmetry was less marked and opposite in direction. Transfer from TP to CP problems was 18% while transfer from CP to TP problems was 26%.

Reed, Ernst, and Banerjii (1974), studying two river-crossing problems, also found asymmetry in transfer of training. In particular, they found that transfer-of-training from the harder problem to the easier problem (43%) was greater than transfer from the easier problem to the harder problem (1%). Notice, however, that for the agent condition in our experiment, transfer from the harder problem to the easier one, that is, from the change problem to the transfer problem, is less than from the easier problem to the harder problem. This may be seen in Table 2 in the columns labeled TA, TA', CA, and CA'. Solution time for the transfer problems is reduced only 6% on the average when they follow solution of a change problem. Solution time for the change problems, however, is reduced by 51% on the average when they follow solution of a transfer problem.

EXPERIMENT 2

A second experiment was performed to provide data on transfer of training from one transfer problem to another and from one change problem to another. The primed problems were not included in Experiment 2 since no significant differences were detected between the primed and unprimed problems in Experiment 1. Otherwise, the problems, procedures, and methods for selecting subjects were identical to those in Experiment 1.

Results

Solution time. Table 3 shows the mean solution time for the problems solved in Experiment 2. Analysis of variance of log-transformed solution times for the first problem solved showed a very significant effect of transfer versus change ($F = 22.48$, $df = 1$, $p < .00002$) and a smaller effect for agent versus patient ($F = 4.82$, $df = 1$, $p < .04$). The interaction of these two variables was not significant. As in Experiment 1, the change problems were about twice as difficult as the transfer problems; while agent problems were slightly easier than patient problems.

Errors. There were no failures to solve either TA or TP problems among 16 and eight subjects, respectively. Two of 14 subjects failed to solve a CA problem presented first and one of 14 failed to solve a CP problem presented first. One of 13 subjects failed to solve a CP problem after successfully solving a CA problem.

Transfer of training. Analysis of variance was performed on the log transformed data for all 8 conditions represented in Table 3. Significant main effects were found for order of presentation ($F = 41.26$, $df = 1$, $p < .00001$) indicating a strong transfer-of-training effect, an effect for transfer versus change ($F = 48.99$, $df = 1$, $p < .00001$), and an effect for agent versus patient ($F = 6.46$, $df = 1$, $p < .02$). The last two effects confirm the results of the analysis of solution times presented above. No interactions were significant.

Transfer of training was about equal in the change and transfer conditions. Among change problems, the second problem was solved in 48.2% less time on the average than the first; while among transfer problems, the second problem was solved 55.9% faster than the first. Within both change and transfer conditions, however, there was marked asymmetry in transfer of training between the

TABLE 3 EXPERIMENT 2:
Solution Times (min)

Order in pair	Problem for which solution time is given			
	TA	TP	CA	CP
First				
Solution time	10.88	16.63	28.08	31.50
Number of subjects	16	8	12	12
Pair in which problem occurred	TA–TP	TP–TA	CA–CP	CP–CA
Second				
Solution time	5.5	6.25	17.83	12.67
Number of subjects	8	16	12	12
Pair in which problem occurred	TP–TA	TA–TP	CP–CA	CA–CP

agent and the patient problems. Transfer from the TA problem to the TP problem was 49.4% while transfer from TP to TA was 62.4%. Similarly, transfer from the CA problem to CP problem was 36.5% while transfer from CP to CA was 59.8%. In contrast to the results of Experiment 1, transfer was greater from the more difficult problems (patient type) to the easier problems (agent type) than the reverse.

In general the transfer of training effects found in Experiment 2, were larger than those found in Experiment 1. The transfer results together with the solution time and error results indicate that the difference between transfer and change problems is much more important to the subject's solution processes than is the difference between agent and patient problems.

Influences of Problem Text on Representation in Experiments 1 and 2

The work sheets used by the subjects in Experiments 1 and 2 were analysed for evidences of differences among subjects in their manner of formulating the problem. Since no instructions were given to the subjects specifying the method for recording their answers, it was hoped that the notations they adopted spontaneously would yield evidence about their internal representations of the problems.

Types of notation observed. Subjects used three major type of notations to describe their solutions:

a. Operator—sequence notation: The solution is described as a sequence of applications of the operators, for example, "The large monster gives his globe to the small monster. Then the medium monster . . . ," etc.

b. State—matrix notation: The solution is described by specifying the state of all the problem elements at each step of the solution. Most frequently the subjects portrayed the sequence of states in a matrix like one of those shown in Fig. 1. The matrix of Fig. 1a is typical of those used by subjects solving transfer

	M	L	S			M	L	S
0	I	S	M		0	L	S	M
1	—	L,S	M		1	L	L	M
2	M	L,S	—		2	L	L	S

|(a)|(b)|

FIG. 1 State-matrix notations used by subjects in solving move and change problem: (a) transfer type; (b) change type. The columns correspond to the fixed attribute; the rows to the successive problem situation after each move (zero is the starting situation). Within the cells are shown the current values of the variable attributes, which either (a) migrate from column to column (transfer type) or (b) change value within a column (change type).

problems. After each successive move, the symbol designating the object moved is literally transferred from one column of the diagram to another.

The matrix of Fig. 1b is typical of those used by subjects solving change problems. After each successive move, the value of a symbol in one of the columns is changed.

From the figure it is seen that whether a matrix depicts a transfer representation or a change representation can be determined without ambiguity.

c. Labeled-diagram notation: The solution is described by presenting a diagram depicting the initial state of the problem together with a sequence of changes depicted either by numbered arrows or by a spatially ordered sequence of crossed-out and redrawn elements in the diagram. See Fig. 2 for an example of labeled-diagram notation.

Table 4 shows that the frequencies with which the three major notational types were used in the first solution in Experiment 1 did not depend in any important way on the type of problem being solved. Further, the solution times for the problems did not appear to vary with the notation type used in the solution. Solution times for the first problem solved were classified by notation type and by problem type for those subjects who used either pure matrix notation or pure operator sequence notation. Labeled diagrams were not used frequently enough to allow analyses. An unequal-n analysis of variance of the log-transformed data revealed neither a main effect nor interactions due to notational type.

Generally, subjects used the same notation or mixture of notations for solving the second problem as for solving the first (91 cases out of 117). The changes that did occur are predominately shifts from operator sequence notation to matrix notation. For the first problem, 43 subjects used operator sequence notation and 57 used matrix notation. For the second problem, 30 subjects used operator sequence notation and 70 used matrix notation.

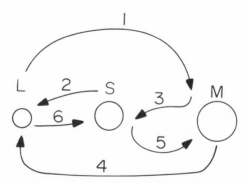

FIG. 2   An example of labelled notation from a solution for Problem TP'. Letters indicate monsters. Circles indicate globes and numbers indicate the order in which transformations were applied.

TABLE 4
Use of Notations in Experiments 1 and 2

	Problem type				
Notation type	TA	TP	CA	CP	Σ
State matrix	18	12	12	15	57
Operator sequence	13	9	11	10	43
Both state matrix and operator sequence	2	3	2	1	8
Labeled diagram	1	0	2	1	4
Labeled diagram and state matrix	1	1	0	0	2
Labeled diagram and operator sequence	0	2	1	0	3
Σ	35	27	28	27	117

While the gross notational types described above did not vary in frequency across problem types, variants within notational types were associated with specific problem types. The matrix notation used for move problems is characteristically different from that used for change problems. In all of the problem solutions we have observed, the transfer form (Fig. 1a) was without exception used in solving the transfer problems and the change form (Fig. 1b) was always used in solving the change problems.

There is no formal reason that the transfer form of the matrix could not be used to represent a change problem. In solving Problem 3 for example, one could let the columns of the matrix represent the globes of different sizes, and the entries in the body of the matrix represent the sizes of the monsters holding the globes. While such a matrix, which has the form of Fig. 1a, is quite adequate for solving the change problems, it was never used by our subjects for those problems.

The operator–sequence notation also shows variants in form that are characteristic of the problem being solved. To identify a move in a monster problem using operator–sequence notation, it is sufficient to designate the object to be transformed and the new state it is to be transformed to. Thus, the subject may designate an operator application by specifying two elements. For example, in Problem TA, a solution might consist of a sequence of statements such as "small globe to big monster." In many cases, however, the subjects specify three elements rather than just two. For example, in Problem TA, statements in the solution frequently have the form "the medium monster gives the small globe to the large monster." Thus we can distinguish notations that mention two elements to identify a move from notations that mention three elements.

Another variation in the form of operator–sequence notation concerns the naming of objects. An object may be designated either by direct naming—that is by specifying an attribute of the object, for example, "the big globe"—or by indirect naming—that is, by specifying a relation of the object to another object

TABLE 5
Variations in Operator Sequence Notation in Experiments 1 and 2

	Transfer				Change			
	Problems							
	TA		TP		CA		CP	
	Object naming		Object naming		Object naming		Object naming	
Number of elements	Direct	Indirect	Direct	Indirect	Direct	Indirect	Direct	Indirect
2	5	0	14	0	0	11	4	7
3	9	1	0	0	2	1	1	0
	14	1	14	0	2	12	5	7

or to an array of objects, for example, "the globe of the large monster," or "the globe on the left."

Table 5 shows the relation between the variant operator sequence notations and the problem solved. Clearly indirect naming is used more frequently in change problems (19 cases out of 26) than in transfer problems (1 case out of 29) (χ^2 = 25.79, p < .005). Further, three elements are named far more frequently for specifying solutions for agent problems (13 cases out of 29) than for patient problems (1 case out of 26) (χ^2 = 10.07, p < .005).

Process Explanations for the Findings

We have hypothesized that the notation a subject uses in solving a problem is related to his internal representation of that problem. We will now present a view of the relation between the internal representation and the notation that is consistent with the variant notations reported above. This view is consistent also with the structure and operation of the UNDERSTAND program.

We propose that the first three sentences of the monster problem text determine a representation of the initial situation which is essentially the same in all of the monster problems. The initial situation has as its most prominent feature a set of monsters. Next in importance is a set of globes which bear a locative relation to the monsters. We suppose that the initial situation is represented as a list of monsters and that each monster has associated with it a list of globes. Early in the process of solution, many of the subjects draw a sketch of the monsters and globes like that shown in Fig. 3. Such sketches can be identified and distinguished from the notation that the subject used to solve the problem in about 60% of cases for the first problem solved. These sketches impose spatial relations of two sorts on the monsters and globes. The first is a spatial association representing the pairing of monsters and globes given in

FIG. 3   An example of a monster-globe diagram for Problem TP.

sentence 3 of the problem text. The second is an arbitrary arrangement of these pairs in a linear ordering which is arrayed either horizontally or vertically. The pairs are ordered either as they are in sentence 3 (text order), or in order of monster size (monster order), or in order of globe size (globe order).

When the subject begins to solve the problem, he chooses one of the three notations to record his answer. We have no information about what determines this choice except to note as we did above that subjects tend to use the same notation in both of their problems. Whichever notation is chosen makes use of some information from the subject's representation of the initial situation.

Both the state—matrix and the labeled—diagram notations incorporate the two sets of objects in the initial situation together with their spatial relations. Thus, these two notations are always monster—globe notations and never monster-size or globe-size notations. Further, the spatial ordering of elements in the matrix or diagram is closely related to the spatial arrangement of elements in the sketch of the initial situation. Table 6 shows that in more than 80% of cases, the ordering of monster—globe pairs in the sketch matches that in the matrix or diagram. Table 7 shows that in more than 90% of cases, the horizontal—vertical orientation of the sketch is identical to the orientation found in the matrix or diagram. Thus, the matrix notation and the labeled-diagram notation are clearly dependent on the initial representation of the situation shown in the sketch.

The association between the forms of the matrix notation shown in Fig. 1 and the problem type depends not on the initial representation, which is the same in all cases, but rather on the relation of the operators in the problem to the initial

TABLE 6
Relation of Ordering in the Diagram of the Initial
Situation and in the Matrix Used for Solution

		Type of ordering in matrix		
		Text	Monster	Globe
Type of ordering in diagram	Text	7	1	2
	Monster	0	12	2
	Globe	0	0	3

TABLE 7
Relation of Spatial Arrangement in the Diagram of
the Initial Situation and in the Matrix Used for
Solution

Spatial arrangement in diagram	Spatial arrangement in matrix	
	Horizontal	Vertical
Horizontal	21	1
Vertical	1	4

representation. Thus the differences in notation related to problem type are due to differences in the way the operators are represented and not to the way the initial situation is represented.

The variations in operator-sequence notation bear a somewhat more complex relation to the initial representation than is the case for the other two notations. However, these variations may be accounted for reasonably well by the following two principles:

1. The monsters are the most important elements in the problem, being the agents of all actions, and therefore must be mentioned. (In 56 of the 59 instances of operator-sequence notation, the monsters are mentioned routinely).

2. Because the complete state is not recorded in this notation, objects should be provided with permanent names so as to identify them unambiguously. That is, an object should be named by a property or relation that does not change in the course of the problem solution. In the change problems, the size of the objects is changed in the course of solution. Thus the big monster at the beginning of the CP problem may become medium or small later in the problem. Hence, only indirect names for the objects are permanent in these problems. This principle, then, may be used to account for the high frequency of indirect naming in change problems.

In the agent problems the agent is distinct from the object being transformed and from the state to which the object is being transformed. In patient problems, however, the agent and the object are identical. Our first principle, therefore, would lead us to expect that transformations would be designated by three elements in agent problems, that is, by agent, objects, and destination, but by two elements in patient problems. This expectation is fulfilled with few exceptions, except for CA problems. This case is largely explainable, however, by the relation between indirect naming and the designation of the agent. In the monster problems, indirect naming frequently involves specifying the relation between the object and the agent. In the CA problems, in fact, all indirect naming was of this sort. A typical transformation might be designated by the statement, "Large monster's globe to large size." Hence, although only two elements are mentioned, one of their names makes reference to the agent. While only two of the subjects used direct naming in the CA problems, both of those subjects used 3 elements in specifying the transformation.

Models of Solution Time Differences

The models below are intended to account for the differences in solution time between transfer and change problems. We will present just two models here; a model for TA problems and a model for CA problems. Models could easily be derived for TP and CP problems but they would be identical to the TA and CA models respectively.

We assume that in solving TA problems, the subject makes use of the following three kinds of goals:

a. to move the globe of size A to the monster of size A;
b. to move a globe away from monster X, so that another globe also held by monster X may be moved;
c. to move a globe away from monster X, so that another globe, Y, can be moved to monster X.

Since the models for executing these three goals are very nearly identical, we will confine our attention to the model for Goal a.

To make the models concrete, we will assume that the subjects are using the matrix shown in Fig. 1a to represent transfer problems and the matrix shown in Fig. 1b to represent change problems. For convenience, we will further assume that the subject first checks Rule 2 and then Rule 3 in testing the legality of a move. The order in which the rules are checked has no implications for our analyses.

Table 8 shows the model for TA problems and Table 9 the model for CA problems. There are two differences between the models that might account for the difference in problem solving. The first is a difference in procedures used for checking whether there are (in TA problems) other globes at a given location or (in CA problems) other globes of a given size. These procedures are invoked in their respective problems at step A1 and again at Step B1. To determine if there are other globes at a given location, requires examining just one cell of the matrix (see Fig. 1a). On the other hand, to determine if there are other globes of a given size requires the subject to scan a row of the matrix (see Fig. 1b). For this reason, we would expect that Steps A1 and B1 in Model 3 would take more time than the corresponding steps in Model 1.

A second difference between the models may be found in Steps A3 and B3. In Model TA, if there are other globes at the specified locus, Globe X is compared in size to those other globes. In Model CA, if there are other globes of the specified size, then rather than comparing globe sizes, the sizes of the monsters holding the globes are compared. This comparison requires one more step of retrieval than does the corresponding comparison in Model TA.

TABLE 8
Model for the Solution of Problem TA

Goal: Move globe X (of size A) to monster Y (of size A)

A. Check Rule 2
   1. Does the monster Z, now holding globe X, hold any other globes?
   2. If not, go to B.
   3. If so; is globe X larger than any of the other globes of monster Z?
   4. If so, go to B.
   5. If not return and report "Blocked at origin, try to remove block."

B. Check Rule 3
   1. Is Monster Y now holding any globes?
   2. If not, go to C.
   3. If so, is globe X larger than any of the other globes of monster Y?
   4. If so, go to C.
   5. If not, return and report "Blocked at destination, try to remove block."

C. Transfer
   1. Delete globe X from monster Z.
   2. Add globe X to monster Y.

TABLE 9
Model for the Solution of Problem CA

Goal: Change globe X (size A) to size of own monster (size B).

A. Check Rule 2
   1. Does any other monster hold other globes of size A?
   2. If not, go to B.
   3. If so, is monster holding globe X the largest of the monsters holding globes of size A?
   4. If so, go to B.
   5. If not, return and report "Blocked at origin, try to remove block."

B. Check Rule 3
   1. Does any other monster hold other globes of size B?
   2. If not, go to C.
   3. If so, is monster holding globe X larger than any other monster holding a globe of size B?
   4. If so, go to C.
   5. If not, return and report "Blocked at destination, try to remove block."

C. Change
   1. Change size of globe X from A to B.

EXPERIMENT 3

Since either or both of these differences could account for the differences in difficulty between move and change problems, we performed Experiment 3 in an attempt to differentiate between these alternatives.

In designing Problems TA2 and CA2, shown in Table 10, we attempted to produce problems that differ in steps A1 and B1 in the same way as problems TA and CA differ, but that do not differ in steps A3 and B3. We have done this by introducing an extra dimension, color. In Problem TA2, instead of comparing the sizes of globes at a given location as in problem TA, the subject must now

TABLE 10
Two Monster Problems

---

a. Monster problem TA2

Three five-handed extraterrestrial monsters were holding three crystal globes. Because of the quantum-mechanical peculiarities of their neighborhood, both monsters and globes come in exactly three sizes with no others permitted: small, medium, and large. Furthermore, globes come in just three colors: white, gray, and black. The medium-sized monster was holding the small white globe; the small monster was holding the large black globe; and the large monster was holding the medium-sized gray globe. Since this situation offended their keenly developed sense of symmetry, they proceeded to transfer globes from one monster to another so that each monster would have a globe proportionate to its own size.

Monster etiquette complicated the solution of the problem since it requires that:

1. only one globe may be transferred at a time;
2. if a monster is holding two globes, only the darker globe may be changed;
3. a globe may not be transferred to a monster who is holding a larger globe.

By what sequence of changes could the monsters have solved this problem?

b. Monster problem CA2

Three five-handed extraterrestrial monsters were holding three crystal globes. Because of the quantum-mechanical peculiarities of their neighborhood, both monsters and globes come in exactly three sizes with no others permitted; small, medium, and large. Furthermore, globes come in just three colors: white, gray, and black. The medium-sized monster was holding the small gray globe; the small monster was holding the large white globe; and the large monster was holding the medium-sized black globe. Since this situation offended their keenly developed sense of symmetry, they proceeded to shrink and expand globes so that each monster would have a globe proportionate to his own size.

Monster etiquette complicated the solution of the problem since it requires that:

1. only one globe be changed at a time;
2. if two globes have the same size, only the darker globe may be changed;
3. a globe may not be changed to the same size as a darker globe.

By what sequence of changes could the monsters have solved this problem?

---

compare the colors of globes of specified sizes. In problem CA2, instead of comparing the sizes of monsters holding globes of a given size as in problem CA, the subject must now compare the colors of the various globes of a given size. Thus, in Problem TA2, Steps A3 and B3 require comparing the size of the globes, whereas in Problem CA2 these steps require comparing the sizes of the monsters who are holding the globes.

If Steps A1 and B1 are the main factors determining problem difficulty then we would expect Problems TA2 and CA2 to yield results like those for Problems TA and CA, respectively. However if Steps A3 and B3 are the main determinants of problem difficulty, then we would expect both Problem TA2 and Problem CA2 to be about as difficult as Problem CA and considerably more difficulty than Problem TA.

Procedure

In Experiment 3, each subject solved only one problem. In all other respects, the procedures were identical to those in Experiments 1 and 2. Fourteen subjects solved Problem TA2 and 13 subjects solved problem CA2. One subject in each condition failed to solve the problem.

Results

The mean solution time for Problem TA2 was 27.07 min and the mean solution time for Problem CA2 was 29.77 min. The difference between the two was not significant by t-test. The solution times for these problems are close to the solution times of 28.48 min for Problem CA in Experiment 1 and 28.08 min in Experiment 2.

General Discussion

The results of Experiment 3 clearly support the hypothesis that the difference in solution times between transfer and change problems observed in Experiments 1 and 2 may be attributed to differences in the difficulty of executing the comparisons in Steps A3 and B3. Further, they offer no support for the hypothesis that the differences are due to differences in difficulty in executing Steps A1 and B1. In other words, the difference between transfer and change problems occurs not because it is harder in change problems to determine if any other globes need to be considered when making a move, but rather because when such globes are found, it is harder to make the appropriate comparisons among globes.

Experiments 1 and 2 have provided a considerable amount of information about transfer of training among the problems. We will discuss just two aspects of these data: (1) the observation that there was generally greater transfer of training in Experiment 2 than in Experiment 1, and (2) the asymmetry of the transfer effects observed in both experiments.

Reed, Ernst, and Banerjii (1974) offer two explanations for the asymmetry of transfer that they found in their study. The first explanation, which concerns a difference between the problem spaces of their two problems, is not applicable in the present study since we have used only isomorphic problems. The second explanation is that while the two problems were solved in the same number of steps, subjects spent more time on the more difficult problem. Thus, in the more difficult problem, the steps are better learned and provide more transfer than in the easier problem. This explanation is consistent with the results of Experiment 2 in which transfer from patient to agent problems was greater than from agent to patient problems and the patient problems were slightly more difficult. However, it is not consistent with the results of Experiment 1 in which the TA problems are much easier than the CA problems but transfer from TA to CA is much greater than transfer from CA to TA.

To analyse the transfer of training effects, we must identify the processes that are facilitated by previous training. Our analysis embodied in the UNDER-STAND program (see Hayes & Simon, 1974) suggests three groups of processes to consider. These are:

1. processes for formulating the initial situation,
2. processes for identifying and representing the operators, and
3. processes for formulating the rules for a legal move.

Since the initial situation is essentially the same in all problems, we would expect that experience with any of the problems would facilitate formulation of the initial situation equally. Thus, it seems unlikely that either the differences in transfer between Experiments 1 and Experiment 2 or the asymmetries of transfer are traceable to the processes for formulating the initial situation.

Similarly, since the processes for identifying "move" and "change" operators are thoroughly overlearned in adults, it seems unlikely that these processes could either benefit enough from transfer or occupy enough time to account for the differences among problems which we have observed.

The final group of processes, the processes for formulating the rules for a legal move, is a much more likely locus for the transfer effects. First, the rules for a legal move are stated in a different way in the text of each of the problem types. Second, the formulation of these rules by the subjects takes considerable time and is known to constitute one of the most difficult parts of formulating the whole problem (Simon & Hayes, 1976). We assume that transfer occurs when the subject, in the course of formulating the rules for a legal move in the second problem recognizes and uses similarities to the formulation of the rules in the first problem. In doing this, the subject must recognize the similarity of two complex structures despite differences in them.

There are two differences between the statements of the rules either or both of which might be responsible for the differences in transfer. One is the difference in the operators—the transfer—change difference. The other is the difference in the way constraints are stated. Constraints are stated either in terms of properties—"The big globe"—or in terms of relations—"The globe of the big monster." Further research will be needed to evaluate the importance of these two differences.

Conclusion

We have shown that differences among the texts of isomorphic problems influence problem solving behavior strongly in three ways:

a. Problems involving transfer operators were solved much more quickly than problems involving change operators.
b. Both the agent—patient variation and the transfer—change variation influence the notation which the subjects use to solve the problems.
c. Transfer between two problems is greater when the difference between the problems is an agent—patient variation than when it is a transfer—change variation.

The differences in solution time between transfer and change problems can be attributed to differences in the difficulty of executing comparison processes when applying the rules for a legal move. The differences in the use of matrix notation in transfer and change problems can be attributed to differences in the relation between the subject's representation of the initial situation and his representation of the operators. Differences in transfer of training among the problems can be attributed to differences in the way the rules for a legal move are formulated.

ACKNOWLEDGMENTS

This research has been supported by Public Health Service Grant MH-07722 from the National Institute of Mental Health and by National Science Foundation Grant GS-38533.

REFERENCES

Fillmore, C. J. The case for case. In E. Bach & R. T. Harms (Eds.), *Universals in linguistic theory.* New York: Holt, Rinehart & Winston, 1968.
Hayes, J. R., & Simon, H. A. Understanding written problem instruction. In L. Gregg (Ed.), *Knowledge and cognition.* Hillsdale, New Jersey: Lawrence Erlbaum Assoc., 1974.
Newell, A., & Simon, H. A. *Human problem solving.* Englewood Cliffs, N.J.: Prentice-Hall, 1972.

Nilsson, N. J. *Problem-solving methods in artificial intelligence.* New York: McGraw-Hill, 1971.

Reed, S. K., Ernst, G. W. & Banerjii, R. The role of analogy in transfer between similar problem states. *Cognitive Psychology*, 1974, 6, 436–450.

Simon, H. A., & Hayes, J. R. Understanding complex task instructions. In D. Klahr (Ed.), *Cognition and instruction.* Hillsdale, N.J.: Lawrence Erlbaum Assoc., 1976.

3
Process of Understanding in Problem Solving

James G. Greeno

The University of Michigan

Most recent work in the theory of problem solving has considered a solution as successful achievement of search (for example, Newell & Simon, 1972; Nilsson, 1971). A well-defined problem presents an initial situation and a goal, and a restricted set of operators that can be used to transform the situation. A solution consists of a sequence of operations that transforms the initial situation into the goal. A problem is difficult to the extent that a solution sequence is hard to find.

Work conducted in an older tradition treated problem solving in a rather different way. Gestalt analyses such as those of Duncker (1945), Köhler (1927), and Wertheimer (1959) emphasized the achievement of understanding in solving problems, showed that failure to solve often is caused by inadequate understanding, and noted that solution often is achieved in occurrence of insight involving sudden realization of critical relations.

This chapter will develop some general ideas concerning understanding in problem solving, and will report the beginning of an effort to represent problem solving with a theory in which understanding has central importance. I will begin by proposing three general criteria that can be used to judge the degree to which understanding has been achieved. I will then indicate the application of these criteria to problem solving, including some brief discussion of some earlier analyses of problem solving. Then I will present some analyses of problem solving in the domain of high school geometry, giving relatively detailed examples that illustrate characteristics of problem solving that correspond to the three criteria of understanding. The performance of the new theoretical problem solver will be described and evaluated in relation to the criteria of understanding.

WHAT IT MEANS TO UNDERSTAND

Of course, various meanings can be given to "understanding." The meaning to be given here is related closely to recent developments in the theory of understanding natural language, notably by Schank (1972) and Winograd (1972). Understanding is a constructive process, in which a representation is developed for the object that is understood. The difference between understanding and not understanding is in the nature of the representation. When a sentence is understood, its internal representation shows what the sentence means. The meaning corresponds to a pattern of relations among concepts that are mentioned in the sentence, and understanding is the act of constructing such a pattern. To do that, the understander relies on a great deal of background knowledge, often including knowledge of what the various words in the sentence refer to, but also more subtle conceptual knowledge that produces constraints and allows inferences about the ways in which concepts are related.

It is important to note that no unique structural representation exists for any input, and this implies that there can be no hard and fast rule for determining whether something has been understood completely. Nonetheless, we can specify ways in which understanding may be incomplete or inadequate for specifiable purposes. I do not propose to give a general and complete theory of understanding here, but I think it would be reasonable to include the following three criteria in such a theory.

First, good understanding involves achievement of a coherent representation. To the extent that some components of the input remain unattached to the rest of the input, the representation will usually be considered incomplete or inadequate. We can also distinguish between representations in which all things are connected, but at a low level, and other representations in which more unity is achieved by the inclusion of some relations that connect large chunks of the input with each other, or of some global thematic concepts that are connected to components throughout the object that is understood. The importance of a high-level relational property is illustrated in the comprehension of analogy. When we understand the sentence, "Tree trunks are straws for thirsty leaves and branches," we do so by finding a property that links the two main topics of the sentence—in this case, a similarity of function, (see Verbrugge, 1976). The importance of a global thematic concept is illustrated in some examples developed by Bransford and Johnson (1973), including a paragraph that begins as follows:

> The procedure is actually quite simple. First you arrange things into different groups. Of course, one pile may be sufficient depending on how much there is to do. If you have to go somewhere else due to lack of facilities that is the next step, otherwise you are pretty well set. It is important not to overdo things. That is, it is better to do too few things at once than too many [p. 400].

As readers who have seen the whole paragraph know, comprehension does not get much better when additional information of this sort is available. However, the whole message makes good sense when one is told that the paragraph is about washing clothes.

A second criterion for understanding is that the internal repressensation should correspond closely to the object that is understood. Coherence can often be achieved at the expense of correspondence, and we all have experienced simple inaccuracies of understanding, where to fill in some aspects of a situation that seemed incomplete, we have drawn conclusions that turned out to be wrong. As with the criterion of coherence, correspondence with the understood object may be examined at several levels. An internal representation may be incomplete or inaccurate because it omits or mismatches some important components of the object, or it may omit or mismatch some important relations that are present among the components of the object.

A third criterion for saying that good understanding has occurred involves the extent to which the understood object and its components are related to the understander's other knowledge. We now know that a great deal of general knowledge is used by a person in achieving even a minimal understanding of information communicated with language. Studies by Kintsch (1974) and Norman and Rumelhart (1975) have emphasized that in understanding a text, many propositions are included in the cognitive representation that are not explicit in the text. Beyond this, it seems reasonable to say that if a person has a greater amount of general knowledge that relates to the concepts in a message, that person will have a stronger understanding of the message. For example, a person who has studied elementary science and has acquired knowledge about the solar system, including gravitation and rotation of planets, has a greater degree of understanding of eclipses and other such events than a person who lacks that knowledge.

GOODNESS OF UNDERSTANDING IN PROBLEM SOLVING

My discussion of understanding in problem solving is based on a general view that in solving a problem a person generates a cognitive representation that is analogous to the structure that is achieved when a person understands something, such as a sentence. Of course, the first thing a person must do about a problem is to understand the problem itself. This requires an internal representation that includes the components of the problem that are given as well as a representation of the problem goal. The process of achieving an initial understanding of a problem is discussed by Hayes and Simon, Chapter 2, in this volume.

Now consider the process of solving a problem that has already been understood in the sense of forming an initial representation. In solving the problem, the person modifies the situation, and eventually achieves the goal of the problem. The solution can be considered as a series of transformations, each of which generates some new components in the problem situation. When the problem is solved, the person has constructed a pattern of relations that connect the components of the situation given initially with the situation that has been achieved. The solution pattern consists of the relations and components that were present in the subject's initial representation of the problem, together with the additional relations and components generated in the process of achieving the problem goal. The solution pattern is thus a cognitive representation of the solved problem, and includes the transformations that were applied as steps in the solution.

When we consider the solution of a problem as a cognitive product, generated by the problem solver, we can evaluate the degree of understanding that is shown in the solution. I give detailed discussion of the three criteria of coherence, correspondence, and connectedness with general knowledge later. Here, I comment briefly on some previous analyses to show the continuity of the present analysis with earlier work.

First, consider coherence. Solutions of problems, consisting of patterns of relations, can vary in the degree to which their components are related in a compact structure. There is a minimum level of coherence required in any solution of a problem; there must be enough connection among components for the solution to work. Beyond that, however, there are different degrees of organization found in different problems, and for some problems there are alternative solutions differing in coherence. A person whose solution of a problem is poorly integrated can be said to lack understanding of the problem, even if the correct answer was obtained.

When a problem or theorem is explained by a teacher, there is generally an effort to communicate the overall structure of relations as much as possible. In discussing this issue, Duncker (1945) distinguished between organic proofs, in which the higher-order relations among the steps are made explicit, and mechanical proofs, which proceed step by step with attention focussed on the justification for deriving each step from preceding statements rather than on the overall plan or structure of the proof. Undoubtedly, teachers who succeed in providing organic proofs generally give their students better understanding of theorems than teachers who give mechanical proofs.

Next, consider the second criterion of understanding, correspondence between the cognitive representation and the object that is understood. Of course, many failures of correspondence are uninteresting. Persons frequently miscopy some information in a problem, or omit some relevant information. Many such errors are probably best explained as random lapses of attention, although some may provide useful indicants of students' lack of an appropriate frame or schema for the kind of problem being presented.

There is a more subtle issue regarding correspondence between the components of a problem and the solution that is found for the problem. This involves the question whether the solution is somehow a natural one in the domain of the problem, or whether the problem has been translated in some way that makes the solution artificial. Wertheimer (1959) was especially concerned with this issue, and supplied several examples of problem solving in mathematics in which a solution based on a learned formula, applied in a mechanical way, seems distinctly different from a solution obtained with good understanding of the problem structure. Wertheimer's best known example is the problem of finding the area of a parallelogram, where he contrasted mechanical use of the formula $A = b \times h$ with a transformation that shows how the parallelogram is related to a rectangle. One interpretation of the difference is that the transformation works directly in the domain of the problem, showing geometric relations between problem components, while the formula extracts problem components and operates on them algebraically, giving an answer that does not come from a coherent pattern of geometric relations.

We clearly need to avoid too simple a characterization of the criterion of correspondence. Transformation of a problem into a new domain, or solution of a problem by decomposing it into subproblems with known solutions, often provides good insight into the structure of the original problem and thus clearly can be productive and indicative of good understanding. I think it is reasonable to judge the solution of a problem to indicate good understanding if the solution pattern includes the important structural properties of the problem in a relatively direct way. Good understanding is often achieved in solutions involving transformations of the problem and sensible constructions that preserve the main structure of the problem. The undesireable cases involve mechanical applications of rules that fail to preserve important relational properties needed for understanding.

Now consider the third criterion of understanding—the degree to which a cognitive structure representing some object is connected with other components of the person's knowledge. It seems a reasonable hypothesis that if concepts in a new structure are connected strongly to other components of knowledge, the person should be able to answer interpretive questions about the new structure and to apply the structure in novel situations. This idea has been useful in interpreting empirical results we have obtained in earlier studies involving instruction in the binomial formula (Egan & Greeno, 1973; Mayer & Greeno, 1972; Mayer, Stiehl, & Greeno, 1975). In that research, we found that if subjects were given instruction that emphasized the meanings of concepts such as trials, outcomes, and probabilities of sequences, subjects were better able to answer questions, identify impossible problems, and solve word problems than were other subjects whose instruction had emphasized computational algorithms.

There have been discussions of problem solving in which a person's ability to solve new problems was proposed as a criterion for deciding that an initial problem had been really solved at all. Katona's (1940) discussion of problem solving and learning has this flavor, and Gagné (1966) suggested explicitly that the label "problem solving" should be reserved for cases in which a new cognitive principle was acquired, as could be evidenced by a subject's ability to solve related problems presented as tests of transfer. In a discussion of Gagné's paper, Newell (1966) objected that solution of a problem in itself often is nontrivial, and that it would stretch terminology undesireably to require evidence of general principles before we say that problem solving has occurred. I think a comfortable resolution is possible. It is quite appropriate to say that problem solving has occurred whenever the solution of a problem has been obtained. On the other hand, when a problem is solved with good understanding, one aspect of that understanding involves recognition of the relation of that problem's solution to some general principle (that may or may not have been known in advance). Therefore, Gagné's suggestion that we assess problem-solving performance by presenting related problems to which we expect successful transfer seems quite an appropriate proposal, if what we want to know is whether the problem solver achieved understanding in the initial situation, in the sense of having the initial solution connected to general components of knowledge.

SOLVING BY GENERATING A COHERENT PATTERN

I present a relatively detailed example that makes the idea of solving a problem by pattern generation concrete, and that illustrates the idea of a coherent solution pattern. I think the idea that problem solving is a process of pattern generation can be applied quite generally and may be quite helpful in understanding relationships between different kinds of problem situations. However, I do not try to support this general theoretical point here. My goal in this chapter is simply to note some basic commonalities between important aspects of problem solving and characteristics of understanding. I hope this first example provides a convincing instance for the idea that in problem solving, as in understanding, a person constructs a cognitive network that incorporates components and relations given in an input, along with other components and relations that are supplied by the person's own knowledge.

I illustrate the process of pattern generation by using a protocol given by a high-school student solving a geometry problem. Using the protocol, along with consideration of the problem itself, I develop a theoretical interpretation of the process of solving the problem, considering the subject's initial understanding as a cognitive pattern, and the various steps in the solution as transformations of the pattern. It is convenient to represent these patterns as networks; the solution will be shown as a series of networks, showing the cognitive elements and relations that I believe were included in the subject's understanding as the solution was achieved. The task given in the problem is to prove the following theorem: if two sides of a triangle are congruent, then the angles opposite those sides are congruent. Another statement of the theorem is: the base angles of an isosceles triangle are congruent.

The most frequent solution of this problem uses an auxiliary line, shown as the dashed line in Fig. 1. It is given that sides $\overline{AC}$ and $\overline{BC}$ are congruent. Construct $\overline{CD}$ as the bisector of $\angle ACB$. Then $\angle ACD$ and $\angle BCD$ are congruent, by the definition of a bisector. Segment $\overline{CD}$ is congruent with itself. Therefore, $\triangle ACD$ and $\triangle BCD$ are congruent, since two pairs of corresponding sides and their included angles are congruent in the two triangles. And it follows that $\angle A$ and $\angle B$ are congruent.

The protocol that I analyze here is presented in Table 1. At the time this protocol was obtained, the class had just completed a unit called "Congruent Triangles," Chapter 6 in the textbook by Jurgensen, Donnelly, and Dolciani (1972). The proof of this theorem was given in the text, and students had worked exercises in which the theorem was used to justify steps in proofs. However, I am confident that the subject had not memorized the proof developed in the protocol.

By the time the subject reached the point marked *1 in the protocol, the components of the problem were identified, including the problem goal. Figure 2

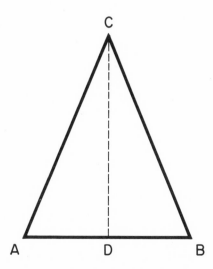

FIG. 1 Diagram drawn to accompany the problem of proving that base angles of an isosceles triangle are congruent.

TABLE 1
Protocol Given by Subject Solving the Base-Angles Problem

E: Try to either remember—or put together, if you can't remember it—the proof of a theorem that was given in the book.
   The theorem is: if two sides of a triangle are congruent ...
S: Wait.
E: Sure. (The subject wrote down, "If 2 sides of Δ≅,")
S: Okay.
E: ... then the angles opposite those sides are congruent.
   (The subject wrote, "then the angles opposite those sides are ≅.")
S: Okay.
E: That's the theorem.
S: And you want me to do the proof?
E: Mm-hm.
S: Okay.
E: And think out loud while you're trying to figure out how to do it.
S: Okay. (Pause) Okay, if two sides of a triangle are congruent—so, draw a triangle.
   (The subject drew a triangle, shaped approximately like the one in Fig. 1.)
E: Okay.
S: ... then the angles opposite those sides are congruent. Okay, so like if I have, Given: triangle ABC (the subject wrote "Given $\triangle ABC$)—I'll letter it A B C (the subject added labels, A, B, and C to the drawing of the triangle)
E: Right.
S: And then I have, Prove ... (wrote "Prove":) Do I already have these two sides given? Okay. Two sides of a triangle are given.
E: Mm-hm.
S: Let me go back to my Given and say that segment AC is congruent to segment BC.
E: Okay.
   (Subject wrote "$\overline{AC} \cong \overline{BC}$.")
S: And I want to prove that angle A is congruent to angle B.
E: Good.
S: All right. Let me write down my Given. Okay. And mark my congruent sides

*1   Okay. So, I want to prove that angle A is congruent to angle B.   C
      (At this point, the subject's paper looked like the following:
      If 2 sides of Δ≅, then the angles opposite those sides are ≅
      Given $\triangle ABC$; $\overline{AC} \cong \overline{AB}$
      Prove: $\angle A \cong \angle B$

---

1. $\triangle ABC$; $\overline{AC} \cong \overline{AB}$ 1. Given
2.

The writing below the line started the formal presentation of a proof, in the format the students had been taught to use.)
S: Now, let's see.
   (Subject drew a vertical line from point C downward.)
E: Why are you drawing a line there?

(Continued)

TABLE 1 *(Continued)*

S: I don't know yet.

E: Okay, fine.

*2   (Subject labeled the point D where the auxiliary line intersects with segment $\overline{AB}$.)

S: Okay, uhm–okay, then I could–if I drew a line . . .

E: Um-hm.

S: That would be the bisector of angle ACB, and that would give me–those congruent angles–no–

    (Pause)

    yeah. Well, that would given me those congruent angles, but I could have the reflexive property, so this would be equal to that.

    (The last remark was accompanied by pointing to the two triangles on either side of $\overline{CD}$.)

E: Okay. Now, before you go ahead and write it all down; when you said you were going to draw the line . . .

S: Yeah.

E: And I said, "Why are you doing that?" and you said you didn't know yet. What do you think happened to give you the idea of making it the bisector?

S: Okay. Well, I have to try to get this–I have to try to get triangle ACD congruent to BCD. Because, if I do that, then angle A is congruent to angle B because corresponding parts of congruent triangles are congruent.

E: So you were drawing the line to give yourself triangles–is that the idea?

*6   S: No, to–to get a side that was in both triangles.

E: Okay.

*7   S: And to get congruent angles.

E: So that's why you drew it as the bisector?

S: Yeah.

E: Yeah; okay.

S: You want me to write it?–it doesn't matter?

E: It doesn't matter.

    (This refers to writing down the individual steps in the format of a formal proof.)

*8   S: I would have side angle side.

E: Yeah.

*9   S: And corresponding parts.

E: Okay.

---

shows these main components in the form of a relational network. Objects such as segments, angles, and triangles are represented as lines in the network, and relations are represented as nodes. The relation of congruence between $\angle A$ and $\angle B$ is shown in dashed lines; this is the problem goal. Figure 2 does not show all the components of the subject's diagram–for example, there is a segment $\overline{AB}$ that is not represented at all, and some relations are omitted, such as $\overline{AC}$ being a side of $\angle A$. We want to represent the components and relations that a subject actually thinks about, and while we can never be completely certain what these are, the representation in Fig. 2 probably is a good approximation.

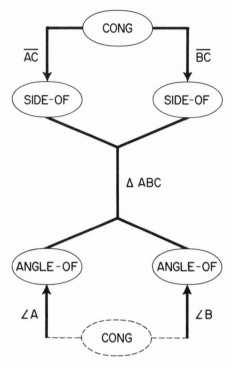

FIG. 2   Cognitive structure corresponding to initial understanding of the base-angles problem.

At the point in the protocol labeled *2, the subject had drawn a segment vertically from point C to the base of the triangle. The subject said, "I don't know yet," when asked why that line was drawn, but I do not believe the construction was aimless. It seems likely that the subject was forming triangles, each containing one of the angles that had to be related in the goal. I hypothesize that the subject formed a subgoal of proving two triangles congruent, with the provision that $\angle A$ and $\angle B$ would be corresponding parts of the two triangles. This is supported by the subject's retrospective comment at point *5. Incorporating this subgoal into the problem representation gives a diagram like Fig. 3. In that representation, the triangles are not specified, other than stipulating that the goal angles should be components of them. The triangles, as well as the relation of congruence between them, are goals at this stage; hence, they are represented in Fig. 3 with dashed lines.

The relation of congruence between the triangles is connected to the relation of congruence between $\angle A$ and $\angle B$. The relation corresponds to a proposition of geometry, linking congruence of triangles to congruence of their corresponding parts. Propositions such as this are used to justify inferences, and using a

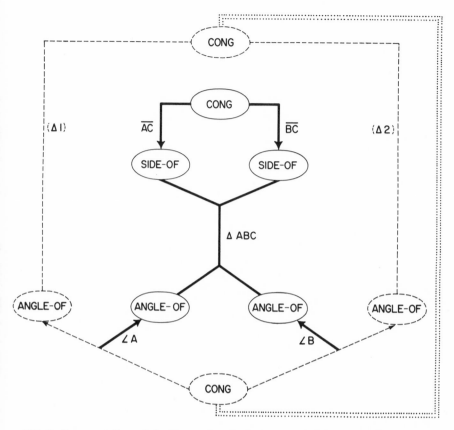

FIG. 3 Representation of the base-angles problem with the subgoal of finding congruent triangles.

proposition such as this to set a subgoal has been a standard method in computational theorem proving in geometry and elsewhere (Gelernter, 1963; Goldstein, 1973; Newell, Shaw, & Simon, 1963). The higher-order relation (that is, a relation between other relations) is shown in Fig. 3 as a double dotted line. I assume that at this point, the subject considered that link as hypothetical— something that might be established by later developments.

Figure 4 shows what the subject's representation of the problem may have been like at point *2, when the auxiliary line $\overline{CD}$ had been drawn. The triangles $\triangle ACD$ and $\triangle BCD$ are now definite, with segment $\overline{CD}$ being thought of as a side of both. However, at this point $\overline{CD}$ may well have been "dangling" in the structure; the subject may not have had a clear idea of how $\overline{CD}$ would fit in other components. In this diagram, $\overline{AC}$ and $\overline{BC}$ are already considered as sides of the two new triangles. There is no direct evidence in the protocol for this

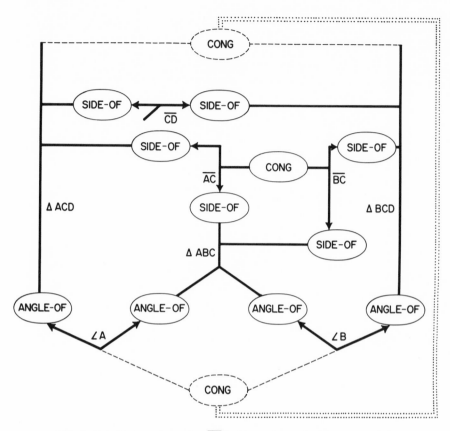

FIG. 4   Cognitive structure after $\overline{CD}$ had been drawn, forming two triangles.

assumption, but the subject's failure to mention anything about those segments later might indicate that this relation seemed obvious all along.

The comments between *2 and *3 in the protocol apparently indicate further thought about $\overline{CD}$, and conclude with specifying $\overline{CD}$ as the bisector of $\angle C$ in $\triangle ABC$, giving congruent angles $\angle ACD$ and $\angle BCD$ in the two triangles. These new components and relations are shown in Fig. 5. Note that $\angle C$ has now appeared explicitly in the representation, since it is the thing whose bisection creates the new angles that are mentioned as being congruent. (The relation CONCAT merely refers to the fact that $\angle C$ is the concatenation of $\angle ACD$ with $\angle BCD$.) The double solid line in Fig. 5 refers to the geometric proposition that when an angle is bisected, the two angles that are formed are congruent.

The subject is not entirely certain about things at *3, presumably because the relations generated this far are still not sufficient to tie the pattern together. At *4, the subject remembers that $\overline{CD}$ is congruent to itself, and that fact (with others already considered) establishes congruence of the two triangles. This is

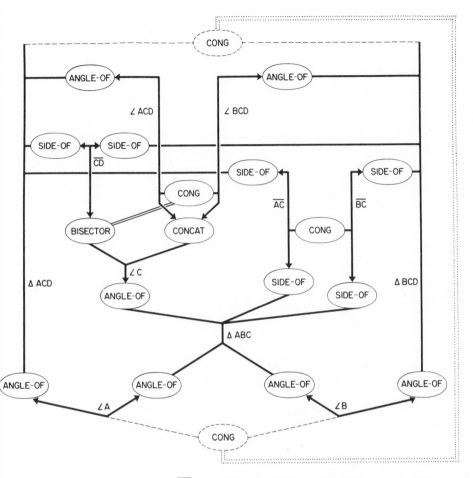

FIG. 5 Cognitive structure with $\overline{CD}$ specified as the bisector of $\angle C$, giving $\angle ACD \cong \angle BCD$.

the main component that was needed to complete the pattern. We can conclude that the final pattern that was achieved had the components and relations indicated in Fig. 6, where congruence between $\triangle ACD$ and $\triangle BCD$ as well as congruence between $\angle A$ and $\angle B$ have been made definite.

The protocol does not provide definite evidence about the exact sequence of events in solving the problem. However, the sequence shown in Figs. 2–6 seems a reasonable reconstruction, especially in the light of some retrospective comments made by the subject. I referred to the comment at *5 earlier, in justification of the hypothesis that the subject set a subgoal of forming congruent triangles. The comment at *6 suggests that the subject thought of the auxiliary line as a common side of the two triangles being formed before thinking of it as the bisector of $\angle C$, and this suggestion is taken into account in the features I incorporated into Fig. 4.

While I am far from confident about the exact sequence of development, I feel quite sure that something like Fig. 6 represents the outcome of problem solving rather accurately.[1] The subject's understanding of the main gist of the proof is indicated in comments at *8 and *9, made after I said it wouldn't matter whether the subject wrote out the complete proof in a formal way. To some extent, these comments involve completion of the problem. The subject had mentioned previously the relations of congruence between pairs of corresponding sides and angles. The comment at *8 probably indicates that the next step after those previously mentioned would involve congruence of the triangles, and then the comment at *9 indicates the last step establishing congruence between the base angles.

We can judge the degree of understanding achieved by the problem solver by considering the properties of the solution pattern. The degree of coherence of the pattern shown in Fig. 6 seems quite good. There is a global thematic relation, the congruence of $\triangle ACD$ and $\triangle BCD$, to which most of the other components of the network relate quite directly. Another focus is around the triangle given in the problem, $\triangle ABC$. An approximate index of compactness can be obtained by counting the number of relations that one would pass through on a minimal path between a pair of objects. For example, to reach $\angle C$ from $\triangle ACD$ one must pass through at least two relational nodes. There are 11 distinct objects represented in the structure, and 20 pairs of objects are directly linked through a single relation. Of the 35 remaining pairs 31 are connected through minimal paths of length two, and the other four have minimal paths of length three.

Concerning the second criterion of understanding, correspondence with the

---

[1] One point about the sequence that seems quite definite is of interest in relation to earlier theories about problem solving in geometry. Gelernter (1963) and Goldstein (1973) developed artificial intelligence systems in which the sequence of events follows a strategy of working backward. The subgoal of finding congruent triangles follows that strategy, but in Gelernter's or Goldstein's systems, the next step would be another subgoal, based on one of the theorems available for proving congruent triangles. For example, there might be a search for components that would provide a proof of congruence by side–angle–side. If that failed, another pattern of congruent parts would be set as a subgoal and tried.

The sequence I have hypothesized involves a more diffuse search for congruent pairs of components once the subgoals of congruent triangles has been set. I think that under the subgoal of congruent triangles, subjects typically just "collect" pairs of congruent segments and angles, with a kind of monitor that checks to see whether the antecedents of any known theorems for congruence have been satisfied. Rather than running consistently in the "top-down" direction, the system apparently alternates in direction, with some general subgoals set from the top but with significant inputs resulting from scanning of available properties and relations, carried out under rather weak constraints. This is a more complicated kind of operation than that considered in previous theorizing, but it corresponds more closely to the performance of subjects who I have observed.

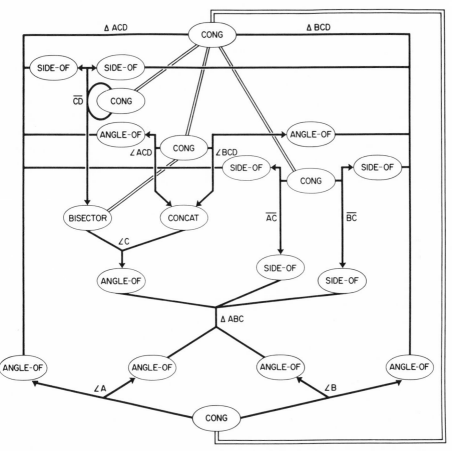

FIG. 6   Final cognitive structure achieved, corresponding to understanding of the solved problem.

real problem, the pattern in Fig. 6 shows a correct set of relationships and thus satisfies at least a simple version of the criterion. However, a more interesting set of issues concerning correspondence arises from the next example to be presented. Concerning the third criterion, connectedness with general knowledge, this first example seems to provide little or no material of interest.

A SYSTEM THAT SOLVES PROBLEMS BY PATTERN GENERATION

Before considering the next example of human problem solving in geometry, I will describe the general features of a new hypothetical system that solves problems using a process of pattern generation. This system is in an early stage of development, but its initial features were selected to try to capture some intuitions about solving problems with understanding, and it is of interest to note the extent to which the features selected for this system succeed in producing solutions that meet the criteria of understanding developed in the first part of this essay. It is convenient to be able to refer to a system by name—I have been calling this one PERDIX.

PERDIX consists of two main components. One is a function called DRAW, which creates structures of information that I assume is available for perception when a subject looks at a geometric diagram. DRAW is not a model of perception, but strong assumptions about the psychology of perception are incorporated in the information that DRAW creates. DRAW creates those entities and relations that I assume can be perceived in a relatively direct way. The interface between DRAW and PERDIX' problem-solving mechanisms is the locus in this system of the standard trade-off between complexity of data structures and complexity of procedures. Whatever structures DRAW creates are available to PERDIX as a kind of raw material for problem solving, and if the material is provided in a more refined form, then less has to be done with it to produce solutions of problems.

PERDIX' other main component is a set of productions that take patterns as conditions and whose actions create new patterns, along with LISP functions that define the patterns in the form of associative structures. The productions are executed by a version of Anderson's (1976) production system ACT, which was designed initially to work in an environment consisting of propositional structures of the kind developed in Anderson and Bower's (1973) theory of human associative memory. One of ACT's main tasks has been to comprehend sentences—that is, to create propositional structures in response to strings of words given as input. Thus an analogy between problem solving and language understanding is built into PERDIX' general operating characteristics.

A major theoretical aspiration for PERDIX is that the knowledge structures it needs to solve problems should be reasonable facsimiles of the kinds of concepts and principles that are taught in classroom instruction. The LISP functions that define patterns for PERDIX correspond to concepts—they are configurations of components related in specified ways. Propositions such as "vertical angles are congruent" are represented as productions and are used to infer relations between components that are not given in the problem, but that are used in solutions of problems. The cleanliness of this distinction between concepts and propositions is much greater in principle than in practice, as will be clear when I describe some details of PERDIX' current operation; but the general separation is valid and quite useful.

PERDIX presently contains knowledge structures required to solve a class of problems involving angles formed by intersecting lines and by parallel lines crossed by a transversal. A brief description follows of the knowledge structures that are used for these problems.

Data Base

The structures created by DRAW are based on the assumption that when a subject looks at a diagram, the perceptible features include angles, segments, and the endpoints of segments. These are included in a relational structure in which segments are associated with their endpoints, and angles are associated with their sides and vertices. In the present version, part–whole relations are specified for segments, but not for angles.

Figure 7 shows a simple diagram, and Fig. 8 shows the relational structure that DRAW creates for that diagram. The nodes marked PNT#, SEG#, and ANG# indicate points, segments, and angles. *P, Q, PQ*, and so on are labels given those geometric objects. Relations between geometric objects are indicated by labels of arcs in the graph.

Input to DRAW includes Euclidean coordinates of each point, and these are used to compute some quantitative properties of angles and segments. The main quantitative property used in the problems PERDIX solves now is a directional property of angles, called "tilt." The tilt of an angle is the direction in which it opens. You could construct the bisector of an angle, and compute its direction vector in polar coordinates; this would be a number between 0 and 2π, and would correspond to the direction in which you would be facing if you stood at the vertex of the angle and looked out directly toward its center. The number computed by DRAW is similar, except it is based on the distance around a unit square (oriented diagonally) rather than a unit circle. The tilt of an angle is always between 0 and 4; for example, an angle with tilt 0 has a bisector that is a horizontal line, and the angle opens to the right. (Directional quantities based on the square can be computed without trigonometric functions. They are quite adequate for use of PERDIX, as will be clear from the description of concepts that PERDIX uses in processing the information in diagrams.) The remaining

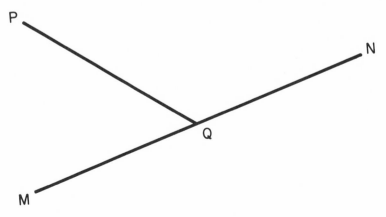

FIG. 7   A geometric diagram.

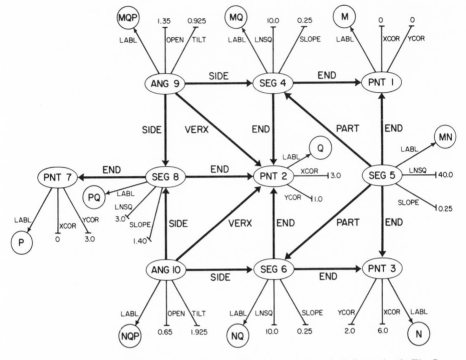

FIG. 8   Relational structure created by DRAW representing the information in Fig. 7.

quantitative properties shown in the diagram include the length (squared) of each segment, the direction vector (in linear polar coordinates) of each segment (called the segment's slope), and the size of each angle (associated with the angle by an arc labeled "open").

DRAW is intended to create information that a person could perceive by looking at a diagram. In its present version, PERDIX uses the orientations of angles as perceptual input. Measures of line segments and angles have been used in previous theories about geometry (Gelernter, 1963; Goldstein, 1973) as guides in selecting plausible subgoals. This is a reasonable use of quantitative information that is not included in PERDIX at this stage. However, inclusion of the measures of segments and angles in the structure created by DRAW anticipates use of that information in future versions of the theory.

Knowledge Structures

The knowledge used by PERDIX in solving problems is in the form of productions. There are two general categories of these. One set of productions identifies relations between angles and finds angles satisfying specified relations. These interact directly with features of the diagram. For example, if Fig. 7 were given, the productions for identifying relations could determine that $\angle MQP$ and $\angle NQP$ have a relation that PERDIX calls "straight angles"; that is, they are adjacent angles whose external sides form a straight line. The other set of productions perform inferences. These productions correspond to propositions such as, "straight angles are supplementary," "vertical angles are congruent," and so on. In Fig. 7, the productions for inference could determine that $\angle MQP$ and $\angle NQP$ are supplementary, or given the measure of $\angle NQP$ as, say, $130°$, the productions for inference could calculate that the measure of $\angle MQP$ is $50°$.

In identifying relations, PERDIX does not directly perceive relations such as vertical angles or corresponding angles. These relations are inferred from relations that involve relations between components of the angles that are related. For example, the relation "straight angles," which applies to $\angle MQP$ and $\angle NQP$ in Fig. 7, is inferred from (i) the fact that both angles have the same vertex, (ii) the fact that segment $\overline{PQ}$ is a side of both angles, and (iii) the fact that the remaining sides, $\overline{MQ}$ and $\overline{NQ}$, are straight-line extensions of each other.

The perceptual machinery used in identifying relations consists of five LISP functions that construct patterns tested in the conditions of productions. First, a pattern called ANGLE identifies the components (sides and vertex) of an angle. Second, EXTSEG requires two segments that are parts of a straight-line segment. (SEG4 and SEG6 in Fig. 8 satisfy this pattern, both being parts of SEG5.) A third pattern, PARANG, requires an angle, and a segment that is parallel to a specified side of the angle. The other two patterns used in identification locate an angle with respect to a segment; one requires that the angle is above or to the right of a segment, the other requires that the angle is below or to the left of the segment. (These properties are based on computations that use the tilt of the angle and the slope of the segment.)

Identification of relations is accomplished by a set of productions organized as a decision network, in the manner of EPAM (Feigenbaum, 1963) or CLS (Hunt, Marin, & Stone, 1966). First, the components of one of the angles are identified, and bound as the values of variables. Next, the components of the second angle are identified through a series of tests that determine whether the second angle has components in common with the first angle. (This device provides tests for features such as having the same vertex, or sharing a side, without requiring an explicit pattern function for that feature.) Depending on what components (if any) are found to be shared by the two angles, the system proceeds to test relations such as EXTSEG and PARANG on the remaining components. To function as an EPAM or CLS net, the system must pass control from one test to another, contingent on the outcomes of previous tests. ACT has a natural device for this; the conditions of ACT's productions include control nodes that must be active for a condition to be satisfied. PERDIX' productions for identifying relations include control nodes that are set when their tests are appropriate.

When PERDIX has to find angles in a specified relation, it uses patterns that consist of conjunctions of the relation's component features. For example, the pattern for alternate interior angles consists of two angles with different vertices, one shared side, the remaining sides parallel, and whose tilts are in opposite directions. Generally, when PERDIX needs to find an angle that is related to some other angle, the angle is needed as a bridge between two angles that are not themselves related directly. Then the patterns that involve specific relations are tested in conjunction with other patterns requiring that angles have a shared vertex or parallel sides, or use the orientation of an angle to conclude that its vertical angle will be nearer to a specified point than the initial angle is.

When a relation between two angles has been identified, PERDIX adds new structure to the data base, representing the relation that has been found. Figure 9 shows the structure that would be added if the angles in Fig. 7 were analyzed. (The symbol g denotes a tag that indicates the specific relationship between ANG9 and ANG10. Without such specific tags, assignment of generic relationships leads to overgeneralization.)

The inferences that PERDIX makes are based on relations that are found in the data base. If PERDIX' current goal were to find a quantitative relation between ANG9 and ANG10, it would test a condition with a pattern that would be satisfied by the structure in Fig. 9. The action of that production is to create new structure in which the relation SUPP (supplementary) is assigned to ANG9 and ANG10. This new structure may provide the solution of the problem, or may be needed for a further step, such as calculating the measure of one of the angles from the measure of the other angle.

In general, PERDIX' mechanisms for making inferences all consist of productions whose conditions are satisfied by the presence of certain relations and whose actions consist of adding other relations to the data base. These inferential productions correspond to two groups of propositions that are learned by

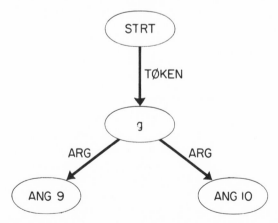

FIG. 9   Relational structure added to the data base by PERDIX when angles in Fig. 8 are analyzed.

students of geometry. The first group are propositions that associate geometric relations with quantitative relations—for example, "vertical angles are congruent"; and "interior angles on the same side of the transversal are supplementary." The second group involve inferences based on quantitative relations—for example, "if A is congruent to B and the measure of A is m, then the measure of B is m"; "if A is congruent to B and B has some quantitative relation with C, then A has that same quantitative relation with C."

Goal Management

In addition to the knowledge PERDIX uses in identifying relations and making inferences, an additional set of productions is engaged in setting goals. These productions constitute PERDIX' strategy for solving a class of problems. Each goal is a structure that is in the data base, consisting of an action, a target, and a pattern. The alternative actions are to find and to prove. The distinction is not a critical one during most of problem solving, but different actions need to be performed at the termination of a problem, depending on which form of problem was given. The pattern usually consists of a relation with arguments, any of which may be in the form of unknown variables. When the goal is to find something, the target is the name of the kind of thing that is needed—for example, when the goal is to find the measure of some angle, the target is ?NUM, indicating that a number is needed. When the goal is to prove something, the pattern is fully specified, and the target is a component of the pattern that will be checked when problem solving has been completed. For example, if the problem is to prove that two angles are congruent, the target will be the relation CONG; then when some quantitative relation between the angles is found, there is a check to see whether it agrees with the target relation.

The memory structure used by PERDIX for goal management is a simple stack. The current goal is a part of the data structure, and its components can be tested as part of a production's condition. To save computation, the system uses control nodes indicating the various kinds of things that goals deal with; this means that the system avoids carrying out expensive pattern matching on the goal structure as it passes by productions that are irrelevant to the current goal.

The main psychological issue in goal management is the sequence in which subgoals are generated when the main goal is not achieved. At this stage, where PERDIX knows about angles and parallel lines, the goals it can create are of four kinds. The simplest goal is to relate two specified angles by a geometric relation. This involves an attempt to find a relation specified in the data base, and if one is not found, the productions for identifying relations are activated. At the next level is a goal to find a quantitative relation between two specified angles. This goal succeeds if the angles are congruent, or supplementary, or complementary. If a quantitative relation is not in the data base, there is a search for some geometric relation from which a quantitative relation could be inferred. If a geometric relation is not in the data base, the goal of finding a geometric relation is set.

A third level of goal is to find the measure of an angle, based on the measure given for another angle. This goal succeeds when the measure of the specified unknown angle is stored in the data base. If the needed measure is not in the data base, there is a search for a quantitative relation between the given and unknown angles. Successful retrieval of such a relation activates a production that assigns measure to the unknown angle. If a quantitative relation is not found, then the goal of finding a quantitative relation is set.

A possible outcome of the analysis of two angles is that they have none of the relations that the system recognizes. When this happens under the goal of finding a quantitative relation, PERDIX sets a goal of finding a bridge angle. PERDIX looks for an angle having a specific relation to one of the angles that were to be related initially. In problems where one angle is given and the other is unknown, PERDIX searches for a bridge that is related to the given angle, thus working forward. (This agrees with the direction of search shown by human subjects.) The bridging relation sought is always one that will permit inference of congruence with the initial angle. Relations of corresponding angles, alternate interior angles, and vertical angles can be sought, and the specific solution to a problem will usually depend on the order in which these are tried. To satisfy the goal of finding a bridge angle, the angle found must be between the two angles that initially were to be related. B can be a bridge angle between A and C if A and B are corresponding angles (or alternate interior angles) and B and C either have the same vertex or a pair of parallel sides. B can be a bridge between A and C if A and B are vertical angles, and the tilt of B is numerically closer to the direction vector between the vertices of A and C. (In other words, the bisector of B points more in the direction of C than does the bisector of A.)

When the current goal cannot be achieved, it is stored in a pushdown stack, and the new goal that is set replaces it as the current goal. When the current goal is achieved, the goal at the top of the memory stack becomes the current goal. The removal of goals from the data structure involves operations that are not compatible with ACT's basic operating characteristics. Ordinarily, when ACT adds structure to the data base, the structure remains there permanently. The modifications of ACT that allow changes in problem goals have been made in a way that restricts their use to goals. That is, the exception to ACT's rule of keeping all its added data structures only applies to the management of goals.

Problems to find or to prove can be given to PERDIX at any of its three main levels of goals. That is, PERDIX can find the measure of an angle with the measure of some other angle given, or it can prove that the measure of an angle is some specified quantity, given the measure of another angle. It can find a quantitative relation between two specified angles, or it can prove that the quantitative relation between two specified angles is as stated. It can also find the geometric relation between two specified angles, and it recognizes a request to prove that a specified geometric relation holds between two angles. In the last case, the reason given is that the angles just have that relationship, although a trace of the process of identifying the relation reveals PERDIX' reasons for the conclusion.

Example

Consider Fig. 10, with the problem to prove that $\angle WPM$ is congruent to $\angle ZQN$. DRAW created a structure of the kind shown in Fig. 8, but of course the number of components and relations was much larger. $\angle WPM$ and $\angle ZQN$ were denoted ANG20 and ANG28 in the structure that DRAW created.

First, PERDIX created a goal corresponding to the problem statement. No quantitative relation was in the data base, so a search was made for a geometric relation between ANG28 and ANG20. The data base had no geometric relation between these angles, so the diagram was analyzed to attempt to find a relation. The outcome of the analysis was that no geometric relation existed. (PERDIX does not know about alternate exterior angles.) The structure in Fig. 11 was then part of the data base. The goal of finding a geometric relation was removed, and PERDIX returned to the goal of finding a quantitative relation.

At this point the structure in Fig. 11 matched the condition of a production that sets a new goal of finding a bridging quantitative relation. There was none in the data base, so a goal of finding a bridging relation was set. When PERDIX solved this problem it was set to look for a corresponding angle first. It found a

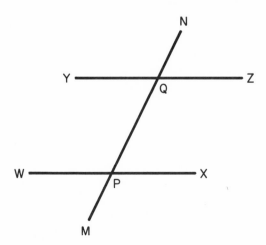

FIG. 10 Diagram for a problem of proving two angles congruent.

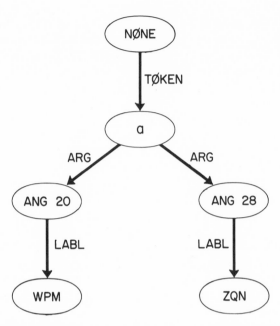

FIG. 11   Relations in PERDIX' data base after analyzing $\angle WPM$ and $\angle ZQN$ in Fig. 10.

corresponding angle with ANG28, identified as ANG19, the angle labeled XPQ. This was added to the data structure, giving the relation indicated as CORR in Fig. 12. This permitted return to the goal of finding a bridging quantitative relation. The relation of corresponding angles matched the condition of a production that creates the relation of congruence. Then the data base contained all the relations in Fig. 12.

The relations in Fig. 12 do not satisfy the goal of finding a bridging quantitative relation; a relation between ANG19 and ANG20 is required. When the diagram was examined, it was found that ANG19 and ANG20 were vertical angles; and this led to the inference that they were congruent. Returning to the goal of finding a bridging quantitative relation once more, the two relations of congruence matched the condition of a production that assigned the relation of congruence to the ANG20 and ANG28. At this point, PERDIX returned to the goal of proving ANG20 and ANG28 congruent, and found the needed relation in the data base. Since the relation found (congruence) matched the target of the goal, PERDIX exited with a message that the needed relation had been found. The complete set of relations generated during problem solving is shown in Fig. 13.

It should be understood that Fig. 13 is not equivalent to a goal tree of the kind generated by GPS. PERDIX' performance is governed by goals, as is true of any problem solver. In solving the example problem, PERDIX explicitly constructed

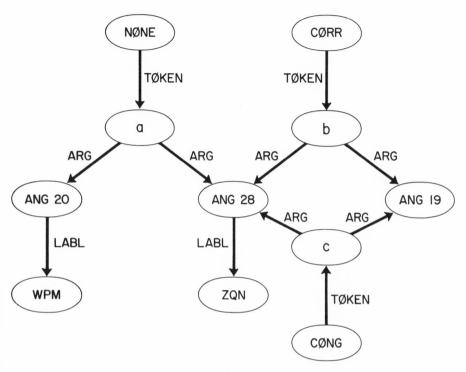

FIG. 12 Relations in PERDIX' data base after $LXPQ$ (ANG19) has been identified as corresponding (and congruent) to $LZQN$.

five distinct goals. These are shown in Fig. 14, enclosed in rectangles; they constitute PERDIX' goal tree for the example problem. (The relational structures that PERDIX added to the data base are shown in Fig. 14 enclosed in triangles.)

SOLUTIONS BY HUMAN SUBJECTS OF A PROBLEM OF PARALLEL LINES

I will now describe a problem that was given to seven high school student subjects, and show the solutions found by the six subjects who successfully solved it. The problem is a more elaborate version of the example just given to illustrate PERDIX' current operation. Since it is in the domain where the current version of PERDIX has relevant knowledge, performance of these subjects can be used to test the adequacy of PERDIX as a theory of human problem solving in this domain. The main new information about human problem solving that will be presented concerns the issue of correspondence between information used in problem solving and information in the problem.

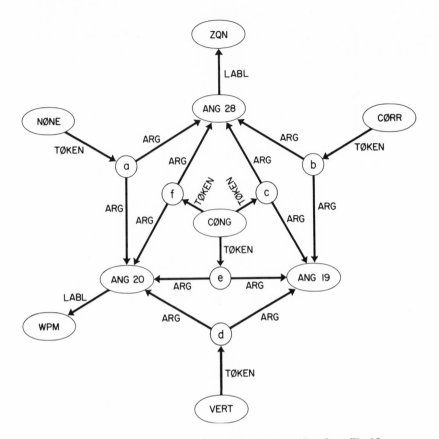

FIG. 13   PERDIX' representation of the solved problem from Fig. 10.

The large diagram and text in Fig. 15 were given. The smaller diagram shows notation that I will use in describing solutions that subjects obtained. Subjects added labels to the diagram, or merely pointed to angles, when they were solving the problems.

The solutions obtained by the six subjects are shown in Table 2. The solutions are given in abbreviated form, indicating only the main steps that occurred. These correspond to relations that were noticed or inferred by the subjects. Most were mentioned explicitly in protocols, although I have maintained a degree of consistency in these records that was not entirely present in the protocols. The additions mainly involve mediating relations of congruence that were not always mentioned. A typical case is the second part of Step 2 in the solution obtained by Subject 1. The subject mentioned that angle $A3$ was congruent to angle $A1$, and I have added the intermediate step of inferring that angle $A3$ was congruent to angle $A6$.

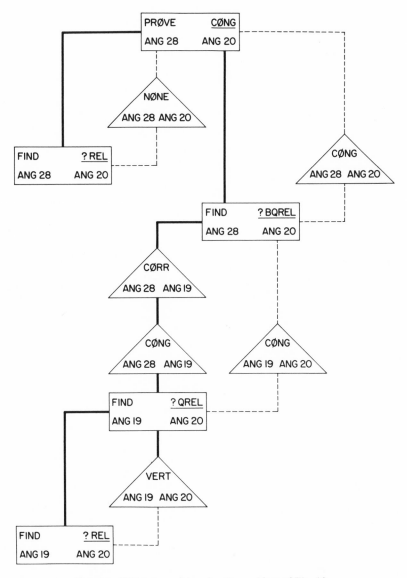

FIG. 14   GPS-type goal tree for the problem of Fig. 10.

PERDIX is capable of generating a variety of solutions for problems like the one in Fig. 15. When PERDIX has the goal of finding a bridging relation, the relations of alternate interior angles, corresponding angles, and vertical angles are tried in some order. The solution generated for a problem like Fig. 15 will depend on that order. The order of trying relations might be a kind of cognitive

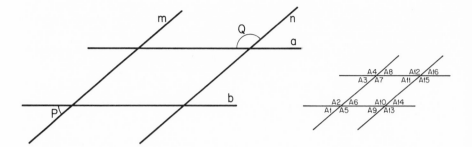

Given a ∥ b and m ∥ n, measure of ∠P = 40°

Find the measure of ∠Q

FIG. 15   Problem of proving angles congruent given to subjects.

set, which we might feel is not a central issue in the psychological structure that is involved in solving problems. Thus, it is of interest to compare solutions given by subjects with solutions that can be generated by PERDIX, varying only the order of trying relations.

PERDIX' ability to generate solutions resembling these human solutions is quite good. Subject 1's solution would be generated exactly either with the order (i) alternate interior (ii) vertical (iii) corresponding, or the order (i) vertical (ii) alternate interior (iii) corresponding. Subject 3's solution would be generated with either of the orders that have corresponding angles first.

Subject 2's performance was somewhat complicated. The solution labeled "initial" was given first. Then, I asked the subject whether the solution had been achieved all at once, or whether there had been stages the subject could recall. The subject then reported that the first solution achieved was different; the subject then described the solution labeled "retrospective." The solution reported first was more economical, and the subject gave it for that reason. Subject 2's retrospective report of the first solution achieved can be simulated exactly by PERDIX if bridging relations are tried in the order (i) vertical (ii) corresponding (iii) alternate interior.

Subject 3's solution departs from the format of PERDIX' performance in that Subject 3 assigned measure to each angle found in the chain of related angles, while PERDIX agrees with the majority of subjects I have observed in deriving a relation between the given and unknown angles, and then computing the measure. This seems a relatively unimportant discrepancy, and could be corrected by revising the order of productions that are concerned with various kinds of subgoals. The sequence of related angles found by Subject 3 would also be found by PERDIX if its order of trying relations had corresponding angles in the first position.

Subject 4's solution also was complicated. The initial solution given contains an error; the subject found a bridging relation consisting of opposite angles in a parallelogram, and this theorem was not available for use. The subject said, "... there's a theorem that says that those two angles will be congruent," and of course there is, but it had not been introduced yet. The subject went ahead and completed a sketch of a solution, then said, "I can give you all the little theorems, except for that one." In doing this, the subject accepted the "missing theorem" as a subproblem, and solved it in the way shown in the revised solution in Table 2. In fact, a solution similar to the revised solution would be generated by PERDIX with the order (i) vertical (ii) alternate interior (iii) corresponding. Step 3 would not occur in PERDIX' solution, because PERDIX would identify the relation of straight angles between $A11$ and $A12$, completing the problem with one fewer bridging relation. The organization of the subject's solution, involving a subproblem of relating $A6$ and $A11$, would not characterize PERDIX' solution.

Subject 5's solution could not be simulated by PERDIX, since a function for alternate exterior angles has not been incorporated. Adding it would not significantly change PERDIX, and the other solutions it generates would be unchanged if alternate exterior angles were simply put last in the order of trying bridging relations.

The relations found in the first three steps of Subject 6's solution were identical to those given by Subject 1; then, Subject 6 failed to identify $A8$ and $A12$ as interior angles on the same side of the transversal. After giving the third step, the subject said, "I was going to figure out if I could get this angle ($A8$) equal to Q, and I figured out there's no way to do that, so I'm going to go by using supplementary angles." The supplementary angle that was found was $A4$. Note that $A4$ is related to the unknown angle $A12$, but the subject failed to identify that these are corresponding angles. Instead, a vertical angle was found, and then the relation of alternate interior angles was identified.

Two modifications would be needed in PERDIX for it to stimulate the sequence of relations in Subject 6's solution. First, the system that identifies relations would have to fail to recognize interior angles on the same side of the transversal and corresponding angles. I have not tried to simulate probabilistic pattern recognition, though there would be little difficulty in doing that. However, the other modification would be more interesting. After Step 3, the subject reached a dead end, as PERDIX would with the reduced identification system. PERDIX would have nothing to do at that point, but the subject apparently generated the goal of finding an angle supplementary to the most recent bridging angle found. The strategy of generating something when all else fails is relatively weak, but is a useful one in many circumstances. Once $A4$ became part of the problem PERDIX, without corresponding angles, would complete the problem as the subject did.

TABLE 2
Solutions by Student Subjects

Step	Subject 1	Subject 2 (Initial)	Subject 2 (Retrospect)	Subject 3
1	(VERT A1 A6) (CONG A1 A6)	(STRT A1 A5) (SUPP A1 A5) (MEAS A5 140)	(VERT A1 A6) (CONG A1 A6)	(CORR A1 A3) (CONG A1 A3) (MEAS A3 40)
2	(ALTINT A6 A3) (CONG A6 A3) (CONG A1 A3)	(CORR A5 A13) (CONG A5 A13) (MEAS A13 140)	(CORR A6 A14) (CONG A6 A14) (CONG A1 A14)	(CORR A3 A11) (CONG A3 A11) (MEAS A11 40)
3	(VERT A3 A8) (CONG A3 A8) (CONG A1 A8)	(ALTEXT A13 A12) (CONG A13 A12) (MEAS A12 140)	(CORR A14 A16) (CONG A1 A16)	(STRT A11 A12) (SUPP A11 A12) (MEAS A12 140)
4	(INTSAM A8 A12) (SUPP A8 A12) (SUPP A1 A12)		(STRT A16 A12) (SUPP A16 A12) (SUPP A1 A12) (MEAS A12 140)	
5	(MEAS A12 140)			
6				

REPRESENTATION OF UNDERSTANDING IN PERDIX

I have reported that PERDIX' capabilities will generate a good approximation to the variety of solution patterns that subjects generate when they solve problems involving angles formed by parallel lines and transversals. However, a more interesting question is whether Perdix represents a process of understanding in its solution of problems. To judge that, we consider the nature of the relational structure that PERDIX generates, including its coherence, correspondence to the features of the given problem, and connectedness to general knowledge structures.

Coherence

I believe that PERDIX' understanding of problems is quite strong as regards its capability of generating coherent solution patterns. PERDIX' method of solving problems is to generate new relations among problem components, eventually

TABLE 2 *(Continued)*

Subject 4 (Initial)	Subject 4 (Revised)	Subject 5	Subject 6
(VERT A1 A6)	Initial	(ALTEXT A1 A8)	(VERT A1 A6)
(CONG A1 A6)	Step 1	(CONG A1 A8)	(CONG A1 A6)
			(MEAS A6 40)
(?REL A6 A11)	(ALTINT A6 A3)	(INTSAM A8 A12)	(ALTINT A6 A3)
(CONG A6 A11)	(CONG A6 A3)	(SUPP A8 A12)	(CONG A6 A3)
(CONG A1 A11)	(CONG A1 A3)	(SUPP A1 A12)	(MEAS A3 40)
		(MEAS A12 140)	
(VERT A11 A16)	(CORR A3 A11)		(VERT A3 A8)
(CONG A11 A16)	(CONG A3 A11)		(CONG A3 A8)
(CONG A1 A16)	(CONG A1 A11)		(MEAS A8 40)
(STRT A16 A12)	Initial		(STRT A8 A4)
(SUPP A16 A12)	Step 3		(SUPP A8 A4)
(SUPP A1 A12)			(MEAS A4 140)
(MEAS A12 140)			
	Initial		(VERT A4 A7)
	Step 4		(CONG A4 A7)
			(MEAS A7 140)
			(ALTINT A7 A12)
			(CONG A7 A12)
			(MEAS A12 140)

achieving a structure that satisfies the requirement of the problem. The structure that is achieved is incorporated into the knowledge base of the problem solver. The record that PERDIX keeps is not a record of its actions, but of the relations that it discovers and infers. The relational information stored during problem solving can constitute a coherent representation of the solved problem, just as a relational structure incorporating the concepts in a sentence can constitute a coherent representation of the meaning of the sentence.

It seems a favorable feature that PERDIX' design makes it possible for problems to be solved with understanding. But a more important feature would be the possibility of representing interesting differences in the coherence of alternative solutions that PERDIX could achieve. In principle, it seems feasible that PERDIX could solve some problems either by generating global relations that provide central conceptual focus, or by generating a sequence of relatively disconnected solution components. As yet, I have not studied problems that admit very large differences in degree of higher-order relational structure in their solutions, but some indication of the potential of the system for such study is

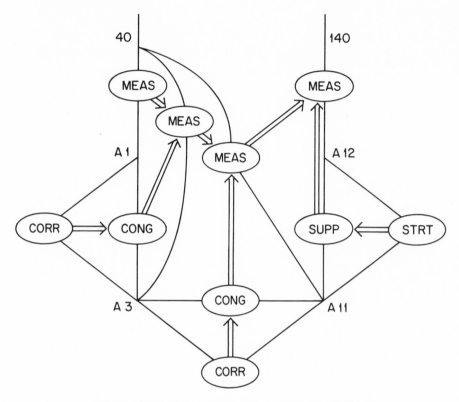

FIG. 16   Graph of the solution pattern obtained by Subject 3.

suggested by one aspect of the solutions of the parallel-lines problem presented here.

One determinant of the coherence of structure achieved by a problem solver is the strategy used in obtaining the solution. As I noted before, Subject 3's solution of the parallel-lines problem was based on a different strategy than PERDIX currently uses. PERDIX derives a relation between the given and unknown angles, while Subject 3 calculated the measure of each angle used in the solution sequence. A graph of Subject 3's solution pattern is shown in Fig. 16, and a graph of PERDIX' solution pattern is shown in Fig. 17.

Intuitively, PERDIX' strategy seems to lead to a somewhat more coherent pattern than does the strategy used by Subject 3. The quantitative relation SUPP between angles $A1$ and $A12$ seems to give at least a weak focus to the structure, with other relations tied in with it. This informal impression is consistent with an analysis of connectedness. Both graphs have six elements, giving 15 pairs, and both graphs have seven pairs linked by single relations. In Subject 3's graph, there are four pairs connected through minimum paths of length two, three pairs

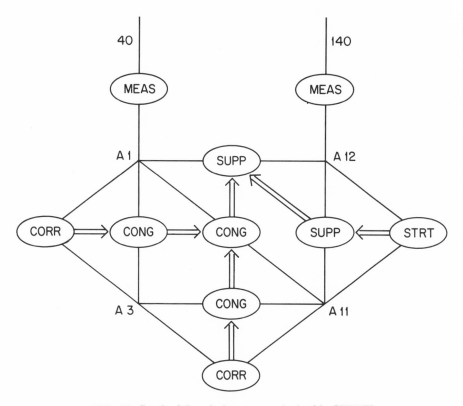

FIG. 17 Graph of the solution pattern obtained by PERDIX.

with length three, and one pair with length four. In PERDIX' graph, there are six pairs connected by minimum paths of length two, and the other two have length three. (The reader may note that an arithmetic step has been omitted—the graphs show no calculation of 180–40. Inclusion of this would have equal effects on the two graphs shown in Fig. 16 and Fig. 17.)

The coherence of a solution pattern will also depend on the specific knowledge structures that are available to the problem solver. An example that has been presented here involves Subject 6's solution of the problem about parallel lines. Subject 6's solution seems to be rather more fragmentary than the others, since it arrived at a kind of dead end at Step 3, and Step 4 seems to be motivated only by the goal of finding some angle that was supplementary to the angle most recently incorporated in the solution. Recall that PERDIX would simulate this solution if some of its knowledge were to be removed—specifically, it would have to fail to identify interior angles on the same side of the transversal, and corresponding angles. In this example, the coherence of PERDIX' solution involves a kind of directness. Using all of its capability to identify relations,

PERDIX (like most of the student subjects) achieves a relatively direct sequence of inferences that leads to the answer. Failure to retrieve a needed relation led Subject 6 to a solution that was less direct, requiring a kind of detour.

Correspondence

The second criterion of understanding is good correspondence with materials of the problem. I am inclined to think that in geometry, there is a more direct correspondence between solutions and problem materials if the transformations that are used and the relations that are generated are spatial rather than algebraic in nature. Numerical and verbal–symbolic operations clearly are needed for many problems in geometry. However, when a choice exists, it generally seems that operations involving spatial relations preserve the sense of the problem to a greater degree than corresponding operations carried out after quantities in a geometric figure have been assigned to variables in equations.

Again, it seems that PERDIX provides a reasonable framework for investigating alternative structures that produce varying degrees of correspondence between solutions and problem inputs. In its present form, PERDIX seems to perform a reasonably meaningful interaction between its procedures for processing information in a diagram and its more propositional knowledge used in making inferences. An important feature seems to be the representation of information in a diagram as a relational structure of the same general form as the representation of verbal propositions. This permits a single production system, based on pattern matching and pattern generation, to govern the activity of both the verbal and spatial knowledge structures used in the solution of a given problem.

On the other hand, in its present form, PERDIX has a rather weak set of analytical procedures for using spatial information. The EPAM-type net that PERDIX uses for identifying relations uses such features as shared sides of angles, and sides that are extended straight lines of other sides, but is seems likely that problem solving in geometry often uses more powerful procedures, such as superposition of figures following rotation or reflection, or judgment of similarity of shape. A set of procedures for analyzing and transforming spatial relations in diagrams would result in a stronger binding of PERDIX' problem-solving process to the geometric materials of problems, and thus would result in stronger understanding in its solutions, in the sense of correspondence to problem materials.

Some evidence showing the need for stronger use of spatial properties is present in the protocols from which the sketches shown in Table 2 were taken. Subject 2's recall of the first solution that was found began as follows: "The first thing I did was I looked across like this, because that's the line of your viewing, because you see *PQ*." (Looking "across like this" meant scanning diagonally between the two marked angles in the diagram.) It is reasonable to conjecture that Subject 2's solution was developed in four stages: first, the subject scanned across the diagram and formed a spatial pattern containing angles P and Q. Angle $A6$ was incorporated in this pattern easily, since it is on a direct line from P to Q. The pattern was incomplete because no known relations could be found to link $A6$ with $A12$, so the spatial pattern had to be expanded to include an angle at one of the other corners. The expansion that was found involved corresponding angles $A14$ and $A16$. Note that $A16$ in this pattern is spatially outside the region in the diagram bounded by the sides of angles P and Q. This feature might have contributed to Subject 2's recognizing that a simpler solution might be available. If the subject reviewed the first solution using the process of scanning back from Q to P, it would seem quite awkward to begin by moving away from the line between Q and P to include angle $A16$; however, the path involving $A10$ and $A5$ would be quite natural moving in that direction.

The importance of spatial features is also evident in Subject 4's protocol. This subject formed a sequence of angles directly along the diagonal, including $A6$, $A11$, and $A16$. Although no theorem was known linking $A6$ and $A11$, these angles are evidently congruent in the diagram, and the subject apparently believed that there was a theorem supporting this although the subject was unable to retrieve the name of the theorem from memory. In trying to supply the reasons for each step, the subject provided a revised solution that included a bridging link between $A6$ and $A11$.

Finally, although the solution found by Subject 5 could have been generated by PERDIX in its present form, the requirement that alternate exterior angles be first on the subject's order of trying relations seems improbable. It seems more likely that Subject 5's elegant solution was found through a scanning process that used spatial relations in the diagram in generating a connected pattern.

It seems to me that these three cases indicate that human subjects use spatial properties of diagrams as an aid in planning solutions. In its present form, PERDIX' planning functions are represented in its goal structure, and this is independent of spatial properties. A changed method of planning that uses spatial features would increase the overall degree of correspondence between PERDIX' solutions and the spatial character of geometry problems. It would probably also increase the power of PERDIX' problem-solving capability.

Problem solving is affected by spatial processing in a second way that PERDIX also fails to represent in its present form. There are strong biases in the identification of many relations and forms. One of these appears in the solutions obtained by Subjects 4 and 6 for the example problem discussed here. This particular bias involves identifying adjacent supplementary angles ("straight angles," in PERDIX' terminology) whose external sides are horizontal in preference to identifying adjacent supplementary angles whose external sides are oblique. Subject 4 found a solution that included $A11$, and $A11$ is directly related to angle Q, but the subject did not identify that relation. Instead, $A16$ was also included in the solution. The external sides of angle Q and $A16$ are horizontal; the external sides of angle Q and $A11$ are oblique. The same kind of bias appeared in Subject 6's solution. Needing an angle supplementary to $A8$, Subject 6 identified $A4$, and the external sides of $A4$ and $A8$ are horizontal. A more direct solution using $A8$ would involve relating $A8$ and $A7$, but the external sides of these angles are oblique.

Preference for use of horizontal lines in spatial patterns appears in many different problems; I think it must be a rather general feature of the spatial processing that subjects use. General features of visual perception suggest that horizontal and vertical axes may be especially salient in organizing a spatial field. In its present form, PERDIX is entirely insensitive to the orientation of lines in a diagram, and this clearly is unrealistic. Incorporating perceptual biases into PERDIX' mechanisms for identifying relations may make PERDIX' general problem-solving capability less powerful in some ways. For example, in its present form, if PERDIX arrived at $A11$, it would always identify the direct relation between $A11$ and angle Q, rather than taking the detour through $A16$ as Subject 4 did. Of course, it is possible that use of horizontal and vertical axes to organize a spatial diagram serves other useful purposes to compensate for the apparent inefficiencies that occur.

Connectedness to General Knowledge

I have not yet included any general knowledge structures in PERDIX that would permit investigation of interesting processes of interpretation or generalization in problem solving. However, the examples that I will sketch briefly in the remaining sections indicate some of the capabilities that should be targets of theoretical development in this regard.

Interpreting word problems. There are two ways in which human subjects show clearly that their knowledge of geometry is connected with general knowledge. First, general concepts are connected to geometric concepts when students interpret word problems. Subjects were given the following problem, accompanied by Fig. 18:

A medieval battle is going on, and your army is trying to attack a castle on the upper side of the river. You have to get across this bridge, but the enemy has the other side and shoots at your soldiers when they try to cross. So you want to set up a catapult at C to fire at T. This line here (the vertical segment marked "150 yd") is a road that goes straight from the bridge back into the territory you have. To set up your catapult, you must know how far its shots must travel. You go along this line here (the horizontal line lowest in the diagram) perpendicular to the road, until you can sight along a

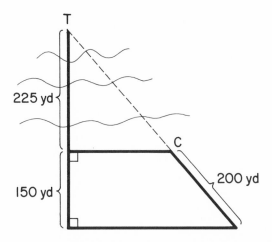

FIG. 18 Diagram accompanying a word problem given to subjects.

line through the place where you want the catapult, directly to the target. Then you measure the distances that are marked here. How far must the catapult shoot?

In working on this problem subjects had no difficulty in translating the information given into a set of geometric concepts. The relevant concepts involved similar right triangles, and subjects made use of those concepts easily. In other problems where diagrams were not presented, subjects showed considerable facility in constructing diagrams representing relevant geometric information from descriptions of ordinary objects such as tables and metal signs.

When subjects encounter a word problem, they typically construct representations that allow them to use geometric knowledge rather directly. In the problem about the catapult, subjects typically recognized the presence of similar triangles, and then applied an algorithm for calculating lengths of sides. The capability shown by this must include coordination of knowledge in geometry with general semantic knowledge. Apparently there is little difficulty in retrieving geometric concepts in response to inputs that do not mention those concepts directly, but specify their properties. The specification may involve quite indirect descriptions, including information about physical objects that is irrelevant to the problem. It should be noted that in the instances I have recorded, students are aware that we are discussing geometry, and this feature of general context probably is quite important in facilitating retrieval of components of the students' geometric knowledge. Nonetheless, the capability of constructing appropriate problem representations for word problems shows that a realistic theory of problem solving must include mechanisms for accessing special knowledge structures through general processes of comprehension and ordinary concepts.

Generalization of principles. The second way in which subjects indicate connections between specialized problem-solving structures and general knowledge involves their ability to apply concepts and propositions to new situations. When principles that have been acquired in relation to one kind of problem can be applied to new kinds of problems, we probably should infer that the generalization is mediated by some more general principles or procedures, and a theory should represent the relationship between the initial structure and those general concepts and principles that support the generalization.

One task that was given to student subjects in geometry required a generalization of the concept of congruence. This concept had been studied in some detail regarding triangles, but had not been examined for any other plane figures. After some discussion about congruent triangles, I showed two irregular quadrilaterals of the same size and shape, and asked subjects what they thought it would mean for the two quadrilaterals to be congruent, and how one might prove congruence for them. In one protocol that was given, the subject generated answers using a physical model. The subject thought about forming a quadrilateral from lines attached to each other with fixed angles. By thinking about the possible ways of deforming a polygon, the subject correctly concluded that congruence could not be proved from congruence of three corresponding sides and one angle, but side-angle-side-angle-side would be sufficient. This subject had also mentioned a physical model in describing the meaning of congruence of triangles, and some abstract properties involving equivalence of size and shape were apparently used to mediate the generalization from triangles to quadrilaterals.

Another subject solved the problem of congruent quadrilaterals by constructing diagonals of both figures, and noting that if information were given permitting proof that both pairs of triangles were congruent, that would also permit a proof that the quadrilaterals were congruent. This creative decomposition of the problem reminds one of Wertheimer's (1959) discussion of the area of a parallelogram, where the problem is transformed in a way that permits use of previous knowledge.

The two solutions sketched briefly here both involve analyses of a novel problem in relation to general knowledge. In the first solution, the analysis involved application of some general concepts of sameness, abstracted from the subject's understanding of congruent triangles. In the second solution, the analysis resulted in a transformation of the problem that permitted use of previously learned procedures. Both kinds of capability represent significant theoretical challenges at this stage of our psychological understanding.

CONCLUSION

In this essay, I have developed some ideas about what it means to solve a problem with understanding, rather than merely finding a correct solution. I have proposed some criteria that I think can be applied generally to occurrences of understanding, and that permit a judgment of how well something is understood. And I have shown how an analysis of problem solving viewed as a process of pattern generation can provide a means of evaluating the goodness of understanding achieved by a problem solver.

I have described the main features of a hypothetical problem solver, PERDIX, and used PERDIX' capabilities as a case study regarding the kinds of processes that might be responsible for understanding in problem solving. PERDIX' main processes are pattern matching and pattern generation. In solving a problem, PERDIX creates a structure of relations among problem components. Depending on the knowledge structures that are applied in reaching the solution, the structure that is generated can give a coherent representation of the problem components, showing how they are related in a compact manner. Thus, PERDIX can satisfy one important criterion of good understanding, the criterion of achieving a representation in which the various components of an object are related in a coherent structure.

Regarding the second criterion of good understanding, correspondence of the representation to the object that is understood, PERDIX manages a meaningful interaction between spatial information taken from a diagram and the procedures (often verbal propositions) that are used in solving problems. However, it seems likely that to represent the degree of understanding in the sense of correspondence that most subjects achieve, PERDIX should have a more powerful set of procedures for transforming and analyzing spatial relations, including procedures in which diagrams are used in the planning of solutions.

The third criterion of good understanding that I proposed is connectedness of a representation to general concepts and procedures in a structure of knowledge. This important issue in the theory of problem solving is not developed at all in the present form of PERDIX.

Conceptualizing problem solving as a process of pattern generation appears to make possible a meaningful analysis of the degree to which an instance of problem solving involves good understanding. There is clearly a good deal of work to be done, beyond the present version of PERDIX, to achieve a good theoretical representation of understanding in problem solving. However, even the present form of PERDIX seems to provide a promising start.

ACKNOWLEDGMENTS

This research was supported by Grant MH25218 from the National Institute of Mental Health. I am grateful for discussions with John Anderson, Clayton Lewis, Paul Kline, and Herbert Simon concerning various aspects of this materal. I am also grateful to six students from a high school geometry class who generously provided thinking-aloud protocols in interviews held weekly during the 1974–75 academic year, and to the administrative officials and geometry teacher in their school for making it possible for me to carry out those interviews.

REFERENCES

Anderson, J. R. *Language, memory, and thought.* Hillsdale, N.J.: Lawrence Erlbaum Assoc., 1976.
Anderson, J. R., & Bower, G. M. *Human associative memory.* Washington, D.C.: Winston, 1973.
Bransford, J. D., & Johnson, M. K. Considerations of some problems of comprehension. In W. G. Chase (Ed.), *Visual information processing.* New York: Academic Press, 1973. Pp. 383–438.
Duncker, K. On problem solving. *Psychological Monographs*, 1945, 58, Whole No. 270.
Egan, D. E., & Greeno, J. G. Acquiring cognitive structure by discovery and rule learning. *Journal of Educational Psychology*, 1973, 64 85–97.
Feigenbaum, E. A. The simulation of verbal learning behavior. In E. Feigenbaum & J. Feldman (Ed.), *Computers and thought.* New York: McGraw-Hill, 1963. Pp. 297–309.
Gagné, R. M. Human problem solving: Internal and external events. In B. Kleinmuntz (Ed.), *Problem solving: Research, method, and theory.* New York: Wiley, 1966. Pp. 127–148.
Gelernter, H. Realization of a geometry-theorem proving machine. In E. A. Feigenbaum & J. Feldman (Eds.), *Computers and thought.* New York: McGraw-Hill, 1963. Pp. 134–152.
Goldstein, I. Elementary geometry theorem proving. Massachusetts Institute of Technology Artificial Intelligence Laboratory Memo No. 280, 1973.
Hunt, E. B., Marin, J., & Stone, P. I. *Experiments in induction.* New York: Academic Press, 1966.
Jurgensen, R. C., Donnelly, A. J., & Dolciani, M. P. *Modern school mathematics: Geometry.* Boston, Massachusetts: Houghton Mifflin, 1972.
Katona, G. *Organizing and memorizing.* New York: Columbia University Press, 1940.
Kintsch, W. *The representation of meaning in memory.* Hillsdale, N.J.: Lawrence Erlbaum Assoc., 1974.
Köhler, W. *The mentality of apes.* New York: Harcourt Brace, 1927.
Mayer, R. E., & Greeno, J. G. Structural differences between learning outcomes produced by different instructional procedures. *Journal of Educational Psychology*, 1972, 63, 165–173.
Mayer, R. E., Stiehl, C. C., & Greeno, J. G. Acquisition of understanding and skill in relation to subjects' preparation and meaningfulness of instruction. *Journal of Educational Psychology*, 1975, 67, 331–350.
Newell, A. Discussion of papers by Robert M. Gagné and John R. Hayes. In B. Kleinmuntz (Ed.), *Problem solving: Research, method, and theory.* New York: Wiley, 1966. Pp. 171–182.
Newell, A., Shaw, J. C., & Simon, H. A. Empirical exploration with the logic theory machine: A case study in heuristics. In E. A. Feigenbaum & J. Feldman (Ed.), *Computers and thought:* New York: McGraw-Hill, 1963. Pp. 109–133.
Newell, A., & Simon, H. A. *Human problem solving.* Englewood Cliffs, N.J.: Prentice-Hall, 1972.
Nilsson, N. J. *Problem-solving methods in artificial intelligence.* New York: McGraw-Hill, 1971.
Norman, D. A., & Rumelhart, D. E. *Explorations in cognition.* San Francisco, California: Freeman, 1975.

Schank, R. C. Conceptual dependency: A theory of natural language understanding. *Cognitive Psychology*, 1972, 3, 552–631.
Verbrugge, R. R. Resemblances in language and perception. In R. E. Shaw & J. D. Bransford (Eds.), *Acting, perceiving, and comprehending: Toward an ecological psychology*. Hillsdale, N.J.: Lawrence Erlbaum Assoc., 1976.
Wertheimer, M. *Productive thinking*, Enlarged edition, New York: Harper & Row, 1959.
Winograd, T. Understanding natural language. *Cognitive Psychology*, 1972, 3, 1–191.

Part II

DECISION PROCESSES

The chapters in this section reflect a contemporary emphasis on cognitive processes in decision making. Much early research in decision making focused on normative models of the decision process in which the behavior of subjects was examined and contrasted with predictions of the models. If subjects failed to perform in accordance with the model, the experimental situation was rejected as inappropriate and new experiments were designed in an effort to encourage subjects to behave as the model specified. A consequence of such concern was that the tasks used and behavior studied became progressively more remote from the tasks and decisions which are found outside the laboratory.

In contrast, the changing emphasis reflected in the following chapters focuses on two important aspects of decision processes. The first is a recognition that subjects have limited capability which has an effect on their ability to process information, the second is that an important class of decision tasks involves cues or stimuli which are of less than perfect validity. Both aspects bear on the relevance and generality of research beyond stylized laboratory settings.

The concern with cues which are of less than perfect validity is a feature of each of the chapters in this section, although each author describes this characteristic differently. Wallsten discusses this aspect in terms of "ambiguous" or "equivocal" information, Castellan discusses "probabilistic" cues or cues with "less than perfect validity," and Schum uses the terminology "inconclusive evidence" and "probabilistic evidence." Decision tasks with such probabilistic characteristics are common in real-world situations involving both specialized tasks such as clinical and medical diagnosis, weather prediction, intelligence evaluation, and ordinary tasks such as interpersonal learning, impression formation, and the evaluation of evidence.

In each of the chapters in this section, the information processing capabilities of people is characterized as a multistep or hierarchical process. The stimuli (or cues, or information) are broken down into components for processing. In the chapters by Wallsten and Castellan this is accomplished by describing the cues in terms of aspects and dimensions, respectively. In Schum's chapter, the evidence is divided into components representing the credibility of the information source and the inferential or diagnostic value of the testimony. Further division results from consideration of the testimony of multiple sources.

Each author makes different assumptions about the manner of combination of information for processing. Wallsten's model assumes that subjects attend to sources of information in terms of their saliency, the most salient source being examined first, followed by the next most salient dimension. Evaluation of information continues until a criterion level of certainty is reached at which time the subject will stop seeking information and make a response. Castellan also describes a model of selective attention. In his model, the subject attends to dimensions in a probabilistic fashion such that attention is focused on dimensions in proportion to their validity. However, instead of successively processing dimensions, only one aspect is evaluated in arriving at a response. Thus, for Wallsten the evaluation of dimensions is in a fixed order of random length, while for Castellan the evaluation is in terms of a random order of fixed length. In Schum's prescriptive model, all information is utilized, but is weighted by source credibility (reliability).

In his chapter, Wallsten outlines the elements of a general algebraic model which is a representation of his heuristic theory about the manner in which persons combine cues and dimensions in decision tasks as a function of their saliency or validity. After presenting the model in some detail, Wallsten describes a series of experiments in which the model has been applied. In Castellan's chapter the present state of development of research in nonmetric multiple-cue probability learning is reviewed, together with related results from research in probabilistic discrimination learning and concept identification studies which utilize misinformative feedback. Particular attention is paid to the crucial role of dimensionality of cues in decision making. Finally, Schum's chapter deals with the application of decision making methodology to inference tasks common in jurisprudence. The methodology utilized applies to a wide range of tasks which have become known as "cascaded" inference tasks.

The chapters in this section make a nice progression. Wallsten examines decision making in what might be called formally abstract tasks, Castellan utilizes tasks which are more representative of the sort encountered in natural settings, and Schum departs from the laboratory entirely and models decision tasks in the real world. Thus, the chapters illustrate a wide variety of contemporary approaches to the study of decision making. Finally, they show how decision making methodology can be useful in gaining a greater understanding of cognitive processes employed in inference behavior.

4
Processing Information for Decisions

Thomas S. Wallsten

University of North Carolina at Chapel Hill

There is some dissatisfaction with many of the current models and theories which purport to describe how humans combine conflicting, equivocal information to arrive at a unique decision. For example, in a review of the use of Bayesian and regression models Slovic and Lichtenstein (1971) wrote that "if we are to pursue this line of research we will have to develop new models and different methods of experimentation [p. 729]." In this chapter, I will discuss the process theory, algebraic models, empirical techniques, and some data that have stemmed from research in our laboratory.

The task is one in which subjects are given a set of data and required to decide which of two hypotheses is more likely correct. The most common (some would say overworked) paradigm along these lines is the book bag and pokerchip experiment in which subjects are shown a sample of red and white chips in order to decide whether the bag from which they were drawn contained, say, 70% red and 30% white chips, or, say, 20% red and 80% white chips. Another example of this task is the situation in which a physician must decide in the absence of an X ray whether a patient more likely has a skull fracture or not, given data such as the patient's length of unconsciousness, degree of retrograde amnesia, display of the Babinski reflex, etc. (Bell & Loop, 1971; Fryback, 1974). A last example of this task is the well known study by Meehl (1959) in which psychologists were required to determine whether a patient was psychotic or neurotic given a profile of scores from the MMPI (Goldberg, 1965).

Although the theory which will follow is limited to describing how one chooses between two hypotheses, it may apply as well to situations in which one is choosing among n hypotheses, where n is greater than two. This would be the case if under such circumstances the subject focused on one hypothesis, X, and chose between it and its complement, not X, or between X and a specific alternative Y. Although there is evidence that subjects consider only a subset of available hypotheses at a time, it remains to be seen whether this particular conceptualization is appropriate.

Before proceeding further, it is necessary to introduce two distinctions which are only occasionally found in the literature. The first, implied in the title of this chapter, is between processing information and making decisions. It is not unreasonable to expect that the cognitive processes involved in combining information are distinct from those involved in arriving at a decision after the information has been assimilated. However, since any behavior which reflects the processing of information also reflects a decision based on that information, models of information processing must be formulated so that their predictions are independent of decision making considerations.

The tack taken in the present work is to assume that when a subject combines information for the purpose of evaluating the likelihood that X, rather than Y, is true, and then provides a response which depends on that opinion, his response is no more than monotonically related to his certainty that X is correct. It is further assumed that the metric properties of the response depend on decision making considerations such as risk aversion and response biases (Wallsten, 1976). Thus, the information processing model is developed and tested at an ordinal level.

The second distinction necessary for our purposes is often made use of, but not often discussed explicitly. It is between what I will call a *heuristic theory* and a *formal model*. This distinction is similar to that expressed in Hoffman's statement (1960) of the paramorphic problem. In 1968 Hoffman wrote: "First, two or more models of judgment may be algebraic equivalents of one another, yet suggest radically different underlying processes. . . . Second, two or more models may be algebraically different, yet be equally predictive, given fallible data [p. 62]." If I understand him correctly, Hoffman (1960, 1968) is suggesting that a judge uses a particular process for combining information, and at best that process can only be approximated by a less than perfectly accurate algebraic model.

Without commenting on that formulation of the problem, I would like to suggest a slightly different one. There exist a variety of levels at which one can theorize about a process. At one extreme is the heuristic theory, in which one's understanding or theorizing is general, heuristic, less than formal, and usually verbal. Many "process theories" are stated at this level. At the other extreme, one's understanding is embodied in a model that is specific, limited in scope, and formally developed. For example, process theories are often formalized in specific computer programs. The models in this chapter will be algebraic, involving various parameters combined in specific ways.

Theorizing at each of the two extremes has advantages and drawbacks. Process theories usually are easily generalizable across situations, but are rarely specified precisely or amenable to rigorous test. Alternatively, formal models often allow specific comparisons between theory and data, but usually cannot be generalized across tasks in a natural way. Examples of the two levels of theorizing exist in the problem area under consideration. Tversky and Kahneman's (1974) set of heuristics, such as anchoring and adjusting, searching memory for available instances, and assessing an event's representativeness, is an example of a heuristic theory. The theory's implications are compelling, but difficult to state and test precisely. On the other hand, the Bayesian (Edwards, 1968) and regression models (Dawes & Corrigan, 1974; Slovic & Lichtenstein, 1971) which have enjoyed some degree of popularity are precise, but of limited applicability.[1]

It is suggested here that theorizing at both levels is necessary for a more complete understanding of a process. The general heuristic theory provides a broad descriptive statement of how the process works and the factors which influence it. The theory should be stated in such a way that when it is applied to a particular situation it can be represented by a well-defined formal model. The theory should be able to specify the conditions under which a particular model will hold, provide an interpretation for the parameters of the model, and suggest how the parameters will vary as a function of experimental manipulations. Conversely, analyzing data according to a particular model will suggest how a theory should be altered.

This interplay between heuristic theory and formal model is not entirely novel. It can be seen, for example, in much computer simulation work, or in work on memory by Greeno (1967; Humphreys & Greeno, 1970) and by Atkinson and Shiffrin (1968).

A PROCESS THEORY

Let us turn, now, to a heuristic process theory which purports to describe how humans combine information for the purpose of inferring which of two hypotheses is more likely correct. The theory, in fact, came about in order to make sense of data analyzed according to certain algebraic models, which will be introduced presently (Wallsten, 1976). However, it is compatible with various

---

[1] Ms. Christa Peterson has pointed out to me that this distinction between heuristic theories and formal models is similar to one advocated by Reese and Overton (1970) in the study of developmental psychology, although unfortunately we use the terms "theory" and "model" in almost opposite fashions. Reese and Overton (1970) base their development on certain views in the history and philosophy of science (e.g., Kuhn, 1970), and speak of models and theories in a manner consistent with that literature. I have attempted to use the terms in a manner that is consistent with phrases often appearing in the research literature, such as "mathematical model" or "computer program model." It is clear that there is a distinction between the levels of theorizing, but it is not clear how the extremes of this distinction should be labeled.

other information processing theories and seems to handle a wide variety of results. After outlining the theory I shall present the models, and then look at various sets of data using the models to obtain answers to questions posed within the context of the theory.

Our theory supposes that the sample of ambiguous information presented to the subject can be considered a complex multidimensional stimulus. For example, in judging applicants for graduate school, one dimension might be an applicant's GRE verbal score, another his GRE math score, a third some portion of a referee's letter, etc. In deciding whether a patient has a skull fracture, one dimension might be unconsciousness, another retrograde amnesia, etc.

Dimensions vary in saliency. The term saliency has the same meaning here as it does in Trabasso and Bower's (1968) work on concept formation, in Garner's (1974) discussion of information processing, or in most modern conceptions of attention (Kahneman, 1973). A salient dimension is one to which a subject is likely to attend, and which is likely to control his behavior. Numerous concept learning experiments in humans (summarized in Trabasso & Bower, 1968) and discrimination learning experiments in other animals (discussed in Mackintosh, 1965) have demonstrated that saliency depends on certain perceptual characteristics of the dimensions, the range of possible dimension values, previous experience, the subjects' set, and other factors.

It is assumed here that when subjects process stimuli for the purpose of evaluating one hypothesis relative to another, the resulting judgment is a function of a subset of the most salient dimensions. It is convenient to assume further that dimensions are processed sequentially in decreasing order of saliency. The most salient dimension provides an "anchor" for the judgment, in Slovic and Lichtenstein's (1968) or Tversky and Kahneman's (1974) use of the term. That is, an initial opinion is formed concerning the relative likelihood of hypothesis X relative to hypothesis Y on the basis of the value of the most salient dimension. This opinion is modified or adjusted in light of the value of the next most salient dimension, and then perhaps modified again given the third most salient dimension, and so on, until either all available dimensions have been processed or until a criterion has been reached. At that point, the subject executes a decision based on his final opinion concerning the two hypotheses X and Y.

Note that it is not assumed that the subject always attends to all dimensions. Rather a stopping rule is hypothesized, whereby the subject only processes the K most salient dimensions, where K is less than or equal to the total number of dimensions available.

The value of each dimension attended to influences the subjective likelihood of the two hypotheses, X and Y, in the following manner. Each dimension value has an association with hypothesis X and an association with hypothesis Y. The stronger the association between a dimension value and a particular hypothesis, the more that value suggests the hypothesis is correct. These associations will be termed aspects. Thus, each dimension level has two aspects.

The strength of association depends in part on the subjective likelihood that the value of the dimension will occur if the hypothesis is true. In this sense, the two aspects of a dimension's value are the subjective correlates of the numerator and denominator of a likelihood ratio. But the strength of an association is assumed to depend on other factors in addition to any measures of conditional likelihood. In particular, aspects, like dimensions, vary in saliency. Thus, given that a dimension is attended to, and a particular value of it is present in the stimulus, the subject may rely more strongly on one or the other of the two aspects. The determinants of saliency discussed in the context of dimensions apply here as well.

To summarize, when a subject processes equivocal information for the purpose of deciding between two hypotheses, he is assumed to evaluate the information, one dimension at a time in decreasing order of salience. He forms an initial judgment on the basis of the two aspects of the value of the most salient dimension. The judgment is adjusted in light of the aspects of the value of the next most salient dimension, etc., until processing stops, because either there are no more dimensions or a criterion has been reached.

This theory is similar in many respects to others already available (Slovic, 1972; Slovic & Lichtenstein, 1968; Tversky & Kahneman, 1974), except, perhaps, that it is spelled out in more detail. However, even with the additional detail the theory becomes testable only when it is embodied in a formal model. The particular structure of the model employed will depend on the features of the theory under consideration and the empirical situation in which it is applied.

THE ALGEBRAIC MODEL

The algebraic model to be introduced now has been developed formally by Wallsten (1976). It is concerned with how aspects and dimensions combine, and with the operation of saliency. The model is neutral with respect to whether processing is serial or parallel, and with respect to how processing is terminated. The model is formulated so that it is relevant to a wide variety of situations, but the data which will be presented all come from the single "overworked" book bag and pokerchip paradigm. This, it will be recalled, is the task in which subjects observe a sample of binary events in order to decide which of two binomial distributions is more likely to be the parent, or to be in effect.

Although numerous investigators have suggested that this paradigm be abandoned (e.g., Winkler & Murphy, 1973), it can be justified for our purposes on various grounds. For one thing, the dimensions of the sample are easy to specify. We will consider each of the binary events in the sample to be a dimension.

Thus, each dimension can take one of two values. It appears unnatural at first to consider each event to be a different dimension. However, this leads to an interesting conceptualization, and provides a bridge to other paradigms.

It is also easy to nominally specify the aspects of the levels of a dimension; they are the parameters of the binomial distributions. Since objective measures of the aspects are available, it is easy to determine whether a change in the subjective value of an aspect is due to a change in its salience or not. Another argument in favor of this paradigm is that if salience can be shown to operate in it, it is a safe bet that dimension and aspect salience are factors in other more complex tasks which are more likely to confront the subject with information overload. Finally, the simple nature of this paradigm allows the derivation of special cases of the general model that are easier to work with, and that give additional insight into the subject's behavior.

We turn now to the model. Two kinds of operations are specified:

1. The two aspects of the value of a dimension compose to yield the diagnosticity of that dimension value.

2. The diagnosticities of a number of dimensions combine to yield the overall diagnosticity of the sample of information.

The first operation can be modeled with a subtractive rule and the second with an additive rule. It should be made clear that the term "diagnosticity" refers to the degree that a subject interprets a dimension value, or a data sample, as favoring one of the two hypotheses. Unless otherwise noted, it will not refer to any objective measures of data impact, such as the ratio of conditional probabilities.

Let the two hypotheses between which the subject is deciding be called X and Y. Without loss of generality, we can refer to the (positive or negative) degree to which a dimension favors hypothesis X over hypothesis Y. If the value of the kth dimension of the sample, $k = 1, \ldots, K$, is labeled E_k, then the two aspects of that value can be represented by real-valued functions $\Phi_1(E_k|X)$ and $\Phi_2(E_k|Y)$, respectively. The first function represents the strength of association between E_k and X and the second represents the strength of association between E_k and Y. The diagnostic strength of dimension k is a function of the difference between the two strengths of association, and can be expressed as

$$\Psi(E_k) = \alpha_k [\Phi_1(E_k|X) - \Phi_2(E_k|Y)] , \qquad (1)$$

where $\Psi(E_k)$ represents the diagnostic strength of dimension value E_k, and α_k is a function which depends on the salience of dimension k and which relates the difference in strengths of association to the diagnosticity of E_k.

Retaining the full generality of the function α_k leads to interesting speculation and research, but in the present context only complicates the presentation of the empirical work without altering the conclusions. Thus, for the remainder of this discussion, we shall assume that the function α_k is a multiplicative one which weights the difference in strengths of association by a nonnegative weight a_k. Then we can express the diagnosticity of E_k as

$$\Psi(E_k) = \phi_{1k}(E_k|X) - \phi_{2k}(E_k|Y), \qquad (2)$$

where $\phi_{ik} = a_k\Phi_i$, $i = 1, 2$.

Considering Eq. (2), note that if E_k is more strongly associated with X than with Y, $\Psi(E_k)$ is positive, and E_k favors hypothesis X to some degree. Similarly, if E_k is more strongly associated with Y than with X, $\Psi(E_k)$ is negative, and E_k favors Y to some degree. The diagnostic strength of E_k depends, therefore, on the salience of dimension k and on the two strengths of association, Φ_1 and Φ_2. The latter, Φ_1 and Φ_2, in turn, reflect both the subjective likelihood of E_k given X and Y, respectively, and the degree of attention, or salience, afforded each aspect.

The judgment based on the most salient dimension is modified by that of the next dimension attended to, and so forth for K dimensions. It is convenient to express the overall diagnosticity of the K dimensions as a sum of the separate values:

$$\Psi(D) = \sum_{k=1}^{K} \Psi(E_k), \qquad (3)$$

where D represents the entire data sample, and $\Psi(D)$ represents its diagnostic weight. Thus, the diagnosticity of the data sample equals the sum of the diagnostic weights of the K dimensions attended to, and is either positive, favoring X to some degree, or is negative, favoring Y to some degree.

The diagnosticity of the data sample can also be written in terms of the aspects of the dimension levels by substituting from Eq. (2) into Eq. (3):

$$\Psi(D) = \sum_{k=1}^{K} [\phi_{1k}(E_k|X) - \phi_{2k}(E_k|Y)]. \qquad (4)$$

In other words, the diagnostic weight of the data sample is equal to the sum of K differences, where each difference is between the two aspects of a dimension value and, implicitly, is weighted by the salience of that dimension. Some of you may recognize Eq. (4) as a special case of the additive-difference model proposed by Tversky (1969) for preference judgments. If α_k had not been restricted, we would have Tversky's model precisely.

The model in Eq. (4) is a composition rule (Krantz & Tversky, 1971). That is, it specifies how the aspects of the sample of information combine to yield the sample's diagnostic weight. It might appear initially that the most appropriate way to investigate the model is with a complete factorial design, manipulating each of the K dimensions and each of the two aspects of each dimension value.

However, even the smallest design is unmanageably large, particularly when considering that the ideal experiment in this kind of research utilizes a within subject design. For example, limiting the number of dimensions to two, allowing each dimension to take on one of three values, and each value to have one of three associations with X and one of three associations with Y, results in 36 parameters to be estimated from data collected in 729 cells, assuming a complete orthogonal design.

Clearly, another approach is called for. We have chosen to hold certain factors constant while varying others completely. This technique has the advantage of providing several special cases of the model, each concerned with a different application, and each evaluated with the power of a full factorial design. So far, we have specified five different special cases of Eq. (4) (Wallsten, 1976), and have run experiments relevant to three of them. The remainder of this chapter will be concerned with two of the cases, discussing six experiments to which they apply.

It is necessary to present at least an informal derivation of the two special cases under consideration, so that their relationship to the main model, Eq. (4), and to each other will be clear. A more formal derivation, and a thorough discussion of how the models relate to others in the literature can be found in Wallsten (1976).

In order to obtain one of the special cases, recall that the task faced by our subjects was to observe a set of binary events and then to decide which of two a priori equally likely binomial distributions had generated them. Let there be n events in the sample, and, as indicated earlier, consider each event to be a dimension. Furthermore, for this case assume that all n events are the same, and therefore, differ from each other only in salience. Then going back to Eq. (4), the two aspects of each of $n - 1$ of the events can be assumed to differ from the corresponding aspects of the remaining event by a constant multiple, allowing a different multiple for each of the $n - 1$ events. Equation (4) can then be rewritten as

$$\Psi(D) = (\phi_1 - \phi_2) + b_2(\phi_1 - \phi_2) + \cdots + b_n(\phi_1 - \phi_2), \tag{5}$$

dropping the second subscript and arguments of the functions for simplicity. Factoring out the common difference gives

$$\Psi(D) = (1 + b_2 + \ldots + b_n)(\phi_1 - \phi_2). \tag{6}$$

The sum of the n coefficients represents the increase in diagnostic weight of n identical events relative to that of a single event, and can be expressed more compactly as $\phi_3(n)$. Equation (6) is then written as

$$\Psi(D) = \phi_3(n) [\phi_1(E|X) - \phi_2(E|Y)]. \tag{7}$$

Equation (7) is a distributive model whose theoretical properties have been thoroughly investigated within the theory of conjoint-measurement (Krantz *et al.*, 1971). It is relatively easy to use this model at an ordinal level by factorially manipulating the number of events n, the hypothesis X, and the hypothesis Y. We have employed this model in four experiments, and will return to it shortly.

The second special case to be considered applies to the situation in which a subject receives samples of events sequentially, and provides a response after each sample. In the simplest version of this case the hypotheses X and Y are held constant over trials. Therefore, the difference between the two aspects of an event is not varied, the separate effects of the aspects cannot be assessed, and it is unnecessary to distinguish them in the model. Thus, it suffices to refer to the diagnostic weight of each event as $\Psi(E_k)$.

If the total number of binary events in each of the sequential samples is held constant at K, all that is left to manipulate is the proportional composition of the sample. Letting the mth data sample be called D_m, and its diagnostic weight $\Psi(D_m)$, it follows that

$$\Psi(D_m) = \sum_{k=1}^{K} \Psi(E_k). \qquad (8)$$

It also follows that the diagnostic weight of M data samples taken together equals the sum of the weights of the separate samples. Letting D refer to the union of the M samples, this can be expressed as

$$\Psi(D) = \sum_{m=1}^{M} \Psi(D_m). \qquad (9)$$

Equation (9) is a simple additive model whose properties also have been explored thoroughly within the framework of conjoint-measurement. This model is evaluated and used by orthogonally varying the composition of each of the M sequential samples. It is the second special case that will be discussed here, and that has been employed in two experiments.

There are two separate, but related questions involved in applying the distributive Eq. (7), the additive Eq. (9), or any composition rule, for that matter, to data. First, does the equation describe the data at an ordinal, nonnumerical level? Various techniques are available for answering this question. One involves assessing the empirical validity of the applicable axioms from the theory of conjoint-measurement. This was done, and the results are available in the original reports of the experiments, which will be referenced as they are discussed.

Another method for evaluating the ordinal data properties relies on nonmetric scaling. Parameter values are estimated, such that when they are combined according to the model, they most closely approximate the rank order of the data. Then the question of whether the equation fits the data is one of goodness of fit. If the fit is bad, then either the process theory is fundamentally wrong, or it has been improperly modeled.

The two descriptive measures of goodness of fit that we have employed are stress and tau. Stress is the standardized square root of the sum of squared differences between model values and a monotonic transformation of the data, whereas tau is the rank order correlation between the model and the raw data. More will be said about these measures, and about how goodness of fit is evaluated statistically when we consider some results.

Given an adequate model, the second question has to do with interpreting the derived parameter values. The parameters represent the effects of aspects and dimension values, as outlined in the process theory. Thus, an appropriate interpretation of the parameters should provide answers to questions raised within the context of the theory, and should provide for modification of the theory. This is not a trivial exercise. First, the derived parameters are unique up to specified transformations, and conclusions that are drawn from inspection of the parameters should be invariant over those transformations. Second, and this is a more subtle point, one would like to interpret the parameter values in such a way that the conclusions can generalize naturally to other situations where the specific model may not apply. If one cannot do this, then there is little to be gained by combining heuristic theories with formal models, as is being attempted here.

THE EXPERIMENTS AND THEIR IMPLICATIONS

The strategy employed in the present research has been to manipulate variables with respect to which the model is neutral, but which within the context of the heuristic theory can be expected to have an effect on information processing, and then to compare parameter values derived under the various conditions. The two variables considered here will be experience and payoffs. Neither variable enters into the algebraic models, yet each can be reasonably expected to influence the number of dimensions processed, and the relative salience of dimensions and aspects, and therefore to have an effect on the derived parameters.

Let us turn now to the experiments, dispensing first with a few details. Subjects were always run independently for a large number of trials, requiring from 2 to 12 sessions of 1–2 hr each, depending on the experiment. On each trial the subject was presented with two a priori equally likely binomial parameters, randomly selected from 16 pairs of parameters. He then observed one or more samples of binary events. After each sample, the subject indicated which parameter he thought more likely to have generated the events, and provided a response with at least ordinal properties concerning the likelihood that his judgment was correct.

The binomial parameters were displayed perceptually, rather than stated numerically to ensure that the subjects understood them. One of the parameters was in fact used to generate the events, and subjects always received honest feedback after each trial. There was no deception involved.

In all studies but the one reported in Wallsten (1972), the experiments were controlled by a computer in a time-sharing mode, using a teletype to present stimuli and to collect responses. Similarly, in all experiments but that one, subjects' salaries were determined entirely by their performance. All of the analyses were conducted on the ordinal data from individual subjects. Only summary results will be given here.

We will consider effects of experience within the distributive model first. For this model, it is necessary to factorially manipulate the hypotheses X and Y and the number of identical events n in a sample. The technique for manipulating X and Y is shown in the top half of Fig. 1. X refers to the hypothesis that is objectively more likely given the data. There are 4 levels of X defining the columns of the right-hand matrix, and nominally designated by the binomial

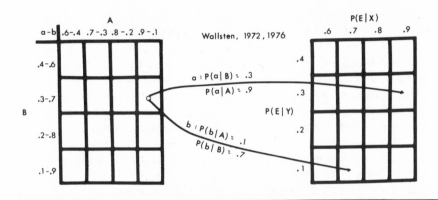

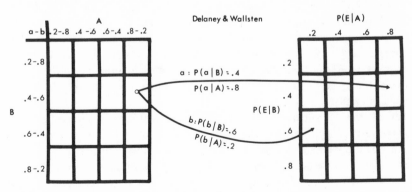

FIG. 1   The relation between the experimental design and the data analysis design for the distributive model.

probabilities .6, .7, .8, and .9. Y refers to the less likely hypothesis, and defines the rows of the right-hand matrix. The four levels are designated by the binomial probabilities .4, .3, .2, and .1.

This factorial arrangement is obtained by pairing one distribution from set B, shown in the rows of the left-hand matrix, with one from set A, shown in the columns of the matrix, as follows. Let the binary events that are sampled be called a and b, and assume for the moment that a single event is sampled, following which the subject responds. Imagine, as indicated in the figure, that the .3–.7 distribution from B is paired with the .9–.1 distribution from A, and that the single event a is sampled. That event has probability .3 given B, .9 given A, and therefore favors A. Thus, the subject's response is entered in the right-hand matrix in the cell designated (.3, .9). When the same pair of distributions is available, but b happens to be sampled, then distribution B is more likely correct. The event b has probability .1 given A, and .7 given B, and the subject's response is entered in the right-hand matrix in cell (.1, .7). In this fashion, the 16 experimental cells in the left-hand matrix yield responses to fill the 16 data cells in the right-hand matrix.

In one experiment (Wallsten, 1972) subjects sometimes observed samples of size one, as just described, and other times saw samples of size two. In two other studies (Wallsten, 1976), the samples were of size one, two, or three. Whenever a sample contained two or three identical events, respectively, the responses were entered in separate data matrices analogous to that on the right side of the top of Fig. 1. This resulted in manipulation of the third factor, sample size n. Often, of course, the random samples of size two and three were not homogeneous. Responses to these samples were collected and analyzed according to a special case of the model that is not under discussion here.

The important features of four experiments utilizing the distributive model are shown in Table 1. We consider now only the first three, which differ primarily in terms of the amount of experience subjects were provided with the task. The studies are summarized in the columns of the table labeled Wallsten (1972), and Wallsten (1976), and for compactness will be referred to as the 1972, 1976-I, and 1976-II studies, respectively. The table shows that the factorial design in the 1972 study consisted of four more likely hypotheses X by four less likely hypotheses Y by two sample sizes n. Each subject was run for 200 problems, after practice. Recall that only a portion of these trials entered into the present analyses, the exact number depending on the random processes which generated the binary events.

Half of the 12 subjects in the 1972 experiment numerically estimated a probability that their decision was correct, and the other half drew a line whose length was proportional to their confidence. Payoffs were not employed. There were large, systematic differences in response magnitude between the two groups, but as expected, no difference in the rank order of the responses. Therefore, it is assumed that information processing was unaffected by response mode, and all 12 subjects are discussed together.

TABLE 1
Summary of Four Experiments
Model $\phi_3 (n) [\phi_1 (E|X) - \phi_2 (E|Y)]$

Study	Wallsten (1972)			Wallsten (1976) Study I			Study II			Delaney and Wallsten (1976)		
Design	X	Y	n	X	Y	n				A	B	n
	4 × 4 × 2			4 × 4 × 3						4 × 4 × 3		
Number of problems	200			960			320			1052		
Response mode	1. probability estimate			Probability estimate converted to gambles						Marschak bidding		
	2. Draw line											
Payoffs	None			Contingent						Contingent and noncontingent		
Number of subjects	12			6			16			6		
Goodness of fit:												
Tau:lo–mdn–hi	.59	.77	.86	.73	.84	.91	.14	.73	.85	.32	.81	.92
z				3.9	4.5	5.0	0.1	3.8	4.6	.33	4.3	5.0
Stress:hi–mdn–lo	.58	.37	.16	.53	.29	.16	.93	.39	.15	.75	.43	.11
z				1.8	3.0	3.7	−.2	2.5	3.7	.70	2.3	3.9
Number of subjects Fit well	8			5			8			5		
Tau:lo–mdn–hi	.73	.79	.86	.76	.86	.91	.75	.81	.85	.65	.81	.92
z				4.1	4.7	5.0	3.9	4.3	4.6	3.3	4.3	5.0
Stress:hi–mdn–lo	.40	.26	.16	.46	.24	.16	.35	.30	.15	.52	.40	.11
z				2.1	3.3	3.7	2.7	3.0	3.7	2.3	2.5	3.9

The corresponding features of Experiments 1976-I and 1976-II can be noted from the table. The difference of current interest over the three studies is in the number of trials run by each subject. In addition, all subjects in both 1976 studies provided probability estimates that their decisions were correct. The estimates were used in a spherical scoring rule (Staël von Holstein, 1970) to obtain gambles specifying (positive or negative) amounts of money to be won, depending on whether the decision was correct or incorrect. Thus, subjects were paid contingent both on their probability estimates and on the correctness of their decision.

Before looking at the effects of experience on the processing of information, it is necessary to determine whether the model describes the data adequately. If it does, then the derived parameter values can be inspected for effects of experience.

A nonmetric scaling technique was used, separately for each subject, to find parameters, or scale values, which, when combined according to the model, best reproduced the rank order of the data. A rank-order correlation of 1 between the model and the data and a stress value of 0 would indicate a perfect fit. A rank-order correlation of 0 and a large stress would suggest that the data are random with respect to the model.

Table 1 shows the median and range of values of tau and stress obtained over subjects within each experiment. The median obtained values of tau were .77, .84, and .73 in the 1972, 1976-I, and 1976-II studies, respectively, and those of stress were .37, .29, and .39, with the ranges given.

It is impossible to determine from these values alone whether the model should be rejected; this is a statistical question for which there are no appropriate statistics. For the two 1976 experiments, we used a Monte Carlo procedure to create and test a null hypothesis, as follows. Fifteen sets of random data were run through the scaling program, and tau and stress were obtained for each. These were used to calculate a mean and standard deviation for both tau and stress for random data. Armed with the two means and standard deviations, it is possible to express the tau and stress obtained from each subject as a standard z score relative to random data. The rows labeled z in the table show how many standard scores *better* than random data the displayed values of tau and stress are. Chebychev's inequality provides an appropriate and very conservative statistical test of the null hypothesis that the data are random. Assuming that the distribution of random values is symmetric, values of z greater than 3.2 occur with p less than .05. If unimodality is also assumed, p drops to less than .02.

Using Chebychev's inequality, plus the axiom analyses which are not reported here, and in Study 1976-I a comparison with the fit of other models, which is also not reported here, the distributive model was not rejected for 8 of the 12 subjects in 1972, for 5 of the 6 subjects in Study 1976-I,[2] and for 8 of the 16 in Study 1976-II (see Wallsten, 1972, 1976). Medians and ranges of tau and stress for the "good" subjects are displayed in the table.

The model failed for half the subjects in Study 1976-II because response variability resulted in unreliable estimates of response rank order. The within cell mean squared deviation of the responses was significantly greater in the "failed" group than in the "good" group ($p < .025$). The reason why so many subjects were so variable is not clear, however.

For those subjects adequately fit by the model, it is appropriate to treat the derived parameters as scale values. The parameter ϕ_1 measures the subjective strength of association between the more likely hypothesis X and the event. Presumably, it depends on the conditional likelihood of the event given X and on the salience of that aspect. The parameter ϕ_2 measures the strength of association between the event and the less likely hypothesis Y, and depends on the corresponding conditional likelihood and salience. The parameter ϕ_3 measures the weight afforded n events relative to that afforded a single event, and therefore reflects the relative salience of additional events. Subjects were run for

---

[2] Since complete data analyses were presented in the original report of Study 1976-I, readers were left to decide for themselves which subjects satisfied the model. The subject indicated here as not being described by the model is identified as subject 3PN by Wallsten (1976).

different numbers of trials in the three experiments, and we can ask what affect this had on the scale values.

The possible effects on ϕ_1 and ϕ_2 are considered first, and are illustrated in Fig. 2. The notation at the top of the figure simply indicates to you that ϕ_1 represents the $(E|X)$ aspect and ϕ_2 the $(E|Y)$ aspect. For each subject, there were 4 levels of ϕ_1 and 4 levels of ϕ_2, each corresponding to an objective conditional probability. When the derived subjective values are plotted as a function of the log of the objective probabilities, three relations between the two functions are possible, as shown in Fig. 2. The slope of the ϕ_1 function can be greater than, equal to, or less than the slope of the ϕ_2 function. Since ϕ_1 and ϕ_2 are unique up to multiplication by a common positive constant, the ratio of the two slopes is invariant over all permissible transformations of the scales.

The first panel in Fig. 2, in which the ϕ_1 slope is greater than the ϕ_2 slope, illustrates the relationship that would appear in a subject's data if the association between the event and the more likely hypothesis X were more salient than that between the event and the less likely hypothesis Y. This is labeled an $(E|X)$ bias, and reflects the fact that a given difference in log probability conditional on the more likely hypothesis X has a greater effect on the scale value than does an identical change in the log probability conditional on the less likely hypothesis Y. Similarly, when the slopes of the two functions are equal there is no bias. When the ϕ_1 slope is less than the ϕ_2 slope, differences in hypothesis Y have the greater effect, and there is an $(E|Y)$ bias. Before proceeding to the data, it may be helpful to mention that for clarity, ϕ_1 and ϕ_2 are plotted as a function of the log probabilities, instead of the arithmetic values, because the optimal Bayesian expression for this task is linear in log probability.

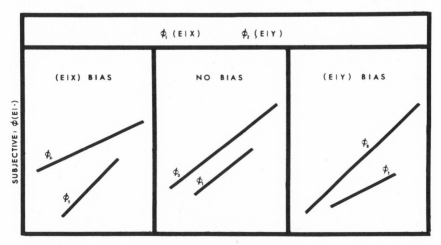

FIG. 2 Theoretical graphs illustrating the three relations possible between the parameters ϕ_1 $(E|X)$ and ϕ_2 $(E|Y)$.

TABLE 2
Effects of Experience: Summary of Parameters

		Leon and Anderson (1974)	Wallsten (1972)	Wallsten, (1976)		
				II	I:1	I:2
$\dfrac{S(\phi_1)}{S(\phi_2)}$	Low		1.14	.80	.55	.32
	Mdn	11.5	1.69	1.3	.87	.79
	High		2.70	4.9	4.7	4.0
$\phi_3(2)$	Low		1.45	1.29	1.03	1.01
	Mdn	1.12	1.56	1.97	1.11	1.40
	High		1.75	2.89	1.22	1.45
$\phi_3(3)$	Low			1.40	1.17	1.26
	Mdn	1.27		2.71	1.35	1.54
	High			3.45	1.51	2.36

The data are shown in the top section of Table 2 labeled $S(\phi_1)/S(\phi_2)$, in terms of the ratio of the ϕ_1 slope to the ϕ_2 slope. Ratios greater than 1 show an $(E|X)$ bias, and those less than 1 show an $(E|Y)$ bias. The experiments are arranged in terms of increasing order of experience on the part of the subjects. Recall that in study 1976-I subjects ran 960 trials. To provide a finer assessment of the effects of experience, the data from study 1976-I were divided into the first 480 and the last 480 trials, and each half of the data was scaled separately for each subject. The slope ratios for the two halves of the experiment are shown under I:1 and I:2, respectively. Also, a slope ratio estimated from mean data published by Leon and Anderson (1974) is included. They ran a study very similar in design to the others under discussion, and obtained scale values with a model which can be derived from the present one. Their subjects ran 392 trials in less than 80 min, about 1 trial every 10 sec. Although their subjects ran more trials than some of ours, I suspect that they had considerably less opportunity to reflect on their behavior.

For the experiments conducted in our laboratory, the table gives the median slope ratio over those subjects described by the model, as well as the largest and smallest obtained ratios. It is evident that as subjects gain experience in the task the slope ratios monotonically decrease generally from greater than 1 to less than 1. This means that initially in forming a judgment based on the binary events, the subjects treated the events' association with the more likely hypothesis as more salient, but that as the subjects gained experience, the association with the less likely hypothesis grew in importance.

One might criticize this conclusion by claiming that the effect appeared simply because of the choice of units on the abscissa. If the scale values had been

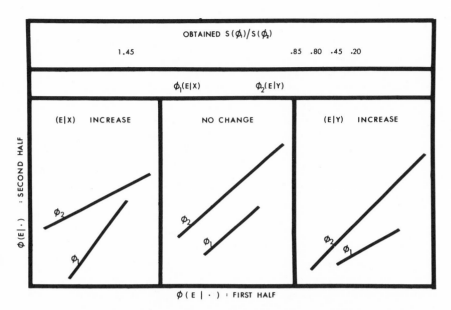

FIG. 3 Theoretical graphs illustrating the three relations possible when $\phi_1(E|X)$ and $\phi_2(E|Y)$ derived from data obtained in the second half of the experiment are plotted as a function of the corresponding parameters derived from data obtained in the first half. The numbers at the top are the empirical ratios of the slope of the ϕ_1 function to that of the ϕ_2 function for five subjects.

plotted as a function of some other objective measure, such as arithmetic probabilities, a different conclusion may have emerged. It can be seen that this criticism is invalid by looking at Fig. 3, which illustrates relations that can appear between the scale values obtained from the two halves of Study 1976-I. Scale values derived from responses obtained in the second half of the experiment are plotted as a function of the scales derived from responses obtained in the first half. In this figure, the curve labeled ϕ_1 connects $\phi_1(E|X)$ values from the two halves of the study, and ϕ_2 connects the $\phi_2(E|Y)$ values.

In the first panel, the slope of the ϕ_1 function is steeper than that of the ϕ_2 function, indicating that the ϕ_1 values are relatively more extreme in the latter half of the experiment than in the former half. If this result were to occur for a subject, it would show that he tended to rely relatively more strongly on the more likely hypothesis X in the second half of the experiment than in the first half. The center panel illustrates identical slopes for the two functions, and represents no change in relative salience between the two aspects. The third panel shows the ϕ_1 slope to be less than the ϕ_2 slope, indicating a relative increase in salience of the less likely hypothesis.

The actual data, in terms of the ratio of the ϕ_1 slope to the ϕ_2 slope for the five subjects fit by the model in Study 1976-I, are shown above the three panels. Four of the ratios are less than 1. This is consistent with the previous analyses, and shows that with experience the subjects came to treat the association with the less likely hypothesis as more salient. The one subject whose reliance on the more likely hypothesis increased, initially relied on it less than any other subject did. Thus, even in the second half of the study, the events' association with the less likely hypothesis was still more salient to him.

Given that a subject reduced his information processing load by not attending to all aspects equally, it is not difficult to understand why the association between the events and the more likely hypothesis initially was more salient, but grew less so with experience until the other association dominated the information processing. Each response consisted of two parts, a binary decision concerning which hypothesis was more likely correct, followed by a probability judgment of some sort. We analyzed the ordinal properties of the latter response. It is reasonable to suppose that in processing information prior to that judgment a subject tended to ignore the hypothesis he had designated as less likely, perhaps feeling that his opinion need not depend on an alternative that was probably not true. However, it was the case in the present design that the objective posterior probabilities varied more steeply as a function of the less likely hypothesis than of the more likely hypothesis. This is illustrated in Fig. 2, where the ϕ_2 graphs cover a wider domain on the abscissa than do the ϕ_1 graphs. In fact, these graphs are not drawn to scale, and the differences are much greater than illustrated. The subjects apparently learned this relation between the two conditional probabilities and the posterior probability, and came to ease their information processing task by relying on the more informative association rather than on the association with the more likely hypothesis.

The effect of experience on the relative weight afforded multiple identical events is not as easy to understand. The medians and ranges of values obtained for ϕ_3 in each of the four experiments are shown in the bottom of Table 2. In Study 1976-II, in which the subjects were intermediate in experience, 2 events were almost twice as diagnostic as 1 (1.97), and 3 events were almost 3 times as diagnostic as 1 (2.71). But, subjects in other experiments, both with less experience and with more experience, treated 2 or 3 events as *not* much more diagnostic than a single event. The only explanation I have is more convoluted than I like.

Recall that subjects in Study 1976-II and in the 1972 study differed not only in experience, but also in that the former group received payoffs contingent on their behavior and the latter group did not. Thus, the former group was motivated to work harder and to attend more consistently to all the dimensions of the information sample than was the latter group. As a result, the former subjects found the second and third dimensions of the sample to be almost as salient as the first, whereas the latter did not. Subjects in Study 1976-I, however, received contingent payoffs exactly as did those in Study 1976-II. It must be assumed, therefore, that since they knew from the beginning they were going to work for about 20 hr, they quickly looked for ways to ease their information processing load, and soon came more or less to ignore dimensions that were all redundant with the first.

Although this post hoc explanation is less than satisfying, it may not be entirely wrong. We used a special case of Eq. (4) that has not been discussed here to analyze the responses of subjects in Study 1976-I to heterogeneous information samples, consisting of two events of one type and one of the other (see Wallsten, 1976, for details). It turned out in that case that two identical events were treated as twice as diagnostic as one. In other words, the subjects who were run for 20 hr did not ignore dimensions of the information sample when the dimensions were not all redundant.

To summarize the results presented thus far, even in this extremely simple decision problem the picture that emerged was that of a subject actively reducing his information processing load. Since the formal model described most subjects' behavior with reasonable accuracy, we are justified in describing the information processing within the framework of the heuristic theory outlined earlier. In those terms, we saw that subjects relied more heavily on one aspect of a dimension value than on the other, and that with experience subjects learned to anchor their judgment on the aspect that was objectively most informative. Furthermore, subjects with little motivation and those settling in for a long grind tended to ease their task by ignoring redundant dimensions of the information. However, when the dimensions of an information sample conflicted with each other, they were not ignored. The conclusion that subjects adopt simplified processing strategies is consistent with a variety of contemporary theories (e.g., Slovic & Lichtenstein, 1968; Tversky & Kahneman, 1974). The interesting additional result that does not appear in other theories is that this is an active process; subjects do not select a strategy and stay with it. The form of the strategy is modified, perhaps even from trial to trial, depending on the characteristics of the particular problem and on what the subject has learned.

We now turn from the effects of experience to the effects of payoffs on the processing of information. The previous experiments demonstrated that salience can be influenced by factors relating in some way or another to objective diagnosticity. However, unless salience can also be shown to be a function of other variables, which are logically independent of data impact, the concept will be of limited use in this context. Accordingly, in light of the literature suggesting that the subjective uncertainty of an event, or an hypothesis, depends in part on its utility (e.g., Irwin & Snodgrass, 1966; Morlock, 1967), Harold Delaney and I thought that information processing might be affected by the association of a unique, positive payoff with one of the hypotheses.

Before discussing that study, it is appropriate to repeat and expand a point already made concerning the effect of payoffs on processing. There was a suggestion in the previous analyses that, other things being equal, when decisions have monetary consequences, subjects attend to more dimensions of the data sample than when decisions are inconsequential. This conclusion is furthered by inspection of the goodness of fit measures of the model. A priori, one would expect a better fit in the 1972 study, where 9 parameters were estimated from the ranking of 32 cells than in Studies 1976-I and II, where 10 parameters were estimated from the ranking of 48 cells. This expectation depends simply on the ratio of data points to parameters. However, in all three of the present experiments the median goodness of fit measures were approximately the same, both before and after individual subjects were categorized as either being described by the model or not. In other words, the model fit better in Studies 1976-I and II than would have been expected given the 1972 results and the ratio of parameters to data points. It is reasonable to assume that this reflects the fact that subjects who were paid on the basis of their decisions more consistently processed more of the dimensions and aspects of the information sample than did subjects who were not so paid.

Thus, it appears that associating payoffs with correct and incorrect decisions tends to increase the *amount* of information processed. We also have some evidence that as long as the payoffs are symmetric with respect to the hypotheses, there are no effects on *relative* salience. Although not mentioned earlier, symmetric payoffs were manipulated in Studies 1976-I and II. In each study, for half the subjects the gambles derived from their probability estimates were such that money was won for correct decisions and lost for incorrect decisions. The other half of the subjects received gambles in which they always won money, but they won more for correct than for incorrect decisions. This manipulation had a profound effect on the magnitude and the range of the probability estimates, which is explainable in terms of risk aversion. However, there was absolutely no effect on the rank order of the estimates, and therefore on any of the model analyses. Thus, it must be concluded that subjects processed information identically in both conditions, but made different decisions on the basis of that processing.

Within that context, the study by Delaney and myself (Delaney & Wallsten, 1976) can be viewed as inquiring whether asymmetric payoffs affect salience, where the asymmetry is obtained by explicitly associating a positive payoff with one of the hypotheses. The design of the experiment is very similar to those already discussed. As before, we shall consider only the distributive case, as illustrated in the bottom of Fig. 1. Note that unlike the prior studies, the sets A and B, defining the left-hand matrix, both contain the same binomial parameters. The sets A and B do differ in an important respect, however, Whenever the parameter from set A was generating the events the subject won money, regardless of the distribution he had judged to be correct. The subject also won or lost money for a correct or an incorrect decision, but the amounts were small relative to what he got when A was the parent. Thus, A is called the "more valuable distribution" and B is the "less valuable distribution."

For a given problem, a distribution from B was paired with one from A, and events were generated according to one of the binomial parameters. As before, the event that occurred determined the cell that was entered in the data matrix on the right. The columns of this matrix are defined by four levels of the more valuable hypothesis, and the rows are defined by four levels of the less valuable hypothesis. Note that the four binomial parameters which nominally designate the levels of each factor are the same, .2, .4, .6, and .8. Thus, when scale values are derived, those for one aspect can be plotted as a function of those for the other, completely ignoring any objective measures.

The details and goodness of fit measures for this study are summarized in the last major column of Table 1. The factorial consisted of four levels of more valuable hypothesis A by four levels of less valuable B by three sample sizes n. The contingent and noncontingent payoffs mentioned earlier were combined in a gamble that depended both on whether A or B was correct, and on which of the two hypotheses the subject actually decided was more likely to be correct. Using the Marschak bidding technique, the subject gave a minimum selling price for his gamble, which provided the ordinal data.

Goodness of fit measures in this study were quite comparable to those in Studies 1976-I and II, as were most other measures; the model was rejected for only 1 of the 6 subjects. Median tau for the remaining subjects was .81, which was 4.3 standard units better than the mean value for random data. Median stress was .40, which corresponded to a z score of 2.5.

The question of whether relative salience was affected by the contingent payoffs can be assessed with the five subjects whose data were fit by the model. Figure 4 illustrates the three relations which could obtain between the parameters ϕ_1 and ϕ_2. The scale value of the event given the more valuable hypothesis, $\phi_1 (E|MV)$, is plotted on the ordinate, and that of the event given the less valuable hypothesis, $\phi_2 (E|LV)$, is plotted on the abscissa. The first panel shows a line with slope greater than 1, which would indicate that a given change in the parameter of the more valuable hypothesis has a larger effect on behavior than does a corresponding change in the parameter of the less valuable hypothesis. In other words, the event's association with the more valuable hypothesis is more salient. This is termed an $(E|MV)$ bias. Similarly, slopes equal to 1 and less than 1 suggest no bias and an $(E|LV)$ bias, respectively.

The obtained slopes are shown immediately above the panels in the line labeled SLOPE. Four subjects showed the expected bias towards the more valuable hypothesis. One subject, however, found the association with the less valuable hypothesis to be more salient. Fortunately, he differed from the other subjects in other respects as well.

Recall that each subject provided a binary response indicating which distribution he thought more likely to be correct given a sample of information. Recall further that very often, information was absolutely undiagnostic; the posterior probabilities were .5–.5. In that case, the first four subjects predicted the more valuable distribution most of the time, as shown in the top line of the data in Fig. 4. However, the one subject whose slope was less than 1 predicted the less

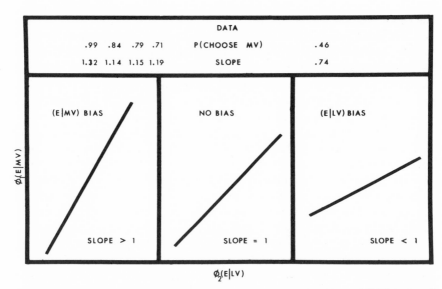

FIG. 4   Theoretical graphs illustrating the three relations possible when ϕ_1 $(E|MV)$ is plotted as a function of ϕ_2 $(E|LV)$. Data from five subjects are given at the top of the figure. $P(choose\ MV)$ refers to the proportion of times each subject stated that the more valuable hypothesis was more likely when in fact the two hypotheses were equally likely. Slope refers to the slope of the best fitting line when ϕ_1 is plotted as a function of ϕ_2.

valuable hypothesis most often in this situation. Thus, the conclusion that one subject tended to focus on the association with the less valuable hypothesis, while the remaining subjects tended to focus on that with the more valuable hypothesis is supported.

Scale values for the relative weight of samples of size two and three were also obtained (median values over subjects of 1.27 and 1.39, respectively), and were indistinguishable from those found in Study 1976-I. Unlike that study, however, when the data were divided into a first half and second half set, all relative scale values remained constant. In other words, the biases just discussed were apparent and unchanged in both halves of the data. This makes sense, since in Study 1976-I one aspect was in fact more diagnostic than the other, but in this study the two aspects were equally diagnostic. Thus, there was no reason to shift attention with experience.

To summarize the conclusions from this study, Delaney and I demonstrated that the salience of an aspect can be manipulated by a factor unrelated to its objective diagnosticity. In this design both aspects in fact contributed equally to the objective measure of data impact, and as a consequence subjects did not alter their strategy with experience. Furthermore, the effect on salience was quite specific, in that the contingent payoff did not cause subjects to process more or fewer dimensions than were processed in Study 1976-I. That is to say, the relative scale values of two and three events were the same in both studies. A number of years ago, Morlock (1967) demonstrated that subjects require less evidence to decide in favor of a desirable hypothesis than in favor of an undesirable hypothesis. The present experiment explains this effect in terms of the nature of the prior information processing.

The empirical work discussed thus far has been concerned with the processing of simultaneously presented identical binary events, and has been easily understood within the framework outlined earlier. However, the apparent success of the distributive model need not imply the validity of the general model from which it was derived. Indeed, originally the distributive rule was obtained from somewhat different considerations (Wallsten, 1972). To establish the viability of the general formulation, it is incumbent upon us to obtain empirical support for as many of the special cases as possible, thereby leaving the general theory and model as a single, parsimonious explanation for a wide variety of findings. In that spirit, a second special case of the general model, appropriate for simultaneous heterogeneous information samples, has also been employed rather successfully (Delaney & Wallsten, 1976; Wallsten, 1976). Rather than discuss that here, however, it will be more informative to apply the theory and model to sequential, as opposed to simultaneous, information processing.

One interpretation of the process theory suggests that when samples of information are presented sequentially, an initial judgment is made after the first sample. This serves as the anchor from which adjustments are made in light of succeeding samples. If it is assumed in general that the most salient dimension is processed first, it might also be the case that the dimension which of necessity is processed first is most salient, and therefore, that primacy effects will be observed.

This prediction is not a necessary one, but with it in mind, Mary Sapp and I used the additive Eq. (9) to look at the sequential processing of equivocal information (Sapp & Wallsten, 1976; Wallsten & Sapp, 1976). Recall that the hypotheses X and Y are not varied over the course of an experiment for this model. Rather, for a given pair of hypotheses, the compositions of the sequential samples are varied orthogonally, so that additivity of the diagnostic weights of the samples can be assessed. In fact, each subject was run in four problems, each consisting of a unique pair of hypotheses. A different problem was presented on each trial, and we later treated each problem as a separate experiment for purposes of analysis. Between problem analyses were also performed, but will not be discussed here (see Wallsten & Sapp, 1976).

The four problems we employed are shown in Table 3, where distributions are labeled along the rows and binary events along the columns. Event a was always more likely given distribution A, and event b was always more likely given distribution B. Figure 5 illustrates the factorial design employed within each of the four problems, separately for the two experiments. In the Wallsten & Sapp

TABLE 3
The Four Problems Employed in the Sequential Studies

	Problem 1				Problem 2	
	a	b			a	b
A	.6	.4	A		.6	.4
B	.4	.6	B		.2	.8

	Problem 3				Problem 4	
	a	b			a	b
A	.8	.2	A		.8	.2
B	.4	.6	B		.2	.8

study, shown in the top half of the figure, subjects received two samples of three events each, and provided a response after each sample concerning the relative likelihood of distribution A. The possible compositions of the first sample are shown along the rows and those of the second sample along the columns of the matrix.

The column labeled blank allows the simultaneous evaluation of two additivity properties of Eq. (9). One property is that the second response differs from the first (at an ordinal level) in an additive fashion, and the other is that the second response is an (ordinal) additive function of the two samples. If the subject's response after the first sample is inserted in the appropriate row of the blank column, and his second response is put in the cell defined by both samples, the two properties jointly imply that the entire matrix should be additive in its rows and columns.

The Sapp and Wallsten study is illustrated in the bottom half of Fig. 5. Subjects received three samples of two events each, and, as before, provided a response after each sample concerning the relative likelihood of distribution A. Although it is possible to analyze the first and second responses exactly as above, this technique breaks down for the third and successive samples. Thus, the matrix shown here is filled only with responses after the third sample, and, according to the model, is additive in its three factors.

The important features and goodness of fit measures for both studies are given in Table 4, which is parallel in form to Table 1. Note in the row labeled Design that P refers to the number of distinct problems in each study, four, and that the factorial design over the first and second and over the first, second and third samples, respectively, are complete within each problem. Subjects in the Sapp and Wallsten study responded after each sample exactly as did those in Delaney and Wallsten, but were paid for each trial according to a randomly selected one of their three responses. A few additional words of explanation are necessary to understand the other experiment. Payoffs were noncontingent, in that subjects received a positive payoff if distribution A was correct and they chose to gamble

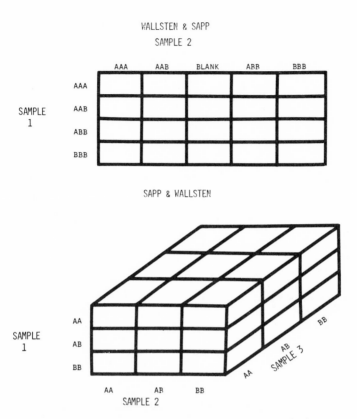

FIG. 5 The factorial designs employed in two studies on sequential information processing.

on that being the case. Specifically, after each of the two samples, the subject chose to gamble either on A being correct or on a simple lottery for the same stake. The probability of winning the lottery was adjusted from trial to trial according to a staircase technique, separately for each of the 80 cells of the design (20 cells per each of four problems), so that a value could be estimated such that the subject was indifferent between gambling on the lottery or on distribution A given the particular pair of hypotheses and sample information. The set of obtained indifference probabilities for a subject provided the ordinal data for analyses. Subjects were paid on each trial according to one of their two responses.

Looking at the results of both studies, nonmetric scaling techniques were used, separately for each of the four problems for each subject, to obtain parameters which, when combined according to Eq. (9), best reproduced the rank order of the data. Thus, four values each of tau and stress were obtained for each subject. Median within subject values were calculated for purposes of summary here, and Table 4 shows the range and medians of the within subject averages for each

TABLE 4
Summary of Two Experiments
Model M
$\sum_{m=1}^{M} \Psi(D_m)$

Study	Wallsten and Sapp (1976)			Sapp and Wallsten (1976)		
Design	1st 2nd P			1st 2nd 3rd P		
	4 × 4 × 4			3 × 3 × 3 × 4		
Number of problems	1040			1148		
Response mode	Choice of gambles			Marschak bidding		
Payoffs	Noncontingent			Contingent and noncontingent		
Number of Subjects	8			8		
Goodness of fit:						
Tau:lo–mdn–hi	.75	.87	.94	.63	.76	.84
z	2.8	3.7	4.2	2.8	4.0	4.7
Stress:hi–mdn–lo	.50	.21	.09	.63	.48	.29
z	2.0	4.2	5.2	3.3	4.5	6.1
Number of subjects well fit	7			6		
Tau:lo–mdn–hi	.81	.87	.94	.69	.79	.84
z	3.2	3.7	4.2	3.4	4.3	4.7
Stress:hi–mdn–lo	.29	.19	.09	.58	.47	.29
z	3.6	4.4	5.2	3.7	4.6	6.1

experiment. As before, we scaled 15 sets of Monte Carlo data for each design, in order to express each obtained measure as a standard score relative to random data. The standard scores of the displayed measures are shown below them. On the basis of the goodness of fit measures for the individual problems, and the axiom analyses which are not reported here, we concluded that the additive model described seven of eight subjects quite well in the first study, and six of eight quite well in the second. Summary goodness of fit statistics are provided for those subjects in the bottom of Table 4. I might add that in the Sapp and Wallsten study, the model was also evaluated for each problem within each subject after the second response. The fit was essentially perfect in all cases.

Sequential effects can be investigated with those subjects for whom the model was not rejected. Since the various sample compositions at each serial position were identical, the scale values at one position can be plotted as a function of those at another. If the derived values for sample i are plotted as a function of those for sample $i - 1$, then a recency effect would appear as a line with slope greater than one. This would reflect the fact that the later sample exerts more control over behavior than does the earlier sample, and therefore has more extreme scale values. Similarly, a slope of one would indicate an absence of sequential effects, and a slope less than one would demonstrate a primacy effect.

TABLE 5
Sequential Effects: Slope of Line Relating Scale Value of Sample i
to That of Sample $i - 1$

	Wallsten & Sapp (1976)	Sapp and Wallsten (1976)		
		After 3 samples		After 2 samples
	2nd vs. 1st	3rd vs. 2nd	2nd vs. 1st	2nd vs. 1st
Low	.853	1.00	1.00	.99
Mdn	.908	1.01	1.02	1.01
High	1.163	1.05	1.05	1.02

Four distinct sets of scale values, one per problem, were obtained for each subject in the Wallsten and Sapp experiment. In each case, the values for sample 2 were plotted as a function of those for sample 1 and a regression line was fitted. The mean of the four slopes was calculated for each subject, and Table 5 gives the range and median of the subject means. Similarly, responses after the third sample in Sapp and Wallsten were used to obtain four sets of scale values for each subject. In this case, third sample scale values were plotted as a function of second, and second sample scale values were plotted as a function of first. Individual regression lines were fitted and mean slopes obtained for each subject, with the overall range and median results as shown in Table 5. Finally, responses after the second sample were also scaled, as already mentioned, with the results summarized in the last column of Table 5. It is not surprising, but is important to add, that the regression lines did provide excellent fits to the points; and that over all plots there was no systematic deviation from linearity.

Table 5 suggests that there may be a modest primacy effect in the first study. Indeed, the mean slope was greater than one for only a single subject. However, it is clear that no sequential effects at all were demonstrated in the second study. The strongest conclusion that can be reached from the two experiments taken together is that if a primacy effect is associated with this task at all, it is an extremely weak one that is susceptible to influence by variables which distinguish the two conditions.

Although our expectation of a primacy effect was not supported, the results have an interesting implication. It should be noted that in general primacy effects have been found when subjects have been given sequential data for the purpose of deciding between hypotheses (Rapoport & Wallsten, 1972; Slovic & Lichtenstein, 1971). The bulk of the research differs from that discussed here in that considerably longer sequences have been used and the effects have been observed in the responses, rather than in derived scale values as in the present studies. It could be the case that primacy would have been observed in the present experiments if the sequence of information had been longer. But it is also interesting to speculate on the differences between the raw responses and the derived scale values.

In that vein, Pitz (1969) suggested as one explanation of primacy effects that the subject is "committed" to his early responses. He is reluctant to change his decision, because he is already publicly associated with it. Our results are consistent with this notion, and suggest that the primacy effects which have been obtained by others may be in the response function, rather than in the information processing. We attempted to look at this in our data, but the studies were not really designed to investigate it, and we did not obtain any conclusive answers.

The lack of a primacy effect should not obscure the fact that the additive model described the data well. Therefore, the general model and theoretical description appear to be appropriate for the sequential case as well as the simultaneous.

SUMMARY AND CONCLUSIONS

By way of a very brief summation, one should be reminded that the power of this approach arises from the concurrent use of a heuristic theory and a formal model. The theory portrays humans as limited, but active information processors who rely on the more salient dimensions and aspects of information samples in deciding between hypotheses. The theory is formulated so that it applies to a wide variety of situations, and can be specifically modeled in each. Two special cases of a particular algebraic model of the theory, suitable for a certain class of tasks, were used quite successfully in six experiments. The success of the models is necessary for the validity of the theory, and suggests that the theory is, indeed, useful. No less important, the theory provides a framework for interpreting the parameters of the models and for generalizing conclusions beyond the single paradigm from which they emerged.

The empirical techniques, and therefore the means for evaluating the conclusions, extend in a natural way to more complex and more interesting situations in which ambiguous information is processed for the purpose of choosing among hypotheses. Experiments to be conducted in our laboratory in the future, and some already completed but not analyzed, are designed to apply the theory and the model to such tasks, involving complex information samples and complex hypotheses.

ACKNOWLEDGMENTS

This work was supported in part by PHS Research Grant No. MH-10006 from the National Institute of Mental Health, in part by Grant No. GB-31028X from the National Science

Foundation, and in part by a University Science Development Program Grant No. GU-2059-Amendment 1 from the National Science Foundation. Thanks are due Peter Ornstein for a detailed reading of an earlier draft of this paper.

REFERENCES

Atkinson, R. C., & Shiffrin, R. M. Human memory: A proposed system and its control processes. In W. K. Spence & J. T. Spence (Eds.), *The psychology of learning and motivation*. Vol. II. New York: Academic Press, 1968. Pp. 89–195.

Bell, R. S., & Loop, J. W. The utility and futility of radiographic examination for trauma. *The New England Journal of Medicine*, 1971, **284**, 236–239.

Dawes, R. B., & Corrigan, B. Linear models in decision making. *Psychological Bulletin*, 1974, **81**, 95–106.

Delaney, H., & Wallsten, T. S. Probabilistic information processing: Effects of a biased payoff matrix on choices and ratings. Manuscript in preparation, 1976.

Edwards, W. Conservatism in human information processing. In B. Kleinmuntz (Ed.), *Formal representation of human judgment*. New York: Wiley, 1968. Pp. 17–52.

Fryback, D. G. Bayes' Theorem and conditional non-independence of data in a medical diagnosis task (Report MMPP: 74-7). Ann Arbor: University of Michigan, Michigan Mathematical Psychology Program, March, 1974.

Garner, W. R. *The processing of information and structure*. New York: Wiley, 1974.

Goldberg, L. R. Diagnosticians vs. diagnostic signs: The diagnosis of psychosis vs. neurosis from the MMPI. *Psychological Monographs*, 1965, **79** (9, whole No. 602).

Greeno, J. G. Paired associate learning with short-term retention: Mathematical analysis and data regarding identification of parameters. *Journal of Mathematical Psychology*, 1967, **4**, 430–472.

Hoffman, P. J. The paramorphic representation of clinical judgment. *Psychological Bulletin*, 1960, **57**, 116–131.

Hoffman, P. J. Cue-consistency and configurality in human judgment. In B. Kleinmuntz (Ed.), *Formal representation of human judgment*. New York: Wiley, 1968. Pp. 53–90.

Humphreys, M., & Greeno, J. G. Interpretation of the two-stage analysis of paired-associate memorizing. *Journal of Mathematical Psychology*, 1970, **7**, 275–292.

Irwin, F. W., & Snodgrass, J. G. Effects of independent and dependent outcome values on bets. *Journal of Experimental Psychology*, 1966, **71**, 282–285.

Kahneman, D. *Attention and effort*. Englewood Cliffs, N.J.: Prentice-Hall, 1973.

Krantz, D. H., Luce, R. D., Suppes, P., & Tversky, A. *Foundations of measurement*, Vol. I. *Additive and polynomial representation*. New York: Academic Press, 1971.

Krantz, D. H. & Tversky, A. Conjoint-measurement analysis of composition rules in psychology. *Psychological Review*, 1971, **78**, 151–169.

Kuhn, T. S. *The structure of scientific revolutions*. (2nd ed.), Chicago: University of Chicago Press, 1970.

Leon, M. & Anderson, N. H. A ratio rule from integration theory applied to inference judgments. *Journal of Experimental Psychology*, 1974, **102**, 27–36.

Mackintosh, N. Selective attention in animal discrimination learning. *Psychological Bulletin*, 1965, **64**, 124–150.

Meehl, P. E. A comparison of clinicians with five statistical methods of identifying psychotic MMPI profiles. *Journal of Counseling Psychology*, 1959, **6**, 102–109.

Morlock, H. The effect of outcome desirability on information required for decisions, *Behavioral Science*, 1967, **12**, 296–300.

116   THOMAS S. WALLSTEN

Pitz, G. F. An inertia effect (resistance to change) in the revision of opinion. *Canadian Journal of Psychology*, 1969, **23**, 24–33.

Rapoport, A., & Wallsten, T. S. Individual decision behavior. *Annual Review of Psychology*, 1972, **23**, 131–176.

Reese, H. W., & Overton, W. F. Models of development and theories of development. In L. R. Goulet and P. B. Baltes (Eds.), *Life-Span Developmental Psychology*. New York: Academic Press, 1970. Pp. 115–145.

Sapp, M. M. & Wallsten, T. S. An additive model and a heuristic theory applied to the sequential processing of equivocal information. Manuscript in preparation, 1976.

Slovic, P. From Shakespeare to Simon: Speculation–and some evidence about man's ability to process information. *Oregon Research Institute Research Monograph*, 1972, **12**, No. 12.

Slovic, P., & Lichtenstein, S. Relative importance of probabilities and payoffs in risk taking. *Journal of Experimental Psychology Monographs*, 1968, **78**, 1–18.

Slovic, P., & Lichtenstein, S. Comparison of Bayesian and regression approaches to the study of information processing in judgment. *Organizational Behavior and Human Performance*, 1971, **6**, 649–744.

Staël von Holstein, C. A. S. *Assessment and evaluation of subjective probability distributions*. Stockholm, Sweden: The Economics Research Institute at the Stockholm School of Economics, 1970.

Trabasso, T., & Bower, G. *Attention in learning: Theory and research*. New York: Wiley, 1968.

Tversky, A. Intransitivity of preferences. *Psychological Review*, 1969, **76**, 31–48.

Tversky, A., & Kahneman, D. Judgment under uncertainty: Heuristics and biases. *Science*, 1974, **185**, 1124–1131.

Wallsten, T. S. Conjoint-measurement framework for the study of probabilistic information processing. *Psychological Review*, 1972, **79**, 245–260.

Wallsten, T. S. Using conjoint-measurement models to investigate a theory about probabilistic information processing. *Journal of Mathematical Psychology*, 1976, in press.

Wallsten, T. S., & Sapp, M. M. Strong ordinal properties of an additive model for the sequential processing of probabilistic information. *Acta Psychologica*, 1976, in press.

Winkler, R. L., & Murphy, A. H. Experiments in the laboratory and the real world. *Organizational Behavior and Human Performance*, 1973, **10**, 252–270.

5
Decision Making with Multiple Probabilistic Cues

N. John Castellan, Jr.

Indiana University

During the last few years research on judgment and decision making has increasingly focused upon careful descriptions and analysis of both the task and the subject. An important class of judgment tasks includes ones in which decisions must be made on the basis of probabilistic information or cues, that is, tasks in which the validity of the stimulus (or cue) is less than perfect. Researchers have approached such problems with a variety of methodologies and techniques, some of which have been extremely valuable in explicating certain aspects of the decision process (cf. Castellan & Lindman, 1975; Peterson & Beach, 1967; Slovic & Lichtenstein, 1971). It is the purpose of this discussion to present one such technique, multiple-cue probability learning, in some detail and provide some insights into related antecedents in cognitive psychology.

The primary focus of research in Multiple-Cue Probability Learning (MCPL) is upon how subjects utilize, and learn to utilize, probabilistic cues or stimuli in making judgments about some distal event. Such tasks are similar to common tasks faced by people during the course of daily living, such as impression formation, in which the person must process information about characteristics in order to form impressions of objects or other persons. The task is also related to more specialized tasks such as diagnostic decision-making in which the person must process cues (symptoms) in order to make a diagnosis. One aspect common to all such tasks is that the cues upon which the judgments are ultimately based are not completely valid—that is, the cues are probabilistic. Further, there is an inherent randomness in the sequences of events that prevents one from using sequential or time-dependent patterns in an effort to learn the task.

As noted above, there are several approaches to the study of how people learn to use probabilistic information. Two general techniques and methodologies which have received wide attention are generally referred to as Bayesian approaches and linear-model techniques including the lens-model approach patterned after the work of Brunswik. A very useful comparative survey of these approaches may be found in the excellent review of Slovic and Lichtenstein (1971). Brehmer (1974) has discussed the relation between several different methodologies. In the Bayesian approach it is often the case that subjects are asked to estimate the probabilities which relate the cues and events. Hogarth[1] (1975) and Manz (1970) have provided critical reviews of such work. A similar approach is that of Pitz in which subjects are required to express their judgments as intervals (e.g., Pitz, 1975). In the linear model (and lens model) approach subjects learn to use cues which are continuous–or at least ordered–to make judgments about continuous or multivalued events. While it is not necessary within the linear-model framework to use such distributions of cues and events, it has been customary to do so because of the sort of judgment task under investigation (cf. Rappoport & Summers (1973) for a useful survey). It is clear from the results of research which has been done that the judgment process is quite complex, and that while some very general statements may be made about performance in such tasks, the information acquisition and processing behavior is very poorly understood. Other methodologies have been proposed and applied. For example, Wallsten (1972) and in Chapter 4 of this book has utilized conjoint measurement models in the study of probabilistic information processing. Hogarth (1974) has proposed a process tracing methodology; Wortman (1970, 1972) has proposed a similar approach to diagnostic judgment.

Experimental paradigms are adopted for a variety of reasons, one of which is the ease with which experimental data relate statements about behavior which follow from some theoretical model. While such justification is certainly valid, it has often been pointed out that the uncritical use of paradigms can lead to tests of theories (or aspects of theories) which ultimately have little substantive value. In an effort to minimize such difficulties, some psychologists and others have argued for more careful choice of experimental designs and that ecological surveys be utilized (e.g., Björkman, 1966, 1969d; Brunswik, 1956; Smedslund, 1955). Dawes (1975) and Winkler and Murphy (1973) have illustrated the importance of such considerations.

One approach to probabilistic judgment tasks has been to attempt to understand the processing of cues by means of varying the feedback to the subject about the task. In particular, are there ways in which the task may be restructured in order to facilitate acquistion and performance? To the extent that this may be done, one may be better able to understand the processing. There have also been repeated pleas from more action-oriented psychologists to use different sorts of feedback in an effort to improve the judgment process and thus

---

[1] The interested reader should be certain to read the discussion of Hogarth's paper which was published at the same time (Edwards, 1975; Winkler, 1975).

affect the general quality of decisions made in natural situations (cf. Björkman, 1972; Castellan, 1974; Hammond, 1971; Hammond & Boyle, 1971). However, in order to make sensible and appropriate inferences about behavior, it is very important to have a thorough understanding of the task itself.

This chapter is concerned primarily with what are termed multiple-cue probability learning tasks, and occasionally called "nonmetric" multiple-cue probability learning tasks. The term has been applied to a variety of contexts, and as will be shown, very similar tasks have been labeled probabilistic discrimination learning and concept identification with misinformative feedback.[2] One precursor of the multiple-cue probability learning paradigm is the probability learning paradigm (Estes, 1964, 1972b), which has been generalized also into sequential processing in which there is information in the sequence of events (Jones, 1971).

NONMETRIC MULTIPLE-CUE PROBABILITY LEARNING: TASK DESCRIPTION

It is useful to begin our discussion with a formal description of the Nonmetric Multiple Cue Probability Learning (MCPL) task. While such a task label is not completely precise, it is more appropriate than the two similar task descriptors, probabilistic discrimination learning and concept identification with misinformative feedback, which will be described more completely in the next sections. The MCPL judgment task may be described as follows.

Suppose a subject is asked to predict which of two events E_1 or E_2 will occur on a trial. On each trial, the subject is presented with one value from each of n binary cue dimensions. On the basis of the cues presented, the subject makes prediction A_1 or A_2. The prediction A_i is correct if it is followed by event E_i. Let C_i be one value of the ith cue and let C_i' denote the other value.[3] On each trial of the experiment, C_i is presented with probability $P[C_i]$; C_i' is presented with probability $P[C_i'] = 1 - P[C_i]$. On each trial event E_i occurs with probability $P[E_i] = \pi_i$. The cue-event contingencies may be described by means of the two conditional probabilities of one event given the cues. Define $P[E_1|C_i]$ to be the probability of event E_1 given presentation of cue C_i. Let $P[E_1|C_i']$ be similarly defined. Then

$$P[E_1] = \pi_1$$
$$= P[E_1|C_i]\, P[C_i] + P[E_1|C_i']\, P[C_i'], \quad i = 1, 2, \ldots, n,$$

[2] It is interesting to note that in reviewing the literature about these two paradigms, it was discovered that there was virtually no overlap in the references cited by the various authors.
[3] If the cue dimension is not binary, it is necessary to indicate the values within a dimension by means of subscripts rather than the convention used here.

are n equations relating the conditional and unconditional probabilities of an event. The various conditional and unconditional probabilities are systematically related (Björkman, 1973; Castellan, 1970) and a small number of them can provide a complete task description. In the case of binary cues and events, the ecological validity of a cue is the phi coefficient (ϕ), or the product–moment correlation, between the event and the cue (Björkman, 1967; Naylor, 1967). The squared validity of the ith cue dimension is given by the following equation:

$$\phi_i^2 = \frac{\{ P[E_1 \mid C_i] - \pi_1 \}^2}{\pi_1(1 - \pi_1)} \cdot \frac{P[C_i]}{1 - P[C_i]}.$$

If the cue dimension and events are independent, then the validity will be zero, and if the event is completely predictable from the cue, the validity is one.

It should be noted that in the discussion above the cues and events were binary; however, the same notation conventions may be used when the number of events is greater than two or the number of values within a given cue dimension exceeds two. In such cases, the ecological validity of cues may be computed as a phi-coefficient, but its interpretation is more difficult as it is no longer a product–moment correlation. However, an advantage of the phi-coefficient is that it is invariant with respect to reorderings of the events or cues, which is desirable when the dimensions are nonmetric.

Since one value from each cue dimension is presented on each trial, a cue pattern consists of the n-tuple of cue values available on that trial. If the cue dimensions are binary, then there are 2^n cue patterns possible as stimuli.

As noted earlier, there is a number of different sorts of experimental tasks which may be called multiple-cue tasks. In the following discussion probabilistic discrimination learning tasks will described first. In these tasks, there is a single cue dimension in that the cue pattern presented on each trial cannot be easily described in terms of more than one dimension. It should be noted that some authors have labeled such tasks as multiple-cue to signify *multiple values on a single dimension* rather than multiple dimensions; Björkman (1973) has summarized some experiments using such tasks. Other authors have stressed the importance of the multidimensionality of the stimuli in order to obtain appropriate task descriptions (e.g., Beach, 1964b; Shepard, 1964; Zeaman & House, 1963). A paradigm that has emphasized the multidimensionality of tasks is concept identification; from this paradigm experiments utilizing misinformative feedback bear upon multiple-cue probability learning. The relevant results from these experiments will be summarized also. Some paradigms that are related, but do not fit easily into either of the two previous categories, are described, and finally, the results of multiple-cue probability learning studies discussed.

PROBABILISTIC DISCRIMINATION LEARNING

Over the period from about 1958 to 1973 approximately thirty papers were published dealing with what generally was termed probabilistic discrimination learning. Perhaps the earliest experiment was that of Popper and Atkinson (1958). In approximately twenty of these experiments the subject's task was to use a single binary cue in order to predict a binary event, and in the remaining experiments the prediction task involved the use of a cue which could take on several values. In general, the cues and events consisted of signal lamps, nonsense syllables, tones, etc. As will become clear in the discussion of the experiments, these experiments are very similar to the Multiple-Cue Probability Learning paradigm and the results provided a foundation upon which to build.

Binary-Valued Single-Cue Tasks

Two central themes appear to dominate the experiments in which a single binary cue was used. One was the problem of stimulus (cue) generalization and discrimination, the other was concerned with asymptotic performance. Table 1 summarizes some of the characteristics of the studies. The following discussion focuses upon those aspects of the results of the studies which relate to the general problem of multiple-cue proability learning.

In most of the early experiments, the base rates of the two-cue values were equal, that is, $P[C_1] = P[C_1'] = .5$. The primary concern was with the event to be predicted and in a typical experiment $P[E_1|C_1]$ was held constant while $P[E_1|C_1']$ was varied across conditions. The primary dependent variable was $P[A_1|C_1]$, which was plotted against $P[E_1|C_1']$, usually at asymptotic response levels. The reasons for such analysis grew out of work on stimulus generalization, the argument being that if there were no stimulus generalization, then $P[A_1|C_1]$, when plotted against $P[E_1|C_1']$ would yield a horizontal line. Predictions from various models (e.g. Burke & Estes, 1957) were that as stimulus overlap and generalization increased, there would be an increase in the slope of the response surface. However, in most studies it was found that the plot of $P[A_1|C_1]$ was not a straight line of varying slope across conditions, but tended to be a U-shaped function with response asymptote slightly above matching when $P[E_1|C_1']$ was close to 0 or 1, and slightly below matching when $P[E_1|C_1']$ was close to .5. Figure 1a summarizes the general form of the results.

In the experiment of Popper and Atkinson (1958), subjects were presented on each trial with one of two cues (nonsense syllables) and were asked to predict whether the event would be an "A" or a "B." The value of $P[E_1|C_1]$ was fixed at .85 and five groups of subjects were run, each with a different value of $P[E_1|C_1']$. The results yielded the U-shaped function plotted in Fig. 1a. The experiment reported by Atkinson, Bogartz, and Turner (1959) set $P[E_1|C_1] = .9$

TABLE 1
Probabilistic Discrimination Learning
1 Binary Cue Dimension, 2 Events

Study	Number of trials	Number of conditions	Parameters varied[a]			
			$P[E_i|C_1]$	π_i	$P[C_1]$	ϕ
Popper and Atkinson (1958)	320	5	part	yes	.5	yes
Atkinson, Bogartz, and Turner (1959)	400	5	part	yes	.5	yes
Atkinson (1961)	400	6	part	yes	.5	yes
Shaffer (1963)	324	3	no	yes	yes	yes
Halpern and Moore (1967)	200	2	yes	yes	.5	yes
Summers (1968)	400	5	yes	yes	.5	yes
Massaro, Halpern, and Moore (1968)	200 or 300	5	yes	yes	.5	yes
Myers & Cruse (1968)	500	9	yes	yes	yes	yes
Björkman (1969a)	120	5	yes	yes	yes	yes
Björkman (1969b, c)	400	2	yes	yes	yes	yes
Björkman (1971a)	300	1	.8	.6	.5	.41
Björkman (1971b)	100	1	.33	.4	.3	.09
Björkman (1971c)	100	2	yes	yes	yes	yes
Bauer (1971a, b)	400	1	.7	.58	.7	.37
Bauer (1972a, b)	200	12	yes	yes	yes	yes
Bauer (1973a) (observed only)	200	2	yes	.5	.5	yes
Bauer (1973b)	200	1	.6	.5	.5	.2

[a]The entry 'yes' for any reference indicates that that parameter was varied across one or more conditions; a numerical entry indicates the value of the parameter when it was not varied. The entry "part" signifies that either $P[E_i|C_1]$ or $P[E_i|C_1']$ was varied.

and varied $P[E_1|C_1']$. The cues and events were signal lamps. Their results are plotted in Fig. 1a. In a subsequent experiment (Atkinson, 1961) the U-shaped function was not found (see Fig. 1b); however, the experimental task was somewhat different in that subjects were required to make an "observing response" prior to predicting the event.

The studies cited above held the base rates of the two-cue values equal. Shaffer (1963), using lights as cues and events, examined the effects of variation in the base rates ($P[C_1]$ and $P[C_1']$) of the cues. She set $P[E_1|C_1] = 1$ and $P[E_1|C_1']$ = .5 and found that the base rate affected the response proportions conditional upon cues, but did not significantly affect the overall response proportions $P[A_1]$. It should be noted that although one cue value was a perfect predictor of the event in her experiment, subjects produced response proportions less than unity. Further, $P[C_1]$ was confounded with $P[E_1]$. Myers and Cruse (1968)

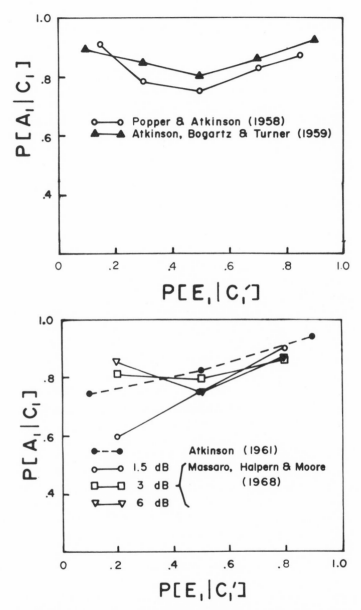

FIG. 1   (a) Response proportions conditional upon cue C_1 as a function of $P[E_1|C_1']$ for two probabilistic discrimination studies. In the Popper and Atkinson study $P[E_1|C_1] = .85$, for the Atkinson, et al. study $P[E_1|C_1] = .9$. In both studies the cue values were highly discriminable.   (b) Response proportions conditional upon cue C_1 as a function of $P[E_1|C_1']$ for two probabilistic discrimination studies. In the Atkinson study the cues were not highly discriminable; in the Massaro, et al. study, discriminability was varied from low (1.5 dB) to high (6 dB).

varied both $P[C_1]$ and $P[E_1|C_1']$ and found that $P[A_1|C_1]$ depended upon both parameters. The ubiquitous U-shaped function was obtained.

Probabilistic discrimination learning tasks using acoustic stimuli were studied by Halpern and Moore (1967) and Massaro, Halpern, and Moore (1968). In the first study the primary concern was with the confusability of the cues; cue similarity was an additional concern in the latter study. Since the second study supported and extended the earlier research, only the relevant portions of the latter will be summarized. It was found that the U-shaped function of $P[A_1|C_1]$ against $P[E_1|C_1']$ depended upon the confusability of the cues. In particular, when the cues (tones) were highly discriminable, the U-shaped function was found; when the cues were highly confusable, $P[A_1|C_1]$ was linear with $P[E_1|C_1']$. Finally, intermediate degrees of confusability yielded independence. These data are also summarized in Fig. 1b. The results of Massaro *et al.* (1968) suggest that the result (a linear function) reported by Atkinson (1961) was due to highly confusable cues. Examination of the procedure used by Atkinson suggests that the effect was due not to the cues per se, but rather the use of lamps, albeit of different color and location, to indicate both the observing response and cues.

The basic experiments were used to test predictions from various models of discrimination learning (Atkinson, 1960, 1961; Burke & Estes, 1957; Lee, 1966; Massaro, 1969; Restle, 1957). In general, such models did not describe the data well except in very restricted situations such as when the cues were highly confusable.

There were a number of subsequent studies of probabilistic discrimination learning which were very similar to those mentioned earlier in that binary cues and events were used, but differed primarily in that more parameters were allowed to vary; in particular, $P[E_1|C_1]$ which had been held constant in most of the earlier studies was allowed to vary. Further, more attention was paid to the cues and the validity of the cue was more systematically varied. Such experiments include that of Summers (1968), those of Björkman, and those of Bauer, which are listed in Table 1. For the purposes of the present discussion, these experiments add little to the general results reported above; however, they make it abundantly clear that responses depend upon cue base rate, cue validity, and event base rate. In most cases, the cues were designed to be highly discriminable so that confusability was not an issue. What was of concern to the researchers, and which will be discussed later, was the effect of learning upon cue compounding, the effect of instructions, and the determination of individual response styles.

There were two basic problems with all of the studies listed in Table 1. First, in each experiment there was only one binary cue dimension, and secondly, in each study in which there was more than one experimental condition, cue validity and event base rate were confounded. The latter problem raises serious questions about the interpretations made of the results. In some of the later studies, when the base rate of the cues was varied across conditions, it resulted in a further confounding of variables.

Multiple-Valued Single-Cue Tasks

In all of the experiments dealing with probabilistic discrimination learning summarized above and in Table 1 a single binary cue and binary event were utilized. The next step was to generalize the experimental task. In these experiments the number of cues was increased; however, rather than increasing the number of dimensions, a single dimension was used and the number of values that the cue could take on increased. Of approximately seven such studies, the cues took on 4–12 values (see Table 2). Unfortunately, the problems simply compounded. Each stimulus was simply a pattern and the confounding of validity and base rate remained. Binary events were still used.

In one of the earliest experiments (Estes, Burke, Atkinson, & Frankmann, 1957) the cues consisted of a set of 12 signal lamps arranged in a row from left to right. The first cue C_i was defined as a randomly selected subset of the lights being lit. The subset was chosen with a "left" bias. For the second value C_i' the subset was chosen with a "right" bias. After three days of training the subjects were tested on single signal lamps and triads of lamps in an effort to determine the amount and type of stimulus generalization. While a precise conceptualization of this experiment in terms of the signal lamps might suggest that there were 12 cue dimensions, the nature of the testing methods used suggests that the proximal cues used may be more easily considered as a single cue with 12 values.

TABLE 2
Probabilistic Discrimination Learning
1 Cue Dimension, 2 Events

Study	Number of values/ dimension	Number of trials	Number of conditions	Comments
Estes, Burke, Atkinson, and Frankmann (1957)	12	592	2	Complex cue
Erickson (1966)	4	480	2	Multiple (E_1, E_2) pairs
Friedman, Rollins, and Padilla (1968)	5	192	2	Tested on compounds
Björkman (1969b, 1969c)	4	800	2	Tested on compounds
Kroll (1970)	4	540	5	
Hanson and Schipper (1971)	4	480	5	Tested on compounds

The results were described in terms of a model for stimulus generalization; the result of importance to the present discussion is that in the final tests on single lights, subject's response proportions tended to match the probability of the event given the cue value presented on a trial.

Of greater interest are the experiments of Erickson (1966) and Kroll (1970). These experiments were described by the authors in terms of "learning several simultaneous probability-learning problems." While such a term is certainly descriptive, it is not necessarily the case that the subjects viewed the tasks in that manner. In both experiments a single-cue dimension was used which could take on four values. While Erickson had separate E_1 and E_2 pairs for each cue value, Kroll used a single pair of outcomes. Their results were quite similar: Subjects' response proportions conditional upon the cue presented tended to exceed the probability of the events given the cue, the variability of the cues tended to reduce response variability, and performing several tasks simultaneously tended to interfere with (inhibit) sequential processing. Kroll's analysis is especially interesting since he measured individual differences in subjects' response strategies in a manner similar to that used by Björkman (1969a).

Multiple-cue values were also used in the studies of Friedman, Rollins, and Padilla (1968), Björkman (1969b, 1969c), Hanson and Schipper (1971), and Schipper (1966, 1967). The central focus of these studies was stimulus compounding. That is, the subject was trained on a sequence in which there was only one cue value presented on each trial; subsequent to training, the subject was presented with nonfeedback trials on which two (or more) of the cue values were presented.[4] While the results were interesting in terms of stimulus compounding, the performance on training trials were similar to that reported by Erickson (1966) and Kroll (1970). Hanson and Schipper found that during the test on compounds the number of elements (closely related to dimensions) in the compound had an effect upon performance.

CONCEPT LEARNING WITH MISINFORMATIVE FEEDBACK

One of the characteristic problems of probabilistic discrimination learning studies is that there is a pervasive assumption that the cues upon which judgments are based are inherently unidimensional. That is, the cues are based upon patterns presented on each trial and if there is any overlap between patterns, then it is something to be estimated as a statistical parameter. While it often may be appropriate to describe the overlap between cues statistically, it is very clearly the case that in a large number of decision tasks, judgments are

---

[4]It should be pointed out that these experiments in stimulus compounding differ from those in which the subject is trained on components and patterns (compounds) at the same time (e.g., Binder & Estes, 1966; Estes & Hopkins, 1961). In such tasks some elements or cues may be probabilistically reinforced; however, a single compound or pattern is not.

based on cues and cue patterns which are described in terms of the attributes from which the cue patterns are presented. The work of Zeaman and House (1963) was virtually alone in stressing the multidimensional aspects of probabilistic discrimination learning. For example, a person is usually described in a multidimensional manner—"an old, friendly, red-haired man" or as a "young female with high blood pressure and anemia." For the purposes of understanding the judgment process it is important to know how these separate proximal cue dimensions are combined into some final judgment of some distal event.

In concept identification tasks careful attention is paid to describing the cues in terms of dimensions, and solutions are based upon some strategy which focuses on either one dimension or some logical rule based on some combination of the dimensions. However, in most concept identification tasks, there exists a solution such that the subject may be correct on every trial. Thus some cue or pattern of cues has perfect validity.

In the late 1950s and early 1960s there was a series of concept identification studies done which used what was termed "misinformative feedback" as part of the experimental design. There were various reasons for such studies, one of the more important of which was to test some of the models of concept identification which postulated all-or-none learning, hypothesis sampling, etc. The introduction of random reinforcements into the learning sequence enabled one to make stronger tests of some of the predictions of the models. However, it is not our purpose to elaborate on such justifications of the experiments since they have separate implications for the study of multiple-cue probability learning.

A typical concept identification experiment with misinformative feedback[5] consists of generating a sequence of cues paired with the determinate outcomes or events. Then, on some probabilistic basis the outcomes are changed. Thus in an experiment with 40% misinformative feedback, outcomes are reversed on 40% of the trials. In the eleven experiments surveyed, (which includes most published studies), the tasks utilized between one and seven binary dimensions; in most cases one dimension was relevant and the remaining cue dimensions were irrelevant. In a small number of these studies, the other dimensions included redundant cues. The percentage of misinformative feedback was varied and its effect was assessed on subsequent trials in which there was no misinformative feedback. The studies are summarized in Table 3. The typical results were that as the percentage of misinformative feedback increased, the slower was the final learning in the determinate stage. The instructions given to subjects were intended to encourage them to infer that the task was solvable and that it was possible to be correct 100% of the time. In several of the experiments it was reported that some subjects maximized during the misinformative feedback stage. Such maximizing may have been due to the instructions given the subjects. There are several problems with such studies when viewed from the point of

---

[5] Misinformative feedback should be distinguished from omission of feedback which consists of omitting all reinforcement on some trials (Bourne & Pendleton, 1958).

TABLE 3
Concept Identification with Misinformative Feedback

Study	Number of dimensions	Number of values/ dimension	Number of trials	True MCPL?	Comment
Goodnow and Postman (1955)	2	5	80	Yes	
Morin (1955)	1	8	240 (or criterion)	Yes	+ feedforward
Bourne and Haygood (1960)	2, 4, 6	2	128	Yes	1 dimension relevant
Pishkin (1960, 1961)	2, 4	2	200	Yes	1 dimension relevant
Johannsen (1962)	2, 4, 7	2	200	Yes	transfer task 1 dimension relevant
Wolfgang, Pishkin, and Lundy (1962)	2, 4, 6	2	240	Yes	1 dimension relevant
Levine (1962)	2	2	0, 10, 30, 60	No	random reinforcement
Bourne (1963)	3	2	600	Yes	1 dimension relevant
Mandler, Cowan, and Gold (1964)	3	6 or 2	72	No	1, 2, or 3 relevant, redundant dimensions
Holstein and Premack (1965)	2, 6	2	0, 6, 20, 40	No	random reinforcement
Trabasso and Staudenmayer (1968)	2	2	16	No	random reinforcement

view of multiple-cue probability learning. First, most of the published data are summarized only in terms of the percentage of correct responses during the misinformative feedback stage; therefore the response proportions conditional upon the cues presented are not known. Second, there were usually relatively few trials. Third, subjects were not informed of the probabilistic nature of the task (an exception was the series of experiments reported by Morin (1955) which will be described below).

The early experiment reported by Goodnow and Postman (1955) set the pattern for the general sort of experiment using misinformative feedback. In their experiment an attempt was made to determine whether probability learning would result in tasks and situations in which the subject expects to be able to find a determinate solution to the problem. Subjects were presented stimuli (cues) which varied on five dimensions; on the basis of which they were asked to make binary predictions. Six groups of subjects, each with a different level of cue validity, were run for 80 trials. The authors suggested that subjects tended to match the conditional event given cue probabilities; however, closer examination of their results indicates that subjects' conditional response proportions exceeded the $P[E_1 | C]$ probabilities when the cues were highly valid and were below those conditional probabilities when the cue validity was low.

In another early experiment, Morin (1955) used four basic experimental groups that received instructions which served to differentially inform the subjects about the nature of the task. One group was told to "solve the problem," another was told that the "equipment does not always tell the truth"; a third group was given similar instructions and an extra signal lamp lit when misinformative feedback was given; the last group was told about both the misinformative feedback *and* meaning of the signal lamp. In addition, each of these basic groups was divided into six subgroups in which the amount of misinformative feedback was varied from 0 to 50%. The cue consisted of a single dimension with eight values (eight lights arranged in an octagonal pattern), and subjects were run for 240 trials or a criterion of perfect concept learning. The results suggested that subjects tended to match or slightly exceed conditional event given cue probabilities except for the group which was given complete information about the task and correction signal. Many subjects in the initial condition failed to solve the task at all.

Bourne and Haygood (1960) reported an experiment which involved the intermittent reinforcement of an irrelevant cue dimension. The task was a concept identification task with one relevant dimension and one, three, or five irrelevant binary dimensions. They varied the rate of intermittent reinforcement of a single dimension. (Subsequent to the intermittent reinforcement of an irrelevant cue, there was a dimensional shift to that cue. The present discussion is concerned only with the first phase.) Although the description of the task was in terms of the intermittent reinforcement, the task was identical to one with misinformative feedback tied to particular cue patterns. Their results showed that accuracy decreased as a function of the number of dimensions and as a function of decreasing cue validity. Since the data were summarized in terms of errors, inferences about conditional probabilities cannot be made.

Pishkin (1960, 1961) conducted one of the more systematic studies of the effect of misinformative feedback in concept identification studies. He noted that most measures of cue validity did not indicate the distribution of misinformative feedback, but only the amount. As part of his design he varied the distribution of misinformative feedback. (That is, 10% misinformative feedback sequences could be structured to give the misinformative feedback on a fixed interval, exactly once in each 10 trials, exactly twice in each 20 trials, etc.) He found that the distribution of misinformative feedback had a significant effect. The more "regular" it was, the better the performance of the subjects. Unfortunately, since only mean errors were analyzed, no inferences may be drawn about conditional probabilities. In addition, the cue-event sequence generation procedure, while controlling for the distribution of misinformative feedback, did not control or examine cue and event base rates. Johannsen (1962) performed a similar experiment and obtained similar results.

Wolfgang, Pishkin, and Lundy (1962) examined the effect of anxiety upon performance in concept identification tasks. Their results, in agreement with all previous studies were that as the amount of irrelevant information increases, misinformative feedback becomes increasingly disadvantageous. While they also found that anxious subjects performed better (closer to maximizing), they also found, as did Morin, that awareness of the presence of misinformative feedback had the effect of leading to faster learning in that subjects reached asymptotic response levels faster.

Levine (1962), in an experiment very similar in design to those described earlier, utilized completely random reinforcements. Unfortunately, since the reinforcements were determined randomly, it is not known whether or not one cue dimension was more valid than another, and it is difficult to make meaningful generalizations to the other experiments reported in this section. Subsequent studies by Holstein and Premack (1965) and Trabasso and Staudenmayer (1968) had the same problem in generalization coupled with a very small number of trials in some conditions.

Bourne (1963) performed an extensive series of experiments to determine the long-term effects of misinformative feedback. While the experiments progressed through several phases, only the first will be described. Subjects were run 200 trials per day for three days on tasks with one relevant and two irrelevant dimensions. The amount of misinformative feedback was 10, 20, or 30%. By means of instructions, subjects were led to believe that there was a solution to the task (on day 4 they were transferred to a different problem with a different amount of misinformative feedback). Bourne reported an intermediate stage of probability matching followed by a level of performance in which 42 of 60 subjects learned to respond consistently on the basis of the partially valid, relevant cue. However, the criterion used by Bourne in order to assess consistent responding was not maximizing; since the true cue validities were not known (or given) an examination of the published results suggests that his estimate is too generous.

Mandler, Cowan, and Gold (1964) utilized tasks of varying difficulty in which the cues were multivalued and could be relevant, irrelevant, or redundant. The experiment is distinguished from those reported earlier in that the base rates of the two events were not equal, $P[E_1] = .67$. They found that subjects tended to probability match the events prior to solution; and, as others have reported, that misinformative feedback retards subsequent learning.

While the results of most of the experiments using misinformative feedback described in this section are useful in a very general sense, most of them suffer from some problems which are critical for the purposes of the present discussion, but not for the original intentions of the researchers. For the purpose of understanding multiple-cue probability learning, perhaps the biggest problem with such experiments with misinformative feedback was that the manner of producing randomness left many experimental parameters uncontrolled. That is, the generation procedure left the base rate of events confounded with the percentage of misinformative feedback, and indices of such confounding were not used. In addition, there was no effort to ensure that the irrelevant cues did not become partially valid as a result of the random reversal procedure. Thus, during the misinformative feedback stage the cue validities were uncontrolled and unknown.

MISCELLANEOUS ENVIRONMENTS AND TASKS

All of the probabilistic discrimination learning tasks discussed earlier involved a single nonmetric cue dimension and binary event outcomes. The multiple-cue tasks in the previous section dealt with stimuli which fit well into a concept identification framework. There have been several other situations and tasks examined within the same general framework of multiple-cue studies but have characteristics which distinguish them from the studies in the earlier categories. A listing of some of these studies is in Table 4. While the list does not include all such studies, an attempt has been made to include a representative sample of the different sorts of studies. Some of the characteristics and results of such studies will be outlined below.

There have been a small number of studies that utilized continuous cue dimensions; for example, Howell and Funaro (1965), Lee and Janke (1965), and Vlek and van der Heijden (1970). In these tasks the cue values presented to subjects were sampled from continuous distributions and were used to predict binary events. Subjects usually made one of two types of response—either a prediction of which category or distribution was sampled, or subjective estimates of the probability that the sample came from a particular distribution. For example, the cues used by Vlek and van der Heijden were representations of human faces and subjects were asked to optimally categorize each face into one of two families. The results of such studies appear to have little direct relevance for tasks involving nonmetric cue dimensions and will not be considered further here. Hogarth (1975) has discussed other implications for such studies.

Another sort of experiment involved tasks in which there were often many cue dimensions (which distinguishes them from the earlier studies) but also multi-valued events. For example, Beach (1964a) used tasks in which three cue dimensions each having 9 or 12 values were used to predict three or five events. Azuma and Cronbach (1966a, 1966b) used a task in which three cue dimensions were employed. The cues consisted of (x, y) coordinate pairs coupled with a binary character. Goldstein, Harmon, and Lesk (1972) used a task in which 21 cue dimensions, each having 3 or 5 values were used to predict multiple events. Like the Vlek and van der Heijden study, they used aspects of human faces as

TABLE 4

Miscellaneous Environments and Tasks

Continuous cue dimensions, binary events
  Howell and Funaro (1965)
  Lee and Janke (1965)
  Vlek and van der Heijden (1970)

Mixed or complex cases
  Beach, (1964a)
    1. 3 cues with 9 or 12 values
    2. 3 or 5 events
  Azuma and Cronbach (1966a, 1966b)
    1. 3 "cues" (x, y) coordinates + binary character
    2. 4 events
  Lanzetta and Driscoll (1966)
  Driscoll and Lanzetta (1965)
  Björkman (1969b, 1969c)
    1 binary cue, 3 events
  Goldstein, Harmon, Lesk (1972)
    21 dimensions, 3–5 values each
    multiple events
  Reed (1970, 1972)
    4 dimensions, 3 values each
    2 events
  Thorngate and Housch (1972)
    3 binary cues, optional stopping of search
  Murray (1971)

Mixed cases (Class 2)
  Robbins and Medin (1971)
  Medin (1972)
  Allen and Estes (1972)
  Allmeyer and Medin (1973)

---

cues. In another series of studies using schematic human faces, Reed (1970, 1972) used faces which varied on four dimensions; each dimension could take on three values. Although several variations were run, subjects were presented with five exemplars of two categories and were required to sort 25 additional faces into the categories. In a comparison of several models, it appeared that the categorizations depend on distance measures which emphasized optimal discrimination. Other than the 10 prototype faces, there was no feedback concerning the accuracy of the categorizations.

Thorngate and Housch (1972) used a simpler task in which they asked subjects to evaluate one to three binary cues on each trial. The subject selected dimensions to observe until a response could be made with some certainty. The optional stopping was used to assess the information processing strategy used by the subjects. Driscoll and Lanzetta (1965), and Lanzetta and Driscoll (1966) utilized tasks in which there was stimulus uncertainty and examined the effect of such uncertainty, stimulus variability, and response uncertainty upon subjective uncertainty, information search, and information processing. The principal results were that subjects continued searching until virtually all information was exhausted, and subjective uncertainty was highly correlated with both stimulus and response uncertainty, and the greater the stimulus uncertainty the faster the subject began seeking information.

Björkman (1969b, 1969c) used a task in which a single binary cue was used to predict one of three events. In this task, only one event value was probabilistically tied to the cue, thus making it easier to assess subsequent cue combinations and cue-event generalization. Murray (1971) performed an experiment in which the subject performed five probability learning tasks simultaneously. However, unlike the experiments of Erickson (1966) and Kroll (1970) described earlier, on each trial the subject was free to pick which one of the cues (slot machines) would pay off. Each alternative had a different probability of winning and subjects tended to choose alternatives as a function of their payoff rate.

Another series of experiments is tangentially related to the work reported this far. Although these experiments vary from one another in some procedural details (Allen & Estes, 1972; Allmeyer & Medin, 1973; Medin, 1972; Robbins & Medin, 1971) they basically consisted of training subjects to associate each value from a set of cues with one event. Subsequently, each pair of cues was presented and judgments had to be made on the basis of what was learned during the single-cue presentation phase. While one purpose of the studies was to separate performance and learning, the results have limited relevance to other research described in this chapter, other than that with suitable instructions and tasks, one can move subjects' response asymptotes almost independently of the cue validities.

MULTIPLE-CUE PROBABILITY LEARNING

A generalization of both probabilistic discrimination learning and concept identification with misinformative feedback leads to multiple-cue probability learning tasks. As pointed out earlier, the rationale for such tasks is not that they generalize some more specialized tasks, rather, such tasks are more natural in that a larger number of analogs in natural situations may be found. Unfortunately, relatively few studies have been done within this paradigm using nonmetric cues and events. (Such is not the case for continuous cues and events, for which there is a virtual plethora of studies.) Table 5 contains a list of the studies. It should be noted that some of the studies of concept identification with misinformative feedback can also be classed as multiple-cue probability learning studies and are so indicated in Table 3.

One characteristic of multiple-cue probability learning tasks is that they require the subject to integrate information from two or more dimensions in which the cue-event validities must be inferred as in concept identification tasks.

TABLE 5
Multiple-Cue Probability Learning

Study	Number of binary cue dimensions	Number of conditions	Comment
Slovic, Rorer, and Hoffman (1971)	7	1	7-point scale for event
Estes (1972a)	3	2	
Castellan (1973)	1, 2, 3	6	1 dimension relevant
Castellan and Edgell (1973)	2	16	
Edgell and Castellan (1973)	2	12	Tested configurality
Castellan (1974)	2	2	Varied feedback
Stockburger and Erickson (1974)	4	2	
Edgell (1974)	1, 2, 3	12	

In a series of experiments in which the validity of each cue dimension was controlled, Castellan and Edgell (1973) found that subjects attend to both dimensions when two dimensions are used. In their experiment two binary cue dimensions were used to predict a binary event. When the validity of one cue dimension was held constant, and the validity of the second dimension was allowed to vary it was found that performance depended upon both dimensions even though subjects could have been as accurate if they had attended to only the most relevant cue dimension. Figure 2 summarizes the data from one set of conditions in their experiment. The validity of one cue dimension was held constant at .8, while the validity of the second dimension was varied. Since there were two binary cues and subjects saw four patterns of cues, the data are summarized as response proportions conditional upon cue patterns. It is clear that the subjects' performance depended upon the validity of both cue dimensions.

While several questions arise from consideration of the subjects' performance in tasks like the one described above, three important ones deal with the effect of irrelevant information, whether the subject is learning patterns per se or learning to respond on the basis of the dimensions which constitute the patterns, and the manner in which learning and/or performance may be facilitated. Each of these issues ultimately deals with the manner in which subjects combine information from various sources in multiple-cue probability learning tasks.

The Effect of Irrelevant Cue Dimensions

The manner in which subjects learn when irrelevant cue dimensions are present can provide clues about the manner in which information is processed in probabilistic situations. While it was found in concept identification studies with misinformative feedback that learning was slowed when irrelevant cues are present, the nature of the cue sequences used did not ensure that the irrelevant

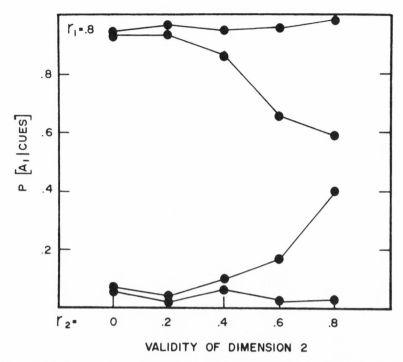

FIG. 2 Response proportions conditional upon cue patterns in a two binary cue probability learning study (Castellan & Edgell, 1973). The validity of one cue dimension was held
constant and the other was varied. (Each column of data represents a different group of
subjects.)

cues remained irrelevant when the misinformative feedback was given. What was
clear was that the irrelevant cues were only less relevant than the relevant cue
dimension.

The effect of irrelevant dimensions was examined in an experiment which
utilized binary cue dimensions and binary events (Castellan, 1973). However, in
each condition only one cue dimension was relevant. Across conditions the
number of irrelevant cue dimensions was varied. Thus subjects were presented
with zero, one, or two irrelevant cue dimensions. The data were then analyzed in
terms of performance conditional upon the relevant cue dimension. It was found
that as the number of irrelevant cue dimensions increased, accuracy and response
asymptotes decreased. It was also observed that the decrement in performance
interacted with the validity of the relevant cue. The response asymptotes are
summarized for several levels of relevant cue validity in Fig. 3. The effect of
irrelevant cues is greatest when the relevant cue is of moderate validity and less
when the relevant cue is of either very high or very low validity. This result
would be expected if the relevant cue is of very high validity, since the task is
then very similar to a concept identification task which subjects are able to solve

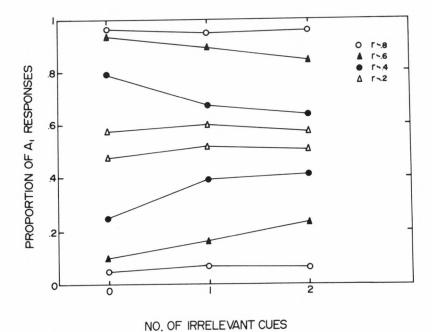

NO. OF IRRELEVANT CUES

FIG. 3   Proportion of A_1 responses conditional upon relevant cue for the last block of 100 trials as a function of relevant cue validity and the number of irrelevant cue dimensions. (The upper and lower curves for each validity level are $P[A_1|C_1]$ and $P[A_1|C_1']$, respectively.) (Adapted from Castellan, 1973.)

when there is one relevant and several irrelevant dimensions. In straight concept identification, the rate of learning is slowed as a function of the number of irrelevant cues. When the relevant cue is of low validity, the subject should have considerable difficulty discriminating between the relevant and irrelevant cue dimensions, thus diminishing the effect. The results reported above indicate that the subjects are doing more than learning *patterns*, since if the subjects were encoding on the basis of patterns only, then the response asymptotes should be horizontal across conditions. While it is true that the number of patterns increases as the number of dimensions increases, for the experiments reported here there would be only two, four, or eight patterns, and while the latter number of patterns may be close to the information processing capacity of subjects, it does not exceed it. Further, the former number of patterns (two and four) are both well within the processing capacity and the effect appears greatest between these conditions. Perhaps the best evidence is in an experiment reported by Edgell (1974) in which the number of patterns was held constant, but their constitution varied. One group of subjects was given a task with two binary cue dimensions and another group was given the same sequence of cues and events, except the two binary cue patterns were mapped onto a single-cue dimension with four levels. There were distinct differences in performance between the two groups.

The Processing of Patterns

Since the experiments with irrelevant cue dimensions make it clear that subjects are not learning patterns only, but are processing the cues in terms of constituent dimensions, it becomes important to ask if subjects are responding on the basis of dimensions only. The experiments described above give at best a partial answer. A more complete answer may be found in studies in which the cue-event validities could be varied.

One of the earliest studies of nonmetric multiple-cue probability learning was that of Slovic, Rorer, and Hoffman (1971) in which a physician's reliance on signs (cues) in making diagnostic judgments was studied. In their study, a group of radiologists judged the malignancy of gastric ulcers on the basis of seven radiological signs. The cues (signs) were binary and indicated the presence or absence of features or characteristics. Judgments were made on a seven-point scale (nonmalignant to malignant). Since the subjects were all experienced radiologists it was assumed that learning had already occurred and that the observed behavior could be considered asymptotic. Each cue had less than perfect validity and it was found that subjects used more than the most valid cue. Further, although in some cases the performances of some radiologists were quite similar, there were marked differences in other cases. There was a marked tendency for the radiologists to make some small use of patterns of cues in making judgments. However, because of the nature of the study, it is not possible to discuss the results in terms of accuracy since the actual events to be predicted could not be controlled by the experimenter.

A second study which did allow for better control of both cue validities and cue and event base rates was done by Estes (1972a). In this study the task was described as a medical diagnostic task; however, the subjects were not professional medical personnel. The task consisted of presentation of three binary cues (symptoms) on the basis of which a binary classification was to be made. One of the purposes of the study was to determine whether subjects process cue information in some additive fashion, or whether processing is done on the basis of patterns. The results were complex but indicated that under some circumstances, subjects were responding on the basis of patterns, while in other circumstances they responded on the basis of individual cues. However, cues, patterns, cue-event validities, and base rates were confounded in this study which resulted in some ambiguities in interpretation.

A better and more complete answer may be found in a set of experiments in which the cues were chosen so that the validity of the cues was held constant, while the validity of the pattern was varied. In a number of experiments it was found that subjects indeed use both the cue dimensions and patterns (Edgell,

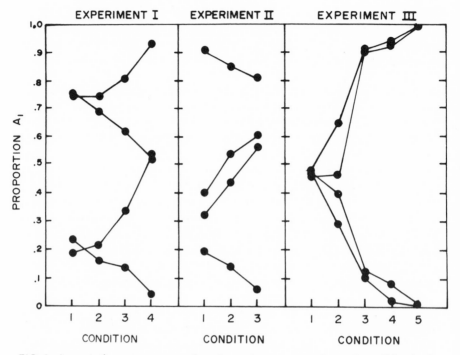

FIG. 4   Asymptotic response proportions for each cue pattern for each condition in the Edgell and Castellan (1973) experiment. In Experiments I and II cue validities were held constant, while pattern validity was varied across conditions. In Experiment III the cue dimensions were irrelevant and only the cue patterns were relevant. (Each column of data represents a different group of subjects.)

1974; Edgell & Castellan, 1973; Stockburger & Erickson, 1974). The data from the Edgell and Castellan experiment are summarized in Fig. 4. In each experiment, there were two binary cue dimensions. The data are summarized in terms of asymptotic response proportions conditional upon the cue patterns. In Experiment I, the first cue dimension was relevant, the second was irrelevant, and the information in the pattern was varied. In Experiment II, both cue dimensions had the same validity, and the validity of the pattern was varied. In the final experiment, the cue dimensions had zero validity, and the validity of the pattern was varied. It is clear from the figure that subjects did indeed process the information in the pattern was well as the dimensions. (If the subjects were processing patterns *only*, then the performance in Experiments I.1 and III.2 would be identical as would the performance on Experiments I.3 and II.2.)

In summary, the results of these experiments show that subjects are pattern or configural information processors if such processing is appropriate for the task, but never at the expense of processing information from the constituent dimensions.

Effect of Feedback Type

In most of the experiments described earlier, the only feedback given to subjects consisted of outcome feedback, that is, feedback which consists of information concerning which event actually occurred on a trial. Many researchers (e.g., Björkman, 1972; Hammond, 1971; Hammond & Boyle, 1971) have argued that other kinds of information about the task may be very helpful in improving performance and facilitating learning. While the effects of instructions upon behavior are well known, the effect of other sorts of feedback have received little attention.

Within the framework of multiple-cue probability learning, Björkman (1971a) examined the effect of presenting the subject with what he termed "feedforward"[6] which was information about the structure of the cue-event contingencies. While it would seem obvious that various amounts of feedforward should produce different predictive policies, he found no systematic relationship between feedforward and optimality of performance. Björkman used two types of feedforward in a task which consisted of one binary cue dimension and binary event. One form of feedforward, termed "ordinal" in that the rank order of cue-event contingencies was given, tended to produce results which were optimal whether or not the rank order information was coupled with outcome feedback. On the other hand, for subjects in the "numerical" condition who were given the probabilities of events conditional upon cues, $P[E_i|C_j]$, feedforward had little effect upon performance. In a recent study Castellan (1974) examined the effect of different types of feedback upon performance. In addition to traditional outcome feedback, subjects were given, in a periodic fashion, one of four types of feedback or feedforward: (a) cue-event validities, (b) cue-response utilization coefficients, (c) a combination of both cue-event validities and cue response utilization coefficients, or (d) the percentage of correct predictions made. In addition, subjects were given such information as short-term feedback (based on the last few trials), long-term feedback (based cumulatively upon all trials), or both short-term and long-term feedback. While the results were complex because of the large number of conditions, the basic finding was that the various sorts of feedback had little effect upon asymptotic performance; however, there were significant effects relating to the rate of learning and an interaction between feedback type and conditions. Two different cue-event sequences were used, each producing different cue-event validities. Of particular interest is that in the condition in which one cue dimension was irrelevant subjects did not learn to ignore that dimension even when the feedback periodically presented the cue-event validities.

---

[6]While a distinction is sometimes made between feedback—information about performance—and feedforward—information about the task—no such distinction is made in this chapter because the classification is more complex and subtle than the dichotomy suggests.

In a more recent study the most promising feedback modes from the Castellan study were adapted to another situation in which subjects were asked to learn to predict in changing environments (Castellan & Swaine, 1975). The feedback types used were outcome feedback, cue-event validities, or the percentage of correct responses. Subjects were run for five days and on each day the task structure changed. For each subject the feedback type was held constant, while the number of cue dimensions and the cue-event validities could change each day. It was found that while there was little difference due to feedback type on the first day, there was an increasing effect of feedback across days. The response proportions conditional upon cue patterns for the three types of feedback on Day 5 are summarized in Fig. 5. It should be noted that the probability of E_1 given cue patterns 2, 4, 6, 7, and 8 was approximately equal and the probability of E_1 given cue patterns 1, 3, and 5 was equal. The differences in responding to patterns 3, 5, and 7 across feedback conditions should be noted. The differences in responding which were found were systematically related to feedback type. However, there appeared to be no simple algorithm for predicting when differences would occur. In fact, it was found that in some cases there were cue reversals in which subjects predicted the less likely event. Current research is focusing on the source of difficulty and its relation to feedback type.

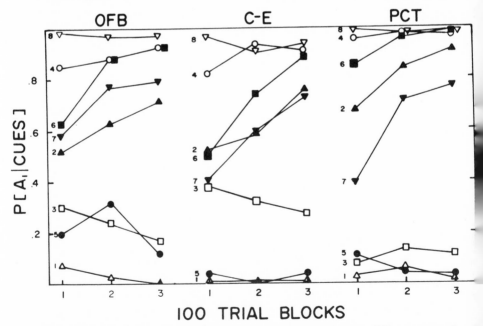

FIG. 5 Response proportions conditional upon cue pattern for three different types of feedback (OFB, outcome feedback; C–E, cue-event validity feedback; PCT, percentage correct feedback). Task involved three binary cues and data in figure are those for Day 5. (From Castellan & Swaine, 1975.)

A few other studies have examined performance as a function of the behavior asked of the subject. For example, Bauer (1972b) found that when subjects were asked to make trial-by-trial predictions such predictions were affected by whether or not the subject also estimated the conditional probabilities of events given the cues. She also found that when subjects made predictions in the absence of outcome feedback, they tended to maximize (Bauer, 1971b, 1972b). This tendency has also been reported by Björkman (1969c, 1973); but was not found by Reber and Millward (1968) in a probability learning task in which cues were not used.

On the basis of the results described in this section, no simple statement about the efficacy of various sorts of feedback may be made. More research is needed in order to specify the effects and judge their potential usefulness in applied situations.

SUMMARY

In this chapter the current state of research in nonmetric multiple-cue probability learning has been summarized. Contributions to an understanding have been made by related research, in particular, probabilistic discrimination learning and concept identification with misinformative feedback.

Although it was found that in the one dimensional tasks the discriminability of the several cue values has an effect upon performance which is predictable, the lack of comparable research in multiple-cue tasks makes generalization about the effect difficult. The research which shows that performance depends upon whether the cues are multidimensional or multivalued—even when highly discriminable—suggests that the coding process is influenced by subjective descriptions and codings of the cues which are not simple labels.

The research in which the information in patterns is varied demonstrates that subjects are neither simple dimension processors nor pattern processors. Rather, the subject learns to process both sources of information when it is indeed appropriate to use such information. On the other hand, subjects in probabilistic judgment tasks do not adopt optimal response strategies. This well-known result extends beyond the failure of subjects to maximize to the result that they are unable to learn to ignore irrelevant information, even when told that the information is irrelevant.

In an effort to enhance understanding of the judgment process, recent work has examined the effects upon performance of different sorts of feedback. Some types of feedback have a large effect upon acquisition and asymptotic performance. While reasonable conjectures lead to appropriate predictions about the effect of particular types of feedback upon learning the judgment task, the effect of different types of feedback upon final performance levels, while large in some cases, appears to be neither systematic nor consistent. This interaction between feedback type and task characteristics has yet to be systematically studied; the available results reinforce the arguments made earlier about choosing tasks which are representative of those about which one would want to generalize.

Models that deal with the multiple-cue probability learning tasks are in a very crude state of development and will be described only briefly. While there is ample evidence that most models derived from probabilistic discrimination learning theories are inadequate, recent work by Norman (1974) on the Zeaman and House model suggests that some generalizations may have reasonable explanatory power. This may be because the model differs from others in that it deals with the dimensionality of the cues. The intuitively appealing model recently proposed by Estes (1972a, b, c) is clearly of some use; however, it does not deal with the problems of multiple dimensions. The hypothesis generation model for multiple-cue probability learning proposed by Castellan and Edgell (1973) appears to provide reasonable accounts of performance. In that model, subjects may make predictions on the basis of information from any of several sources—the individual cue dimensions, cue patterns, or event base rates. That model, which postulates a two stage judgment process, has been applied with good results to experiments in which the diagnosticity of patterns and cues is varied (Edgell, 1974; Edgell & Castellan, 1973; Stockburger & Erickson, 1974). Tasks can be used in which the model will clearly fail—for example, the model is unable to deal with the effect of different sorts of feedback. However, the basic assumptions of the model still apply and should be examined. A multistage model, similar in many features, has been proposed by Wortman (1972).

The models which give the best accounts of performance in multiple-cue probability learning have at least one of two things in common: they include some meaningful representation of the dimensionality of the cues, and/or imply multiple stages of processing of cues and events. Both aspects are present in the models proposed by Castellan and Edgell (1973), Norman (1974), and Zeaman and House (1963), and the latter aspect is included in the models of Atkinson (1960), Hogarth (1974), and Wortman (1972). While these models differ in how they deal with these aspects, their relative success appears to depend upon inclusion of one or both of them.

It is only through the use of suitable models that we will come to good understanding of the judgment process in probabilistic cue tasks. Such models, together with the contributions and insights from other methodologies, should enable the construction of task environments which will lead to the facilitation of learning of judgment tasks in practical situations.

ACKNOWLEDGMENTS

Preparation of this chapter was supported in part by National Institutes of Health Grant MH-23563. The author would like to thank S. E. Edgell for his comments on an earlier draft of this manuscript.

REFERENCES

Allen, G. A., & Estes, W. K. Acquisition of correct choices and value judgments in binary choice learning with differential rewards. *Psychonomic Science*, 1972, 27, 68–72.

Allmeyer, D. H., & Medin, D. L. Reward information and cue selection following multiple-cue probability learning. *Journal of Experimental Psychology*, 1973, 99, 426–428.

Atkinson, R. C. A theory of stimulus discrimination learning. In K. J. Arrow, S. Karlin, & P. Suppes (Eds.), *Mathematical methods in the social sciences*. Stanford, California: Stanford University Press, 1960. Pp. 221–241.

Atkinson, R. C. The observing response in discrimination learning. *Journal of Experimental Psychology*, 1961, 62, 253–262.

Atkinson, R. C., Bogartz, W. H., & Turner, R. N. Supplementary report: Discrimination learning with probabilistic reinforcement schedules. *Journal of Experimental Psychology*, 1959, 57, 349–350.

Azuma, H., & Cronbach, L. J. Cue-response correlations in the attainment of a scalar concept. *American Journal of Psychology*, 1966, 79, 38–44. (a)

Azuma, H., & Cronbach, L. J. Concept attainment with probabilistic feedback. In K. R. Hammond (Ed.), *The psychology of Egon Brunswik*. New York: Holt, Rinehart & Winston, 1966. Pp. 258–276. (b)

Bauer, M. Effects of absolute and conditional probability judgments on prediction in probabilistic inference. *Umeå Psychological Reports*, 1971, No. 52. (a)

Bauer, M. Prediction and probability judgment in a cue-probability learning task during two non-feedback phases. *Umeå Psychological Reports*, 1971, No. 54. (b)

Bauer, M. Bias in estimates of conditional probabilities and betting behavior as a function of relative frequency and validity of cues in a cue-probability learning task. *Acta Psychologica*, 1972, 36, 337–347. (a)

Bauer, M. Relations between prediction- and estimation-responses in cue-probability learning and transfer. *Scandinavian Journal of Psychology*, 1972, 13, 198–207. (b)

Bauer, M. Inference strategies in Bayesian tasks not requiring high scale-level responses. *Umeå Psychological Reports*, 1973, No. 61. (a)

Bauer, M. Prediction strategies in non-metric probability learning tasks when feedback is omitted. *Umeå Psychological Reports*, 1973, No. 62. (b)

Beach, L. R. Cue probabilism and inference behavior. *Psychological Monographs*, 1964, 78 (5, Whole No. 582). (a)

Beach, L. R. Recognition, assimilation, and identification of objects. *Psychological Monographs*, 1964, 78 (6, Whole No. 583). (b)

Binder, A., & Estes, W. K. Transfer of response in visual recognition situations as a function of frequency variables. *Psychological Monographs*, 1966, 80 (23, Whole No. 631).

Björkman, M. Predictive behavior: Some aspects based on an ecological orientation. *Scandinavian Journal of Psychology*, 1966, 7, 43–57.

Björkman, M. Stimulus-event learning and event learning as concurrent processes. *Organizational Behavior and Human Performance*, 1967, 2, 219–236.

Björkman, M. Individual performances in a single-cue probability learning task. *Scandinavian Journal of Psychology*, 1969, 10, 113–123. (a)

Björkman, M. Response consistency as a function of cue congruency of stimulus compounding. *Umeå Psychological Reports*, 1969, No. 5. (b)

Björkman, M. Policy formation in a non-metric task when training is followed by non-feedback trials. *Umeå Psychological Reports*, 1969, No. 6. (c)

Björkman, M. On the ecological relevance of psychological research. *Scandinavian Journal of Psychology*, 1969, 10, 145–157. (d)

Björkman, M. Policy formation as a function of feedforward in a non-metric CPL-task. *Umeå Psychological Reports*, 1971, No. 49. (a)

Björkman, M. Consistency of subjective estimates of relative frequency and probability in cue probability learning. *Umeå Psychological Reports*, 1971, No. 51. (b)

Björkman, M. Consistency of a predictive policy under cue-event reversal. *Umeå Psychological Reports*, 1971, No. 55. (c)

Björkman, M. Feedforward and feedback as determiners of knowledge and policy: Notes on a neglected issue. *Scandinavian Journal of Psychology*, 1972, **13**, 152–158.

Björkman, M. Inference behavior in non-metric ecologies. In L. Rappoport & D. A. Summers (Eds.), *Human judgment and social interaction*. New York: Holt, Rinehart, and Winston, 1973. Pp. 144–168.

Bourne, L. E., Jr. Long term effects of misinformative feedback upon concept identification. *Journal of Experimental Psychology*, 1963, **65**, 139–147.

Bourne, L. E., Jr., & Haygood, R. C. Effects of intermittent reinforcement of an irrelevant dimension and task complexity upon concept identification. *Journal of Experimental Psychology*, 1960, **60**, 371–375.

Bourne, L. E., Jr., & Pendleton, R. B. Concept identification as a function of completeness and probability of information feedback. *Journal of Experimental Psychology*, 1958, **56**, 413–420.

Brehmer, B. Inductive inferences from uncertain information. *Umeå Psychological Reports*, 1974, No. 78.

Brunswik, E. *Perception and the representative design of experiments*. Berkeley, California: University of California Press, 1956.

Burke, C. J., & Estes, W. K. A component model for stimulus variables in discrimination learning. *Psychometrika*, 1957, **22**, 133–145.

Castellan, N. J., Jr. Determination of joint distributions from marginal distributions in dichotomous systems. *Psychometrika*, 1970, **35**, 439–454.

Castellan, N. J., Jr. Multiple-cue probability learning with irrelevant cues. *Organizational Behavior and Human Performance*, 1973, **9**, 16–29.

Castellan, N. J., Jr. The effect of different types of feedback in multiple-cue probability learning. *Organizational Behavior and Human Performance*, 1974, **11**, 44–46.

Castellan, N. J., Jr., & Edgell, S. E. An hypothesis generation model for judgment in non-metric multiple-cue probability learning. *Journal of Mathematical Psychology*, 1973, **10**, 204–222.

Castellan, N. J., Jr., & Lindman, H. R. Contemporary approaches to judgment. In F. Restle, R. M. Shiffrin, N. J. Castellan, H. R. Lindman, & D. B. Pisoni, (Eds.), *Cognitive theory*. Vol. 1. Hillsdale, N.J.: Lawrence Erlbaum Assoc., 1975. Pp. 103–106.

Castellan, N. J., Jr., & Swaine, M. Long-term feedback and differential feedback effects in non-metric multiple-cue probability learning. Indiana Mathematical Psychology Program, Report No. 75-7, 1975.

Dawes, R. H. The mind, the model, and the task. In F. Restle, R. M. Shiffrin, N. J. Castellan, H. R. Lindman, & D. B. Pisoni (Eds.), *Cognitive theory*. Vol. 1. Hillsdale, N.J.: Lawrence Erlbaum Assoc., 1975. Pp. 119–129.

Driscoll, J. M., & Lanzetta, J. T. Effects of two sources of uncertainty in decision making. *Psychological Reports*, 1965, **17**, 635–648.

Edgell, S. E. Configural information processing in decision making. Indiana Mathematical Psychology Program, Report No. 74-4, 1974.

Edgell, S. E., & Castellan, N. J., Jr. Configural effect in multiple-cue probability learning. *Journal of Experimental Psychology*, 1973, **100**, 310–314.

Edwards, W. Comment on "Cognitive processes and probability assessment." *Journal of the American Statistical Association*, 1975, **70**, 291–293.

Erickson, J. R. On learning several simultaneous probability-learning problems. *Journal of Experimental Psychology*, 1966, **72**, 183–189.

Estes, W. K. Probability learning. In A. W. Melton (Ed.), *Categories of human learning.* New York: Academic Press, 1964. Pp. 89–128.

Estes, W. K. Elements and patterns in diagnostic discrimination learning. *Transactions of the New York Academy of Sciences*, 1972, 34, 84–95. (a)

Estes, W. K. Research and theory on the learning of probabilities. *Journal of the American Statistical Association*, 1972, 67, 81–102. (b)

Estes, W. K. The product rule for stimulus and outcome frequencies in probability learning. Paper presented at Psychonomic Society Meetings, St. Louis, Missouri, November 4, 1972. (c)

Estes, W. K., Burke, C. J., Atkinson, R. C., & Frankmann, J. P. Probabilistic discrimination learning. *Journal of Experimental Psychology*, 1957, 54, 233–239.

Estes, W. K., & Hopkins, B. L. Acquisition and transfer in pattern vs. component discrimination learning. *Journal of Experimental Psychology*, 1961, 61, 322–328.

Friedman, M. P., Rollins, H., & Padilla, G. The role of cue validity in stimulus compounding. *Journal of Mathematical Psychology*, 1968, 5, 300–310.

Goldstein, A. J., Harmon, L. D., & Lesk, A. B. Man-machine interaction in human-face identification. *The Bell System Technical Journal*, 1972, 51, 399–427.

Goodnow, J. J., & Postman, L. Probability learning in a problem-solving situation. *Journal of Experimental Psychology*, 1955, 49, 16–22.

Halpern, J., & Moore, J. W. Two choice discrimination learning as a function of cue similarity and probability of reinforcement. *Journal of Experimental Psychology*, 1967, 74, 182–186.

Hammond, K. R. Computer graphics as an aid to learning. *Science*, 1971, 172, 903–908.

Hammond, K. R., & Boyle, P. J. R. Quasi-rationality, quarrels, and new conceptions of feedback. *Bulletin of the British Psychological Society*, 1971, 24, 103–113.

Hanson, B. L., & Schipper, L. M. Numerosity in probability learning and decision making with multiple equivalent predictors. *Psychonomic Science*, 1971, 22, 199–201.

Hogarth, R. M. Process tracing in clinical judgment. *Behavioral Science*, 1974, 19, 298–313.

Hogarth, R. M. Cognitive processes and the assessment of subjective probability distributions. *Journal of the American Statistical Association*, 1975, 70, 271–289.

Holstein, S. B., & Premack, D. On the different effects of random reinforcement and presolution reversal on human concept identification. *Journal of Experimental Psychology*, 1965, 70, 335–337.

Howell, W. C., & Funaro, J. F. Prediction on the basis of conditional probabilities. *Journal of Experimental Psychology*, 1965, 69, 92–99.

Johannsen, W. J. Concept identification under misinformative and subsequent informative feedback conditions. *Journal of Experimental Psychology*, 1962, 64, 631–635.

Jones, M. R. From probability learning to sequential processing: A critical review. *Psychological Bulletin*, 1971, 76, 153–185.

Kroll, N. E. A. Learning several simultaneous probability learning problems as a function of overall probability and prior knowledge. *Journal of Experimental Psychology*, 1970, 83, 290–315.

Lanzetta, J. T., & Driscoll, J. M. Preference for information about an uncertain but unavoidable outcome. *Journal of Personality and Social Psychology*, 1966, 3, 96–102.

Lee, W. Conditioning parameter model for reinforcement generalization in probabilistic discrimination learning. *Journal of Mathematical Psychology*, 1966, 3, 184–196.

Lee, W., & Janke, M. Categorizing externally distributed stimulus samples for unequal molar probabilities. *Psychological Reports*, 1965, 17, 79–90.

Levine, M. Cue neutralization: The effects of random reinforcements on discrimination learning. *Journal of Experimental Psychology*, 1962, 63, 438–443.

Mandler, G., Cowan, P. A., & Gold, C. Concept learning and probability matching. *Journal of Experimental Psychology*, 1964, 67, 514–522.

Manz, W. Experiments on probabilistic information processing. *Acta Psychologica*, 1970, 34, 184–200.

Massaro, D. W. A three state Markov model for discrimination learning. *Journal of Mathematical Psychology*, 1969, 6, 62–80.

Massaro, D. W., Halpern, J., & Moore, J. W. Generalization effects in human discrimination learning with overt cue identification. *Journal of Experimental Psychology*, 1968, 77, 474–487.

Medin, D. L. Partial information and choice behavior in differential reward magnitude learning. *Psychonomic Science*, 1972, 27, 73–76.

Morin, R. E. Factors influencing rate and extent of learning in the presence of misinformative feedback. *Journal of Experimental Psychology*, 1955, 49, 343–351.

Murray, F. S. Multiple probable situation: A study of a five one-armed bandit problem. *Psychonomic Science*, 1971, 22, 247–249.

Myers, J. L., & Cruse, D. Two-choice discrimination learning as a function of stimulus and event probabilities. *Journal of Experimental Psychology*, 1968, 77, 453–459.

Naylor, J. C. Some comments on the accuracy and the validity of a cue variable. *Journal of Mathematical Psychology*, 1967, 4, 154–161.

Norman, M. F. Effects of overtraining, problem shifts, and probabilistic reinforcement in discrimination learning: Predictions of an attentional model. In D. H. Krantz, R. C. Atkinson, R. D. Luce, & P. Suppes (Eds.), *Contemporary developments in mathematical psychology*, Volume I. San Francisco: Freeman, 1974. Pp. 185–208.

Peterson, C. R., & Beach, L. R. Man as an intuitive statistician. *Psychological Bulletin*, 1967, 68, 29–46.

Pishkin, V. Effects of probability of misinformation and number of irrelevant dimensions upon concept identification. *Journal of Experimental Psychology*, 1960, 59, 371–378.

Pishkin, V. Transmission of information as a function of misinformation feedback distribution. *Psychological Reports*, 1961, 9, 255–263.

Pitz, G. F. Bayes Theorem: Can a theory of judgment and inference do without it? In F. Restle, R. M. Shiffrin, N. J. Castellan, H. R. Lindman, & D. B. Pisoni (Eds.), *Cognitive theory*. Vol. 1. Hillsdale, N.J.: Lawrence Erlbaum Associates, 1975. Pp. 131–148.

Popper, J., & Atkinson, R. C. Discrimination learning in a verbal conditioning situation. *Journal of Experimental Psychology*, 1958, 56, 21–25.

Rappoport, L., & Summers, D. A. (Eds.), *Human judgment and social interaction*. New York: Holt, Rinehart & Winston, 1973.

Reber, A. S., & Millward, R. B. Event observation in probability learning. *Journal of Experimental Psychology*, 1968, 77, 317–327.

Reed, S. K. Decision processes in pattern classification. University of California, Los Angeles, Department of Psychology Technical Report No. 32, 1970.

Reed, S. K. Pattern recognition and categorization. *Cognitive Psychology*, 1972, 3, 382–407.

Restle, F. Theory of selective learning with probable reinforcements. *Psychological Review*, 1957, 64, 182–191.

Robbins, D., & Medin, D. L. Cue selection after multiple-cue probability learning. *Journal of Experimental Psychology*, 1971, 91, 333–335.

Schipper, L. M. Context effects in probability learning and decision-making. *Psychological Reports*, 1966, 18, 131–138.

Schipper, L. M. Extreme probabilities in learning and decision making. *Journal of Experimental Psychology*, 1967, 73, 149–151.

Shaffer, J. P. Effect of different stimulus frequencies on discrimination learning with probabilistic reinforcement. *Journal of Experimental Psychology*, 1963, 65, 265–269.

Shepard, R. N. On subjectively optimum selection among multiattribute alternatives. In M. W. Shelly, II, & G. L. Bryan (Eds.), *Human judgments and optimality*. New York: Wiley, 1964. Pp. 257–281.

Slovic, P., & Lichtenstein, S. Comparison of Bayesian and regression approaches to the study of information processing in judgment. *Organizational Behavior and Human Performance*, 1971, **6**, 649–744.

Slovic, P., Rorer, L. G., & Hoffman, P. J. Analyzing use of diagnostic signs. *Investigative Radiology*, 1971, **6**, 18–26.

Smedslund, J. *Multiple-probability learning*. Oslo, Norway: Akademisk Forlag, 1955.

Stockburger, D. W., & Erickson, J. R. Probabilistic discrimination learning with dimensionalized stimuli. *Organizational Behavior and Human Performance*, 1974, **11**, 157–171.

Summers, S. A. Alternative bases for choice in probabilistic discrimination. *Journal of Experimental Psychology*, 1968, **76**, 538–543.

Thorngate, W., & Housch, S. Information seeking and information processing in a multi-cue judgment task. University of Alberta, Department of Psychology, Report No. 72-5, 1972.

Trabasso, T., & Staudenmayer, H. Random reinforcement in concept identification. *Journal of Experimental Psychology*, 1968, **77**, 447–452.

Vlek, C. A. J., & van der Heijden, L. H. C. Aspects of suboptimality in a multidimensional probabilistic information processing task. *Acta Psychologica*, 1970, **34**, 300–310.

Wallsten, T. S. Conjoint-measurement framework for the study of probabilistic information processing. *Psychological Review*, 1972, **79**, 245–260.

Winkler, R. L. Comment on "Cognitive processes and probability assessment." *Journal of the American Statistical Association*, 1975, **70**, 290–291.

Winkler, R. L., & Murphy, A. H. Experiments in the laboratory and the real world. *Organizational Behavior and Human Performance*, 1973, **10**, 252–270.

Wolfgang, A., Pishkin, V., & Lundy, R. M. Anxiety and misinformative feedback in concept identification. *Perceptual and Motor Skills*, 1962, **14**, 135–143.

Wortman, P. M. Cognitive utilization of probabilistic cues. *Behavioral Science*, 1970, **15** 329–336.

Wortman, P. M. Medical diagnosis: An information-processing approach. *Computers and Biomedical Research*, 1972, **5**, 315–328.

Zeaman, D., & House, B. J. The role of attention in retardate discrimination learning. In N. R. Ellis (Ed.), *Handbook of mental deficiency*. New York: McGraw-Hill, 1963. Pp. 159–223.

6

The Behavioral Richness of Cascaded Inference Models: Examples in Jurisprudence

David A. Schum

Rice University

INTRODUCTORY COMMENT

For a number of years I have been a student of evidentiary processes in inference. The inference tasks of interest to me are those in which individuals revise, on the basis of inconclusive evidence, their opinions about the relative likeliness of two or more hypothesized events. Although the general study of inference has occupied philosophers and probability theorists for centuries, a systematic study of the behavior of individuals performing inference tasks is only a recent undertaking. The past fifteen years have witnessed a fairly vigorous empirical study of human performance in probabilistic opinion–revision tasks. A large number of studies have been performed in laboratory settings using quite abstract inference tasks; a smaller number of studies have been performed in simulated inferential or diagnostic systems; a small but growing number are being performed in actual or natural settings such as in medical diagnosis, weather prediction, and intelligence–evaluation centers.

Much of the empirical research on human inference performed in laboratory and simulation settings has been focused on human ability to aggregate probabilistic evidence of given or prescribed inferential value. Probability revisions made by individuals in these evidence–aggregation tasks have been compared with corresponding formally ideal revisions prescribed by Bayes' rule. Certainly, no one has ever expected perfect correspondence between subjective and formally ideal revisions. A more natural expectation is that subjective revisions are sometimes stronger and sometimes weaker than ideal revisions. One hopes, however, that such deviations are systematically related to various characteristics

149

of inference tasks under experimental control. The results of early studies of subjective probability revisions were indeed systematic and aroused considerable interest because conservative subjective probability revision was a rather consistent result. *Conservatism* in this context means a probability revision of smaller magnitude than Bayes' rule says is justified by the evidence. A conclusion reached on the basis of early studies was that such conservatism is a universal characteristic of human probabilistic inference. This conclusion now appears unjustified since excessive probability revisions (those stronger than Bayes' rule says is justified by the evidence) are consistently observed in a variety of conditions, particularly in those "cascaded" inference tasks which this chapter is all about. (For general reviews of research on subjective probability revision, see Rapoport & Wallsten, 1972; Slovic & Lichtenstein, 1971.)

Research on subjective probability revision has certainly not been slighted when it comes to critical commentary. There has always been widespread scepticism regarding the accuracy of conclusions about behavioral processes made on the basis of subjective numerical judgments. Thus, our studies of subjective probability revisions partake of the same criticisms frequently directed at procedures such as magnitude estimation in psychophysics. Another kind of criticism concerns frequent attempts to alter normative or prescriptive models, such as Bayes' rule, in order to make them "descriptive" of human behavior. The argument is that these alterations only account for data and have little or no explanatory power (e.g., Green, 1968). A more recent criticism (Winkler & Murphy, 1973) is that there is now an overabundance of laboratory studies. Although these authors do not object to laboratory studies per se, they believe that certain experimental paradigms are overworked and that more research is necessary on inference behavior in natural settings.

Another criticism concerns the generally simplistic nature of the inference task paradigms studied in many laboratory and simulation settings. Many of our laboratory and simulation tasks seem to be distant relatives of inference tasks individuals actually perform in a variety of contexts. If we wish our conclusions from laboratory research to apply to inference behavior in natural settings like medical diagnosis and jury behavior, we must be prepared to study tasks of much greater complexity than those typically found in laboratory research. In considering complex inference in contexts such as jurisprudence and medicine, intuition often falters as we try to decide what variables or processes are of importance. Fortunately, probabilistic opinion revision, as an intellectual process, seems susceptible to formal analysis. When it can be performed, a formal analysis of a behavioral task, apart from being interesting in its own right, is a very useful prelude to empirical studies of how people actually perform the task. Such formal analyses help to support or to correct intuition about requisite task variables and how they combine. The essence of my criticism is that we have perhaps been tardy in putting available formal techniques to use in the study of complex inferential processes. This criticism leads me to the substance of my general comments about cascaded inference.

CASCADED OR HIERARCHICAL INFERENCE

A requisite in the formal study of probabilistic opinion revision is the establishment of appropriate conditioning patterns or probabilistic linkages among events of concern. We suppose that there is a class $H_1, H_2, \ldots, H_i, \ldots, H_n$ of disjoint hypothesized events (or simply "hypotheses"); one is asked to make initial judgments of the relative likeliness of the H_i and then to revise these judgments on the basis of *observable* events or evidence. The H_i represent states or processes not observable to us, at least not at the time when inferences are required. Now, we encounter several problems in determining appropriate patterns for conditioning or revising opinion about the unobservable H_i on the basis of observable evidence. The first problem is that it is sometimes difficult to decide which one of several possible events properly conditions opinions about the H_i in some behavioral situation. Defining an appropriate conditioning event involves judgmental issues not resolved by the formal mechanism prescribing the *process* of conditioning. The celebrated "prisoners problem" is an example of an instance in which there are several alternative definitions of a conditioning event, each of which appears plausible as a representation of the behavioral process under study (Pfeiffer & Schum, 1973). Unfortunately, the formal model for the process of conditioning does not specify which alternative event definition exactly characterizes the behavioral process under investigation.

The second problem involves the nature of the conditioning pattern or probabilistic linkage between observable evidence and hypotheses. In some cases, which I believe are fairly rare in natural settings, there is a direct or simple linkage between observables and hypotheses. In its pristine form, Bayes' rule involves simple or direct conditioning patterns of the form $P(E|H_i)$, where E is some observable event whose occurrence can be established beyond doubt. In other cases, the linkage between observables and hypotheses is indirect and involves one or more intermediary stages in an inferential hierarchy. In these cases we say that the inference task is *cascaded* or *hierarchical* in nature (several examples are discussed below). At each stage or level in the hierarchy the nature of the probabilistic linkage must be carefully prescribed. The formal mechanism underlying such prescription makes use of the concepts of independence and of conditional independence between two or more events. These concepts are easily and frequently confused; appropriate prescriptions about event independence and conditional independence also involve judgmental issues not resolved by the formal mechanism prescribing the process of conditioning. In summary, the formal analysis of a complex inference task is an exercise in careful definition of conditioning events and painstaking analysis of conditioning patterns.

Virtually all of the tasks in early studies of subjective probability revision had three characteristics in common. The first is that probabilistic inferences were made about hypotheses in a single disjoint, and usually exhaustive, class. Second, there was an absence of uncertainty about which one of several possible conditioning events in some specific class had actually occurred. For example, suppose that at a certain stage a subject was required to revise his opinions about the likeliness of each H_i on the basis of events E or E^c (E^c = complement of E), only one of which could occur. Experimental procedures eliminated any subject uncertainty about which of these events had actually occurred. Third, there were *direct* or simple linkages between the inferential events in each one of several event classes and the hypotheses. For example, suppose one of the events in $\{E, E^c\}$ occurred on one revision trial and one of the events in $\{F, F^c\}$ occurred on another revision trial. By "direct linkages" I mean that each of the events in both classes was conditioned only by the H_i; formally this means that the two event classes were conditionally independent, given each H_i. The prototypical experiment having these three characteristics is the familiar "bookbag and poker chip" experiment (e.g., Phillips & Edwards, 1966).

In other studies (e.g., Schum, 1966; Schum, Southard, & Wombolt, 1969) somewhat more complicated conditioning patterns were studied by incorporating conditional nonindependence among classes of inferential events. In this case there are probabilistic linkages among event classes as well as linkages between event classes and the hypotheses. For example, given event classes $\{E, E^c\}$ and $\{F, F^c\}$, event F might be conditioned by event E as well as by each H_i; that is, $P(F|H_i \cap E) \neq P(F|H_i)$. These studies incorporating conditional nonindependence still typically involved single H_i classes and no uncertainty about which inferential event occurred.

Illustrated in Fig. 1 are three examples of cascaded or hierarchical inference tasks. They differ in important ways from the tasks mentioned above. First, consider Case 1, in which the relative likeliness of H_1 and H_2 is to be revised on the basis of event D or D^c. Events D, D^c are inconclusive, that is, they both have nonzero probability under H_1 and under H_2. Now suppose that the source of information, about the occurrence or nonoccurrence of D, is not perfectly reliable. The source of information might be a human observer or a mechanical sensor. The person making inferences about H_1 and H_2 uses the source's reports or testimony about the occurrence or nonoccurrence of event D. Because the source is unreliable to some degree, we must distinguish between the occurrence or nonoccurrence of *event* D and the source's *report* of the occurrence or nonoccurrence of D; let D_i^* be the report or testimony from source i that event D occurred and let D_i^{c*} be the report from source i that event D did not occur. The inference task in this case is cascaded because there is an additional source of uncertainty. Not only is there uncertainty about $\{H_1, H_2\}$ because $\{D, D^c\}$ are inconclusive, but there is also uncertainty about events $\{D, D^c\}$ because *reports* $\{D_i^*, D_i^{c*}\}$ are inconclusive. That is, source i sometimes reports D_i^* when D^c is true and reports D_i^{c*} when D is true. In this case, as far as the person making the inference about $\{H_1, H_2\}$ is concerned, the "observables" or bases for inference are the *reports* D_i^* or D_i^{c*} and not the *events* D or D^c.

Case 2 in Fig. 1 presents an additional problem. Suppose we intend to use information about a person's blood type as a basis for inferring susceptibility to diabetes. We then wish to use our inferences about susceptibility to diabetes as a

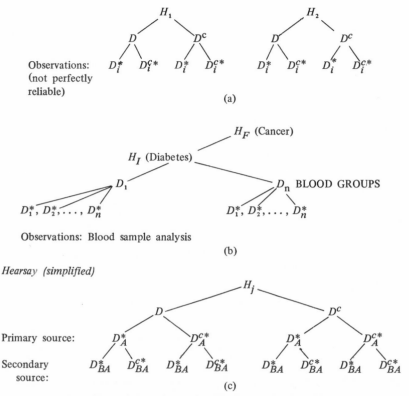

FIG. 1   Hierarchical linkages: (a) Case 1; (b) Case 2; (c) Case 3.

basis for inferring susceptibility to a certain form of cancer. There are four stages in this inferential hierarchy. First, since laboratory-based blood group classification procedures are not error free, we distinguish between the *report* D_k^* that a person's blood group is k and the actual *event* D_k^* that his blood group is k. These reports are the "observables" in inferences about intermediate hypotheses H_I regarding diabetes; inferences about H_I are then used as a basis for final inferences H_F about cancer. In this case there are two classes of hypotheses. In fact it could be argued that there are three if $\{D_1, \ldots, D_n\}$ is considered hypothetical. However, direct inferences about blood groups are usually bypassed in the conditioning process.

Case 3 differs from Case 1 because the inference-maker receives information about $\{D, D^c\}$ not from the primary observer A but from a secondary source B who receives a report from A about what A observed. Second-hand or "hearsay" evidence forms a basis for many inferences in natural settings. In fact, in many cases the inference-maker is more than twice removed from the actual occurrence of inferential events. The use of hearsay evidence is carefully restricted in legal proceedings. However, each one of us bases opinions about current events on patently hearsay evidence such as newspaper, radio, and television reporting. In Case 3 in Fig. 1, D_{BA}^* is the report from secondary source B that primary source A reported the occurrence of D, D_{BA}^{c*} is the report from B that A reported the nonoccurrence of D. Case 3 is a highly simplified representation of hearsay. For example, A might not have made an observation but, nevertheless, made a report to B. As another example, B may say that A reported D^* when A, in fact, said nothing at all to B.

Several of us have been studying the formal requisites of cascaded or hierarchical inference tasks such as those illustrated in the three fairly simple cases in Fig. 1. In addition, there is growing interest in the empirical study of human performance in cascaded inference tasks. Recently, an entire issue of the journal *Organizational Behavior and Human Performance*, was devoted to formal and empirical studies of cascaded inference (Peterson, 1973). A person interested in the study of cascaded inference has a choice from a smorgasbord of interesting and challenging issues. I have chosen to study the formal relationship between the credibility or reliability of sources of evidence and the inferential value of their testimony or reports. My belief is that imperfect credibility of sources of evidence is a basic feature which makes most, if not all, actual inference tasks cascaded in nature.

The basic objective of our formal work is to study the manner in which information about source credibility and information about the inferential value of the event being reported combine to determine the inferential value of the source's report or testimony. By "inferential value" I mean the extent to which an event or a report causes one to revise his estimate of the relative likeliness of two or more hypotheses. A useful measure of the inferential value of an *event D* in inferences involving hypotheses H_i and H_j is the familiar likelihood ratio

$$L_D = \frac{P(D|H_i)}{P(D|H_j)} \ .$$

As I have mentioned, there are many cases in which our opinions about the relative likeliness of H_i and H_j are conditioned by a *report D** not the *event D*. We have been led to consider expressions we call *adjusted likelihood ratios* Λ; for some report or testimony D^*,

$$\Lambda_{D^*} = \frac{P(D^*|H_i)}{P(D^*|H_j)}$$

prescribes the inferential value of D^*. In its expanded forms Λ_{D^*} shows the manner in which source credibility information and information about event impact combine to determine the inferential value of testimony D^*.[1]

[1] Much of my work on relating credibility and the inferential value of testimony stems from many conversations with Paul Pfeiffer, Mathematical Sciences Department, Rice University, whose helpful and patient assistance I gratefully acknowledge.

ADJUSTED LIKELIHOOD RATIO AND THE INFERENTIAL VALUE OF TESTIMONY

Using the concept of adjusted likelihood ratio, Λ, my colleagues and I have examined, in a variety of cases, formal relationships between source credibility and the inferential value of testimony. There are two major dimensions in the classification of our work to date. The first concerns the complexity of inferential event classes. In some cases one may only be concerned about the occurrence or nonoccurrence of an event D, that is, about the binomial event class $\{D, D^c\}$. In other cases further partitioning of an event class is required as, for example, in Case 2 in Fig. 1 where there are $n > 2$ possible blood groups in the multinomial event class $\{D_1, D_2, \ldots, D_n\}$. The other dimension concerns the number of sources or witnesses to the occurrence of events in some class. Having access to more than one source or witness to events in some class is a frequent occurrence in many inference tasks. This case is especially interesting since it can involve both confirming and contradictory testimony about which one of two or more events in some class actually occurred.

Using Λ, we have studied the formal relationship between witness (source) credibility and the inferential value of testimony in the case involving a single source and a binomial event class (Schum & Du Charme, 1971); in the multi-source, binomial event class situation (Schum & Kelly, 1973); and in the more general multisource, multinomial event class situation (Schum & Pfeiffer, 1973). The latter case leads to quite lengthy expansions of Λ. For reasons of ease in relating our work to credibility issues in jurisprudence I will restrict my attention to binomial event classes but will discuss both the single and the multi-source cases. In addition, I will not present the details of the expansions of in these cases but simply cite references which contain the necessary detailed expansions.

Single Witness, Binomial Event Class

We wish to determine the extent to which *reports* D^* or D^{c*} from a single witness, about binomial *events* D, D^c , allow us to revise our opinions about the relative likeliness of the hypotheses[2] :

H_G: defendant guilty as charged;
H_I: defendant innocent of charge.

Discussed below are various expansions of the adjusted likelihood ratios Λ_{D*} and Λ_{D^c*}. These expansions make it clear that the inferential value[3] of

---

[2] I am aware of the fact that the partition $\{H_G, H_I\}$ may not always be adequate in actual legal proceedings (see Tribe, 1971).

[3] The term in jurisprudence corresponding to inferential value is "probative value." Since much subsequent discussion will relate to jurisprudence I will use the latter term except when discussing inference in general.

testimony D^* or D^{c*} depends upon the two classes of information summarized in Table 1. Part A of Table 1 contains information about the probative value of *events* D, D^c . For example, the probative value of *event D*, regarding inferences about H_G and H_I, is contained in the conditional probabilities $P(D|H_G)$ and $P(D|H_I)$. As mentioned above, the likelihood ration L_D is frequently a useful measure of inferential or probative value. If

$$L_D = \frac{P(D|H_G)}{P(D|H_I)} = 1,$$

then D has no probative value. If $L_D > 1$, D is more likely under H_G then under H_I, that is, D points inferentially towards H_G. If $L_D < 1$, D points toward H_I. However, we will shortly discover a large class of instances in which we must have the conditional probabilities themselves and not simply their ratio.

In order to discuss the credibility-related values shown in Part B of Table 1 we must first consider four possible ways in which reports $\{D^*, D^{c*}\}$ can be conditioned. First, suppose that the reports $\{D^*, D^{c*}\}$ are conditioned neither by events $\{D, D^c\}$ nor by the hypotheses $\{H_G, H_I\}$. It is easily shown that $\Lambda_D{}^*$ = $\Lambda_{D^c*} \equiv 1$ in this case; in other words, D^* and D^{c*} have no probative value. Next, suppose that reports $\{D^*, D^{c*}\}$ are conditioned by $\{H_G, H_I\}$ but not by events $\{D, D^c\}$; in this case

$$\Lambda_D{}^* \equiv \frac{P(D^*|H_G)}{P(D^*|H_I)} \quad \text{and} \quad \Lambda_D{}^{c*} \equiv \frac{P(D^{c*}|H_G)}{P(D^{c*}|H_I)} .$$

This is a curious circumstance since either of these ratios can be greater than or less than one, that is, D^* and D^{c*} could have inferential value. However, this case can be regarded as pathological in jurisprudence, since if it could be shown that the testimony of a certain witness is independent of the events that could occur, given H_G or H_I, the testimony would be rejected on grounds of incompetency. We might, for example, find some person who makes no observations but simply guesses about the occurrence of $\{D, D^c\}$. We might discover that he guesses D more often for guilty defendants than he does for innocent defendants. Although his testimony would have inferential value in a statistical sense, his testimony would have no probative value in a juridical sense.

The remaining two conditioning patterns are of interest to us. First suppose that reports $\{D^*, D^{c*}\}$ are conditioned by events $\{D, D^c\}$ but not by either of the hypotheses $\{H_G, H_I\}$. When this is true, we have the four conditional probabilities shown in Case 1 of Part B in Table 1. For convenience I will label these four values with terms common in the literature on signal detection theory, even though they may seem foreign in some juridical examples. The four credibility-related conditional probabilities are:

h = hit rate $= P(D^*|D)$,
f = false positive rate $= P(D^*|D^c)$,

TABLE 1
Information Necessary to Determine the Probative Value of Testimony from a Single Witness about Binomial Events

Information about the probative value of events D, D^c

H_G H_I

$P(D|H_G)$	$P(D|H_I)$	$L_D = P(D|H_G)/P(D|H_I)$
$P(D^c|H_G)$	$P(D^c|H_I)$	$L_{D^c} = P(D^c|H_G)/P(D^c|H_I)$

Credibility-related information

Case 1: $\{D^*, D^{c*}\}$ conditioned by $\{D, D^c\}$ but not by $\{H_G, H_I\}$

D D^c

$P(D^*|D) = h$	$P(D^*|D^c) = f$
$P(D^{c*}|D) = m$	$P(D^{c*}|D^c) = c$

Case 2: $\{D^*, D^{c*}\}$ conditioned by $\{D, D^c\}$ and by one or both of $\{H_G, H_I\}$.

	H_G				H_I	
	D	D^c			D	D^c
D^*	$P(D^*|D \cap H_G)$ $= h_G$	$P(D^*|D^c \cap H_G)$ $= f_G$	D^*		$P(D^*|D \cap H_I)$ $= h_I$	$P(D^*|D^c \cap H_I)$ $= f_I$
D^{c*}	$P(D^{c*}|D \cap H_G)$ $= m_G$	$P(D^{c*}|D^c \cap H_G)$ $= c_G$	D^{c*}		$P(D^{c*}|D \cap H_I)$ $= m_G$	$P(D^{c*}|D^c \cap H_I)$ $= c_I$

m = miss rate = $P(D^{c*}|D)$,
c = correct rejection rate = $P(D^{c*}|D^c)$.

Now, if reports $\{D^*, D^{c*}\}$ are conditioned only by events $\{D, D^c\}$ and not by $\{H_G, H_I\}$, this means that there is no inferential or probative value in the reporting behavior itself and that all of the *potential* probative value of the reports resides in the events; how much of this potential value "carries over" to the reports or testimony depends upon the four credibility-related values listed above (formal justification of this argument is found in Schum, 1975).

Finally, it is easy to imagine many situations in which the four values shown above might be dependent upon the guilt or innocence of a defendant. For example, a witness might be a relative or friend of the defendant or he might be serving as a prosecution witness in order to improve his own position. These situations find formal expression by supposing that reports $\{D^*, D^{c*}\}$ are conditioned by events $\{D, D^c\}$ *and* by *either* or *both* of the hypotheses $\{H_G, H_I\}$. Case 2 in Part B of Table 1 illustrates the further conditioning of testimony by H_G and H_I; h_G, for example, refers to "hit-rate conditional upon H_G." When the four credibility-related values are conditioned by one or both of $\{H_G, H_I\}$ it can be shown that reports $\{D^*, D^{c*}\}$ can have probative value in *excess* of that contained in the events $\{D, D^c\}$. The reason is that the reporting behavior itself is conditional upon H_G or H_I and thus acquires probative significance.

We can now discuss the adjusted likelihood ratios for reports D^* and D^{c*}. First consider Case 1 in Table 1 in which the credibility-related values are not conditioned by H_G or H_I. [This means that $h_G = h_I, f_G = f_I, m_G = m_I$, and $c_G = c_I$]. In this case we can write the adjusted likelihood ratios

for the report D^*:

$$\Lambda_{D^*} = \frac{P(D|H_G) + (h/f - 1)^{-1}}{P(D|H_I) + (h/f - 1)^{-1}}, \quad \text{for } h \neq f \text{ and } f \neq 0, \tag{1a}$$

for the report D^{c*}:

$$\Lambda_{D^{c*}} = \frac{P(D|H_G) + (m/c - 1)^{-1}}{P(D|H_I) + (m/c - 1)^{-1}}, \quad \text{for } m \neq c \text{ and } c \neq 0. \tag{1b}$$

For Case 2 in Table 1 when there is conditioning of the credibility-related values by either or both of $\{H_G, H_I\}$ we can write the adjusted likelihood ratios

for the report D^*:

$$\Lambda_{D^*} = \frac{P(D|H_G)(h_G - f_G) + f_G}{P(D|H_I)(h_I - f_I) + f_I}, \tag{2a}$$

for the report D^{c*}:

$$\Lambda_{D^{c*}} = \frac{P(D|H_I)(m_G - c_G) + c_G}{P(D|H_I)(m_I - c_I) + c_I}. \tag{2b}$$

(Details of the necessary expansions of Λ in these four cases are given in Schum & Du Charme, 1971.)

The relationship between witness credibility (expressed in terms of the conditional probabilities discussed above) and the impact of his testimony can be conveniently studied by comparing Λ_{D^*} and L_D. By varying the credibility-related values given above in the four equations we can study how the probative force of testimony compares with the probative force of the event being reported. For perfectly reliable sources whose credibility-related values do not depend upon $\{H_G, H_I\}$, $\Lambda_{D^*} = L_D$ and $\Lambda_{D^{c*}} = L_{D^c}$. Such examinations of Λ_{D^*} relative to L_D have allowed us to draw some important conclusions about witness credibility and the impact of testimony:

1. The first conclusion is that Λ_{D^*} and $\Lambda_{D^{c*}}$ depend upon the conditional probabilities $P(D|H_G)$ and $P(D|H_I)$ and *not* upon their ratio L_D. This means that Λ is sensitive to the *rarity* of the event being reported. It happens that L_D suppresses information about the rarity of event D. For example, consider event

D_1 with $P(D_1|H_G) = 0.90$, $P(D_1|H_I) = 0.10$ and $L_{D_1} = 9.0$. Then consider D_2 with $P(D_2|H_G) = 0.009$, $P(D_2|H_I) = 0.001$, and $L_{D_2} = 9$. Event D_2 is a rare event, that is, one with small likelihood under both hypotheses considered. It is easily shown that a fixed reduction in source credibility weighs more heavily upon the testimony of a rare event than it does upon testimony of an event which has substantial probability under H_G or H_I. In short, the probative value of testimony depends upon the rarity of the event being reported. If we fix h and f in Equation (1a), $\Lambda_{D_1}* > \Lambda_{D_2}*$ even though $L_{D_1} = L_{D_2}$. Thus, our adjusted likelihood ratios make explicit a consideration about testimony which was of concern but elusive in several early studies of credibility and testimony (Todhunter, 1865).

2. A second conclusion is that the general effects of even modest reductions in source credibility weigh heavily upon the impact of testimony. The more probatively important an event is, the more crucial is witness credibility. Consider the two examples summarized in Table 2. In each case, suppose a witness of reasonable credibility for whom $h = 0.98$ and $f = 0.05$. His report is $D*$ in each case. Comparing Λ_{D*} and L_D in each case, we first see that the rather slight credibility reduction causes probative value of report $D*$ in Case a to be 10% smaller than the probative value of the event, which in this case is reasonably small. In Case b, however, the same slight reduction in credibility causes the probative value of report $D*$ to be 98% smaller than the probative value of the event, which in this case is very large.

Results of recent empirical investigations suggests that the extent of reductions of probative value with decreased credibility may be counterintuitive. For example, in one of our empirical studies subjects systematically failed to diminish the impact of testimony in a manner consistent with source credibility (Schum, Du Charme, & DePitts, 1973).

3. Inspection of the four equations reveals certain conditions I formerly labeled "pathological" but do not any longer for reasons discussed below. One already mentioned reason concerns the case in which credibility-related values are contingent upon hypotheses. In this case the probative value given by Λ_{D*} can be greater than the probative value of L_D. Another case involves what I shall term "impact reversals." This term refers to instances in which an event D may point inferentially, say, to H_G but the report $D*$ may point inferentially to H_I. These reversals occur when false positive rates (f) are greater than hit rates (h).

TABLE 2
Adjusted Likelihood Ratio Calculations for Examples
Mentioned in the Text

	$P(D|H_G)$	$P(D|H_I)$	L_D	Λ_{D*}
Case a	0.9	0.3	3	2.70
Case b	0.999	0.001	999	19.22

Many Witnesses, Binomial Event Class

It frequently happens that more than one source, or witness is queried about the occurrence or nonoccurrence of some event. We are faced with the task of determining the probative or inferential value of the *joint* testimony. Again, let us consider the binomial class of events $\{D, D^c\}$ and the probative value information in Part A of Table 1. Suppose we have n witnesses $\{W_1, W_2, \ldots, W_i, \ldots, W_n\}$ to the occurrence or nonoccurrence of D. It is important to be clear about the fact that they all witness the occurrence or nonoccurrence of the *same* event, that is, each witness' testimony is about events in $\{D, D^c\}$. Suppose also that we have the credibility-related values shown in Cases 1 or 2 in Table 1 for each witness.

Now, their joint testimony consists of the report class $\{R_1, R_2, \ldots, R_i, \ldots, R_n\}$, where any $R_i = D_i^*$ or D_i^{c*}. Of course, the witnesses may not all agree about whether D occurred or not. Suppose r of the witnesses report D^* and $n - r$ of the sources report D^{c*}. When $r = 0$ or $r = n$ we have *confirming testimony.* When $r \neq 0$ or $r \neq n$ we have *contradictory* testimony. Let

J = set of r witnesses who report D^*
K = set of $n - r$ witnesses who report D^{c*}.

Their *joint* testimony F^* can be expressed as

$$F^* = \left[\bigcap_{j \, \epsilon \, J} D_j^* \cap \bigcap_{k \, \epsilon \, K} D_k^{c*} \right] .$$

Our objective is to determine the probative value of F^* given the probative value of events, D, D^c and credibility-related information about each of the n witnesses. (A detailed formal treatment of this problem is found in Schum & Kelly, 1973.)

It happens in this multiwitness case that there are two conditional independence issues to consider. The first concerns the conditioning of credibility-related values by H_G or H_I. This possible conditioning must be determined for each witness. The other issue concerns whether or not any subset of the witnesses has had any influence upon the reporting behavior of any other subset; in other words, have any of the witnesses coalesced or cooperated in their testimony? We can combine these two issues into a single statement about conditional independence. Consider the class $\{R_1, R_2, \ldots, R_n, H_x\}$, where any $R_i = D_i^*$ or D_i^{c*} and $x = G, I$. If this class is conditionally independent, given D and given D^c, for H_G and H_I, for any subclass of the R_i and for $x = G, I$,

$$P\left(\bigcap_{i=1}^{n} R_i | D \cap H_x \right) = P \left(\bigcap_{i=1}^{n} R_i | D \right)$$

$$= \prod_{i=1}^{n} P(R_i | D),$$

$$P\left(\bigcap_{i=1}^{n} R_i | D^c \cap H_x\right) = P\left(\bigcap_{i=1}^{n} R_i | D^c\right)$$

$$= \prod_{i=1}^{n} P(R_i | D^c) .$$

For the illustrations I will discuss in a later section of this chapter I need only consider the special case in which (a) no witness' credibility related-values depend upon H_G or H_I, (b) the witnesses do not coalesce or cooperate. Under these assumptions we can write the adjusted likelihood ratio for joint testimony F^*

when all n sources report D^*:

$$\Lambda_{F^*} = \frac{P(D|H_G) + V_1}{P(D|H_I) + V_1} , \tag{3a}$$

where

$$V_1 = \left[\prod_{i=1}^{n}\left(\frac{h_i}{f_i}\right) - 1 \right]^{-1}$$

(h_i and f_i are the hit and false positive rates, respectively, for witness i).

when all n sources report D^{c*}:

$$\Lambda_{F^*} = \frac{P(D|H_G) + V_2}{P(D|H_I) + V_2} , \tag{3b}$$

where

$$V_2 = \left[1/\prod_{i=1}^{n}\left(\frac{c_i}{m_i}\right) - 1 \right]^{-1}$$

(subscript i refers to witness i).

Equations 3a and 3b involve *confirming* testimony. The remaining case involves *contradictory* testimony in which J is the set of r sources who report D^* and K is the set of $n - r$ sources who report D^{c*}. In this case,

$$\Lambda_{F^*} = \frac{P(D|H_G) + V_3}{P(D|H_I) + V_3} , \tag{3c}$$

where

$$V_3 = \left[\frac{\prod\limits_{j \in J} \dfrac{h_j}{f_j}}{\prod\limits_{k \in K} \left(\dfrac{c_k}{m_k}\right)} - 1 \right]^{-1}$$

The same conclusions reached about Λ in the single-witness case apply to the multiwitness case as well. There is, however, one unique feature of multiwitness Λ. In the confirming case when all n sources agree, there is no question about which hypothesis is favored by their joint testimony F^*. For example, if event D is more probable under H_G than under H_I and all n sources report D^*, then the joint report F^* is more probable under H_G (i.e., F^* "favors" H_G). [There is an exception which involves the "pathological" case in which $h < f$]. In the contradictory case, however, we face the problem of determining the inferential *direction* of the joint report F^*; that is, which hypothesis does F^* favor. Suppose again that D is more probable under H_G than under H_I. This implies that D^c is more probable under H_I than under H_G. Further suppose that r sources report D^* and $n - r$ sources report D^{c*}. We wish to determine whether F^* favors H_G or H_I. This determination is made on the basis of the aggregate credibility

$$A_J = \prod_{j \in J} \left(\frac{h_j}{f_j} \right)$$

of the r reporting D^* and the aggregate credibility

$$B_K = \prod_{k \in K} \left(\frac{c_k}{m_k} \right)$$

of the $n - r$ sources who report D^{c*}. The determination of inferential direction in the binomial case, where D favors H_G and D^c favors H_I, is straightforward. If $A_J > B_K$, then F^* favors H_G; if $B_K > A_J$, then F^* favors H_I. The important fact is that the aggregate credibilities A_J and B_K, rather than the number of witnesses r and $n - r$, determine the probative direction and strength of the joint testimony F^*.

It is comforting to learn that this very issue of determining the probative direction and strength of joint contradictory testimony has been treated by our legal system in a formally consistent manner. The courts have held that the number of witnesses presented on either side is not sufficient, by itself, to establish the weight of testimony. Jury members are to be advised that the credibility of witnesses on either side is crucial in determining the weight of testimony (Cleary, 1972).

REVELATIONS ABOUT CASCADED INFERENCE IN JURISPRUDENCE

Recently, I began to consider what I shall term the *behavioral richness* of adjusted likelihood ratio expressions like those discussed in the preceding section. In the present context a *behaviorally rich* formal expression is one that has enough flexibility to make it applicable to a wide variety of actual inferential situations. If Λ is behaviorally rich, it will successfully capture the essence of source credibility in its relation to the inferential value of reports or testimony in a wide variety of cases. I shall *not* use the term *behavioral richness* to indicate how satisfactory Λ is in describing actual human behavior in inference tasks. Indeed, our formalizations of Λ were not developed to serve such descriptive purposes.

In evaluating the behavioral richness of Λ I was led, quite naturally, to consider the rules of evidence in jurisprudence. This collection of rules or principles regulates the admissibility, relevancy, weight, and sufficiency of evidence in legal proceedings. The collection of evidentiary rules is not static but undergoes revision in the light of experience. While reading in this fascinating area I discovered many interesting things. One is that the study of what we have called *cascaded* or *hierarchical* inference is not a new venture. One cannot read very far in the literature devoted to juridical evidentiary processes before encountering the name John Henry Wigmore. For many years Wigmore was one of the foremost American scholars in the area of evidentiary processes in jurisprudence. In a book entitled *Principles of Judicial Proof* (first published in 1913) Wigmore distinguishes between *simple* and what he calls *catenated* inference tasks. It is apparent that his *catenated* and our *cascaded* inference tasks are the same. Wigmore's analysis of catenated inference was indeed systematic but not formal in nature. At several points in his work he lamented the fact that science has not provided formal rules for combining information in complex cases (J. H. Wigmore, 1931). I will later return to Wigmore's concern about the use of probability theory in jurisprudence.

Another revelation concerns the details of the relationships between source credibility and the inferential value of reports or testimony. There are several conditions I used to think were pathological in the sense that they would rarely, if ever, be encountered in actual inferences. For example, in many inferential tasks it is difficult to imagine employing a mechanical sensor or human observer whose false-positive rate exceeded his hit rate, or employing one whose credibility-related values depend upon the hypotheses being entertained. However, cases which appear pathological in many medical diagnosis and intelligence-analysis tasks are actually rather commonplace in jurisprudence. In part, the problem involves the manner in which much legal evidence comes into existence. Witnesses may have vested interests in trial outcomes or have other self-serving objectives. My belief is that the inference task facing a juror is as complex, and often bizarre, as any inference task in existence. My further belief is that, if our formal representations are behaviorally rich in jurisprudence, they will be rich in any inferential context.

A final revelation was that our formalizations of adjusted likelihood ratio appear to be rich or flexible enough to handle all of the *general* considerations found in the rules of evidence which apply to witness credibility and the probative value of testimony. Justification for this claim is the subject of the next section.

THE ADJUSTED LIKELIHOOD RATIO AND GROUNDS FOR IMPEACHMENT AND SUPPORT OF WITNESS CREDIBILITY

The particular area within the rules of evidence which is relevant to our present work is termed *grounds for impeachment and support of witness credibility*. In this area are found the processes and rules involved in diminishing or in establishing witness credibility in order to reduce or to preserve the probative value of the witness' testimony. In judicial proceedings, the party offering a witness presumes that his testimony should receive full probative value. In our (Anglican) judicial system the task of diminishing this probative value falls upon counsel for the opposing party. By cross-examining the witness or by calling other witnesses the opposing counsel seeks information which either discredits the witness in some way or contradicts the substance of his testimony. Parenthetically, it may be noted that the opposing counsel may, for a variety of reasons, choose not to attempt credibility impeachment even when there appear to be good reasons for doing so (Keeton, 1973). Attempts to impeach, if they miscarry, often work to the advantage of the party summoning the witness. In the interests of fairness, counsel for the party summoning the witnesses is given opportunity to restore his witness' credibility in order to preserve the probative force of the original testimony. This third stage is called *redirect* but might also be called *rehabilitation* (Wigmore, 1935).

Within our judicial system there appear to be five major grounds for impeaching or discrediting the credibility of a witness. Detailed discussions of these grounds, together with illustrative cases, are to be found in the seven juridical references I have included at the end of the reference list. My present task is to show how all five of these grounds for impeachment find *direct* expression or representation in the formulations of adjusted likelihood ratio. At the close of the preceding section I claimed that these formalizations were behaviorally rich in this area of jurisprudence. I did *not* claim that applications or extensions of our formalizations *in any specific case* would be easy or straightforward. Indeed, I will later illustrate how tedious and painstaking such a task might often be.

Following is a discussion of the five major grounds for impeachment and how each finds expression or representation in Λ. I have not listed these grounds in any order of importance.

Defect in Capacity

One ground for credibility-impeachment involves demonstration of a defect in the capacity of a witness to observe, remember, or recount the events being reported. Samuel Johnson once remarked that the force of testimony could be likened to the force of an arrow shot from a long bow; its force depends upon the strength of the hand that draws the bow. One suspects that severe observational, memory, or reporting deficiencies might be grounds for judging a witness to be incompetent (a judgment made by the court rather than by the jury). However, there appears to be increasing reluctance on the part of courts to dismiss witnesses on incompetency grounds.[4] Presumably, this means that greater burden is placed upon opposing counsel and members of the jury. In Λ, defects in capacity are represented by the relative magnitudes of h and f for testimony D^*, and by the relative magnitudes of c and m for testimony D^{c*}. For example, in Equation (1a) for testimony D^*, as h and f become close in value the term $(h/f - 1)^{-1}$ grows large and "swamps" the probative value of event D as expressed by the conditional probabilities $P(D|H_G)$ and $P(D|H_I)$. Thus, Λ_{D^*} becomes smaller than L_D. It is important to note that our four credibility-related values (h, f, c, m) do not distinguish among various causes for defects in capacity. For example, a substantial false–positive value or a low-hit value might be indicative of observational inaccuracy, memory lapses, reporting inaccuracy, or any combination of these factors. In short, our credibility-related values reflect any factor or factors which reduce testimonial accuracy.

Bias

An essential fact about evidence in legal proceedings is that it is presented by disputing parties. Human nature being what it is, the law recognizes the virtually infinite variety of ways in which testimony can be biased depending upon the motives of the witness. Among the more common sources of bias are kinship or friendship with the defendant, hostility toward the defendant, pecuniary or other self-interest (e.g., paid testimony of "experts," witness for the state to avoid prosecution), and corruption or mutual influence among two or more witnesses. Thus, biasing effects will involve both single and multiwitness formalizations.

Considering the testimony of a single witness, there are several ways in which bias can be incorporated in our formalizations. The first way is sufficiently obvious that it is easily overlooked. Suppose a witness who would testify D^* whether D or D^c occurred and whether H_G or H_I was true (e.g., event D might favor H_I and the witness might be a close friend or relative of the defendant). Formally, $P(D^*|H_G) = P(D^*|H_I) = P(D^*) = 1.0$. Such a case might be called "perfect bias" since the unconditional probability of the report D^* equals one; that is, the witness reports D^* no matter what else is true. In this case $\Lambda_{D^*} \equiv 1.0$. In fact, the same result is achieved whenever $P(D^*|H_G) = P(D^*|H_I) = P(D^*)$, even if $P(D^*) \neq 1.0$. In this case the report D^* does not depend upon events D or D^c, and has equal likeliness under H_G and H_I, the result is that $\Lambda_{D^*} \equiv 1.0$.

---

[4] See *Cleary, McCormick on Evidence* (1972) and *Rules of Evidence for U.S. Courts and Magistrates* (July 1, 1973, Rule 601).

A second way of incorporating bias involves possible conditioning of the four credibility-related values by H_G and H_I. Equation 2a, for report D^*, shows that when h and f are made close in value under either hypothesis, Λ_{D^*} depends to a greater extent upon the values f_G and f_I than upon $P(D|H_G)$ and $P(D|H_I)$. It seems natural to suppose that a linkage between false—positive tendency and $\{H_G, H_I\}$ can reflect bias of some sort.

In considering the testimony of a single witness there is yet another way in which bias can be incorporated in our formulations of Λ. There may be some specific event or report relative to the prior behavior of the witness which conditions his present testimony and, thus, affects the probative value of this testimony. The procedure for incorporating such conditioning events is discussed below under character impeachment (Ground 5).

When there are several witnesses to events in $\{D, D^c\}$ there is the possibility that the witnesses decide among themselves what to report. For example, three witnesses all report D^*. One of the witnesses reports D^*, not because he observed event D, but because he was bribed or threatened into reporting D^*. Such "corruption" or mutual influence among witnesses to events in $\{D, D^c\}$ finds direct expression in Λ by means of the conditional independence considerations discussed prior to Equations 3a, 3b, 3c.

Conflicting and Contradictory Evidence

Another natural characteristic of evidence given by parties in dispute is that testimony given by one side either conflicts with or contradicts testimony given by the other side. There appears to be a subtle distinction to be made between *conflicting* and *contradictory* evidence.[5] Webster's dictionary says that conflicting things are at variance with each other while contradictory things are exactly opposite in character. I am going to discuss four basic cases involving credibility issues in conflicting and contradictory evidence. The first two cases make clear the distinction between conflicting and contradictory evidence.

Case a.   In many inferential situations, particularly in jurisprudence, not all of the evidence points toward the same hypothesis. Suppose, in a certain legal proceeding, that event D points toward H_G [i.e., $P(D|H_G) > P(D|H_I)$], and event E points toward H_I [i.e., $P(E|H_I) > P(E|H_G)$]. Suppose one witness W_1 reports D^* and another, W_2, reports E^*. This is a case of *conflicting* evidence since the two reports are at variance with respect to inferential direction. Suppose that D^* is conditioned only by events $\{D, D^c\}$ and, possibly, by hypotheses $\{H_G, H_I\}$; suppose that E^* is conditioned only by events $\{E, E^c\}$ and, possibly, by hypotheses $\{H_G, H_I\}$. Also suppose that events $\{D, D^c\}$ and $\{E, E^c\}$ are conditionally independent under H_G and H_I. This means that there is no probabilistic linkage between the two events, the two reports, or the

[5] Such a distinction was not made in an earlier paper (Schum & Kelly, 1973).

reports from one witness and the events reported by the other. In this case we can simply determine Λ_{D*} and Λ_{E*} using Eq. (1a) if reports are not conditioned by $\{H_G, H_I\}$ or using Eq. (1b) if they are. Their joint probative value is given by the product $\Lambda_{D*} \times \Lambda_{E*}$. In determining Λ_{D*} and Λ_{E*}, the credibility of W_1 and W_2 can be attacked individually for reasons of bias, capacity defect, etc. However, the testimony of one witness is not used to attack the other's credibility.

Case b. Suppose one or more witnesses on one side of a legal dispute report $D*$; then, one or more witnesses on the other side report D^{c*}. Here we have a case of directly opposing or *contradictory* testimony. Equation (3c) prescribes the probative value and direction of the joint testimony of all witnesses. The discussion accompanying Equation (3c) shows how the probative value and direction of the joint testimony are determined by the aggregate credibility of witnesses on either side and by the probative value of the events being reported. This example does involve credibility impeachment of one side by the other since, for example, providing competent witnesses who say D^c occurred acts typically to *reduce* the probative value of testimony from witnesses who said that D occurred (except in those cases in which $h < f$).

Case c. Now suppose two event classes $\{D, D^c\}$, $\{E, E^c\}$ with the following characteristic, events D and E cannot both occur; formally $D \cap E = \phi$. Suppose D = the event that the defendant was at the scene of the crime in Muleshoe, Texas, and E = the event that the defendant was in Bloomington, Indiana at the time the crime was committed. Witness W_1 reports $D*$ and witness W_2 reports $E*$. Clearly, at least one of the witnesses is lying or confused. This seems to be a case of *conflicting* testimony since $E \neq D^c = D^c E \uplus D^c E^c$. In this case we define adjusted likelihood ratio $\Lambda_{D* \cap E*}$ for the joint testimony $D* \cap E*$. In its expanded form $\Lambda_{D* \cap E*}$ reveals some very complicated conditioning patterns, as expected. For example, we must determine whether h and f values for each witness are conditioned by hypotheses, by the event the other witness reports, and by the report the other witness makes.

The fourth case involves conflicting and contradictory statements made by a single witness at different times. This situation occupies separate status in the rules of evidence; it is discussed below.

Prior Inconsistent Statements

One of the most effective and frequently employed methods of credibility-impeachment is a demonstration that the witness on a previous occasion has made statements inconsistent with his current testimony. Presumably these prior statements could either conflict with or contradict his current testimony. How we proceed depends upon whether or not the witness admits making a prior inconsistent statement. Let us first suppose that the witness admits to making a prior statement which *contradicts* his current testimony. Today on the witness stand he tells us that the street light at the scene of the accident was on (D^*). Two months ago, immediately after the accident, he told an investigating officer that the light was off (D^{c*}). Reminded of this inconsistency he admits making contradictory statements. Probatively, the joint report $D^* \cap D^{c*}$ has no significance; in fact, Λ is indeterminate in this case.

Next, suppose the witness admits to a prior statement which *conflicts* with his current testimony. Today on the witness stand he reports D^*; reminded by the opposing counsel, he admits making report E^* on a previous occasion. Suppose, as in Case c above, events D and E cannot both occur. The adjusted likelihood ratio $\Lambda_{D^* \cap E^*}$ can be defined and examined as in Case c above. One interesting feature is that the credibility-related values for reports D^* and E^* all refer to the same witness.

Now suppose a witness W_1 who refuses to admit making the prior statement which either conflicts with or is contradictory to his current testimony. In order to impeach his credibility we have to summon another witness W_2 who could testify that W_1 made the prior assertion in question. The testimony of W_2 is, of course, *hearsay* evidence. Hearsay evidence is a Pandora's box which I shall only open a wee crack in this chapter. My difficulty in determining formal representations for the probative value of hearsay mirrors the difficulty our legal system faces in deciding whether or not to admit hearsay; some forms of hearsay are admissible and others are not.

Case 3 in Fig. 1 is an illustration of the simplest possible case I can think of involving hearsay. It is simplified by the assumptions (a) that primary source A always makes an observation of events $\{D, D^c\}$ (b) that A always makes one of the reports $\{D^*_A, D^{c*}_A\}$ to secondary source B, and (c) that secondary source B always reports one or the other of A's possible reports. Let D^*_{BA} = the report from B that A reported D^*. Suppose our hypotheses are $\{H_G, H_I\}$. In this simple case there are two conditional independence issues:

(a) Are A's reports conditioned by $\{H_G, H_I\}$?
(b) Are B's reports conditioned by $\{H_G, H_I\}$ or by $\{D, D^c\}$?

Under the assumption that A's reports are conditioned only by $\{D, D^c\}$ and B's reports are conditioned only by $\{D^*_A, D^{c*}_A\}$, the probative value of hearsay report D^*_{BA} is prescribed by

$$\Lambda_{D^*BA} = \frac{P(D|H_G) + V}{P(D|H_I) + V} , \qquad (4)$$

where

$$V = [h_A/f_A - 1]^{-1} + [(h_B/f_B - 1)(h_A - f_A)]^{-1}$$

(h_A and f_A are credibility-related values for A; h_B, f_B are credibility-related values for B).

The term V in Equation (4) is interesting because it shows an interaction between the credibilities of the primary and secondary sources. Even if B is highly credible (i.e., h_B much larger than f_B), there can be little probative value unless A is credible. The reader with interests in jurisprudence might wish to compare Equation (4) with the definition of *hearsay* given in *McCormick On Evidence* (1972 ed.) on p. 584. This definition says that the value of hearsay depends upon the "out-of-court" asserter, source A in our case. It seems apparent that the credibility of B also is relevant in determining probative value.

Character

The character of a witness has been regarded as relevant circumstantial evidence in impeachment or support of credibility. The opposing counsel is generally permitted, in cross-examining the witness, to introduce evidence regarding the witness' prior misconduct provided that such evidence relates to the witness' credibility. It appears that judges have great discretionary powers in deciding what evidence to admit. Such decisions are obviously difficult to make except in extreme cases in which an overzealous counsel embarks upon generalized character-assassination.

In our formulation of Λ, character-impeachment can be represented by appropriate conditioning of testimony $\{D^*, D^{c*}\}$ by the events representing the prior behavior of the witness. I will give two examples. The first example will serve the additional purpose of showing a second way in which *bias,* as a ground for impeachment, can be represented. Such an example was promised in the discussion of bias (Ground 2).

Case a. Let D^* represent current testimony from a witness that event D occurred. Let E represent a prior event, whose occurrence is not in doubt, and which either indicates prior misconduct of the witness or a reason for bias. For example, there is a case on record in which the credibility of a witness to a trolley-car accident was attacked in 1967 on the basis of his prior felony conviction for pandering in the year 1955.[6] In this case D^* represents his testimony about event D, and E represents the 12-year old pandering conviction. As an example of bias, let D^* represent testimony favoring the innocence of a defendant in a felony case. Let E be the event that the defendant owes the witness a large sum of money (which the witness would stand no chance of

[6] McIntosh vs Pittsburg Railways Co. *Supreme Court of Pennsylvania*, 1968, 423 Pa. 123, 247 A. 2d 467.

recovering if defendant were jailed). In either case we can define

$$\Lambda_{D^*|E} = \frac{P(D^*|H_G \cap E)}{P(D^*|H_I \cap E)} \quad .$$ (5)

Expansion of Equation (5) reveals the following conditional independence issues:

1. Are $\{D, D^c\}$ and $\{E, E^c\}$ independent *event* classes conditional upon $\{H_G, H_I\}$?
2. Are reports $\{D^*, D^{c*}\}$ conditioned by prior events $\{E, E^c\}$ or by hypotheses $\{H_G, H_I\}$?

If such conditionings do not take place $\Lambda_{D^*|E}$ becomes Λ_{D^*} as shown in Eq. (2a); if, further, report D^* is not conditioned by H_G, H_I $\Lambda_{D^*|E}$ becomes Λ_{D^*} as shown in Eq. (1a).

Incidently, in the pandering case, a lower court allowed (over objection) attempts to impeach by bringing up the 12-year old pandering charge. It is comforting to discover that, upon appeal, a new trial was awarded by a higher court. Comments made by the appeals court are worth reporting:

> The logical connection between pandering and not testifying truthfully in auto accident litigation twelve years later completely escapes us. It would be surprising if any statistical correlation at all could be found between panders of twelve years ago and witness stand liars today. Indeed it is difficult to see why someone who was convicted of pandering twelve days ago necessarily would be more likely to lie on the witness stand than any other randomly chosen citizen. If there is any connection at all, its probative value is so slight as to be clearly outweighed by the prejudice created.

Examination of Eq. (5) reveals an important consideration. There are often more conditional independence issues than meet the eye. The judge quoted above talks only about the second conditional independence issue noted above; there is, however, another issue concerning the *event* classes involved. If an inferential problem like this one is posed correctly, the formalization Λ tells precisely what must be demonstrated in order to establish or impeach credibility.

Case b. My final example may be incorrectly placed. It appears to involve character impeachment but it could also involve contradiction. Wigmore (1935, p. 181) quotes an old maxim "falsus in uno, falsus in omnibus" (false in one matter, false in every matter). The essential idea is that one lie causes perpetual ruin of a person's credibility. Wigmore goes on to remark that this maxim reflects "primitive psychology" and deserves to be abandoned. Nevertheless, prior falsehood is sometimes admitted for credibility-impeachment purposes. Again let D^* represent current testimony by a witness. Let E^{c*} be some prior statement by the witness that E did not occur; it is definitely known that E did occur. E^{c*} might be the report by the witness that he was never convicted of a felony. Careful background investigation reveals that he was. The probative value of current testimony D^*, conditioned by the joint event ($E^{c^*} \cap E$), can be assessed using $\Lambda_{D^*|Ec^*} \cap E$. The expansion, though tedious, is straightforward and reveals four separate conditional independence issues (which I will not trouble you with). By noting the conditions under which $\Lambda_{D^*|Ec^*} \cap E$ becomes equal to Λ_{D^*} as given in Eq. (1a) we determine exactly those probabilistic linkages we need to establish in order to change the probative significance of D^* in the light of the witness' previous false testimony.

SUMMATION

I have attempted to demonstrate, without placing too great a strain on your imagination, the behavioral richness or flexibility of a formal tool for incorporating credibility information in cascaded inference tasks. The basic objectives of our formal research are to seek better understanding of certain basic inference issues and to set the stage for more and better research on human inference. My purpose has never been to seek reforms in the rules of evidence in jurisprudence. I say this in hopes that I will not be drawn into the current controversy over the use of probability theory in legal proceedings (e.g., Cullison, 1969; Finkelstein & Fairley, 1970; Tribe, 1971). Indeed, I have been repeatedly impressed by the similarity between legal prescriptions, based upon experience, and our formal prescriptions. I should think, however, that continuing formal and empirical studies of inference ought to be of interest to jurists as well as to psychologists and others. Surely, there is widespread sympathy for the thousands of citizens, from all walks of life, who perform exceedingly complex inferential and decision tasks as jurors. If jurors can be better informed about the nature of their task, the parties involved in legal dispute will surely benefit as well.

I claimed at the outset that, although I could demonstrate behavioral richness of our formulations, I could not guarantee easy implementation of these formulations in any given actual case. This difficulty arises not because the mathematical operations are difficult, but because actual cases usually involve very large collections of events and very complex conditioning patterns. Indeed, the major ingredient in applying our formalizations to actual cases seems to be dogged determination on the part of the analyst. Wigmore (1931, p. 7) argued that logicians have provided "canons of reasoning" for specific single inferences but not for total masses of contentious evidence in judicial trials. I don't know whether or not Wigmore knew of Bayes' rule and its potential application, in sequential fashion, to streams of evidence. Our present work extends the range of application of Bayes' rule since Λ can be incorporated directly in Bayes' rule for the purpose of sequential revisions of posterior odds. To be a rewarding exercise for jurists in their analysis of cases, formalization of entire cases, even if possible, may not be necessary. Formalization of specific crucial aspects of a case may be tractible and very informative, for example, about the necessary conditioning patterns. In discussing the study of legal science, Keyser (1929) emphasized that mathematical methods can never tell what the law is or ought to be. However, he said,

> An ensemble of experience-given propositions (like those constituting any existing branch of law) never gets so thoroughly examined and criticized and understood as when the ensemble is submitted to the severe processes of mathematicization.

One obvious simplification in my examples of the behavioral richness of the adjusted likelihood ratio, Λ, concerns the use of binomial event and report classes. Although we have extended Λ to the general case of discrete event classes (Schum & Pfeiffer, 1973), the connection between Λ and the five grounds for impeachment exists but is less easy to illustrate. Another simplification is that we have expressed Λ for *simple* events. However, a witness' testimony is frequently not the report of a *simple* event but of a *compound* event $D = \bigcap_{i=1}^{n} D_i$. Each additional detail in the testimony adds another event to this intersection. Of course, some of the detail may be probatively irrelevant and may be safely ignored in an analysis of the probative value of the testimony.

Finally, I cannot yet answer the question about whether or not our increased formal understanding of aspects of cascaded inference will lead to better research on human inference. The answer to this question depends upon the quality of our imagination in designing research and, of course, on our perserverence, since we are now abstractly examining human inference tasks which begin to approximate in complexity those inference tasks performed so often in so many natural settings.

REFERENCES

Cullison, A. Identification by probabilities and trial by arithmetic. *Houston Law Review*, 1969, 6, 484–502.

Finkelstein, M. O., & Fairley, W. B. A Bayesian approach to identification evidence. *Harvard Law Review*, 1970, 83, 489–517.

Green, B. F. Descriptions and explanations: A comment on papers by Hoffman and Edwards. In B. J. Kleinmuntz (Ed.), *Formal representation of human judgment*, Wiley, New York, 1968.

Keyser, C. J. On the study of legal science. *Yale Law Journal*, 1929, 38. (Reprinted in *Readings in Jurisprudence*, Hall, J. (Ed.), Bobbs-Merrill Co., Indianapolis, 1938).

Peterson, C. R. (Guest Editor) Special issue on cascaded inference. *Organizational Behavior and Human Performance*, 1973, 10(3), Dec.

Pfeiffer, P. E., & Schum, D. A. *Introduction to applied probability*. New York: Academic Press, 1973.

Phillips, L. D., & Edwards, W. Conservatism in a simple probability inference task. *Journal of Experimental Psychology*, 1966, 72, 346–357.

Rapoport, A., & Wallsten, T. S. Individual decision behavior. *Annual Review of Psychology*, 1972, **23**, 131–176.

Schum, D. A. Inferences on the basis of conditionally nonindependent data. *Journal of Experimental Psychology*, 1966, **72**, 401–409.

Schum, D. A. On the weighing of testimony in judicial proceedings from sources having reduced credibility. *Human Factors*, 1975, **17**, 172–182.

Schum, D. A., & Du Charme, W. M. Comments on the relationship between the impact and the reliability of evidence. *Organizational Behavior and Human Performance*, 1971, **6**, 111–131.

Schum, D. A., & Kelly, C. W. A problem in cascaded inference: Determining the inferential impact of confirming and conflicting reports from several unreliable sources. *Organizational Behavior and Human Performance*, 1973, **10**, 404–423.

Schum, D. A., & Pfeiffer, P. E. Observer reliability and human inference. *IEEE Transactions on reliability*, 1973, **R-22**, 170–176.

Schum, D. A., Du Charme, W., & DePitts, K. Research on human multistage probalistic inference processes. *Organizational Behavior and Human Performance*, 1973, **10**, 318–348.

Schum, D. A., Southard, J. F., & Wombolt, L. F. Aided human processing of inconclusive evidence in diagnostic systems: A summary of experimental evaluations. *AMRL Technical Report 69-11*. Aerospace Medical Research Laboratory, Wright-Patterson AFB, Ohio, May, 1969.

Slovic, P., & Lichtenstein, S. Comparison of Bayesian and regression approaches to the study of information processing in judgment. *Organizational Behavior and Human Performance*, 1971, **6**, November, 649–744.

Todhunter, I. *A history of the mathematical theory of probability*. Cambridge: Macmillan & Co., 1865.

Tribe, L. H. Trial by mathematics: Precision and ritual in the legal process. *Harvard Law Review*, 1971, **84**, 1329–1393.

Wigmore, J. H. *The principles of judicial proof.* Boston: Little, Brown, 1931.

Winkler, R. L., & Murphy, A. H. Experiments in the laboratory and the real world. *Organizational Behavior and Human Performance*, 1973, **10**, 252–270.

JURIDICAL REFERENCES ON CREDIBILITY, IMPEACHMENT, AND SUPPORT

Cleary, E. W. (General Editor) *McCormick on evidence.* St. Paul: West Publishing, 1972.

Keeton, R. E. *Trial tactics and methods.* Boston: Little, Brown, 1973.

Maguire, J. M., Weinstein, J. B., Chadbourn, J. H., & Mansfield, J. H. *Cases and materials on evidence.* Mineola, New York: Foundation Press, 1973.

McCormick, C. T., Elliot, F. W., & Sutton, J. F., Jr. *Evidence: cases and materials.* St. Paul, Minnesota: West Publ., 1971.

Rothstein, P. F. *Evidence in a Nutshell.* St. Paul, Minnesota: West Publ., 1971.

Supreme Court of the United States, *Rules of evidence for United States courts and magistrates.* 1 July, 1973.

Wigmore, J. H. *A students' textbook of the law of evidence.* Brooklyn, New York: Foundation Press, 1935.

Part III

COGNITIVE DEVELOPMENT

There can be little doubt that cognitive development is an important and essential area of investigation in modern cognitive psychology. The well-known insights of Piaget on the thought processes of young children as well as the strong claims about the biological basis for human language by Chomsky have generated new and important research concerning the course of cognitive development. The role of the environment as well as the cognitive predispositions that the child brings to the learning situation are seen in a somewhat different light today than ten or fifteen years ago.

Each of the chapters in this section deals with a somewhat different topic in cognitive development. The first chapter by Elissa Newport is concerned with the role of mothers' speech to young children. For a number of years following Chomsky's remarks on the issue it was taken for granted that the linguistic environment plays only a relatively minor role in language acquisition. As the argument went, all that is necessary for language acquisition is that the child be exposed to a sufficient corpus of linguistic input so that the appropriate structures can develop. Within the last few years, psychologists and psycholinguists have begun to study quite intensively the speech directed to young children and have found that it has certain properties that may well serve a special function during the language acquisition process. In her chapter, Newport reviews these findings cautiously and places them in perspective with a number of other facts having to do with what the child must learn from the corpus of utterances presented in order to acquire the grammar of natural language.

The second chapter by Rochel Gelman deals with how young children reason about small numbers. Although the ability of the young child to abstract and deal with numerical representations of objects appears to be limited in some ways, Gelman shows that these children can and do use reasoning principles. By means of a series of clever "magic" experiments Gelman has been able to demonstrate that very young children know something about numerical equality and order as well as having available a set of heuristic procedures for dealing with the operations of addition and subtraction. These results are, of course, somewhat at variance with the kinds of findings obtained by Piaget in his well-known conservation tasks with young children. However, Gellman's work indicates that children can reason about numbers and that these principles may very well serve as the basis for more complex mathematical processes as the child develops.

The final chapter in this section is by Herman Buschke, who has studied verbal learning in children for a number of years. Buschke has developed a number of new experimental paradigms which provide important information about the course of verbal learning in terms of storage, retention and retrieval processes. What Buschke shows in this chapter is that young children learn a good deal more than what is revealed in traditional types of verbal learning tasks. Moreover, he has shown that with children, as well as adults, recall failure is due primarily to retrieval failure and not in discriminating list items from items not on the list. Buschke also points out the need for individualized testing conditions in recall experiments with children in order to facilitate retrieval processes. This seems to be particularly crucial in developmental studies of memory processes where subjects may be at somewhat different stages of development with regard to the use of different retrieval strategies.

7

Motherese: The Speech of Mothers to Young Children

Elissa L. Newport

University of California, San Diego

The acquisition of language most certainly depends to some degree on the linguistic environment: the child acquires whatever language is spoken to him. However, Chomsky (1965) has pointed out how slight this dependence may be. What the child must learn is not presented to him in any direct way. He is exposed merely to a sample of speech sounds, but he must project this sample onto an infinite set of utterances of the language. Further, he must construct a mapping between the speech events and the form (whatever that is) in which concepts are represented in his head. Worse, even the speech data directly presented to the learner may be a poor basis for discerning language patterns, for real speech is often garbled. The incompleteness and degeneracy of the speech data, and the indirect relation between these and conceptual structure led Chomsky to hypothesize that the child must be innately endowed with knowledge of the formal characteristics of human language. On this view, few, if any, characteristics of the environment would be crucial for learning.

More recently, psychologists have begun to investigate the actual characteristics of mothers' speech to children and have formed a strikingly different view of the nature of the linguistic environment and its impact on the learning process. They have suggested that mothers produce a special language (technically, a special speech *register*) when speaking to children. For convenience's sake we have named this kind of speech "Motherese." The first question to ask must be a linguistic one: what is the nature of this "language" that is directed to young children?

Motherese: A Simpler Language Corpus?

Shipley, Smith, & Gleitman (1969) have proposed that the interaction between mother and child may function to restrict the complexity of the speech forms from which the child must learn the language. First, they suggest that the child limits his effective language environment by such strategies as repeating (that is, rehearsing) utterances which are slightly beyond his current productions while ignoring excessively complex or unfamiliar speech. This selection of utterances to be processed requires little from the child in the way of preprogrammed abilities: he is likely *incapable* of processing long and complicated material, for example, due to short-term memory limitations. Furthermore, the authors suggest that adults are sensitive to the fact that the child ignores complex speech; wanting the child's attention, they select from their own repertoires utterances which are lexically and constructionally simple. Thus a new picture of the language acquisition situation begins to emerge: both the mother and the child filter the corpus so that the speech used by the child as data is appropriate in its complexity to what the child is learning. The child responds to utterances which are a bit beyond the current generative capacity of his rule system. In her turn, the mother, attempting to communicate with an unsophisticated listener, produces utterances at the level of complexity to which he will respond. In sum, the effective language environment may itself be quite specialized for language learning, thus reducing the requirements for specialization in the child. This of course leaves intact the problem of how the child relates the language to the structure of internal concepts. While Shipley *et al.* (1969) propose that the child could learn the forms of English from an ideal corpus, they give no proposal for how he might grasp what any of its utterances mean. This chapter likewise leaves the problem of meaning untouched.

It appears on first examination that the simplicity of speech to children may solve many of the problems of language acquisition. There is accumulating evidence that speakers produce a different set of utterances to young children than to more mature listeners. Several investigators have studied white middle-class mothers talking to their language-learning children (ages 8–33 mos.). Without exception they have found radical differences between child-directed and adult-directed speech. Higher and more variable pitch (i.e., fundamental frequency) acoustically differentiates child-directed speech from adult–adult speech (Phillips, 1970; Remick, 1971), so that in principle the child need not process the latter at all. Speech to children is slower (Broen, 1972; Phillips, 1970; Remick, 1971), with pauses after each sentence. It is also more careful, with less than one dysfluency per hundred words (Broen, 1972). Thus child-directed speech is adjusted for intelligibility. Further, the vocabulary of Motherese is comparatively restricted and concrete (Phillips, 1970; Remick, 1971; Broen, 1972).

Grammatically, speech to young children consists almost entirely of well-formed sentences (Brown & Bellugi, 1964). The utterances are short (Baldwin & Frank, 1969; Phillips, 1970; Snow, 1972), in part because they are rarely complex or compound in clausal structure (Baldwin & Frank, 1969; Phillips, 1970; Remick, 1971; Snow, 1972), and in part because of the rarity of modifiers (Phillips, 1970) and optional constituents (Pfuderer, 1969). Further, subject nouns are frequently deleted from otherwise well-formed sentences (Remick, 1971), and many utterances consist only of a single word (Broen, 1972). Such simplifications and restrictions on Motherese no doubt reduce the language acquisition problem in quantity. But all the qualitative issues remain for a child presumed literally to be learning a language he did not come equipped knowing. Even to acquire an uninterpreted syntax, the child would have to recover deep structures not represented in speech. Again we note that the real task in language acquisition involves more (or less!) than deriving an uninterpreted formal structure. He must map the syntactic structures of English onto conceptual structures which, whatever they are, are not identical to those of syntax. Some authors argue that there are interactional sequences between mother and child which may help to reduce this difficulty as well. Brown, Cazden, and Bellugi (1969) noted that when children produce one- and two-word "telegraphic" utterances which omit inflectional endings and syntactic function words (for example, "Mommy sock"), mothers very often expand the utterance into its full adult form (for example, "Mommy is putting on your sock"). Thus the child receives immediate feedback which supplies him with the appropriate surface forms for intended meanings. In addition, when the mother produces an utterance to which the child fails to respond, she frequently repeats the content in some new surface variant. For example, when a wh-question ("What is the dog biting?") fails to receive a reply, she may next produce an *occasional question* ("The dog is biting what?") (Brown et al., 1969). In addition to providing the child with another opportunity to process the utterance, she may thereby give him information about which segments of the utterance are constituents, and further above the range of surface structure options permitted by the language on a given underlying structure. Fully 20% of the mother's utterances to a young child may be repetitions of this sort (Snow, 1972).

Studies of black (Baldwin & Frank, 1969; Drach, 1969; Kobashigawa, 1969) and white (Snow, Arlman-Rupp, Hassing, Jobse, Joosten, & Vorster, 1976) working-class mothers, mothers of quite different cultures and language groups (Blount, 1971, 1972), and even nonparents (Snow, 1972; Sachs, Brown, & Salerno, 1972) reveal that much the same kind of speech is directed to children by any adult. Furthermore, even 3- and 4-year-old children, who in some cultures are the primary caretakers of younger siblings (Slobin, 1968a), produce this type of speech to young language-learners (Sachs & Devin, 1976; Shatz & Gelman, 1973). Thus, it is entirely conceivable that much of the uniformity seen in language acquisition may arise from the regularity with which speakers adjust their utterances to the needs of the language learner. This adjustment is at least in part due to the immediate response or nonresponse of the child. Snow (1972), like Shipley *et al.* (1969), found that children's attention drops sharply to complex adult speech. However, even in the absence of a differentially responding listener, both 4-year-olds and adults can speak Motherese. That is, they talk differently to a doll when told it is "a baby" than to the same doll when told it is "a grownup" (Sachs & Devin, 1976). Speakers need remarkably little experience with young children to know how to speak in this fashion. Nonparents perform similarly to parents (Snow, 1972), and 4-year-olds without younger siblings perform identically to 4-year-olds with 2-year-old sibs (Shatz & Gelman, 1973).

Superficially, at least, it would appear that speakers modulate the syntactic complexity of their speech when they are talking to very young children. On this view, we must grant the sophisticated speaker—in addition to his undoubted implicit knowledge about grammatical utterances in his language—something further: he must know the relative complexity of his own possible utterances and must be able to select from them just those utterances which are appropriate to the listener's level of sophistication. This hypothesis seems implausible; not every mother is a professional linguist. But a less bizarre account of Motherese is also consistent with the findings reported above: speech modification may result from any of a number of nonsyntactic constraints on the mother–child interaction, such as the adoption of a particular conversational role or a restriction of message content. On this view, the observed syntactic simplifications would appear as *indirect side effects*. In short, many characteristics of Motherese (and common sense) suggest that mothers are trying to communicate—here and now—with their children, rather than trying to produce exemplary English syntax. For example, on the basis of his study of Luo and Samoan children, Blount (1972) suggests that the frequencies of various sentence types in conversation depend heavily on the social and conversational status of the speaker (for example, the mother is the socially superior member of the speech interaction) rather than on the linguistic needs of the listener (for example, his need to learn Luo syntax). Blount notes that Luo and Samoan children are considered conversational inferiors who do not initiate activities. Therefore they are characteristically asked wh-questions and given commands. Middle-class American children, he says, are considered able to make decisions regarding activities, and thus are more often asked yes/no questions. Such findings raise the possibility that the form of Motherese derives directly from the general needs of communication.

Gelman and Shatz (1974, 1976) have proposed an explanation of Motherese that is consistent with, but rather more general than, Blount's. Their analysis is based on the distinction made by Grice (1975) and Searle (1969) between propositional and conversational meaning. While propositional meaning is a function of the form of the utterance itself, conversational meaning is a function of the context and the conversational agreements into which speaking partners enter as well.[1] Gelman and Shatz hypothesize that the speaker's selection of

[1] For example, an utterance like "Can you open the window?" is syntactically a yes–no question; however, said when there is no reason to suppose that the speaker genuinely wonders about the listener's physical abilities, nor to suppose that the speaker is violating a rule of speaking sincerely, it functions conversationally not as a question at all but as an action directive.

utterances appropriate for particular contexts is made on the basis of conversational meaning. They show, in particular, that 4-year-olds talk differently to 2-year-olds and to adults, even though the subject matter (how to use a complicated toy) stays about the same. The child attempts to direct the behavior of the 2-year-old, but does not presume to do this to the adult. Artifactually, the syntax to the 2-year-old is simpler overall. However, there are many instances in which speech to the 2-year-old is syntactically complex but conversationally simple. The converse is never found. Shatz and Gelman (in press) suggest that this constraint on the meanings the speaker intends to convey to the child is in fact only one of a system of constraints that operate on conversational interactions (Grice, 1975). Even the selection of form within a given conversational meaning may not be syntactically based. For example, politeness may govern whether directives are expressed as imperatives or questions.

The effect of this conversational system, then, is that speech to young children will be simplified syntactically only to the extent that such simplification happens to result from constraining conversational interaction. It follows that the linguistic environment may not always be ideal for the special purpose of acquiring syntax.

Purpose of This Study

Of course the primary interest of a description of maternal speech is in the light it may cast on the nature of language acquisition. Fodor (1966) and others have suggested that the degree of structure we find in the linguistic environment is inversely related to the structure we must impute to the child's mind: the more directly the environment presents what the child must learn, the less we must grant the child in advance. Thus by comparing what is known about the input to the child with what is known about his output, we may deduce something about the little black box in between.

There are now many investigations of the child's output (his speech at various points in time). But relatively little is known about the input (what he hears). Only recently have investigators begun to describe speech to young children. One approach (the one that will be taken here) is to describe the environment from the point of view of its producer, the mother. What is the process by which the mother produces her speech to the child? If she modulates the syntactic complexity of her utterances with some precision, she will thereby produce a linguistic environment which may be simple for the acquisition of syntax by the child. If, on the other hand, she modulates instead the kinds of messages conveyed by those utterances (for example, always tell the child what to do) rather than their syntactic complexity, the result may then be rather different: the linguistic environment of the child may be simple for message-derivation but not necessarily for the direct acquisition of syntax. Finally, if she modulates many aspects of her utterances, each with different priorities, the resulting environment may not be strikingly simple at any one of these levels for the child.

We will consider three topics:

1. *Nature of mothers' speech to young children.* What is the most systematic description we can give of the means by which the mother as speaker modulates her speech to her child? In our view, the process is best described by a multifactor hypothesis. Speech modification occurs through a set of interacting factors that shape the output: these include speaker status (as in Blount, 1972), constraints on conversational meaning (as in Gelman & Shatz, 1974, 1976), and listener deficits in processing capacity and language knowledge (as in Shipley *et al.*, 1969; and others).

2. *Adjustment of mothers' speech to young children.* To what extent, and by what means, is this speech adjusted to child listeners as they mature in language sophistication as well as in age? Adjustment will be examined in two ways. *Gross adjustment* of speech to age-class of the listener will be examined by comparing speech to the group of child listeners with speech of these same mothers to the experimenter. *Fine adjustment* of speech to particular child listeners will be examined through a correlational analysis of the relations between properties of maternal speech and those of child speech. We will argue that the nature of adjustment in fact confirms a multifactor hypothesis of speech modulation: while some features, because of their function, will be adjusted very finely to the linguistic competences of listeners, others will be adjusted instead to nonlinguistic cognitive competences, and yet others will be adjusted only to age class.

3. *The effect of mothers' speech on young children.* Finally, having tried to examine Motherese systematically from the point of view of the speaker, we will turn to its effects on the listener. Given this system of speech modification to children and the resulting linguistic environment, what conclusions can we draw about the process by which the child might acquire language? Since the environment appears to be shaped by a multiplicity of purposes, and therefore is not perfectly simple at any single level of analysis, we will conclude that we can envisage the helpfulness of the linguistic environment only within the constraints of some fairly extensive prior structure in the child.[2]

---

[2] The primary purpose of the present study is a description of the structural properties of Motherese and of the adjustment of these properties to the characteristics of the young listener. I have already indicated that Motherese is not characterizable as a language teaching dialect (cf. Skinner, 1957). Yet, whatever the mother's motivation for using Motherese, it is of course, in the end, the child's primary data source for the acquisition of his native tongue—syntax and all. A direct study of the effects of properties of Motherese on the course of language growth is therefore clearly appropriate. This issue is discussed elsewhere (Newport, Gleitman, & Gleitman, in press).

METHOD

Subjects

The subjects were 15 white middle-class mother-child pairs. Possible effects of the listener's sex on maternal speech style were avoided by selecting only mothers of female children.[3]

The mothers. Mothers were all housewives at least during the child's first years. All completed at least two years of college (in fact all but four had bachelor's degrees), and five had done graduate work before having children. Their husbands were all professionals; seven had MDs or PhDs. In short, the speakers studied here were all either graduate students or part of the highly educated segment of the population found in university communities. They were contacted through graduate housing at the University of Pennsylvania or through Nursing Mothers Association of Philadephia.

The child listeners. The original subject population consisted of 18 mother–child pairs. Half of the children were firstborn and half later-born. They fell into three age groups: 12–15 months, 18–21 months, and 24–27 months. Three subjects (one firstborn and two later-born) were lost during testing because the family moved.[4] Thus, the remaining subjects here reported on were 15 children: 3 1-year-olds, 6 18-month-olds, and 6 2-year-olds. All children spent almost all their time with their mothers.

Analyses of the children's speech were performed over the entire transcripts. Each child's syntactic sophistication was estimated through scoring:

1. mean length of utterance, in morphemes,[5]
2. upper bound—the longest utterance in morphemes,
   and the subcomponents of MLU:

[3] Phillips (1973), in a study undertaken after the present study was run, has found no effect of listener sex on maternal speech complexity.

[4] Subjects were recorded again, six months later, for a longitudinal study of the consequences of maternal speech styles on acquisition rate (see page 215 of this chapter and Newport, Gleitman, & Gleitman, in press). For purposes of continuity between the two studies, subjects were included in the analyses reported here only if they completed the second recording session as well.

[5] In counting morphemes an attempt was made to examine the entire transcript for a given child to determine whether the use of a particular adult morpheme was in fact productive in the child's usage as opposed to being part of a large memorized unit. The child was given credit for only those morphemes which were used productively in his speech (e.g., "can't" was counted as one morpheme in cases where it appeared to function for the child as a unitized negative element and was counted as two morphemes only when the child elsewhere produced such auxiliaries as "can," "will," "won't," etc.). Single-word yes–no replies to questions were omitted from the analysis. Otherwise, Brown's procedure (1973) was followed.

3. mean number of noun phrases per utterance,
4. mean number of morphemes per noun phrase,
5. mean number of words per noun phrase,
6. mean number of inflectional endings per noun phrase (4–5),
7. mean number of verbs per utterance,
8. mean number of morphemes per verb constituent,
9. mean number of words per verb constituent,
10. mean number of conjugational morphemes per verb constituent (8–9).

Vocabulary size was estimated as follows:

11. total number of word types (as opposed to tokens) produced during the interview (Nelson, 1973).

A description of the 15 children's speech is presented in Table 1. The average child in this study was producing many single-word utterances but also a large proportion of multiword and multimorpheme utterances. The children ranged from the very beginnings of one-word speech to fairly sophisticated multiword speech. Table 2 presents Pearson product moment correlations among the various child language measures. These indices generally correlate with one another quite highly. The children's syntactic sophistication, as measured by MLU and its subcomponents, does however show some degree of independence from age and vocabulary size. That is, although older children and children with large vocabularies tended to have more syntactic sophistication, these trends are

TABLE 1
Child Speech

	Mean	Range
MLU	1.65	1.00–3.46
UB	4.67	1–9
NP/Utt	1.02	.80–1.47
Morph/NP	1.17	1.00–1.46
Wds/NP	1.09	1.00–1.35
Vb/Utt	0.23	.00–.65
Morph/Vb	1.17	1.00–1.75
Wds/Vb	1.13	1.00–1.48
Vocab	83.67	3–210

Legend:
MLU: mean length of utterance   Wds/NP: words/noun phrase
UB: upper bound   Vb/Utt: verbs/utterance
NP/Utt: noun phrases/utterance   Morph/Vb: morphemes/vb
Morph/NP: morphemes/noun phrase   Wds/Vb: words/vb
                                        Vocab: vocabulary size

TABLE 2
Intercorrelations Among Child Variables

	Age	MLU	UB	NP/Utt	Wds/NP	Infl/NP	Vb/Utt	Wds/Vb	Infl/Vb
LU	.47	—							
B	.45	.93**	—						
/Utt	.30	.81**	.73**	—					
ds/NP	.41	.84**	.82**	.58*	—				
l/NP	.68**	.59*	.56*	.61**	.36	—			
/Utt	.56*	.86**	.88**	.58*	.71**	.42	—		
ds/Vb	.25	.65**	.62**	.81**	.42	.54*	.51*	—	
l/Vb	.44	.90**	.83**	.86**	.61**	.50*	.84**	.70**	—
cab	.59*	.53*	.59**	.18	.48	.43	.61**	.14	.43

gend

LU:	mean length of utterance	Infl/NP:	inflections/noun phrase
B:	upper bound	Vb/Utt:	verbs/utterance
/Utt:	noun phrases/utterance	Wds/Vb:	words/vb
ds/NP:	words/noun phrase	Infl/Vb:	inflections/vb
		Vocab:	vocabulary size

$p < .05.$
$p < .01.$

rarely statistically significant.[6] Thus it is possible to examine mothers' speech in relation to a variety of aspects of these child listeners: in particular, it is possible to ask whether mothers' speech is finely tuned to the age or rather to the language sophistication of the child listeners; and if to language sophistication, whether it is tuned to vocabulary size or to syntactic competence.

Apparatus

The equipment consisted of a Sony TC 126CS stereo cassette tape recorder with external microphone which was set on a centrally located table. One channel was used to record ongoing conversation among mother, child, and experimenter. The other channel was connected to a hand-held frequency generator which the experimenter used to mark each of the mothers' utterances. Depressing one of two buttons on the frequency generator silently recorded a tone on the tape. A high tone indicated an utterance to the experimenter; a low tone indicated an utterance to the child. Appropriate cues such as direction of the mother's gaze

[6] Intercorrelations among the language indices, partialling out age, can be found in Table 2' in Newport (1975). When age is partialled out, intercorrelations among the language scores become rare. MLU and upper bound still correlate with almost all the individual syntactic indices, but correlations between the syntactic subcomponents tend to disappear. Vocabulary size is unrelated to all other aspects of linguistic sophistication.

and content of the message were used to determine to whom the utterance was directed. This procedure avoided possible circularity in using the dependent measures to separate the two classes of utterances during transcription.

Procedure

All mothers were initially contacted by telephone and were told that the experimenter was studying language acquisition and wanted to tape-record the child's speech with only the mother present. The experimenter then visited the home for recording sessions. The mothers were not informed until the end of the sessions that their own speech was of interest. During sessions, the tape-recorder ran for 1½–2 hr, while both mother and child stayed in whatever room the mother deemed most convenient (usually the living room). For approximately half the session the experimenter engaged the mother in conversation; for the rest of the time, the mother was left free to interact with the child. Conversation among the three participants was as natural as possible, with no particular set of topics or situations chosen by the experimenter.

Coding of Mother's Speech

The interest of this study was in examining the syntactic structure of maternal speech in relation to particular characteristics of child listeners. Many of the analyses performed here therefore look at features of maternal speech which have previously been examined in speech to children within a narrow age range, and which have been hypothesized to change in relation to the child's linguistic competences. In particular, the well-formedness and syntactic complexity of the utterances, the distribution of sentence types, and the frequency of maternal self-repetition were examined. In addition, a new analysis of the relations between deep and surface structure was performed. Fodor and Garrett (1967) and Fodor, Bever, and Garrett (1974) have suggested that psychological, rather than linguistic, complexity of an utterance for adults is best predicted by the explicitness with which the underlying structure configuration is represented in the surface structure of the utterance. For example, actives (e.g., *The boy hit the girl*) are easier to understand than passives (e.g., *The girl was hit by the boy*) because the passive "departs from the 'canonical' (base structure) English sentence order in which the first noun phrase is the subject and the second noun phrase is the object." In general, a sentence will be easier when we increase "the extent to which its surface structure exhibits the grammatical relations among the parts of the sentence in the appropriate form for semantic interpretation" (Fodor, Bever, & Garrett, 1974, p. 326). That is, utterances which retain as much as possible of the deep structure form should be easy to process. It seems reasonable to hypothesize that such utterances should as well be the ones which are syntactically simplest for acquisition of the language, since underlying structures must be constructed by the young child on the basis of surface structure clues. An additional evaluation of the structural characteristics of maternal speech, then, looked at the relationship of the surface structures of utterances to their underlying representations. Details of these analyses are provided below.

The entirety of the 15 interviews (15 mother–child pairs), each consisting of $1^1/_2$–2 hr of conversation among the mother, her child, and the experimenter, were transcribed by a research assistant. Normal English punctuation was used to note intonation patterns. Utterance boundaries were determined subjectively by intonation contour and pauses in the stream of speech; therefore, syntactic boundaries were not always judged to coincide with the utterance boundaries. Analyses of maternal speech (1–4 below) were performed on portions of the transcripts. Analyses of mother–child discourse (5 below) were performed on the entire transcripts.

Ten- to 20-min segments of each interview were independently transcribed by the experimenter and checked for accuracy by relistening and comparison with the first transcription. The segments were each approximately 100 utterances from mother to child and 50 utterances from mother to experimenter. These segments were the corpora on which Analyses 1–4 were based.[7]

Utterances of the mother to the two listeners were coded according to the following:

1. *Well-formedness.* Utterances were classified as either:

    a. *unanalyzable:* incomplete utterances broken off midstream, or either partially or wholly unintelligible.

    b. *ungrammatical:* ill-formed even in colloquial speech; commonly acceptable but technically ungrammatical colloquial speech, e.g., "Wanna go?", was not scored in this class.

    c. *stock expressions:* idioms, "yes," "no," "oops."

    d. *sentence fragments:* isolated constituents or phrases, e.g., "the ball," "the one I knew."

    e. *grammatically acceptable utterances.*

The proportion of utterances falling into each of these categories was then computed for each mother.

2. *Sentence complexity.* Only the sentence fragments and grammatical utterances were scored for:

---

[7] A second set of segments, each 100 utterances from mother to child chosen from a different portion of the transcripts, has recently been analyzed for purposes of cross-validating the findings reported in this chapter. The results are almost identical to those contained herein.

a. *surface structure length:* mean length of utterance in words.

b. *deep structure complexity:* mean number of underlying sentence nodes per utterance, that is, mean number of underlying propositions, roughly equivalent to the mean number of main verbs per utterance.[8] Utterances may have more than one sentence node either by being syntactically complex or by being a run-on of more than one sentence with no pause or terminal intonation between sentences. Run-on utterances were scored as syntactically complex since the naive listener (that is, the child) presumably would have no way of determining that utterance boundaries occur in the absence of acoustic features such as silence and falling intonation.

c. *semimodals:* mean number of catenatives, e.g., gonna, wanna, hafta, usta. These verbal forms behave in many ways like auxiliaries rather than main verbs[9] and thus were scored as the former rather than the latter in S-node measures. This separate scoring, however, permits some evaluation of their contribution to the complexity of child versus adult directed speech.

3. *Surface sentence type.*   Only the grammatical utterances were classified as either:

a. *declarative.*

b. *deixis:* an utterance of the form

$$\left.\begin{array}{l}\text{``that}\\\text{this}\\\text{here}\\\text{there}\end{array}\right\} \text{ is } N,\text{''}$$

or any transformational variant thereof, that is, an explicitly referential utterance which points to an object and gives its name.

c. *imperative.*

d. *wh- question.*

e. *yes—no question.*

For each mother the proportion of grammatical utterances falling into each of these categories was computed.

4. *Surface structure—deep structure relations*

a. Each of the grammatical utterances was classified as to the degree and type of deformation in surface structure of the deep structure

---

[8] Prenominal adjectives were not counted as derived from a separate underlying S-node, since there is no evidence that such forms are psychologically complex for adult listeners. Otherwise, S-nodes were determined as in a Chomskian (1965) grammar.

[9] See Shatz and Gelman (1973, p. 16).

frame.[10] Pronominalization and contraction, scored separately below, were not counted as deformations for this analysis; they both preserve clear traces of the relevant underlying structural items in the appropriate locations and thus were judged not to deform surface structure.

1. *no deformations*
   (a) *declarative*, for example, "John went to school."
   (b) *deixis*, for example, "That's a ball."
2. *minor movements only:* negation, particle or dative movements, for example, "She gave Lissa the ball."
3. *deleted constituents only*
   (a) *auxiliary:* "do" or "do you" in yes–no questions, for example, "Wanna go to the store?"
   (b) *subject NP:* in imperatives, for example, "Throw the ball."
   (c) V P: verb ellipsis, for example, "He is." "John can."
   (d) *other.*
4. *auxiliary movement only:* in yes–no questions, for example, "Can you go to school?"
5. *wh- replacement and movements:* in wh- questions, for example, "Where did he go?"
6. *complex:* major movements, for example, passives, or combinations of the above within a clause
7. *multiclausal combinations:* utterances composed of more than one clause, each of which fell into one of Categories 2–6.

b. Miscellaneous common transformations
   1. mean *number of pronouns per utterance.*
   2. mean *number of contractions per utterance.*
   3. proportion of datives undergoing *dative movement.*
   4. proportion of particles undergoing *particle movement.*

5. *Discourse features: repetition and imitation.* Two discourse features of the mothers' speech were coded: self-repetition and imitation. For this analysis, the entirety of the transcripts of mothers' speech over the interviews was used instead of the smaller segments utilized for the coding categories described thus far. This expansion of the data base was necessitated by the fact that an analysis

---

[10] Fodor *et al.* (1974) discuss the concept of deformations only in outline, with several specific examples but no catalogue of the deformations which may occur in English. The analysis of deformations performed here was therefore created by the author. Coding categories were determined inductively on the basis of those types of deformations which in fact appeared in the corpora. Those types which are logically possible but do not appear here as categories simply failed to occur in the speech collected for this study. This analysis omitted "What's that?" utterances, as they may be analyzed by the children as a unit even though deformationally they are extremely complex. Because of the high frequency of these utterances and the likelihood that this analysis would overrate their complexity, they were omitted altogether.

of repetition and imitation require a large number of utterances. By definition, the smallest instance of either of these categories involves two utterances. In actual fact, some instances comprised as many as ten utterances. Each utterance was classified as either:

a. *self-repetition:* any maternal utterance which follows another maternal utterance by no more than 10 utterances (by any speaker) and which conveys the same meaning as the original. Each of these was then subclassified as:
   1. *exact repetition.*
   2. *exact plus:* an exact repetition with additional lexical items as well.
   3. *partial repetition:* the lexical items of the repetition are a subset of those of the model.
   4. *partial plus:* a partial repetition with additional lexical items as well.

b. *imitation:* any maternal utterance which follows a child utterance by no more than 10 utterances (by any speaker) and which conveys the same meaning as the original. Each of these was then subclassified as:
   1. *exact imitation.*
   2. *exact plus:* known elsewhere in the literature as "expansion" (Brown *et al.*, 1969).
   3. *partial imitation.*
   4. *partial plus.*

c. *neither* of the above.

The proportion of maternal utterances falling into each of these categories was computed for each mother.

DESCRIPTION OF MOTHERESE

Motherese as a Simple Language

Utterances directed to young children form a remarkably well-formed and clearly articulated corpus. As shown in Table 3, a full 77% of the utterances are nonanomalous examples of the productive conversational language between mother and child: 60% of the utterances are grammatical[11] sentences, while another 17% are grammatical sentence fragments, that is, sentential constituents spoken in isolation. Of the remaining 23% of the utterances, 19% are primarily occurrences of a small set of nonproductive "stock" utterances ("thank you," "yes," "no," "oops," "uh-oh"), while only 4% are truly unanalyzable because of unintelligibility of one or more of the words or interruption of the utterance in midstream. Only one utterance out of a total of approximately 1500 spoken by

[11] Throughout this chapter the term "grammatical" is used in the sense of grammatical as informal conversational speech.

the 15 mothers is ungrammatical in the serious sense: a garbled utterance, not part of the language.

This strikingly low proportion of anomalous utterances (0% ungrammatical, 4% unanalyzable) is consistent with other recent empirical investigations of the speech of mothers to young children (Broen, 1972; Drach, 1969; Phillips, 1970; Remick, 1971; Snow, 1972). The high proportion of sentence constituents spoken in isolation has also been reported previously (Broen, 1972; Snow, 1972). The high proportion of stereotyped stock expressions has not been noted elsewhere, but it fits neatly enough into the general picture of a well-controlled and clean set of utterances—in clear contrast to Chomsky's (1965) notion of a linguistically chaotic corpus.

In terms of complexity, the corpus is again strikingly clean and well-ordered. Broen (1972) has shown that actual silences fall consistently and only between sentences, thus allowing the naive listener to segment the speech stream into sentences on the basis of acoustic cues alone. The data here support this finding: utterances (as segmented by intonation contour as well as pauses) are run-on sentences only 1% of the time. Thus the corpus is a simple one in two ways. First, the acoustically isolable units are in fact individual sentences. Second, these sentences are themselves simple in clausal structure.

The fact that about one-fifth of the utterances are stereotyped expressions indicates that a goodly portion of these utterances are simple in a special sense: in addition to being very short (almost all one word apiece), they are syntactically unanalyzable, since their meanings are by assignment and not by composition of their parts. In this sense they are not syntactic objects at all. Nearly as frequent (17%) are single sentence constituents, primarily nouns or noun phrases. These utterances are slightly more complex than the preceding class; although they too are frequently unanalyzable (i.e., one-morpheme utterances), they consist of those items from which the more complex utterances of the language

TABLE 3

Mean Proportion of Utterances in Each Category of Well-Formedness
to Child and Adult Listeners

	Mother to child	Mother to experimenter	Difference[a]
Grammatical	.60	.58	NS
Sentence fragments	.17	.09	$t = 2.23$*
Ungrammatical	.00	.05	$t = 5.40$***
Stock expressions	.19	.19	NS
Unanalyzable	.04	.09	$t = 3.16$**

*$p < .05$.   **$p < .01$.   ***$p < .001$.

[a]Differences between proportions to the two listeners were tested by correlated t tests.

TABLE 4
Sentence Complexity to Child and Adult Listeners

	Mother to child	Mother to experimenter	Difference[a]
Surface length (MLU)	4.24	11.94	$t = 10.22^*$
Deep structure complexity			
(No. S-nodes/utterance)	1.16	2.66	$t = 9.93^*$
No. semimodals/CI	.09	.03	$t = 5.00^*$

$^*p < .001$.
[a]Differences between speech to the two listeners were tested by correlated t tests.

are constructed. That is, "oops!," a stereotype, is not a morpheme that occurs as part of sentences, while "doggie," a fragment, consists of an item which can be embedded in full sentences. The remaining 60% of the utterances are short and clausally simple grammatical sentences. As Table 4 shows, the grammatical sentences average 4.24 words apiece in surface structure length and have only 1.16 underlying clauses (S-nodes). A full 84% of these utterances are one-clause sentences. Once again, these findings support other recent studies (Drach, 1969; Phillips, 1970; Snow, 1972).

Brevity and structural simplicity are achieved in Motherese in a variety of ways over and above the predominance of one-clause sentences. Nine percent of the utterance clauses contain semimodals (for example, *wanna, hafta, gonna*) which can function in the adult language similarly to main verbs taking complement clauses and can also function as catenative modals. These forms appear in Motherese almost exclusively in their catenative modal-like form (for example, "Do you wanna play?" "We're gonna go.," and almost never "Do you want me to play?"). Thus one more way in which maternal utterances maintain structural simplicity while preserving some semantic flexibility is by using verb qualifiers as syntactically simpler catenative modal auxiliaries rather than as more complex main verbs.

Motherese as More Than a Simple Language

The results so far suggest that indeed Motherese may be a language which is uniformly simple in syntactic structure. However, when one looks at the structure of the individual utterances in detail, the notion of formal simplicity begins to dissolve.

Simple functions, complex forms. As shown in Table 5, utterances to young children range rather broadly across the possible classes of sentence type. Most of the grammatical utterances, a full 44%, are questions (including 6% "What's that?" and 2% "Is that a *N*?"), 30% are declaratives, 18% are imperatives, and

TABLE 5
Mean Proportion of Sentences of Each Surface Sentence Type to Child
and Adult Listeners

	Mother to child	Mother to experimenter	Difference[a]
Declarative	.30	.87	$t = 13.25^*$
Imperative	.18	.02	$t = 5.67^*$
Deixis	.16	.02	$t = 4.93^*$
Statement	.08	.02	
Wh- question	.06	.00	
Yes–no question	.02	.00	
Wh- question	.15	.01	$t = 6.28^*$
Yes–no question	.21	.08	$t = 4.52^*$

$^*p < .001$.
[a]Differences between proportions to the two listeners were tested by correlated t tests.

8% are statement *deixes* ("That is a *N*"). These proportions are roughly comparable to those found by other investigators (Broen, 1972; Drach, 1969; Remick, 1971; Sachs *et al.*, 1972; Snow, 1972). This wide distribution of sentence types appears primarily to arise from the communicative function of utterances to young children. Mothers quite frequently direct the activity of the child, query the child's needs, and display the child's competence for observers; thus, their utterances are frequently imperatives, question directives, motivational questions, and requests for well-practiced behaviors.

Although mothers universally engage in directing the child's activities, the particular surface form of these communications (that is, whether as questions or imperatives) may depend to some degree on the cultural attitudes toward children (Blount, 1972). In middle-class American culture (where Blount claims children are credited as conversational peers) an enormous proportion of yes–no questions, wh- questions, and even declaratives function conversationally as directives to action (Holzman, 1972; Shatz, 1974). For example, "Will you put the truck on the table?" or "Why don't you put the truck on the table?" said to a two-year-old is almost never a request for information, but rather a directive. Such directives differ from the imperative not in terms of whether they intend to issue a command but rather in terms of "politeness" or degree to which they will tolerate disobedience. That is, much of the variety in sentence types at the level of syntactic structure may be more uniform at the level of conversational, or intended, meaning. Surely the straight imperative form would be a better cue to intended literal meaning than these indirect directives.[12] Probably it would be syntactically more transparent as well. Yet the more complex form appears in

[12] But see Shatz (1975).

Motherese in response to the dictates of conversational rules (Gelman & Shatz, 1974, 1976).

In addition to such social functions of mothers' speech, some of the sentence types may have an explicit language-teaching function: deictic utterances state for the child the linguistic object (the name) corresponding to an object in the world. A full 16% of the sentences are, syntactically as well as functionally, a form of deixis. On a more liberal definition of deictic sentences (that is, including all sentence fragments that name an object and all utterances that direct the eye to a referent, e.g., "look at the *balloon*" and "see the *mailbox*?") a full 28% of the utterances are deictic. In addition another 5% are verb deixis, analogous to noun deixis in pointing to an action and giving its name (e.g., "He is *sitting.*" "What's he *doing?*"). In sum, one-third of the utterances from mother to child function to direct the child's attention to naming. This informal look across syntactic types at functionally similar utterances is in general accord with the suggestions above. The wide range of sentence types in Motherese seems to arise in the service of nonsyntactic constraints on mother—child interaction, which may, at least at times, supercede syntactic constraints.

Some further qualifications: Simple processing, complex forms. When one looks at maternal utterances in terms of syntactic processing, a few *more* qualifications on the notion of "simplicity" begin to appear. Overall, utterances to children tend, with some significant exceptions, to preserve in surface structure a relatively clear representation of the deep structure; in Bever's (1970) heuristic processing terms, the sentences tend to preserve canonical English form (Noun [actor]-Verb [action]-optionally, Noun [object]). Fodor and Garrett (1967) and Fodor *et al.* (1974) have argued that, since a listener in comprehending a sentence must use the surface structure form to reconstruct the underlying structure, or meaning, of that sentence, the psycholinguistic complexity of the sentence is a function of the explicitness with which the surface structure represents the underlying structure, in other words, the degree to which it preserves the deep structure form. It seems reasonable to expect that the same relative complexities should hold for the young child constructing underlying structures from surface forms. Table 6 shows that, apart from "What's that?" utterances,[13] over one quarter of the utterances from mother to child are as undeformed a representation of underlying structure form as a surface structure could possibly be. Of course no utterance can be a totally explicit representation of an underlying structure: numerous obligatory transformations apply in the generation of surface structures, not to mention phonological recodings (Chomsky, 1965). Nevertheless, 26% of the utterances undergo no additional movement or deletion transformations. Another 6% of the utterances differ

---

[13] Although this utterance seriously violates canonical form, it often occurs in routinized form and appears to be learned by young children as a single unit; thus for purposes of this analysis all occurrences of "What's that?" were simply eliminated.

TABLE 6

Mean Proportion of Utterances and Clauses in Each Category of Deformations from Canonical Form to Child and Adult Listeners[a]

	Mother to child (% utterances)	Mother to child (% clauses)	Mother to experimenter (% clauses)	Difference[b]
Undeformed	.26	.28	.45	$t = 4.19$***
Declarative	.19			
Deixis	.06			
Minor movement (negation, particle, or dative movement)	.06	.07	.10	NS
Deletions	.25	.33	.26	NS
Affirmative imperative	.13			
Negative imperative	.01			
Do ± you deletion (yes–no question)	.06			
Verb ellipsis	.02			
Other	.03			
Auxiliary movement (yes–no question)	.13	.14	.06	$t = 3.55$**
Wh- replacements and movements (wh- question)	.15	.16	.10	$t = 2.42$*
Complex deformations	.00	.00	.04	$t = 2.64$*
Multiclausal combinations	.13	–	–	–

*$p < .05$.   **$p < .01$.   ***$p < .001$.

[a]This analysis omits "What's that?" utterances. Totals do not reach 100% because of rounding error.

[b]T tests here compare M to E with M to C deformations per *clause*, since M to E speech differs from M to C speech so radically in clauses per utterance.

from underlying structure form only in minor movements (e.g., particle movement or dative movement, as discussed below). Only one utterance in all of the samples has complex deformations (e.g., passivization or intraclausal combinations of the other categories). In fact, of the remaining 68%, a full 42% have surface structure forms entirely dictated by sentence type: for these utterances, deformations from underlying or canonical form are due either to imperative subject-deletion (e.g., "you" in "Shut the door."), yes–no question auxiliary inversion (e.g., "Can you sing a song?"), or wh-question formation (e.g., "Where is the boy?"). Thus the first qualification on the notion of simplicity is as discussed above: the range of sentence types in mothers' speech to children does entail syntactic complexity in the corpus; to this degree, utterances are certainly not structurally simple. But within these constraints, utterances directed to children are fairly undeformed: only 17% of the utterances have any type of optional transformation from deep structure form.

What leads to the further qualifications on the notion of "simplicity" in Motherese is the nature of the deformations comprising this 17% of the utterances. Included in this set of utterances are: 6% which are yes–no questions whose auxiliary (always "do") and sometimes subject (always "you") has been deleted (e.g., "Want a cookie?"); 2% whose VP has been elliptically deleted (e.g., "He can," "It is"); and 6% which differ from an undeformed version only in having negation (e.g., "John didn't hit the boy"), particle movement (e.g., "You can put the box down."), or dative movement (e.g., "You give Lissa the truck"). With the exception of negation (which is clearly not a stylistic or optional insertion), all of these deformations have properties which may make them appropriate for child listeners. Although complex in syntactic terms, they may simplify psychological processing. Consider, for example, particle movement and dative movement. As Table 7 shows, 60% of all dative constructions in maternal speech undergo dative movement, while 100% of all particles are moved. Such movement is certainly predominant in this speech style and may in fact be the standard rather than the derived form. In heuristic terms, particle movement makes utterances simpler by moving the particle out of the way of the action–object sequence (Bever, 1970); perhaps dative movement is similar in properly grouping "give" verbs with their recipients rather than with their objects. In similar terms, auxiliary, subject, and VP deletions are complex in both linguistic and psycholinguistic terms if one considers them only from the point of view of syntax: the interpretation of such utterances must involve the recovery of those constituents which have been deleted. But in a more general psychological sense these utterances are simple: they are shortened, and perhaps thereby easier to process, through the deletion of items which are understandable in the discourse context (e.g., *Child*: "I can reach it." *Mother*: "You can?"). In sum, utterances of mothers to young children by and large violate canonical form because of sentence type or ease of processing; rarely, if at all, is canonical form violated merely as a stylistic option.

TABLE 7
Mean Frequencies of Minor Transformational Variations to Child and Adult Listeners

	Mother to child	Mother to experimenter	Difference[a]
Datives with dative movement (%)	.60	.70	NS
Particle constructions with particle movement (%)	1.00	.53	$t = 5.53$*
Pronouns/utterance	1.08	2.23	$t = 7.71$*
Pronouns/clause	.92	.85	
Contractions/utterance	.40	.65	$t = 4.18$*
Contractions/clause	.34	.32	NS

*$p < .001$.
[a]Differences to the two listeners were tested by correlated t tests.

Motherese as Simple Discourse

Finally, the discourse structure of mother–child conversation is remarkably repetitive. As Table 8 shows, discourse very often consists of recurrences of previous utterances. A full 23% of the mothers' utterances are complete or partial repetitions of one of their own previous utterances, while another 11% are imitations of a child utterance; only 66% of the utterances are new to the ongoing discourse. Children certainly attend to and comprehend only some fraction of what is said to them; mothers appear to adapt to this by repeating their utterances when attention lapses and by varying them slightly when the child fails to understand the previous version. In short, the mother as a conversational partner is careful not to lose her listener. The frequency of such self-repetition accords with that found by previous investigators: Kobashigawa (1969) found that 34% of the utterances of one mother were repetitions, while Snow (1972) reported an average of 19% complete or partial repetitions plus 14% semantic repetitions in the speech of 12 mothers to their 2-year-old children. In addition to repeating herself, the mother simplifies discourse structure by frequently repeating the child's utterances. Again, this may function to maintain at least a primitive conversational interaction with a partner who, if unaided, can do little more than offer disconnected comments on the here-and-now world.

Brown and Bellugi (1964) have examined maternal expansion of the child's utterances (corresponding here to "exact-plus imitations") and have reported that two of their three mothers produced such expansions 30% of the time. In the present study, however, only 11% of the mothers' utterances are imitations, and only half of these are expansions. Over the 15 mothers, the highest percentage of expansion by any mother is 12%, whereas two mothers do no expanding at all.[14]

---

[14] It should be noted that Brown's statistics and those presented here are not directly comparable: Brown presents the frequency of maternal expansion over child utterances, while the present figures represent the frequency of maternal expansion over mother utterances. It is further possible that the discrepancy between Brown's results and those presented here is due to a discrepancy in the age of the child subjects: expansion increases with age of the child listener (see the next section); however, so does the number of child utterances. Thus it is unlikely that expansion in this sample of mothers will reach 30%.

Another possible explanation for the greater frequency of expansion in Brown's data is that it is an artifact of transcription: in Brown's study, parental expansions (i.e., translations) to the *experimenter* may have been considered maternal expansions. In the present study mothers were encouraged to interact with the child in as natural a way as possible, and when mothers began translating child speech for the experimenter, the latter quickly reassured the mother that she was able to understand the child. Furthermore, many of the mother's utterances, particularly in nonobvious cases, were marked on the tape as adult versus child directed on the basis of direction of the mother's gaze, etc., so that the transcriber frequently had direct information at points when determining listener might otherwise have been difficult. In sum, it is highly unclear whether 30% expansion is common for mother-to-child interactions.

TABLE 8
Mean Proportion of Mother-to-Child Utterances Which
Are Self-Repetitions and Imitations of the Child

Self-repetition		Imitation	
Exact	.08	Exact	.05
Exact plus	.04	Exact plus	.05
Partial	.04	Partial	.00
Partial plus	.08	Partial plus	.01
Total	.23	Total	.11

An Attempt at Synthesis: A Multifactor Description of the
Structure of Motherese

A sensible account of the syntactic structure of maternal speech appears to require considerations of speaker status and associated conversational role, as well as of the general processing capacity and specific linguistic abilities of the listener. The particular syntactic facts of Motherese examined here seem best described by the following set of factors:

1. *Function of the conversation.* The variety of action directives (e.g., requests for well-practiced behaviors, motivational questions, as well as simple commands) results in surface sentence type being widely distributed among declaratives, deixes, imperatives, and questions. This distribution of sentence types means in turn that a large proportion of utterances from mother to child have surface forms which are, to this extent, rather deformed representations of underlying structure, having undergone such operations as subject deletion (imperative), auxiliary inversion (questions), and wh- attachment and fronting (wh- questions).

2. *Means for accomplishing the conversational function with a deficient listener.* General processing limitations (e.g., limited attention span, short-term memory capacity and comprehension) of the child listener result in utterances frequently being repeated and almost always being short. In part, the brevity of these utterances is achieved through syntactic simplicity: utterances typically consist of single constituents or single clauses and furthermore have few optional modifier elements such as adjectives, adverbs, and prepositional phrases; both of these simplifications shorten the number of words in surface structure. In addition, however, utterances are shortened by the deletion of deep structure constituents, for example, the auxiliary and "you" in yes—no questions.

3. *Formal simplicity.* Finally, within these functional constraints Motherese is structurally simple. Utterances to children are well-formed and clearly articulated; and, with the exceptions due to 1 and 2 above, they are undeformed representations of underlying structure.

This study thus accords in many details with descriptions of mothers' speech to children by other investigators; it differs from them primarily in viewing syntactic simplification at least in part within the framework and constraints of the communicative interaction between mother and child. Previous investigations have tended to focus on the relevance of mothers' speech to language acquisition and have argued that syntactic simplification and repetition are primarily adjustments to the needs of language learning, that is, "ways of making grammatical structure transparent" (Snow, in press).

Recently Snow (in press) has suggested that the semantic limitations of maternal speech produce its grammatical simplicity, and this may indeed be part of the story. Gelman and Shatz (1974, 1976) have argued convincingly that a system of context-sensitive conversational rules similarly yields syntactic simplification as a characteristic artifact.[15]

Whatever one's view of the basis of Motherese, that view will lead to the prediction of syntactic simplification; positions differ in whether they see this simplification as the primary basis of speech adjustment or as a secondary effect of the function of the conversation. They differ in addition in the naturalness of the account provided for occasional exceptions to syntactic simplification. The present investigation argues that both views are in part correct and necessary for fully describing speech to young children: conversational functions determine the outlines of maternal speech, but within these outlines syntactic simplicity itself determines the remaining details.

ADJUSTMENT OF MOTHERESE TO LISTENERS

It is clear that mothers do indeed speak in special ways to young children. It has been argued that this speech can be described in terms of modifications suited to communicating special kinds of messages with a special class of listeners. How well in fact do mothers adjust their speech to the characteristics of those listeners? First, which of the characteristics of their speech do they adjust even

[15] One possible way of examining whether in fact it is the case that the basis for maternal adjustment is through conversational rather than directly syntactic simplification is to study the nature of Motherese across languages whose syntactic expressions of the same conversational styles differ. (Such a technique is analogous to that suggested by Slobin (1973) for evaluating conceptual versus syntactic complexity of constructions in child speech.) One might expect, for example, that in cultures where similar conversational roles are given to young children but whose languages differ in syntactic means for expressing yes–no questions (e.g., French, where the yes–no question can be asked by only adding "est-ce que" to the front of the sentence, compared to English, which requires auxiliary fronting), the frequency of yes–no questions in speech to children will not differ if the adjustment of maternal speech is made on the basis of conversational requirements but will differ if made on the basis of syntactic complexity. No such investigation of maternal speech has as yet been done, although there are now enough data on maternal speech across languages that such a study could be made.

Susan Williamson of the University of Pennsylvania has recently begun a doctoral dissertation on maternal speech in Tamil which will examine these questions directly.

grossly, to adults versus children? Second, given that they do adjust a variety of characteristics of their speech to such radically different listeners, to what extent do they further adjust these same characteristics more finely, to individual children who differ in age as well as linguistic sophistication?

Gross Adjustment: Motherese versus Adult Speech

Everyday experience as well as previous investigations tell us that mothers speak differently in an enormous number of ways to adults than they do to children; that is, they adjust their speech at least grossly to listeners. Nevertheless, for completeness, let us compare the speech of mothers to children as described above with the speech of the same mothers to the experimenter.

Speech to adults, like that to children, is overwhelmingly well formed. The frequently supposition that the linguistic environment consists of sloppy, fragmented utterances is then contradicted not only by the nature of mothers' speech to children but also by the nature of adult speech; see also Labov (1966) for supporting evidence. As Table 3 shows, 58% of the utterances to the experimenter are fully grammatical sentences, a proportion not significantly different from that to children. However, the proportion of grammatical sentence *fragments* spoken to adults is slightly but significantly less than that to children (9 versus 17%), thus making the overall proportion of nonanomalous examples of the language slightly less in speech to the adult (67 versus 77%). The reason for this difference evidently lies in the greater proportion of ungrammatical (5 versus 0%) and unanalyzable (9 versus 4%) utterances. In sum, there is a significant difference in well-formedness between child-directed and adult-directed speech, at least under the assignment of constituent fragments to the class of grammatical utterances. Nonetheless, adult-directed speech is largely grammatical and contains relatively few mumbles and disfluencies. Apparently, the only speech which is highly ungrammatical is the conversation of academics (or perhaps, of generative grammarians).[16]

Speech to adults and speech to children differ radically in syntactic complexity, as shown in Table 4. In average surface length in words, the two sets of utterances are completely nonoverlapping; in average deep clausal complexity, the two corpora overlap for only one mother. In no case does any mother speak to her child with the complexity of her own speech to the experimenter; in general, speech to children is a drastically simplified register. Not only are utterances to adults much more frequently multiclausal, but in addition the frequency of semimodals is significantly reduced; in other words, complex verbs are used more frequently and they are more often used in their more complex forms.

---

[16] Lila Gleitman has pointed out to me that this may be a less frivolous remark than it seems: complexity of content, requiring in turn a more complex interweave of prepositions in complex and compound sentences, may quite naturally cause processing problems not found in everyday conversation.

Likewise, speech to children and speech to an adult differ sharply in surface sentence type. As Table 5 shows, speech to adults consists almost entirely of declaratives, a few yes–no questions, and almost no other sentence type, as compared to the balanced variety of sentence types used to children. Again, conversational explanations make good sense of these data: adults treat each other as conversational peers who exchange information (and occasionally question each other, seeking information). Even the few deictic utterances from mother to the experimenter are metalinguistic rather than true primary deixis (e.g., when the child says "a-ao," the mother says "that was 'radio'."), offering relevant information rather than language instruction. Adults (at least recently acquainted adults) do not use conversation to order each other about.[17]

Speech to adults differs in terms of surface representations of deep structure from speech to children (Table 6) as a function both of sentence type and syntactic complexity. As described above, conversational role (exchanging information with adults versus directing behavior of children) accounts for the fact that adults receive significantly more undeformed surface structures (declaratives) and fewer clauses with auxiliary movement (yes–no questions). However, even apart from this effect, adult- and child-directed speech differ. Although adults and children hear utterances with deletions equally frequently, the types of deletion differ: adults hear clauses with constituents obligatorily deleted through embedding transformations (e.g., complement subject deletion, "John wants [John] to change jobs."), while children hear clauses with "do you" deleted from yes–no questions and subjects deleted from imperatives. "Do you" deletion (e.g., "Wanna play with the doll?") never occurs to the adult listener (e.g., "Do you live near here?"). Furthermore, complex permuting deformations occur significantly more to the adult listener (e.g., "Was he hit by a car?"). Thus adult-directed speech is not only functionally different than child-directed speech; within these functional constraints it is more complex in syntactic terms.

In sum, Motherese on some dimensions is a simple and well-formed subset of adult speech. Utterances to children are shortened and simplified by reducing the number of clauses per utterance, by deleting ordinarily optional and obligatory constituents, and by reducing the number of optional stylistic deformations in surface structure.

Yet there are features of Motherese that cannot be described merely as speech to adults simplified. Surface sentence types are more widely distributed in child-directed than in adult-directed speech. Further, transformations like auxiliary deletion occur only in child-directed speech and not at all in adult-directed speech, while others (such as particle movement) occur significantly more frequently in child-directed speech. Of course it is also obvious that the discourse features of repetition and imitation are unique to child-directed speech. In short, mothers adjust their speech in particular ways (not all of which

---

[17] Except perhaps in the most indirect and disguised fashion: "I think Susie's getting crabby," that is, take your tape recorder and go home.

are syntactic) for listeners who differ in age and status as well as cognitive and linguistic sophistication. Speech to adults is neither intended to direct the listener's behavior nor adjusted to extreme processing limitations; thus the adult corpus consists of unrepeated information-exchanging declaratives which, although most of the time well-formed and intelligible, are more loosely controlled in these respects and are much longer and more complex.

Fine Adjustment:
Motherese to Particular Child Listeners

As we have seen, mothers, clearly speak differently to children and adults. But it does not necessarily follow from this that they adjust their speech differentially when they deal with children of somewhat different ages and language sophistication.

If it is true, as suggested above, that speech modifications to children involve a set of adjustments rather than just one, it then follows that these adjustments may be made somewhat independently to listeners whose status and linguistic fluency are not perfectly associated. To take some obvious examples, one may issue directives to uncooperative garbagemen (although not necessarily in three-word sentences), while with colleagues who are nonnative speakers of English, simple syntax (although certainly not commands) would be appropriate.

In a less trivial vein, this position suggests that such factors may be adjusted independently to the relevant aspects of child listeners. The fashion in which speakers in fact adjust properties of their utterances to gradations of age, linguistic, and cognitive sophistication of child listeners will be discussed below. We will see that while some aspects of mothers' speech are differentiated to such gradations, others are not.

Table 9 presents Pearson product moment correlations between aspects of maternal speech and a variety of characteristics of the child listeners. In general, neither well-formedness nor sentence complexity seem to be adjusted to features of the child listeners. Utterances do not become gradually less grammatical or more structurally complex as listeners mature. They do, however, become longer; surface sentence length alone is correlated with child age.[18] This finding

---

[18] On cross validation with another speech sample, some of the correlations between well-formedness measures and child language, although still not significant, were larger than those reported here. Even if one takes these trends seriously, however, the basic nature of the arguments made here does not change; the direction of these trends is inappropriate for notions of fine adjustment to listener competence. In this set of results, while sentence fragments were less frequent to more sophisticated listeners, grammatical sentences were more frequent to more sophisticated listeners; in sum, the proportion of nonanomalous examples of the language heard by child listeners did not change. Mothers' mean length of utterance became significantly longer in response to a greater number of measures of language sophistication; but deep structure complexity still failed to correlate with any aspects of the child at all. Otherwise correlations were approximately the same as in the original set of results reported here.

corroborates Phillips (1970), who found that the number of words per utterance in mothers' speech to 28-month-olds was greater than that to 18-month-olds. This lengthening of utterances to older children in the present samples is apparently a function of the fact that constituents are less often deleted, for reasons to be discussed below, rather than that sentences are in general more complex.

In contrast, the proportions of the various sentence types do show relations to characteristics of the individual child. The proportion of declaratives is correlated with child age, MLU, and NP complexity; the proportion of imperatives is correlated with almost every characteristic of the child listeners measured here. In short, as children mature, utterances directed to them are more frequently declaratives rather than imperatives. The proportion of deictic utterances increases with child vocabulary size; that is, the larger the child's vocabulary, the more frequently the mother engages in explicit object naming.[19] The frequency of questions, on the other hand, shows no adjustment to the child listener. This lack of developmental pattern in overall question frequency agrees with the findings of Remick (1971), for speech to 16- to 30-month-olds, and with those of Holzman (1972). When Remick looked at questions functionally, rather than syntactically, developmental patterns emerged. Questions with "no answer expected" (including action directives, like "Will you hand me the Kleenex?," as well as informational questions beyond the child's capacities) declined in frequency with the child's age; yes–no questions and questions intended to elicit speech increased. Similar age-related changes in the frequencies of test questions and real questions were reported by Holzman. Remick's and Holzman's results, in conjunction with the correlations between sentence type and child sophistication found here, suggest that, in general, sentence types may change systematically in response to fine changes in the function of maternal speech.

In terms of deformations of the utterances from canonical form, maternal utterances show a variety of correlations with child features. Many of these relations are due to the effects, described above, of sentence type: undeformed utterances (declaratives and deixes) increase in frequency, while imperatives decrease in frequency, as children mature. These categories here, as in the analysis above, show correlations with several aspects of child syntactic sophistication. In contrast, the overall proportion of utterances with deletions, and particularly those with auxiliary deletion, correlates only with child age and vocabulary size: the older the child, the less frequently utterances directed to him are missing constituents. The frequencies of minor transformations, except that of particle movement (which has no variance to child listeners), correlate

[19] It is conceivable that this correlation says only that the measure of vocabulary size is strictly an artifact of how often the mother made deictic statements; however, if this were indeed the case, one would expect such a correlation primarily with the frequency of maternal deictic questions ("What's that?") and not with the frequency of maternal deictic statements ("That's an apple."). In fact the reverse is true. Thus this explanation of the correlation will be considered no further.

TABLE 9
Simple Correlations Between Maternal Speech and Child Age and Language

	Child									
Mother	Age	MLU	UB	NP/Utt	Wd/NP	Morph/NP	Vb/Utt	Wd/Vb	Morph/Vb	Vocab
Well-formedness										
Grammatical	.01	.01	.00	-.19	-.04	-.04	-.09	-.04	-.07	-.06
Sentence fragments	-.04	-.12	-.09	.00	.03	-.09	.04	-.06	-.02	.14
Ungrammatical	.24	-.03	-.05	-.05	.41	.21	-.04	.00	-.05	-.08
Stock expressions	.15	.34	.28	.41	.20	.38	.27	.37	.32	.11
Unanalyzable	-.40	-.50	-.45	-.22	-.47	-.50	-.45	-.47	-.49	-.50
Sentence complexity										
Surface length (MLU)	.53*	.40	.36	.18	.29	.44	.27	.23	.25	.49
Deep structure	.28	.22	.18	.21	.02	.27	.06	.15	.15	.43
Complexity (# S nodes/utt)	-.17	.11	.21	.16	.29	.26	-.11	.09	.06	-.25
Semimodals/Cl										
Sentence type										
Declarative	.53*	.51*	.41	.33	.45	.69**	.45	.35	.37	.24
Deixis	.09	-.03	.15	-.24	.15	-.01	.17	-.06	-.07	.62*
Imperative	-.51*	-.58*	-.65**	-.35	-.53*	-.53*	-.72**	-.57*	-.62**	-.72**
Wh question	.15	-.29	-.29	-.19	-.25	-.22	-.34	-.08	-.11	.10
Yes–no question	-.23	.25	.38	.34	.20	.00	.42	.33	.38	-.07

Surface structure—Deep structure relations
Deformations from underlying form

Undeformed	.40	.57*	.59*	.19	.63**	.62	.67**	.33	.36	.49
Declarative	.46	.48	.40	.22	.52	.48^A	.50	.21	.30^A	.16
Deixis	-.16	.17	.33	-.01	.13	-.19^A	.30	.20	.13^A	.48
Deletions	-.56*	-.25	-.36	.04	-.22	-.24	-.41	-.26	-.27	-.57*
Affirmative imperative	-.41	-.50	-.61*	-.20	-.47	-.14^A	-.66**	-.46	-.51*^A	-.69**
Negative imperative	-.56*	-.34	-.28	-.14	-.32	-.32^A	-.44	.01	-.32^A	-.41
Do ± you	-.75**	-.15	-.20	.04	-.13	-.45^A	-.20	-.15	-.05^A	-.41
Vb ellipsis	.55*	.73**	.63*	.76**	.43	.59*^A	.69**	.68**	.85****^A	.37
Auxiliary movement	.00	-.13	.07	-.26	.01	-.21	.16	.01	-.03	-.05
Minor movement	.18	.15	.11	-.04	.12	.10	.29	-.07	.14	.12
Wh-replacements	-.02	-.41	-.51*	-.32	-.49	-.45	-.50	-.26	-.23	-.18
Complex deformations	.00	.00	.00	.00	.00	.00	.00	.00	.00	.00
Multiclausal combinations	.35	.19	.20	.24	-.01	.24	.04	.14	.16	.51*
Minor transformations										
Pronouns/Utt	.53*	.53*	.45	.45	.49	.73**	.32	.38	.39	.51*
Contractions/Utt	.38	-.01	-.01	-.33	.07	.15	.03	-.18	.15	.67**
Dative movement	.22	.30	.32	.25	.16	.31	.15	.15	.21	.50*
Particle movement	.00	.00	.00	.00	.00	.00	.00	.00	.00	.00
Repetition & imitation										
Exact repetition	-.62**	-.43	-.60**	-.15	-.38	-.56*	-.63**	-.36	-.38	-.69**
Exact plus repetition	-.24	-.50	-.45	-.41	-.40	-.50	-.41	-.36	-.39	-.29
Partial repetition	-.42	-.48	-.38	-.27	-.43	-.51*	-.55*	-.29	-.36	-.66**
Partial plus repetition	-.31	-.30	-.40	-.25	-.20	-.35	-.47	-.37	-.37	-.43
Total repetition	-.55*	-.51*	-.59*	-.22	-.44	-.60*	-.68**	-.40	-.42	-.69**

(Continued)

205

TABLE 9 *(Continued)*

Mother	Child									
	Age	MLU	UB	NP/Utt	Wd/NP	Morph/NP	Vb/Utt	Wd/Vb	Morph/Vb	Vocab
Exact imitation	.28	-.16	-.10	-.39	-.25	-.21	.18	-.18	-.14	.48
Exact plus imitation	.56*	.17	.26	-.19	.19	.19	.46	-.17	-.05	.79***
Partial imitation	.58*	.64**	.59*	.70**	.54*	.61**	.72**	.63**	.71**	.20
Partial plus imitation	.54*	.88***	.82***	.82***	.65**	.73**	.83***	.70**	.85***	.52*
Total imitation	.51*	.19	.25	-.11	.08	.12	.50	.01	.12	.72**

*$p < .05$.   **$p < .01$.   ***$p < .001$.   A: correlations with inflectional measures only (i.e. morphemes–words)

Legend–Child speech measures

MLU:	mean length of utterance
UB:	upper bound
NP/Utt:	noun phrases/utterance
Morph/NP:	morphemes/noun phrase
Wds/NP:	words/noun phrase
Vb/Utt:	verbs/utterance
Morph/Vb:	morphemes/vb
Wds/Vb:	words/vb
Vocab:	vocabulary size

highly with the child's vocabulary size. In sum, those deformations affecting the processing of utterances change in frequency with nonsyntactic aspects of the child's growth.

Finally, the frequency of maternal self-repetitions shows correlations with age, aspects of syntax, and vocabulary size; mothers repeat themselves less as children become more competent in a variety of spheres. Imitations differ according to type: expansions (*exact plus*) increase with age and vocabulary size, while partial imitations increase with almost every aspect of child growth.

The Multifactor Hypothesis
Extended to Gross and Fine Adjustment

In terms of the communication purposes ascribed above to the Motherese corpus, these patterns of gross and fine tuning continue to make sense. Mothers attempt to direct the child's behavior less as the child matures, and the nature of the direction changes with child sophistication. This changing functional basis of the conversation as the child matures has the following effects on the structure of maternal speech:

1. *Function of the conversation.* Change in the extent and nature of behavior directives with age results in systematic variation in surface sentence type as listeners mature. Action directives as a whole decrease; thus while simple commands (imperatives) decline, information-exchanging declaratives increase. Within the broad class of action directives, however, the type of directive may change as well. Many of the newly introduced declaratives may not functionally be information exchanges but rather indirect directives, as in "The block goes there." Questions, which do not change in frequency over this period when looked at only in overall syntactic form, may nevertheless show changes with maturity of the listener in the way in which they direct behavior (e.g., more indirect forms, or more motivational questions). Finally, object naming, an activity which eventually drops out in conversation with mature listeners, increases in frequency with the child's vocabulary size during this period of development; that is, mothers adjust the frequency of their object naming quite specifically to the child's interest in naming.

This changing distribution of sentence types with listener-change means in turn that deformations in surface representation of underlying structure change to some extent correspondingly: that is, the proportion of undeformed utterances (declaratives and deixes) increases with listener sophistication, while the proportion of utterances with deletions (imperatives) declines.

2. *Means for accomplishing the conversational function with listeners of different abilities.* Increasing processing capacities (e.g., extended attention span, short-term memory capacity and comprehension) of the child listener result in a decreasing frequency of maternal self-repetitions and increasing sentence length.

Increasing length with listener sophistication apparently results not from increasing clausal complexity but from the declining frequency of deleting deep-structure constituents such as subjects in the less frequent imperative sentences and, particularly strikingly, the auxiliary and "you" in yes–no questions.

3. *Formal simplicity.* Except for simplifications that arise artifactually from just these functional constraints, structural complexity of the Motherese corpus does *not* change systematically with listener sophistication. Utterances to children within this range of sophistication are equally well-formed, clearly articulated and stylistically undeformed representations of underlying structure.

Some supporting evidence for multiple factors: The nature of adjustment. We have suggested above that if speech modification to children involves a set of factors rather than just one, then these adjustments may be made somewhat independently, each to the relevant aspects of listeners. In fact the findings of the correlational analysis support this suggestion: those features of maternal speech hypothesized to arise directly from conversational constraints on maternal speech (Factors 1 and 2) are adjusted in a continuous way to aspects of the listeners, while those features hypothesized to arise directly from syntactic constraints (Factor 3) are adjusted only grossly, to adults versus children.

The grossness with which directly syntactic, or formal, simplification is made in turn suggests several possibilities. First, the characteristics of the listener (e.g., the child's syntactic competence) to which such adjustment is made may be only loosely monitored by the speaker. Alternatively, the speaker may have only a rough measure of control over her own syntactic complexity; she may be able to monitor the listener's syntax precisely but be unable to monitor her own output in these terms. Of course, it may be that there is loose monitoring of both.

In contrast, nonsyntactic adjustment of the conversational interaction (that is, simplification of conversational function and processing of utterances) is made in a finely graded way to aspects of the listeners. That is, mothers' notions of social and cognitive appropriateness, if not their notions of syntactic appropriateness, are sensitively tuned to their listeners. In fact the details of the correlational analysis lend support to the further distinction between conversational features relating to listener status and function of the interaction (Factor 1) versus those relating to listener processing limitations (Factor 2). The former (e.g., distribution of surface sentence type and associated deformations, as well the frequency of maternal self-repetition) are adjusted to a wide variety of characteristics of the child listener, including his age as well as linguistic competence. The latter (e.g., utterance-shortening deletions and contractions, expansion, and deixis) are adjusted only to the listener's age (and its cognitive concomitants) or vocabulary size. That is, while the function of the conversation appears to be regulated in detail by the precise nature of the interaction between mother and child, the adjustment of the psycholinguistic difficulty of individual utterances appears to be regulated more narrowly by the listener's nonsyntactic cognitive deficits.

In sum, there is a set of somewhat independent constraints operating to make the adjustment of maternal speech to its listeners. Each of them appears to involve the speaker's monitoring of different qualities of the listener, each with varying degrees of sensitivity.

IMPLICATIONS OF THE STRUCTURE OF MOTHERESE
FOR LANGUAGE ACQUISITION

Having attempted to describe something of the nature of Motherese and the ways it is produced by its speaker, we can now turn to the point of view of the listener. The thrust of the discussion thus far is that the structure of this corpus may be well-suited for getting the child to pick up his toys or take his foot out of the wash. But, although cleanliness may be next to Godliness, it will surely not in itself guarantee the acquisition of language. How could the child learn English if all he hears is Motherese?

The debate on the nature of language acquisition has centered around the question of whether language competence is primarily preprogrammed, or learned on the basis of the linguistic environment. It is within the context of this rationalist—empiricist debate that an interest in the nature of mothers' speech to children has arisen. Chomsky (1965) and others (Bever, Fodor, & Weksel, 1965) found support for the view that language is preprogrammed in the child by claiming that mothers' speech, unlike adult speech, is too degenerate and complex a corpus to support learning by inductive generalization. In response to this claim, more recent investigators (Brown & Bellugi, 1964; Phillips, 1970; Snow, 1972; and others cited above) have maintained that mothers' speech to children is radically different from adult speech, in particular that it is a clean and well-ordered corpus, carefully graded in complexity for the child's current competence and therefore well-suited for learning by inductive generalization.

From the point of view of language acquisition, Motherese may be examined in at least three ways: first, in general terms as a corpus which may or may not have properties suiting it for easing learning; second, as a sequence of corpora which change over time as the child matures and whose degree of adjustment to the child's linguistic competence may be important for programming the course of learning; and third, as a set of corpora produced by mothers each with different listener-sensitivities, whose individual differences may predict individual differences in the rate of child learning. That is, each mother produces a sequence of Motherese corpora as her child matures; the general properties of these corpora, and the nature and degree of their tuning over time may be relevant for the course and rate of child language acquisition.

General Properties of Motherese

Earlier investigations have shown that, as a result of listener-dependent speech modifications, Motherese is a language which is grammatically well-formed, syntactically simple, and repetitious. Although investigators have assumed— correctly I think—that the primary intent of such speech modification is to maintain the child's attention and comprehension, most have made two additional, and related, assumptions as well: that the basis for speech modification to young listeners is syntactic, and thus that, whatever the primary intent of the mother, the result is a corpus that will be simple for purposes of learning syntax. That is, they have assumed that the modifications resulting from attempts to maintain attention and the like are precisely the ones that will simplify the corpus for acquiring syntax (see in particular Remick, 1971; Sachs *et al.*, 1972; Snow, 1972). The present study, although finding many of the same details of mothers' speech, argues that the corpus is shaped by a set of communication purposes, and thus by a set of modifications as well. The nature of speech adjustment to the child is through a selection of utterances that are socially and psychologically, as well as syntactically, appropriate; in fact the former appear to dominate, so that syntactic simplicity operates only within their constraints. What results from this set of maternal intents and their associated effects on speech is a corpus which may or may not be helpful for acquisition.

In many ways Motherese does in fact appear to be a language well suited for inductive learning. Grammaticality and intelligibility are high and thus potentially useful for acquisition. In addition, a large proportion of utterances in these mothers' speech samples are sentence constituents spoken in isolation. Snow (1972) has suggested that these sentence fragments may give the child useful information regarding the constituent structure of full sentences. Further, in this study as well as in many preceding it, almost all the utterances of mothers to children are short and syntactically simple, and are well distributed across the sentence types of the language. With the exception of utterance-shortening deletions and manipulations of surface structure constitutents involved in varying sentence type, utterances to children are remarkably explicit and undeformed representations of deep structure.

Finally, the discourse structure of Motherese may contribute to language acquisition. Brown and Bellugi (1964) have suggested that parental expansion may provide the child with a timely presentation of just those surface structure elements which his current utterances lack. It has also been suggested (Kobashigawa, 1969; Snow, 1972) that maternal self-repetition may be beneficial for language acquisition by providing the child with sequences of utterances whose meanings are the same but whose surface structures differ, that is, sequences of utterances which display for the child in an organized fashion the surface structure variations possible for a given deep structure. In the present study, as in those cited above, maternal self-repetition occurs quite frequently: an average of 23% of the mothers' utterances are self-repetitions, with the youngest children receiving as much as 51% repeated utterances.

There are, however, ways in which these same features may be viewed as counterproductive, or at best indifferent, for language acquisition, having arisen for other purposes. As cited above, utterances of mothers to children are short. In part the brevity of these utterances is achieved through syntactic simplicity. In addition, however, utterances are shortened by the deletion of deep structure constituents, for example, the auxiliary and "you" in yes–no questions, the subject in imperatives, and the object in a variety of sentence types. Whether shortening utterances through deletion, particularly deletion of constituents which are obligatorily present in the adult language, is a structural simplification or complication is not obvious. There is evidence that young children will fail to attend and respond to lengthy utterances (Shipley, Smith & Gleitman, 1969; Snow, 1972). Furthermore, there is evidence in adult sentence processing that some types of deletion (e.g., deep structure subject deletion in passives, "The ball was hit," Slobin, 1968b) make sentence processing easier. However, other types (e.g., relative pronoun or complement sentence-introducer deletion, Fodor & Garrett, 1967) make adult sentence processing more difficult. Fodor and Garrett suggest more generally that any deletion which makes the deep structure of the sentence less obvious will make the sentence more difficult to process, since the construction of the deep structure must proceed from surface structure clues. Furthermore, deletion of *any* kind may cause additional difficulties for the language learner since he presumably will be able to learn about the structure of his language only through the occurrence of surface structure elements; those that consistently fail to occur (e.g., auxiliaries) should not be learnable, even if their deletion might otherwise reduce the complexity of sentence processing for the mature listener. Thus it is conceivable that such modulations of speech to language learners may be somewhat counterproductive for learning, even though they may serve the here-and-now function of maintaining the child's attention, keeping an otherwise lengthy sentence within the limits of the child's short-term memory span, or stressing the elements of the sentence to which a response is desired.

In addition, utterances to children are well-distributed across the sentence types of the language. Thus a relatively large proportion of the utterances children hear have surface structures which are rather deformed representations of underlying structure in the language. Wh- questions in English, for example, have the questioned constituent replaced by a wh- word, fronted, and in addition reverse the order of the subject noun and the first member of the auxiliary. Whether or not such utterances are a hindrance to language learning, it seems unlikely, or at least untested, that they are more helpful to the learner than a larger proportion of declaratives might be.

Similarly, imitation and repetition may be less useful for acquisition than has been imagined. Some attempts have been made to test experimentally the effect of expansion on child language acquisition, essentially by giving large numbers of expansions to a group of children, and comparing their subsequent language growth to a control group. The results with young children have uniformly been negative (Cazden, 1965; Feldman, 1971), while those with older children are positive (Nelson, Carskaddon, & Bonvillian, 1973) but possibly artifactual.[20]

There has been no long-term test of the effects of self-repetition on acquisition. However, some evidence suggests that (at least in the short run) self-repetition serves the function of communication in the here-and-now but has no effect on the *growth* of comprehension (Newport & Gleitman, 1976). Three mothers were asked to give their two-year-old children commands, which the mothers generated themselves. We then looked at the probability of the child's response, indicating some comprehension of the utterance, across exact and partial maternal self-repetitions. The question of interest was whether the probability of a response increases with the number of repetitions the mother presents to the child, that is, whether the comprehension of the child *grows* as a function of repetition. Of course the cumulative probability of a response increases with the number of maternal repetitions; but this is banal and obvious: saying something five times instead of once increases the overall likelihood that a response will be made, since there is some probability on each trial that the child will make a response regardless of whether he even heard the other occurrences of that message. But does the conditional probability of a response increase? That is, on any *particular* occurrence of an utterance, is the probability of a response by the child greater if it is preceded by other occurrences of that message than if it is not? Is it greater if preceded by four other occurrences than by two others? Table 10 presents these conditional probabilities as a function of the position of the utterance in the repetition sequence, for all sequences to which the child ever responded. The answer to the question posed is clearly *no*: for all three subjects the probability of a response to a given utterance is entirely independent of the number of preceding utterances in the repetition sequence. The explanation is simple. Children surely attend to and comprehend only some fraction of what is said to them; mothers may adapt to this by repeating their utterances when attention lapses. Eventually, then, one utterance may elicit a response, regardless of the effects or even the presence of the preceding utterances. The mother's interest in repetition is clear: the overall likelihood of eliciting a response from the child is obviously greater with repetition than without. But this effect is apparently only due to giving the inconsistent, or stubborn, listener more chances to respond and not to the instructive effects of

---

[20] See a discussion in Newport (1975). In brief, the control group for the Nelson *et al.* (1973) study may not have been sufficiently familiarized with the test situation; such familiarization is known to affect measures of language sophistication (Cazden, 1972, Appendix). Since this chapter was written, however, Keith Nelson (personal communication) has informed me that a new experiment supports his previous findings of an effect of expansions and recast sentences on language growth.

TABLE 10
Proportion of Correct Responses by the Child to Serial
Position in Mothers' Repetition Sequences
Successful Sequences Only

	Position					
	1	2	3	4	5 & 6	Overall
Subject 1	.35	.27	.38	.27	.44	.35
Subject 2	.59	.39	.32	.54	.50	.48
Subject 3	.41	.51	.43	.44	.43	.43
Mean	.45	.39	.38	.42	.46	

repetition on the comprehension of a new form. A child who manages only to process bits and pieces of utterances (Shipley *et al.*, 1969) could scarcely be expected to hold some sequence of whole utterances in mind for comparison and learning. This result appears to be a strong argument against the view that repetition helps language acquisition.

In short, the properties of Motherese do not support the claim that it is a teaching language. It is a language for the convenience of the mother, not for the education of the child.

The Nature of Adjustment of Motherese
to Child Listeners of Increasing Sophistication:
A Look at Fine-Tuning Theories
of Language Acquisition

This skepticism about Motherese as a teaching language finds further support in the data on fine adjustment. Several previous investigators of maternal speech (e.g., Phillips, 1970; Remick, 1971; Snow, 1972) have suggested that the linguistic environment of young language learners is not only well-suited in a general way for the needs of acquisition but that in addition it is finely tuned to the particular stage of acquisition of its listeners. According to this view, the child's linguistic environment is at all points of development one small step ahead of him in complexity, thus specifying precisely what he will learn next. The few studies (Pfuderer, 1969; Phillips, 1970; Remick, 1971; Shatz & Gelman, 1973) which have compared speech to young children of various levels of sophistication have only done so for children who differ in *both* age (and cognitive ability) and language sophistication; the present study is the first to look at speech as a function of these child variables individually. A fine-tuning theory obviously presupposes a fine adjustment of the mother's speech to the child's linguistic competence rather than to his age, cognitive sophistication, status, or physical babyishness. But, as seen above, this fine adjustment is precisely what we did *not* find.

The primary argument against fine-tuning comes from an examination of the source of mother's adjustments: as seen above, the different features of maternal speech, because they may arise through any of several communicative functions, may be adjusted in varying degrees to different properties of the listeners. Thus there will be no general statement one can make about the *degree* of adjustment of the linguistic environment to its listeners or the *aspects* of its listeners to which it is adjusted. Further evidence against the fine-tuning hypothesis comes from the sizes and directions of the particular relations between maternal speech characteristics and child sophistication. As already mentioned, few measures of either well-formedness or syntactic complexity are adjusted at all to child sophistication. Length of mothers' utterances does indeed increase with child competence, as it should for such a hypothesis. But this increase occurs because few of her utterances are imperatives, or questions with auxiliaries deleted. Her utterances do not become propositionally more complex as children mature. While the proportion of imperatives in speech to young children is relatively high and decreases with language sophistication, the proportion of declaratives is relatively low and increases with sophistication; these relations are just those that would be predicted by a functional explanation of speech adjustment but not by a syntactic tuning hypothesis. In short, although speech to children is (though messily) somewhat simpler in syntactic structure than is speech to adults, it is imperfect indeed in its tuning to the differing syntactic sophistication of children.

An Alternative Approach:
Individual Differences in the Degree of Adjustment
of Motherese to Child Listeners

If the suggestions herein are correct, that the linguistic environment is shaped by a multiplicity of purposes and therefore is not perfectly structured at any single level of analysis, there appears to be no avoiding the attribution of fairly extensive prior structure to the language learner himself. Although Motherese is simple in many ways, there are enough qualifications and complications that the problem of language acquisition as raised by Chomsky (1965) essentially remains intact.

Does this mean that the child is so richly endowed with the structure of language that he could learn to speak English if the mother in fact produced long, complicated sentences? Could he learn to speak English even if she produced those sentences backwards? The answer is certainly no. Despite the messy details, mothers who communicate with their children all succeed to some degree in adjusting the linguistic environment to the competence of the child;

communicative adjustment, whatever its origins, will very probably produce for the child a speech corpus that is roughly appropriate to his needs as a language learner. This provision of the right "ballpark" of complexity may indeed be required.

Furthermore, an examination of universals of early language acquisition makes suggestions about the nature of the prior structure which the learner brings to the task of acquisition. In particular, the child may be equipped with a set of linguistic and cognitive processing strategies which he applies to his input, regardless of the peculiarities of the particular language to which he is exposed (Bever, 1970; Ervin-Tripp, 1973; Slobin, 1973). In that case individual differences among mothers in the extent to which they (incidentally) produce speech appropriate for the application of such strategies may help or hinder the learner; that is, individual differences in maternal speech style may affect the rate and form of acquisition within some narrow (but nonetheless interesting) constraints. A direct attack on the question of the effect of the linguistic environment on language growth will examine differences among children in ease of acquisition as a result of such individual differences in their mothers' provision of a linguistic environment. This work will be reported elsewhere (Newport, Gleitman, & Gleitman, in press).

Conclusion

It has been demonstrated that Motherese is different from adult-directed speech. Motherese is characterized by brevity, propositional simplicity, and remarkable absence of phonologically and syntactically anomalous utterances; thus it may in fact be simple for communicating messages or for satisfying maternal notions of conversational structure. But the facts do not secure that this difference of Motherese from a haphazard set of utterances will solve the crucial question of how to acquire English from a corpus.

ACKNOWLEDGMENTS

This chapter is based on a doctoral dissertation submitted to the University of Pennsylvania. I wish to thank Lila and Henry Gleitman for their invaluable participation in every conceivable aspect of this work; Marilyn Shatz for her careful reading of an earlier version of this chapter and more generally for the influence her ideas have had in shaping mine; Elizabeth Shipley, John Jonides, and Rochel Gelman for their encouragement, advice, and discussions at a variety of stages along the way. Careful and countless hours of transcribing and analysis were contributed by Suzanne Hale. The research was supported by NIMH Grant #RO23505 to Henry Gleitman and Lila Gleitman and by Spencer Foundation Research awards from the University of Pennsylvania to me. Cross-validation and continued analyses performed during the time of writing this chapter were supported by Academic Senate Research Grant #936 awarded to me by University of California, San Diego.

REFERENCES

Baldwin, A. L., & Frank, S. M. Syntactic complexity in mother–child interactions. Paper presented at the Society for Research in Child Development, March 1969.

Bever, T. G. The cognitive basis for linguistic structures. In J. R. Hayes (Ed.), *Cognition and the development of language.* New York: Wiley, 1970.

Bever, T. G., Fodor, J. A., & Weksel, W. Theoretical notes on the acquisition of syntax: A critique of "Contextual Generalization." *Psychological Review,* 1965, 72, 467–482.

Blount, B. G. Socialization and prelinguistic development among the Luo of Kenya. *Southwest Journal of Anthropology,* 1971, 27, 41–50.

Blount, B. G. Parental speech and language acquisition: Some Luo and Samoan examples. *Anthropological Linguistics,* 1972, 14, 119–130.

Broen, P. A. The verbal environment of the language-learning child. *ASHA Monographs,* 1972, no. 17.

Brown, R. *A first language: The early stages.* Cambridge, Massachusetts: Harvard University Press, 1973.

Brown, R., & Bellugi, U. Three processes in the child's acquisition of syntax. *Harvard Educational Review,* 1964, 34, 133–151.

Brown, R., Cazden, C. B., & Bellugi, U. The child's grammar from I to III. In J. P. Hill (Ed.), *Minnesota Symposium on Child Psychology Vol. II.* Minneapolis: University of Minnesota Press, 1969.

Cazden, C. B. Environmental assistance to the child's acquisition of grammar. Unpublished education doctoral thesis, Harvard University, 1965.

Cazden, C. B. *Child language and education.* New York: Holt, Rinehart & Winston, 1972.

Chomsky, N. *Aspects of the theory of syntax.* Cambridge, Masschuetts: MIT Press, 1965.

Drach, K. M. The language of the parent: A pilot study. Working Paper no. 14, University of California, Berkeley, 1969.

Ervin-Tripp, S. Some strategies for the first two years. In T. E. Moore (Ed.), *Cognitive development and the acquisition of language.* New York: Academic Press, 1973.

Feldman, C. F. The effects of various types of adult response in the syntactic acquisition of 2- to 3-year-olds. Unpublished manuscript, University of Chicago, 1971.

Fodor, J. A. How to learn to talk: Some simple ways. In F. Smith & G. A. Miller (eds.), *The genesis of language.* Cambridge, Massachusetts: MIT Press, 1966.

Fodor, J. A., & Garrett, M. Some syntactic determinants of sentential complexity. *Perception and Psychophysics,* 1967, 2, 289–296.

Fodor, J. A., Bever, T. G., & Garrett, M. *The psychology of language: An introduction to psycholinguistics and generative grammar.* New York: McGraw-Hill, 1974.

Gelman, R. & Shatz, M. Rule-governed variation in children's conversations. Unpublished manuscript, University of Pennsylvania, 1974.

Gelman, R. & Shatz, M. Appropriate speech adjustments: The operation of conversational constraints on talk to two-year-olds. In M. Lewis & L. Rosenblum (eds.), *Communication and language: The origins of behavior.* Vol. V. New York: Wiley, 1976.

Grice, H. P. Logic and conversation. In P. Cole & J. L. Morgan (Eds.), *Syntax and semantics, Vol. 3: Speech acts.* New York: Academic Press, 1975.

Holzman, M. The use of interrogative forms in the verbal interactions of three mothers and their children. *Journal of Psycholinguistic Research,* 1972, 1, 311–336.

Kobashigawa, B. Repetitions in a mother's speech to her child. Working paper No. 14, University of California, Berkeley, 1969.

Labov, W. On the grammaticality of everyday speech. Paper presented at the Linguistic Society of America, 1966.

Nelson, K. *Structure and Strategy in Learning to Talk. SRCD Monographs,* 1973, 38, no. 149.

Nelson, K. E., Carskaddon, G. & Bonvillian, J. D. Syntax acquisition: Impact of environmental acquisition in adult verbal interaction with the child. *Child Development*, 1973, 44, 497–504.

Newport, E. L. Motherese: The speech of mothers to young children. Unpublished doctoral dissertation, University of Pennsylvania, 1975.

Newport, E. L., & Gleitman, H. Maternal self-repetition and the child's acquisition of language. Paper presented at the Boston University Conference on Language Development, 1976.

Newport, E. L., Gleitman, H., & Gleitman, L. R. Mother, I'd rather do it myself: Some effects and non-effects of maternal speech style. In C. Ferguson & C. E. Snow (Eds.), *Talking to children*. Cambridge, England: Cambridge University Press, in press.

Pfuderer, C. Some suggestions for a syntactic characterization of baby talk style. Working paper no. 14, University of California, Berkeley, 1969.

Phillips, J. R. Formal characteristics of speech which mothers address to their young children. Unpublished doctoral dissertation, Johns Hopkins University, 1970.

Phillips, J. R. Syntax and vocabulary of mothers' speech to young children: Age and sex comparisons. *Child Development*, 1973, 44, 182–185.

Remick, H. The maternal environment of linguistic development. Unpublished doctoral dissertation, University of California, Davis, 1971.

Sachs, J., Brown, R., & Salerno, R. Adults' speech to children. Paper presented at the International Symposium on First Language Acquisition, Florence, Italy, 1972.

Sachs, J. & Devin, J. Young children's use of age-appropriate speech styles in social interaction and role-playing. *J. Child Language,* 1976, 3, 81–98.

Searle, J. R. *Speech acts: An essay in the philosophy of language*. Cambridge, England: Cambridge University Press, 1969.

Shatz, M. The comprehension of indirect directives: Can two-year-olds shut the door? Paper presented at the Linguistic Society of America Meeting, 1974 (in *Pragmatics Microfiche,* Dec. 1975).

Shatz, M. How young children respond to language: Procedures for answering. *Papers and Reports on Child Language Development*, 1975, 10, 97–110.

Shatz, M., & Gelman, R. *The Development of Communication Skills: Modifications in the speech of young children as a function of listener. SRCD Monographs*, 1973, 38, no. 152.

Shatz, M., & Gelman, R. Beyond syntax: The influence of conversational rules on speech modifications. In C. Ferguson and C. E. Snow (Eds.), *Talking to children*. Cambridge, England: Cambridge University Press, in press.

Shipley, E. S., Smith, C. S., & Gleitman, L. R. A study in the acquisition of language: Free responses to commands. *Language*, 1969, 45, 322–342.

Skinner, B. F. *Verbal behavior*. New York: Appleton-Century-Crofts, 1957.

Slobin, D. I. Questions of language development in cross-cultural perspective. Working paper no. 14, University of California, Berkeley, 1968. (a)

Slobin, D. I. Recall of full and truncated passives in connected discourse. *Journal of Verbal Learning and Verbal Behavior*, 1968, 1, 876–881. (b)

Slobin, D. I. Cognitive prerequisites for the development of grammar. In C. Ferguson and D. Slobin (Eds.), *Studies of child language development*. New York: Holt, Rinehart & Winston, 1973.

Snow, C. E. Mothers' speech to children learning language. *Child Development*, 1972, 43, 549–565.

Snow, C. E., Arlman-Rupp, A., Hassing, Y., Jobse, J., Joosten, J., & Vorster, J. Mothers' speech in three social classes. *Journal of Psycholinguistic Research,* 1976, 5, 1–20.

Snow, C. E. Mothers' speech research: An overview. In C. Ferguson & C. E. Snow (Eds.), *Talking to children*. Cambridge, England: Cambridge University Press, in press.

8
How Young Children Reason about Small Numbers

Rochel Gelman

University of Pennsylvania

INTRODUCTION

There is now considerable evidence that preschool-aged children can form accurate number-based representations of set sizes of 1–4 and sometimes 5 (Beckmann, 1924; Descoudres, 1921; Gelman, 1972a; Gelman & Tucker, 1975; Lawson, Baron, & Siegel, 1974; Smither, Smiley, & Rees, 1974). The conclusion that the representation is number based rests on the fact that the child's response—be it an absolute judgement, choice, construction of a set like the standard, etc.—can be shown to be independent of the linear extent of an array, the relative density of items in an array, and the kinds, for example, heterogeneous versus homogeneous, in an array. In other words, where care is taken to control for the possibility that the child might use nonnumerical criteria, the child is still able to perform successfully, indicating thereby an ability to use a number-based criterion.

It is now clear that the young child is able to respond to the numerosity per se of the array. This is not to say that he will always base his responses on the number of items in the array and do so without difficulty. Even within the range of 1–5 items, the larger the set the less the tendency for the young child to focus on a number-based criterion (Gelman, 1972a) or assign the correct number word (Gelman & Tucker, 1975). And the extent to which the child is influenced by heterogeneity is clearly related to experimental conditions (Gelman & Tucker, 1975; Siegel, 1973). The point simply is that the young child *can* and often does form accurate number-based representations of small sets. This is to be contrasted with the fact that larger set sizes (6 or more items) are seldom represented in terms of their numerosity. A number of investigators have documented

TABLE 1
Number of Subjects out of 48 Who Gave Correct Absolute
Judgment[a]

Age and exposure time	Number of items in display						
	2	3	4	5	7	11	19
3 years							
1 sec	33	28	9	8	1	0	0
5 sec	41	38	21	16	10	1	0
1 min	41	40	28	27	20	16	5
4 years							
1 sec	44	37	23	17	4	2	1
5 sec	44	41	29	21	11	3	1
1 min	45	42	37	32	19	19	7
5 years							
1 sec	47	43	33	23	9	6	1
5 sec	44	44	37	26	19	8	2
1 min	47	46	42	38	27	19	8

[a]Details of the procedure used to obtain these data are in Gelman and Tucker (1975). The data for set sizes 2–5 were reported in that paper; those for set sizes 7, 11, and 19 are reported here for the first time.

the young child's tendency to judge the larger arrays on the basis of their length (e.g. Gelman, 1972a; Piaget, 1952; Smither *et al.*, 1974). And we find a marked decrease in the young child's ability to give accurate answers when judging the absolute number of items contained in larger arrays—even when they are given one minute to answer (See Table 1).

Why the Small Number Limit?

The fact that the young child's ability to form number based representations appears to be limited to the small number range has led to the suggestion that the young child's concept of number is "intuitive" or "perceptual" (e.g., Pufall, Shaw, & Syrdal-Lasky, 1973; Gast, 1957). My understanding of this position is two-fold: First there is the view that young children represent the number of items in an array by means of a direct perceptual apprehension mechanism, sometimes referred to as subitizing (e.g., Neisser, 1967). Second, there is the idea that young children have yet to develop an ability to reason about numbers, to understand say, that there are transformations under which the numerosity of a set remains invariant.

The hypothesis that young children might subitize the numerosity of small arrays derives in part from the assumption that adults do. In a summary of evidence from experiments on adult judgments of various set sizes (e.g., Jensen, Reese, & Reese, 1950; Kaufman, Lord, Reese, & Volkmann, 1949; Saltzman & Garner, 1948), Klahr (1973) draws attention to two factors. Adult subjects respond more quickly to small set sizes than they do large set sizes ($N \geqslant 5$ or 6). Further the reaction time (RT) function is different for the two ranges. The slope of the RT function in the small range is widely assumed to be flat (Neisser, 1967). Although upon close inspection it is not flat, it is indeed shallow—on the order of 40 msec per item (Klahr, 1973). In contrast, the slope for set sizes that are larger than five is on the order of 300 msec per item (Klahr, 1973). Figure 1 presents a schematic plot of these results. Klahr and Wallace (1973), like others (e.g., Neisser, 1967) use the difference in slopes to infer the working of different processes when subjects represent arrays of small set sizes as opposed to large set sizes. Small sets are subitized, larger sets are counted. According to Klahr and Wallace, the slight increase in the time needed to respond to each successive set size in the small number range reflects the time to retrieve the verbal label from the serial list of small number words. Thus, it is implicitly assumed that the time taken to represent each of the stimulus sets within this range is constant.

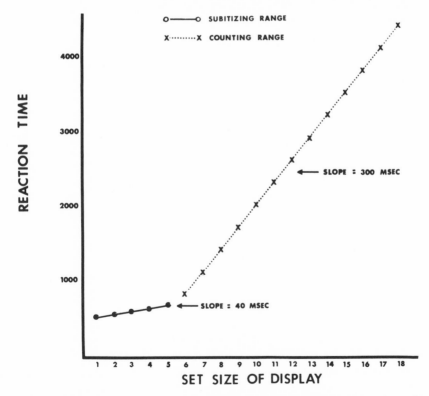

FIG. 1   Schematic presentation of the relationship between reaction time and set size. (Based on Klahr, 1973.)

Presumably then, the representation of number within this range involves a perceptual process akin to a direct apprehension one. In contrast, the authors assume that the representation process of large sets involves a counting mechanism. The counting mechanism "requires the coordination of processes that notice each object while generating the sequence of number names. When there are no more objects to be noticed, the current name is assigned to the collection of objects" (Klahr & Wallace, 1973, p. 305).

Putting together the findings that young children can represent the number of small sets but have difficulty with large sets, the inference can be made that young children subitize before they count (Klahr & Wallace, 1973). The young child's ability to deal with small numbers reflects the working of the subitizing process; their inability to deal with large numbers represents their failure to count. Presumably then, small numbers are not counted. But is this the case? The answer appears to be no.

Some years ago Beckmann (1924) advanced the hypothesis that the young child counts to represent a given small number before he shifts to relying on a subitizing-like process. Beckmann cited the fact that the younger the child, the greater his tendency to count aloud when answering questions about the number of items in an array. And I (Gelman, 1972a) noted a tendency for three- and four-year-olds to count aloud in order to determine whether unexpected variations in the properties of small sets (e.g. increases in length or number) corresponded to an actual change in number.

Counting-aloud data do not allow one to conclude that the child who counts fails to use a perceptual process like subitizing when estimating small numbers (Klahr & Wallace, 1973). They do however indicate that a young child *can* and *will* count in order to estimate. Indeed, it now seems to be the case that young children are better able to estimate small sets when tested under conditions which maximize their chances of using a counting procedure (Gelman & Tucker, 1975). Thus, for example when 3-year-olds are required to indicate how many things are in linear two-dimensional arrays of 2, 3, 4, or 5 items, the longer the exposure time of the array, the greater the accuracy scores. And, as might be expected, the greater their tendency to count aloud.

Thus, the fact that the preschooler's ability to represent numbers is limited does not appear to be due to their inability to use a counting procedure. I suspect that the assumption that the small number limit reflects a reliance on a perceptual process is what underlies Piaget's assumption that the young child's understanding of number is intuitive and not governed by a set of reasoning principles. The remainder of this chapter is given over to the presentation of my view that, even though the young child's manifested understanding of small number may be limited to the small number range, the nature of the understanding is a highly abstract one: one that contains many of the fundamental components of arithmetic reasoning. I will review the evidence on how young children reason about small numbers and outline the reasoning principles that must be available to the young child in light of these data.

A Number Reasoning Task for Young Children

Much of the evidence on how young children reason about small numbers comes from a series of "magic" experiments that I have conducted, some of which have been reported elsewhere (Gelman, 1972a, b; Gelman & Tucker, 1975) and some of which will be summarized here for the first time. Accordingly, I begin by summarizing the basic experimental paradigm. A fuller description is available in Gelman 1972b.

In all cases, the procedure involves a two-phase experiment. In the first phase, children are shown two plates containing different numbers of small plastic toys, for example, one rabbit on one plate and two rabbits on the other plate or three mice on one plate and five mice on the other plate. The experimenter designates one of these plates "the winner" while simply pointing to it—making *no reference to number*. The other plate is designated the "loser," again there is no reference to number. Phase 1 then continues as an identification game. The plates are covered with cans and the cans are shuffled. If a child appears to be keeping track of the covered winner, as in a shell game, the shuffling continues until the child appears to have lost track. When the shuffling stops, the child is asked to guess where the winner is, then lift this chosen can and verify the correctness or incorrectness of his guess. In the event that he has guessed incorrectly and recognizes this, that is, says that the uncovered plate is in fact the designated loser, he is immediately allowed to uncover the other plate. When the other plate is uncovered, he is again asked if it is the winner. The child's identification receives immediate feedback from the experimenter. If a child erroneously identified a "loser as the "winner," the experimenter says "no, that's the loser," covers the plates up again and begins reshuffing them. Whenever the child correctly identifies the winner plate as the winner, he receives verbal feedback and a prize. Then, the plates are recovered and reshuffled; the child is encouraged to help with the shuffling on half of the trials.

It should be emphasized that the feedback is based on the child's correct or incorrect identification of a plate once he has uncovered it and *not* upon his guesses. Each uncovering of a plate is counted as a trial. Thus, when a child uncovers the loser plate, correctly identifies it as such and then uncovers the winner plate, that sequence counts as two trials. The purpose of running what is basically an identification experiment in the form of a game is twofold: Firstly, the game-like nature of the task is extremely effective in engaging the young child's interest. Secondly, it builds a strong trial-to-trial expectation for one set on one plate and the other set on the other plate.

The first phase of the experiment, which we have just described, continues for at least 11 trials. On three of these trials, the child is asked to justify his identification. This serves to determine what the child takes to be the definitive properties of the sets. As reported elsewhere, the child's answers to these probes makes it clear that he almost always defines the sets in terms of their *numerosity* and he does so spontaneously. Thus, despite the fact that the experimenter makes no mention of number, the child says a plate wins (or loses) because it contains a given number of items (e.g., "It wins because it has three, 1–2–3.")

The second phase of the experiment begins when the experimenter *surreptitiously* alters some property of one or both of the expected sets. In some experiments the experimenter alters the spatial arrangement of one set, making it long and less dense or shorter and more dense. In other experiments, the experimenter alters the color or identity of one of the elements in one of the expected sets. And in still other experiments, the experimenter alters the number of elements in one or both of the expected sets, by adding or subtracting one or more elements.

From the child's standpoint, Phase 2 is just a continuation of Phase 1—until he discovers that neither plate contains a set that is identical in every way to what had been the winner set. In Phase 2 the child is also asked to identify the plates as "winner" or "loser." When the child has uncovered the altered winner plate, he is asked a series of questions: Which plate is the "winner" and why; has anything happened and if so, what; how many objects are presently on the plates, how many objects used to be on the plates; can the game proceed; does the game need fixing, and if so how it can be fixed. If the child says the game has to be fixed and suggests he needs certain items in order to do so, he is given a handful of items that include what he needs to fix the game plus several additional items.

Everything the child says is tape-recorded for later transcription. The experimenter also rates the degree of the child's surprise in Phase 2 on a 3-point rating scale (0 = no discernible surprise; 1 = some surprise; 2 = very surprised) and makes notes about any striking aspect of the child's behavior, for example, search behavior. The criteria for assigning a surprise score can be found in Gelman (1972b).

We treat the way the child responds to the surreptitious changes introduced in Phase 2 as our basic evidence for drawing conclusions about the nature of the young child's ability to reason about number. For it provides the opportunity for the child to respond to these changes in a way that involves the integration of his representation of the Phase 2 events with his established representation of the Phase 1 events. Thus for example, the child who confronts an unexpected change in number can (and does) postulate the intervention of addition or subtraction operations (e.g. "Another mice came!") to explain the discrepancy between the expected and encountered events. And reasoning about number involves the ability to integrate and relate numerical representations, one to another. Given that the child does integrate the events of Phase 1 and Phase 2, the way in which he does so can provide insight into the nature of his reasoning principles. For presumably it is the availability of reasoning principles that allows the child to decide how events x and y can be tied together.

As we have shown (e.g., Gelman 1972a; Gelman & Tucker, 1975) young children do treat the sets they encounter in Phase 2 in terms of numerical expectancies developed during Phase 1 and transformation that might have occurred between the two phases. Changes in the expected set that do *not* involve changes in number, for example, lengthening, shortening, substitution of an item of another color or identity, are often noticed. Yet they are typically classified as irrelevant with respect to number, as evidenced by the statements to the effect that the plate is still the winner-plate because it has the expected number and that the change does not matter. In contrast changes in the expected sets that *do* involve changes in number, for example, addition or subtraction are typically classified as relevant to number. For the children indicate that the altered Phase 2 set is no longer the winner-plate because it has a different number, one larger or smaller than the expected number. Moreover, they explain the change in terms of the number-relevant operations that they say must have intervened (e.g., "It's 1−2−3, three now, was two! Another one flew in. How did that happen?")

Further evidence that the event encountered in Phase 2 is integrated with the expectancy carried forward from Phase 1 comes from the children's responses to questions about fixing the game. The majority of subjects who have participated in our magic experiments are able to provide accounts as to how they (or someone else) could alter the set in a way as to make it like the original one. This is illustrated in the following protocol:

D.S. (4,7) (The subject participated in the Gelman & Tucker, 1975, experiment which involved starting with a 3-item heterogeneous—two green mice and a soldier—and a 2-item homogeneous array—two green mice. The 3-item array was designated the winner. In Phase 2 it was altered to produce a 3-item homogeneous array—three green mice.)
(Experimenter asks subject)
You take this (a mouse) *off and put on a soldier. Where's a soldier?* (Experimenter gives subject extra objects, including soldiers). *"How about two winner ones?"* (*S* places the soldier on the 2-mouse plate and says:) *"This is gonna be a winner plate too. Both have three things."*

Given that children as young as three (and sometimes two and a half) years provide such evidence, the question becomes; what is the nature of the young child's numerical reasoning? I organize the answer to this question in terms of the kinds of reasoning principles that guide the young child's ability to integrate numerical representations vis-à-vis the potential or actual effects of transformations.

THE REASONING PRINCIPLES

In this section I outline the set of arithmetic reasoning principles available to the young child. The reasoning principles that I grant the young child can be divided into three categories: (1) the relations; (2) operators; and (3) principles of "reversibility." It is my view that the observed behavior of the young child warrants the assumption that he organizes numerical comparisons in terms of the relations of equality and order; that he can classify many of the transformations that can be performed on a set as either identity preserving operations or the number changing operations of addition and subtraction; and that he has a principle of solvability which enables him to undo the effects of addition and subtraction. The latter principle and knowledge about events that can serve to cancel the effects of irrelevant transformations allow the child to relate reversible operations that can be performed on sets.

Before returning to a detailed treatment of these particular principles, it is well to indicate the domain of our inferences. The assumption that these principles are available is based on the behavioral evidence at hand. If the child's behavior is such as to warrant the granting of that principle, then the principle is granted. This is done on the assumption that the behavior could not occur were there no such principle available to the child.

Despite the fact that I require some behavioral evidence before granting a reasoning principle, I do *not* require the child to pass all potential tasks that embody that principle. As long as the child manages to perform successfully on a task in which his probability of doing so would be zero under assumption of no competence, I see no choice but to grant at least some competence. An illustrative case might be helpful.

As stated I am concerned with the question of whether preschoolers have any arithmetic reasoning principles. For the sake of argument, let us take the position that they do not. One might conclude that preschoolers lack arithmetic reasoning principles on the basis of their performance on a number conservation task, a task which they fail (Piaget, 1952). In the conservation task the child is typically shown two arrays of N items each. When the perceptual features of the array, for example, length and spacing between items are identical the young child admits to numerical equivalence. But when the perceptual properties of one array are altered, for example, one row is made longer, the young child denies that the numerosities of the arrays are still equivalent. One might conclude on the basis of such results that the young child lacks the reasoning principles that make it possible for him to treat number as invariant. But does he? In the magic experiment we demonstrate that a child of this age says a *noted* change in the length of a set of objects does not change the number therein. Further he says that addition and subtraction do change number, the former serving to increase and the latter to decrease the number of objects in an array. Add to this the fact that he never saw the transformations being performed. Rather he confronted length and number changes when he was expecting no such changes. To explain them, he himself *postulates* the intervention of the various transformations. It would seem impossible for him to do all of this without the availability of some reasoning principle(s) and supporting process(es) which organize his responses to number. He may not know how to pass the number conservation task but he obviously has some ability to treat number as invariant. What is the nature of this ability?

The Relations

In describing the quantitative relationships between the Phase 1 and Phase 2 winner-displays that children confront in the magic paradigm, the children decide that they either contain the same number and (are therefore both winners) or different numbers. If they decide the Phase 2 numerosity deviates from that encountered in Phase 1, they also indicate the direction of the deviation. Therefore I assume that when young children compare small sets x and y they recognize that the numerosities of the sets are either equal or not. If not, that is, if $x \neq y$, the children recognize that x and y satisfy an ordering relation $(>)$ such that $x > y$ or $y > x$. The evidence for assuming the availability of these reasoning principles is as follows.

Equality. In reasoning about number, the young child recognizes numerical identity. That is, he recognizes that his representation of the numerosity of one set (the expected one) is identical to his representation of the numerosity of another set. As an immediate consequence of the recognition of identity in numerical representations, the child recognizes a numerical equivalence between sets. The evidence that children recognize an equality relation in the number domain comes primarily from those magic experiments in which the "winning" array was transformed in a fashion that was irrelevant to number. In these experiments, children unexpectedly encountered arrays (varying in set size from 2 to 5 items) that had been lengthened or shortened, or that had an item of different color or kind substituted for one of the original items. In nearly all cases, children regarded the altered array as equivalent to the original array, that is, as still the "winner." When those children who noticed the transformation were probed as to the justification for their judgment of equality, they characteristically indicated that, although some attributes of the array had changed, the number had remained the same. In other words, the reason that the altered array was the same as the original array was based on the equality of their numerosities. Thus children for example would say, "They moved out. It still wins. It's three now and it was three before."

A second line of evidence that children recognize an equivalence relation in the number domain comes from one of the studies reported by Gelman and Tucker (1975). When asked to reverse an identity change transformation, half the subjects ended up constructing *two* perceptually dissimilar arrays whose numerosities were equivalent to the numerosity of the original winner plate and said that they now had two "winners" because both had the same number as the expected "winner" plate. (See D.S.'s protocol on page 225). Notice here that the children were spontaneously constructing an equivalence based on numerosity and not simply recognizing it.

If an equality relation did not form part of the principles that guide the child's reasoning about numerosity it is difficult to understand what would lead the child to say that the numerosity of the altered set was equal to the numerosity of the original set. It would be even more difficult to understand the child's constructing a further set (out of heterogeneous items) that was equivalent in number but few, if any, other properties. Thus I assume that the child's behavior is guided by a principle which says that two numerosities may or may not satisfy an equality relation.

The assumption that an equality relation forms part of the child's reasoning principles leaves entirely open the procedure or algorithm by which the child decides whether two numerosities that he has encountered in the real world do or do not satisfy the relation. I am inclined to the position that judgments of numerical equality (and nonequality) in the magic task rest on a counting procedure.[1] For there is a noticeable tendency for the children to count when they encounter the altered array (Gelman, 1972a) and/or where they are asked to justify their judgments. As an illustration consider the answer of E.B. (3,11) who participated in a displacement condition of an experiment using a 5-mouse plate as the winner. He encountered a shortened 5-mouse plate in Phase 2 and when he did, said:

They crushed together. (Is it the winner?) *Yes.* (Why?)
Because 1–2–3–4–5... . Were 5. Now is 5.

Similarly children tended to confirm judgments of nonequivalence by a counting procedure as did T.P. (3,9) who said: "Can I count? 1–2–3 . . . Supposed to be 1–2–3–4 . . ." Given that they are able to make judgments of numerical nonequality, it seems reasonable to suppose they might also be able to indicate the direction of the nonequality, that is, indicate which of two arrays represents the larger set size.

Order. It appears that preschool children in fact recognize that when numerosities are not numerically equivalent, then they are numerically ordered. In other words, given two numerical representations (x and y) of two nonequivalent sets so that $x \neq y$, the child assumes that either x is more than y or y is more than x. That is the child behaves as if an ordering relation ($>$) holds between two nonequivalent numerosities.

---

[1] Briefly, by the counting procedure we mean the integration of (a) a one–one principle which regulates the assignment of unique tags; (b) a repeatable order principle which regulates the order of tag assignment; (c) a cardinal principle which governs the assignment of a representation to the set; and (d) a principle which serves to define what is to be counted.

Some of the evidence for this statement comes from the magic experiments in which the "winning" plate was transformed by either addition or subtraction of elements. In all of these studies children not only recognized the resulting inequality, they gave unequivocal evidence of recognizing what might be called the direction of inequality. When items had been subtracted, the children's comments and repair behavior showed that they recognized the transformed array was less than the original array. When items had been added the children understood that the transformed array was more than the original array (Gelman, 1972a, b).

Further evidence for postulating that the young child appreciates an ordering relation comes from an experiment that Merry Bullock and I are conducting this year. Again the magic paradigm is employed. In Phase 1, children are shown a 1-mouse and 2-mouse plate. Half the subjects in each age group (3- and 4-year-olds) are told the 1-mouse plate (less) wins and half are told the 2-mouse plate (more) wins. As before, there is no mention of number or quantity during Phase 1. The children spontaneously identify the winner and loser on the basis of number for example "that loses, it has 2; that wins, it has 1." In the magic phase subjects encounter a 3-mouse and a 4-mouse plate. The question is whether subjects will decide that the winner plate can be the one that honors the relationships of "more" or "less" (depending on which one they were reinforced for). The answer is yes. So far we have run 43 children between the ages of 3,0 and 4,11; all but seven decided that the "winner" plate was the one which honored the quantitative relation they were originally reinforced for. In other words, children who were reinforced for the 1-item plate in Phase 1 said the 3-mouse plate won in Phase 2; likewise those children who were initially reinforced for the 2-item array chose the 4-item array in Phase 2. There was no effect of age or reinforcement condition ($<$ or $>$) on choice behavior. Thus the children inferred that the numerical ordering relations between the winning and losing plates in Phase 1 could be generalized in Phase 2.[2]

Siegel (1974) showed that preschoolers can consistently respond to a $<$ or $>$ number relationship in a discrimination learning paradigm, indicating an ability for subjects of this age to recognize the ordering relation between simultaneously present arrays. The Bullock and Gelman experiment confirms Siegel's results. In addition, it indicates that 3- and 4-year-old children can use an ordering relation in an inferential manner. For, despite the fact that they initially judged the winning and losing arrays on the basis of their absolute set

---

[2] Although there was no effect of reinforcement condition or age as measured by choice behavior, one other response did show effects of these variables. Generally, when children were asked to explain their choices they were unable to do so. Still, 8 children (6 of whom were 4-year-olds) were able to provide answers that involved the use of relational terms. Given that such a term was used, it was used by the older children in the 'more' condition. Only one of these children referred to "less" in their justification; the rest referred to "more", "many", "a lot."

size they made Phase 2 choices solely on the basis of the ordering relation. When confronted with the fact that neither Phase 2 array was of the same absolute value as expected, the children chose that array which honored the same relationship as did the original winner. It should be noted that although this is an inference based upon the recognition of an ordering relation, it need not be taken as an instance of a transitive inference (Gelman & Gallistel, in preparation).

In sum, when comparing small sets young children recognize that their numerosities are either equal or not. If the sets are *not* numerically equivalent, then in the child's reasoning: If $x < y$, then the set with x items is more numerous; if $y > x$, then the set with y items is more numerous. The representations x and y appear to involve the use of a counting procedure.

The Operations

As just indicated, the magic experiments show that the child has certain numerical reasoning principles that integrate his previous experience with present experience. The recognition of numerical equivalence and order form an important part of these principles, in that they organize comparisons between present and past experiences. However, the young child's reasoning about numerosities is not limited to the drawing of comparisons. The child interprets the results of these comparisons by means of a scheme that categorizes possible real world manipulations into number-relevant and number-irrelevant ones. The possible number-relevant manipulations are subcategorized into ones that decrease and increase numerosity. The recognition that a given array is now either, more than, less than, or equivalent to the original numerosity leads the child to postulate the intervention of an operation drawn from the appropriate class in the operation classification scheme. Thus judgments of equivalence go hand in hand with reference to manipulations that do not affect numerosity and judgments of nonequivalence go along with the postulation of manipulations that do affect numerosity; judgments of nonequivalence go along with the postulation of manipulations that do affect numerosity. Since the categorization of possible manipulations in this way plays much the same role in the child's reasoning that the operations play in formal treatments of arithmetic, we refer to these categories as *operators* (cf. Gelman, 1972a).

Identity. As the magic experiments (e.g. Gelman, 1972a; Gelman & Tucker, 1975) have demonstrated, when children reason about numerosity, they recognize that there exists a large class of operations (manipulations) that can be performed on a set without altering the numerosity of the set. When called upon to explain unexpected spatial rearrangements, color changes, and item substitutions, they postulate operations having no effect on numerosity. When probed, the children will typically state that these operations do not affect numerosity.

Thus the children recognize that there exists a class of operations (which I will symbolize, I) and that whenever a member of this class of operations operates on a set, the numerosity of the set is not changed. It is appropriate to emphasize here that the child's behavior does not always demonstrate the existence of such a classification scheme in his number reasoning. For example, in the well-known experiments of Piaget (1952) children do not give evidence of recognizing number identity operators. However, in the magic experiments young children clearly do recognize the existence of number-identity operations, that is, operations which do not alter number.

We do not know the limits of the class of identity operators in the young child. In the adult, this class has no limit since it includes all operations except for those few that are specifically assigned to the class of number altering operations. We know that, for the young child, surreptitious transformations involving the lengthening or shortening of a linear array, changing the color, and/or identity or an item in the array are all explained in terms of identity operators. Thus, the class of identity operators is already quite extensive.

Addition and subtraction. As mentioned in the introductory remarks on operators, the young child's numerical reasoning also involves recognition of operators that *do* alter numerosity, that is, operations that are distinct from the class of identity operators. These are the operations of addition and subtraction. As summarized in Gelman (1972a; 1972b), when young children confront an unexpected increase in numerosity they postulate the intervention of addition. In other words, they state that something must have been added. Similarly in the subtraction experiments they say that something must have been removed. And that the children know that these operations alter number in a systematic way, that is, to increase or decrease it, is further demonstrated by their repair behavior. When asked how to "fix" the effect of addition they indicate that a subtraction operation is called for; likewise the effect of a subtraction operation can be repaired by adding. The following protocol demonstrates the kind of results we are referring to here.

V.B. (4,4) (Subject participated in subtraction condition of an unpublished experiment involving a 5-mouse and a 3-mouse plate in Phase 1. The 5-mouse plate was the winner and changed to a 3-mouse plate in Phase 2).

Phase 1: (Why win?) *Case there's 1–2–3–4–5.* (Why lose?) *Cause 1–2–3!*
Phase 2: (Uncovers first 3-mouse plate. Win?) *No . . . 3 mouses.* (Okay which plate wins?) She points to remaining can and lifts it. (Win?) *Wait! There's 1–2–3* (Is that the plate that wins?) *No?* (Why?) *Because it has 3. It has 3!* (What happened)? *Must have disappeared!* (What?) *The other mouses.* (Where did they disappear from?) *One was here and one was here.* She points to spaces on the nontransformed plate.–(How many now?) *1–2–3*

(How many at beginning of game)? *There was 1 there, 1 there, 1 there, 1 there, there 1.* (How many?) *5—this one is 3 not but before it was 5—*(V. what would you need to fix the game?) *I'm not really sure because my brother is real big and he could tell* (What do you think he would need?) *Well, I don't know . . . Some things come back.* (Experimenter hands V. some objects including four mice.) V. puts all four mice on one plate. *There.. Now there's 1–2–3–4–5–6–7! No . . . I'll take these* (points to two) *off and we'll see how many.* V. Removes one and counts *1–2–3–4–5, no 1–2–3–4, Uh . . . there were 5, right?* (Experimenter says right.) *I'll put this one here* (on table), *then we 'll see how many there is now.* V. takes one off and counts *1–2–3–4–5. 5! 5.*

V. B's protocol does more than demonstrate her understanding of the role of subtraction vis-à-vis number. It also illustrates the young child's organized use of the reasoning principles. For V.B. clearly stored in memory a representation of the expected numerosity of the winner-plate. When confronted with the altered array, she obtained a representation of its numerosity. She compared the numerosity of the altered array with the stored representation of the numerosity of the winner-plate. She "decided" that the equivalence relation did not hold between these two representations of number. This decision was yoked to the conclusion that some items had been removed or "disappeared." And she revealed her knowledge about the relationship between addition and subtraction, and how they serve to undo each other.

That the children behave as if they know that addition and subtraction cancel each other leads us to postulate the availability of a reasoning principle that allows the child to "reverse" the effects of operations.

The Solvability Principle

In the magic experiments, children encountered sets whose numerosity was either more than (the addition experiments), less than (the subtraction experiments) or the same as (the displacement, color and identity change experiments) the numerosity they expected. As noted, the children reliably indicate the nature of noted discrepancies, the operations that cause a change and whether the change is relevant or irrelevant to number. I now turn attention to the fact that the children know how to eliminate the discrepancies encountered.

When asked to "fix" discrepancies, the children make cogent suggestions, ones that they are typically able to carry out. For example, children indicate that a decrease in length, "they squeezed together" can be undone by an increase in length "if you spread them out."

Or when they encounter a red mouse instead of the expected green mouse, they suggest the need for a further substitution, this time of a green mouse for the red mouse present in Phase 2. That the children know how to undo the effects of number-irrelevant transformations indicates an ability to organize various nonnumerical transformations that can be applied to events. Such knowledge in its own right does not allow us to conclude that young children know that the operations of addition and subtraction reverse each other or how such knowledge might be used. These issues require that we focus on the manner in which our subjects proceed to repair the effects of unexpected additions or subtractions.

When confronted with the discrepancy between an actual numerosity (represented as x) and an expected numerosity (y) subjects show that they know that x can be converted into the original numerosity (y) by the application of either an addition or subtraction operation. When $x < y$ they specify the need to add; when $x > y$ they talk about and engage in subtraction. In cases where addition or subtraction are called for and the difference between x and y is equal to 1 (as in all or our published experiments), the children specify not only the operation (addition or subtraction) the is appropriate but also the number of items (1) to be added or subtracted.

This latter observation, that is, subjects specify that addition (or subtraction) of 1 item is cancelled by the subtraction (or addition) of 1 item, might be taken as evidence for the position that children of this age already know that the addition or subtraction of a given number of items, x, is uniquely cancelled by the application of the reverse operation on a set size of x. This would amount to assuming that young children have a precise notion of the inverse, an assumption which I am not prepared to make. For me to take this position I would have to be able to demonstrate that young children know not only that one item has been added (or subtracted) but likewise the exact number that has been added (or subtracted) when $x > 1$. However, I have evidence to the contrary. When the difference between the expected and encountered numerosities becomes greater than 1, the children *can* indicate that some number of items greater than 1 must be added or subtracted *but* they are far from precise about the exact value of the number required. This is demonstrated in a magic study that I have already referred to here but have not published yet. Therefore I briefly summarize the details of what I call the 3 versus 5 study.

Summary of the 3 versus 5, take away 2, study. Fifty-four (30 3-year-olds and 24 4-year-olds) children were tested in Phase 1 of the magic experiment. In this phase, a 3-mouse plate, consisting of 3 green mice in a linear row, served as the "loser." A 5-mouse plate, consisting of 5 green mice in a row was identified as the "winner." As in other experiments, the difference in number was redundant to either a difference in length or density. Whether the items on each plate

TABLE 2

Summary of Phase 2 Reactions in 3 versus 5, Take Away 2 Magic Experiment

Condition and age	N	Who say they win (%)	Correct on why win or lose[a] (%)	Searchers (%)	Surprise score[b] ($\bar{X}$)	Who notice change[c] (%)	Noticers who adequately explain change[d] (%)
Subtraction							
3 years	16	12.5	75.0	68.8	1.22	93.7	80.0
4 years	16	0.0	100.0	87.5	1.44	100.0	93.7
Displacement							
3 years	8	100.0	87.5	0.0	.88	50.0	75.0
4 years	8	100.0	100.0	0.0	.88	100.0	75.0

[a]Subject is counted here only if indicates number has or has not changed from expected $N = 5$.

[b]Maximum score for subject is 2 on scale of 0 (no discernible surprise), 1 (some noticeable surprise) or 2 (very noticeable surprise).

[c]As evidenced by *any* indication of noticing, for example, surprise, explicit statement, hesitation or negative statement about the winner's status.

[d]The subject has to indicate the nature of the intervening transformations.

had the same or different distance between them was counterbalanced. Six of the 3-year-olds were dropped after Phase 1 for failing to reach the criterion of five out of six correct identifications. This left an equal number of children in each age group with the respective median ages being 3 years, 7 months and 4 years, 7 months.

Of the remaining 48 subjects, 32 were assigned to subtraction and 16 to displacement conditions and this was done so that there were equal numbers from each age group. Children in the subtraction conditions encountered a winning plate that had 3 mice, that is, two less than expected. Whether the items were removed from the ends of the original row of the second and fourth positions of the original row was counterbalanced. Children in the displacement conditions encountered a shortened or lengthened row, a factor which was also counterbalanced. All remaining details of the procedure were as outlined in the introduction. Phase 1 results compare to those we find in other studies. Thirty-four of the children made no identification errors at all. The mean number of errors for the 8 3-year-olds who erred at least once was 1.4; the mean error score for the 6 4-year-olds who erred was 1.5. As in previous experiments, there was a striking tendency for the children to spontaneously define the "winner" and "loser" in terms of their absolute number. All but six children (three in each age group) talked in terms of their numerosity. Clearly the children established an expectancy for number. How did they react to the unexpected changes they encountered in Phase 2?

In most ways, the children who participated in this experiment treated the Phase 2 events just like children who participated in other displacement versus subtraction experiments. As shown in Table 2, displacement children treated the effects of this transformation as irrelevant. They said they still won because the number of items was as expected; if they noticed the change in length they could suggest an operation that produced it. Children in the subtraction condition treated the surreptitious change in number to be a violation of their expectancy for the 5-mouse plate as winner. The altered array did not win because it only had three items; the change in number produced considerable surprise and search behavior; and it was assumed that somehow items were removed from the Phase 1 display (see V.B.'s protocol above). Thus the children behaved as we expected; they revealed an ability to make inferences about the sorts of operations that could produce the transformations they encountered.

I introduced the presentation of this 3 versus 5 take away 2, experiment by summarizing one way in which the results of this experiment differed from those in which the intervening subtraction or addition involved only one item. In the experiments where we removed or added one item, children were precise about the size of the deviation. Furthermore, they were precise about the number of items—one—that needed to be added or subtracted to "fix" the game. In the current experiment, where they expected a set size of five and encountered one with only three items, they were nowhere near as precise on these counts. They knew *some* items had been removed and generally gave evidence of knowing that it was more than one item that was missing. Thus in one of several ways 26 of 32 subtraction children talked of more than 1 missing item e.g. *"They* gone.," *"Some* came out."; "Has to be *some more."* Yet only six children could state that terms like *they, some,* and *some more* had the specific numerical reference of *two.* In other words the ability to compute, in their head, the specific number required to solve for the difference seems to be poorly developed in preschool children. Yet, that they clearly recognize that the difference can *in principle* be solved for, is shown in the way they "fix" the game.

When asked how to go about fixing the game, all but two children indicated the need to add some items. When given four mice, only four children knew to take just two of them. The rest began by taking a variable number, be it one, three or four and placing that number on a display. What followed was a sequence of counting, adding, or subtracting, counting, etc.,—much like that illustrated in V.B.'s protocol. Eventually a total of 11 of 16, 4-year-olds produced a five item array and declared it like the original. Only 4 3-year-olds met this criterion. Despite the fact that many children did not end up with a 5-mouse plate, all but three ended up with a "winning" array that had more than 3 items, arrays ranging from 4 to 7 in set size. Thus although the children knew to add items they did not necessarily know exactly how many were needed to repair the game.

Implications of the 3 versus 5 repair behavior: A principle of solvability. What does the above experiment add to our understanding of the young child's arithmetic principles? It shows that the principle that guided the young child's repair behavior in the initial magic experiments was not limited to differences of only one. Despite the fact that young children are not very good at specifying larger differences, they are able to indicate in some way that it is a difference that is greater than 1. Further they know how to begin to remove the difference. Thus in the present experiment almost all of the children in the subtraction condition knew that they should add some items. Not knowing the exact number they typically proceeded through a trial and error sequence of adding/subtracting and counting.

I hesitate to take these results as evidence for granting the children a precise concept of the inverse. Still, there is much in the behavior that warrants the postulation of some principle of reversibility, that is, some principle which leads the child to recognize that addition is what undoes the effect of subtraction and to furthermore proceed to attempt to alter the arrays in a systematic fashion. What then is the simplest principle that explains the repair behavior? I think it is a *principle of solvability,* or the "you can get there from here" principle. Put more formally, this is a principle which states the following: *given two sets* S_n *and* S_m *such that* $n < m$, *there exists a set* S_e *that when added to* S_n *will produce* S_m *and there exists a proper subset* S_d *of* S_m *that when subtracted from* S_m *will produce* S_n.

If I had evidence that the children thought the numerosity of S_e to be equal to that of S_d, I could say that they have a precise concept of the inverse. This is a question for further research. For now, the solvability principle as stated simply requires the child know to add and subtract to solve for a difference. It leaves unspecified the exact size of the difference. One might ask how it is the child arrives at the difference. We have already indicated the answer. Recall that children tend to count when working with the reasoning principles of equality and nonequality. Likewise when solving for an removing differences in numerosity children tend to employ a counting algorithm (see V.B.'s protocol). In other words, the child carries the principle of solvability into practice via algorithms that involve counting. Since the child is far from adept at these algorithms (Gelman & Gallistel, in preparation) there is many a slip between principle and practice. Yet the principle seems clearly at work.

SUMMARY

I began by focusing on the fact that the young child's ability to abstract a numerical representation of a set of objects is limited. In general, the young child seems to be able to use a number based representation for small set sizes. This observation leads some to deny the young child the ability to reason about number. Presumably there is little to reason about if the numbers are small. I accept the limited ability to abstract a numerical representation of arrays. I do not agree that this limits the child's use of small numbers to the "perceptual" or "intuitive" domain. For one, the young child can and does count small sets. Further, the evidence from magic experiments leads to the postulation of a set of arithmetic reasoning principles that young children use to reason about small numbers. These principles allow for inferences about numerical equality and order; operators that do or do not alter set size and procedures for reversing the effects of addition and subtraction. These principles may not be as advanced or sophisticated as those we attribute to older children and adults. Nevertheless they are reasoning principles. The evidence dictates some ability for the young child to reason about numbers. It seems that there is little to be gained by efforts to explain it away. Instead the effort that is called for is one that focusses on how principles like those we describe serve as the foundation for the development of more complex and extensive principles of arithmetic reasoning.

ACKNOWLEDGMENTS

A more extensive treatment of the issues covered in the chapter can be found in Gelman and Gallistel (in preparation). The research reported here and the preparation of the manuscript were supported by PHS Grant No. NIHHD-04598 and a John Simon Guggenheim Foundation fellowship. I thank: The children, parents, teachers, and administrative staffs of

Chestnut House, Har Zion-Wynnefield Nursery School, S. Paley Day Care Center, St. Mary's Cooperative School and the YM—YWHA Broad Street Nursery School—all of the Greater Philadelphia area; Marsha F. Tucker and Merry Bullock who helped collect and analyse data for the new studies presented in this chapter and Dan Osherson for his careful reading of an earlier draft of this chapter.

REFERENCES

Beckmann, H. Die Entiwicklung der Zahlleistung bei 2–6 jährigen Kindern. *Zeitschrift für Angewandte Psychologie*, 1924, **22**, 1–72.

Descoudres, A. *Le développment de l'enfant de deux à sept ans*. Paris: Delachaux & Niestlé, 1921.

Gast, H. Der Umgang mit Zahlen und Zahlgebilden in der frühen Kindeit. *Zeitschrift für Psychologie*, 1957, **161**, 1–90.

Gelman, R. The nature and development of early number concepts. In H. W. Reese (Ed.), *Advances in child development and behavior*. Vol. 7. New York: Academic Press, 1972. (a)

Gelman, R. Logical capacity of very young children: Number invariance rules. *Child Development*, 1972, **43**, 75–90. (b)

Gelman, R., & Tucker, M. F. Further investigations of the young child's conception of number. *Child Development*, 1975, **45**, 167–175.

Gelman, R., & Gallistel, C. R. *Arithmetic reasoning in the young child*. In preparation.

Jensen, E. M., Reese, E. P., & Reese, T. W. The subitizing and counting of visually presented fields of dots, *The Journal of Psychology*, 1950, **30**, 363–392.

Kaufman, E. L., Lord, M. W., Reese, T. W., & Volkmann, J. The discrimination of visual number. *American Journal of Psychology*, 1949, **62**, 498–525.

Klahr, D. Quantification processes. In W. G. Chase (Ed.), *Visual information processing*. New York: Academic Press, 1973.

Klahr, D., & Wallace, J. G. The role of quantification operators in the development of conservation of quantity. *Cognitive Psychology*, 1973, **4**, 301–327.

Lawson, G., Baron, J., & Siegel, L. The role of number and length cues in children's quantitative judgments. *Child Development*, 1974, **45**, 731–736.

Neisser, U. *Cognitive psychology*, New York: Academic Press, 1967.

Piaget, J. *The child's conception of number*. New York: Norton, 1952.

Pufall, P. B., Shaw, R. E., & Syrdal-Lasky, A. Development of number conservation: An examination of some predictions from Piaget's stage analysis and equilibrium model. *Child Development*, 1973, **44**, 21–27.

Saltzman, I. J., & Garner, W. R. Reaction time as a measure of span of attention. *The Journal of Psychology*, 1948, **25**, 227–241.

Siegel, L. S. The role of spatial arrangement and heterogeneity in the development of concepts of numerical equivalence. *Canadian Journal of Psychology*, 1973, **27**, 351–355.

Siegel, L. S. Development of number concepts: Ordering and correspondence operations and the role of length cues. *Developmental Psychology*, 1974, **6**, 907–912.

Smither, S. J., Smiley, S. S., & Rees, R. The use of perceptual cues for number judgment by young children. *Child Development*, 1974, **45**, 693–699.

9
Retrieval in the Development of Learning

Herman Buschke

Albert Einstein College of Medicine

Multitrial free-recall learning, in which a list of items is repeatedly presented for free recall in any order, should provide a useful paradigm for investigating the development of verbal learning (Jablonski, 1974). Although the use of such conventional free-recall learning has shown that the number of items recalled increases over trials and that recall increases with age (Cole, Frankel, & Sharp, 1971), it has been difficult to account for either of these findings, because the continuing presentation of all items before each recall trial obscures and confounds components of learning that must be analyzed to account for total recall. Theoretical analysis and empirical investigation of free-recall learning have therefore been limited to constructing models that predict total recall functions, and to evaluation of factors that may affect total recall, by manipulating the conditions of learning and the material to be learned. This chapter describes the analysis of developmental changes in verbal learning provided by the alternative paradigms of selective and restricted reminding (Buschke, 1973) which show what happens during such learning in terms of storage, retention, retrieval, and stages of learning that are differentiated by consistent and random retrieval.

The essence of these paradigms is that they allow subjects to show what they have learned by recall without further presentation. Spontaneous recall without presentation shows true retrieval from long-term storage. Separating retrieval from long-term storage and immediate recall of just presented items (Craik, 1968, 1970; Glanzer, 1972; Glanzer & Cunitz, 1966; Tulving, 1964; Waugh & Norman, 1965) makes it possible to evaluate storage and retention, as well as retrieval itself (Buschke, 1973; Tulving, 1964; Tulving & Colotla, 1970; Tulving & Pearlstone, 1966), and to analyze the development of learning in terms of two stages of item and list learning shown by random and consistent retrieval (Buschke, 1974b, c; Fuld & Buschke, 1976; Kintsch & Morris, 1965).

The aims of this chapter are to show how the development of free-recall learning can be investigated by analysis of its components; to show how these components account for increasing recall with age; to point out that learning is demonstrated by consistent retrieval from long-term storage without presentation, not by total recall; to argue for the use of extended recall with paradigms that let subjects show learning by recall without presentation, to obtain maximum retrieval for accurate evaluation of storage, retention and retrieval in the development of learning; to indicate how the use of cognitive presentations establishes certain conditions that must be assumed in developmental studies of verbal learning, and provides experimental control of cognitive processing during presentation; to emphasize that evaluation of competence depends on performance, analysis of learning depends on successful retrieval.

To show how verbal learning can be analysed in terms of its components, we begin with the analysis of an individual learning protocol, followed by discussion of how consistent retrieval shows list learning and differentiates two stages of learning. To illustrate how differences in recall can be accounted for by these components, the differences in children's learning of related and unrelated items is analyzed in terms of storage, retention, retrieval, and stages of learning. The general applicability of these methods of analysis for investigation of developmental changes in learning is shown by comparative analysis of free recall learning by children, young adults, and older adults. The increasing recall of 5- through 9-year-old children is then described in terms of these components, using the paradigms of restricted reminding and selective reminding, which demonstrate true retrieval in learning by recall without presentation, as well as conventional free recall, which does not show learning directly. Having shown that verbal learning does not require continuing presentation before every recall attempt, the function of presentations as instructions is illustrated by use of cognitive presentations which permit evaluation of cognitive processing in learning and assure us that subjects have attended to each item, have thought about each item, know the items, and can retrieve them from permanent memory. The concluding comments emphasize the importance of performance in evaluating competence and summarize the critical role of retrieval in studies of the development of learning.

ANALYSIS OF INDIVIDUAL LEARNING

The best way to explain the use of these new paradigms for free recall learning is by analysis of a typical individual learning protocol. Analysis of individual protocols is also the best way to see what happens during learning; the more customary analysis of pooled data is useful for statistical evaluation, but may not provide an adequate description unless individual learning is carefully analyzed first.

NAME: ___M. B.___   DATE: _26 Feb. 1975_

RESTRICTED REMINDING, VERBAL   AGE: _7 (Oct. 6)_ SEX: _F_

TRIALS

Figure 1 is a hand-completed "restricted reminding, verbal" recall protocol form. The grid lists 20 items (rows) across 12 trials (columns), with stippled cells indicating presentations and numbers indicating recall order, followed by summary score rows. Best-effort reading of the legible entries:

#	Item	1	2	3	4	5	6	7	8	9	10	11	12
1	CANDLE	3				12	5	8	8	9	9	9	11
2	BOOK •		3	10	3	2	6	1	1	1	1	1	1
3	POT			4	6	6	11	12	11	5	13		6
4	BOTTLE		8	3		11	10	11	9	12	15	12	15
5	COTTON	2											
6	CIGARETTE	5				10	5	9	2	14	7	4	8	9
7	BOX •	6	6	8	8	4	1	14	12	8	7	5	14
8	FEATHER		5							13	3	2	4
9	STONE			5	7	7	13	10	15	14			7
10	MAT •				2	1	8	7	13	6	5	10	5
11	BATTERY				1								
12	NICKLE			5				13		14	16	14	10
13	KNIFE				6								
14	SHIRT	4				10	4	9	7	10	12	7	13
15	STICK			2		13	7	5	6		11	13	14
16	NAIL				1	14	10	2	11	10	11	12	
17	ORANGE •	4	9	4	3	3	4	4	2	6	4	2	
18	ROPE		2		9	9	12	6	5	4	8	6	8
19	HORN		1										
20	GRASS •	1	7	11	5	8	2	3	3	3	2	3	3

Score	1	2	3	4	5	6	7	8	9	10	11	12
TOTAL RECALL	6	8	11	10	13	14	14	14	15	16	14	16
INITIAL RECALL	6	12	18	20								
RETRIEVAL		2	5	8	13	14	14	14	15	16	14	16
TOTAL STORAGE		5	10	15	16	16	16	16	16	16	16	16
RANDOM RETRIEVAL		0	1	2	3	3	3	3	2	3	1	3
RANDOM (ITEM) STORAGE		3	6	9	6	5	5	5	3	3	3	3
ADDITIONAL LIST LEARNING		0	0	2	5	6	6	6	8	8	8	8
INITIAL LIST LEARNING		2	4	4	5	5	5	5	5	5	5	5
TOTAL LIST LEARNING		2	4	6	10	11	11	11	13	13	13	13
CUMULATIVE RECALL FAILURES		3	5	9	9	9	10	11	12	12	14	14
RECOVERIES			0	2	6	7	8	9	11	12	12	14

FIG. 1 Typical free recall verbal learning of restricted reminding, when each item is presented only until it has been recalled once. Presentations are shown by stippling. Numbers show recall order.

Figure 1 shows the protocol of a 7-year-old girl who learned this list of 20 unrelated items (Cole *et al.*, 1971) by the paradigm of *restricted reminding*. In restricted reminding each item on the list is presented only until it has been recalled just once. The stippled cells in Fig. 1 show the items presented on each trial. The numbers on each trial show the order in which items were recalled. A number in a cell means that item was recalled on that trial; no number in a cell means that item was not recalled on that trial. On the first trial all 20 items were presented by reading them aloud to the subject at a 2-sec rate for verbal free recall. Because this subject recalled 6 items on the first trial, only the other 14 items not yet recalled were presented again on the second trial. At the end of the second trial, she had recalled 12 items at least once, either on Trial 1 or Trial 2 or both. Therefore, only the 8 items she had not yet recalled were presented again on Trial 3. At the end of Trial 3 she had recalled 18 of the 20 items at least once and was therefore reminded on Trial 4 of only the 2 items she had not yet recalled at all. Since she recalled all 20 items at least once by the end of Trial 4, there were no more presentations at all, so that all recall on Trials 5 through 12 is recall without presentation that shows retrieval from long-term storage.

Numbers in stippled cells show recall with presentation on that trial. Numbers in cells without stippling show recall without presentation. Such recall without presentation demonstrates retrieval from long-term storage (Buschke, 1973), identifying a critical component in verbal learning. Retrieval from long-term storage demonstrates previous storage. For example, the last item (grass) was recalled without presentation on Trial 2. Its retrieval from long-term storage on Trial 2 indicates that it must have been stored when last presented on Trial 1. Similarly, the first item (candle) also must have been stored on Trial 1 even though it was not recalled again until Trial 5, since its spontaneous retrieval from long-term storage, without any further presentation after Trial 1, shows that it must have been stored when last presented. Retrieval from long-term storage will show storage on or before the last presentation of an item when storage and retention are not obscured by any further presentation after the initial recall of each item. The spontaneous recovery of the first item (candle) on Trial 5 also shows that it must have been retained in storage despite recall failures on Trials 2, 3, and 4. Spontaneous retrieval without further presentation shows continuing retention as well as initial storage on or before the last presentation of an item.

Storage is indicated in Fig. 1 by the dashed and continuous underlining that shows the items in storage at the beginning of each trial. Storage is shown as continuing throughout learning because the nearly complete recovery of all stored items after recall failures has shown that retention generally is excellent (Buschke, 1974a, b, d). This is illustrated in Fig. 1 by the boxed circles that mark the spontaneous recovery of stored items after previous recall failures. This subject eventually recovered all recall failures, indicating that such recall failures were due to retrieval failure and that information about these items was retained in storage despite such recall failures. We do not know whether items that were only recalled once immediately after presentation, such as the fifth item (candle), were stored or not. The arrows indicate the onset of perfectly consistent retrieval without any further presentation on all remaining trials. Storage related to such consistent retrieval is shown by the continuous underlining; long-term storage prior to the onset of such consistent retrieval is indicated by the dashed underlining.

The asterisks in some cells represent retrieval after very long pauses. This subject used *extended recall*, for which she was given as much time and encouragement on each trial as necessary to obtain the maximum retrieval possible. It is extremely important to obtain maximum retrieval at each point in learning to accurately evaluate storage and retention as well as retrieval itself. Since retrieval is difficult, it is necessary to encourage subjects to persist in attempts at retrieval even after recall of any more items seems impossible. It is necessary to do this right from the onset of learning, since each subject must learn that it really is possible to retrieve more items even after any further recall seems impossible, and to prevent subjects from retrieving only some convenient subset of well-rehearsed items. Extended recall on the first trial may last for a long as 5 min; recall on later trials is usually shorter because the rate of retrieval increases during the course of learning. The items marked with asterisks presumably represent items that would not have been retrieved without such extended recall.

The course of such verbal learning can be analyzed in terms of retrieval and storage by counting the number of items retrieved from long-term storage on each trial by recall without presentation (retrieval), and by counting the total number of (underlined) items that have been retrieved from long-term storage at least once (storage). Retrieval from long-term storage allows us to identify the onset of storage on or before the last presentation of that item, and to demonstrate its continuing retention despite any recall failures by its spontaneous recovery without further presentation. For example, on Trial 2 two items were retrieved without presentation. At the onset of Trial 2, at least five items were available in long-term storage, as demonstrated by their spontaneous recovery without any further presentation after Trial 1 (Items 1, 6, 7, 14, and 20). Retention can be evaluated by counting the cumulative number of recall failures and the spontaneous recoveries (boxed circles) of stored items, to show that most recall failures are recovered spontaneously without further presentation.

Retrieval and storage can be analyzed further by distinguishing between those items in long-term storage that are consistently retrieved on all recall attempts and those items retained in storage that are not retrieved consistently. The development of consistent retrieval can be evaluated by counting the total number of items marked by arrows to show the trial from which they are consistently retrieved. Storage of consistently retrieved items is marked by continuous underlining that begins with an arrow. Storage and retention of items that are not consistently retrieved is marked by dashed underlining, so that the effectiveness of such random retrieval can be evaluated separately; this is indicated in Fig. 1 as random retrieval and random (item) storage. Consistent retrieval and storage are called "list learning" in Fig. 1 for reasons that will be discussed. Consistent retrieval or total list learning is composed of the initial list learning of those items that were consistently retrieved from their initial recall on (indicated by the large dots in Fig. 1), and the additional list learning of those items that were not consistently retrieved until later.

CONSISTENT RETRIEVAL AND LIST LEARNING

The reason for distinguishing between consistent retrieval and inconsistent or random retrieval is that these appear to reflect different stages of learning. Consistent retrieval from long-term storage is of interest because it may provide us with a reasonable and easily calculated measure of *list* learning. We have not had a measure of list learning, although we have had measures of subjective organization that may reflect whatever organization may be involved in list learning. The difficulties inherent in measures of subjective organization have been discussed elsewhere (Buschke, 1976; Frankel & Cole, 1971; Pellegrino & Battig, 1974). The main difficulty with such measures is that they do not really seem to capture the degree of organization apparent in learning protocols. More direct evaluation of list learning would be useful for analysis of list learning, and would also provide a measure of organization if list learning reflects increasing organization of information in memory. When a subject can recall all of the items in a list on every attempt, without any further presentation, we would conclude that the entire list has been learned. The difficulty in evaluating list learning is to estimate how much of the list has been learned before the entire list has been learned. However, our conception of learning the entire list indicates that if a subject can recall *some* of the items in the list on every attempt, without any further presentation, then *those* items have been learned as a list. It therefore seems reasonable to regard consistent retrieval without any further presentation as an indication of list learning. Consistent retrieval presumably means that the retrieval of such items has been integrated with the retrieval of other items so that they are no longer subject to the inhibiting effects of recall (Roediger, 1974).

The distinction between consistent retrieval and inconsistent or random retrieval can be justified by asking how an item reaches the stage of consistent retrieval. Does retrieval of an item get better and better until it can be consistently recalled all of the time? No. Random retrieval does not improve prior to the abrupt onset of consistent retrieval, indicating that random and consistent retrieval reflect different stages of learning (Buschke, 1974b, c; Bower & Theios, 1963; Evans & Dallenback, 1965; Fuld & Buschke, 1976; Kintsch & Morris, 1965; Waugh & Smith, 1962). This can be shown in two ways. The first is to evaluate the probability of random retrieval on successive trials. The dashed underlining in Fig. 1 indicates those items in long-term storage that have not yet reached the stage of consistent retrieval. We can count the number of such items available in random storage for random retrieval on each trial and the number of such items actually retrieved on each trial, to determine whether the probability of such retrieval increases during the course of learning. This is shown in the left panel of Fig. 2. It is apparent that random retrieval of either list does not improve over successive trials. However, it might be argued that this way of evaluating random retrieval over trials is not fair, because such apparent lack of

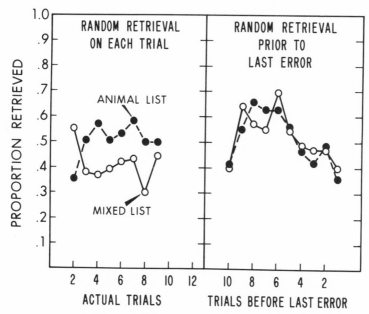

FIG. 2 Random retrieval on each trial (left), and random retrieval before the abrupt onset of consistent retrieval (right).

improvement might be due to greater difficulty in retrieving "harder" items left in random storage after "easier" items had reached the stage of consistent retrieval. Therefore more conventional backward learning curves were constructed for each subject, as shown in the right panel of Fig. 2. Since such backward learning curves show the retrieval of all items on each trial prior to the onset of consistent retrieval, such curves are not affected by item or subject differences. The backward learning curves in the right panel of Fig. 2 also do not show improvement in random retrieval prior to the abrupt onset of consistent retrieval. It therefore seems reasonable to regard consistent and random retrieval as indications of different stages of learning.

STAGES OF RETRIEVAL

The view that consistent retrieval can reasonably be regarded as an indication of list learning has already been discussed. It also seems reasonable to interpret random retrieval as an indication of a stage of *item* learning, in which the retrieval of such items has not yet been integrated with the retrieval of other items. Learning to recall a list of items already known to the subject can reasonably be regarded as involving selective retrieval of that set of items from the subject's permanent memory (Buschke, 1975b). Figure 3 illustrates one

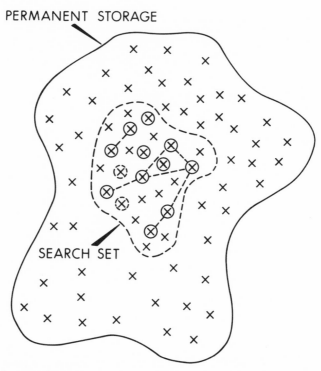

FIG. 3 Schematic illustration of selective retrieval from permanent storage by random and consistent retrieval. Tagged items (closed circles) may be randomly retrieved by random search at first, then consistently retrieved when retrieval scheme (dashed connections) is developed during learning.

useful way to think about such selective retrieval. It is as though the subject first tagged certain items, which must be found during retrieval. The Xs indicate items in the subject's permanent storage. For certain lists, such as those in a single category, selective retrieval may be confined to a more restricted search set. List items are circled by dashed and closed circles. Closed circles indicate items that have been tagged, so that they can be recovered by random search that results in random retrieval; this stage might be interpreted as item learning. As learning progresses the subject may generate retrieval schemes, suggested by dashed lines connecting some circled items, that permit the consistent retrieval interpreted as list learning. Consistent retrieval does not necessarily imply consistent order of recall from trial to trial. One advantage of consistent retrieval as an indication of list learning is precisely that it does not assume that list learning, or any organization involved in list learning, must be reflected by increasing consistency in order of recall from trial to trial. Such an assumption often is either unnecessary or false; increasing organization can lead to greater flexibility in retrieval, not less.

While the interpretation of stages of selective retrieval illustrated by Fig. 3 seems reasonable (Shiffrin & Atkinson, 1969), other interpretations are possible (Restle, 1965). Although the data in Fig. 2 indicate that random and consistent retrieval may represent different stages of learning (Restle, 1965), those data do not demonstrate that random retrieval reflects item learning and consistent retrieval reflects list learning. Such data may also be consistent with an interpretation of random and consistent retrieval in terms of two stages of item learning. However, interpretation of random and consistent retrieval in terms of item and list learning is reasonable and useful. Regardless of how these stages of retrieval are interpreted, the distinction between random and consistent retrieval allows us to appreciate that consistent retrieval demonstrates completed learning, and permits analysis of verbal learning in terms of the following components: the number of items retained in long-term stoarge for random retrieval (random storage); the number of such items retrieved from random storage (random retrieval); the number of items consistently retrieved from their initial recall (initial list learning); the number of items transferred from the first stage of random retrieval to the second stage of consistent retrieval (additional list learning).

Such an analysis of learning in terms of stages of retrieval is useful because it does not depend upon the distinction between storage and retrieval. The difficulty with analyzing verbal learning only in terms of storage and retrieval is that the evaluation of storage and retrieval may be interdependent. Accurate evaluation of storage depends on retrieval and successful retrieval may depend on the adequacy of storage. It may not always be clear whether poor storage is due to inadequate encoding or to ineffective retrieval, or whether poor retrieval is due to ineffective retrieval or to inadequate storage that makes subsequent retrieval difficult.

ACCOUNTING FOR DIFFERENCES IN RECALL

Analysis of learning in terms of the components demonstrated by random and consistent retrieval is illustrated by a study that compared children's recall of related items with their recall of unrelated items. A list of 20 animals and a mixed list of 20 unrelated items (Cole et al., 1971) were learned by ten 7–10-year-old children (mean age = 8.6, SD = 1.17). Both lists were learned in counterbalanced order by each child, in test sessions at least a week apart. Because it would be difficult to show persuasively that different children have the same cognitive abilities necessary for such learning, a within-subjects design was used to minimize the effect of individual differences. Each child was tested individually by the same examiner. The items were presented verbally at a 2-sec rate for verbal free recall in any order; the subjects' recall was recorded by the examiner. Both lists were learned by restricted reminding, presenting each item only until it was recalled once, in order to obtain the spontaneous retrieval without presentation necessary to compare learning in terms of its components. Extended recall was used to maximize retrieval on each trial.

Analysing the recall of related and unrelated items is of interest for several reasons. Learning to recall selected items that are already known presumably involves selective retrieval of such items from permanent memory. Subjects can confine their search for selective retrieval of single-category items to a well-defined search space when recalling a list of animals, but not when recalling a list of unrelated items (Laurence, 1967). Comparing the retrieval of single-category items and unrelated items may indicate whether such learning is affected by the set of alternatives from which items are to be retrieved, as well as by the number of items to be retrieved (Shiffrin, 1970). Retrieval of unrelated items also shows that such phenomena as spontaneous recovery after recall failure (Buschke, 1974a, d) are not due to some kind of guessing that might be possible if the items were all from a single category (Buschke, 1975a).

The first (left) panel of Fig. 4 shows that total recall of the animal list was greater than total recall of the mixed list of unrelated items (Laurence, 1967). Although this difference in total recall is significant $[F(1, 96) = 24.0, p < .001]$, it is rather modest, indicating that recall in such verbal learning is more a function of the number of items to be retrieved than of the number of items from which the list items are selectively retrieved (Shiffrin, 1970).

The second panel of Fig. 4 accounts for the difference in total recall of the animal and mixed lists in terms of storage and retrieval. This panel shows that the greater total recall of animals was due to both greater storage and greater retrieval of the animals. The discrepancy between storage and retrieval, and the increasing spontaneous retrieval of unrelated items in the mixed list, as well as the single-category items in the animals list, shows that there really are retrieval difficulties in such learning and that spontaneous retrieval can occur without

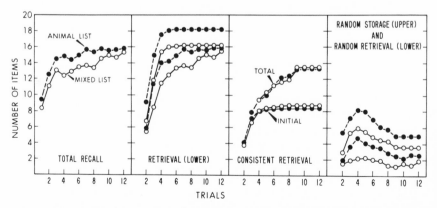

FIG. 4   Total recall, long-term storage and retrieval from long-term storage, initial and total consistent retrieval (list learning), and random storage and random retrieval (item learning).

guessing. The discrepancy between storage and retrieval is due to the occurence of retrieval failures. The increase in retrieval without further presentation shows continuing retrieval of items that were spontaneously recovered from storage after recall failure.

The last two panels account for greater recall of the animals by analysing storage and retrieval in terms of the two stages of learning shown by random and consistent retrieval. The third panel of Fig. 4 shows no difference between the animal and mixed lists in terms of either initial or total consistent retrieval (list learning). The last panel on the right of Fig. 4 shows more random storage and retrieval of the animals. This seems reasonable, since it would seem easier to find additional animals by random retrieval, that is, by thinking of items in that category and determining whether they belong to the list (Laurence, 1967).

There were significant order effects in learning the two lists. Separate analyses of total retrieval in first and second lists learned showed that the greater retrieval of animals in the first list was due to more random storage and random retrieval. However, in the second lists the greater retrieval of animals was due to more consistent retrieval. These differences in the components of first and second list learning indicate that these subjects did use strategies, although the nature of the strategies is obscure, and that such learning-to-learn effects may involve changes in strategies.

Nearly all recall failures after storage were recovered spontaneously without further presentation, as illustrated by the boxed circles in Fig. 1. Since spontaneous recovery after recall failure shows that such recall failures are due to retrieval failure, spontaneous recovery after recall failure also shows that retrieval is a critical component of such learning (Buschke, 1974a, d; Erdelyi & Becker, 1974; Shapiro & Erdelyi, 1974). The most difficult aspect of retrieval seems to be the initial spontaneous recovery of an item from storage, since the retrieval of spontaneously recovered items usually is maintained quite well after their initial retrieval without presentation (Buschke, 1975a).

Retrieval is also critical for successful investigation of verbal learning. In the absence of retrieval we simply don't know what happened during learning. When an item is not retrieved we do not know whether that item was not stored, was stored but not retained, was stored and retained but not found, or was stored, retained, and found, but not discriminated as a list item. On the other hand, when an item is retrieved after recall failure we know that item was stored, retained, found, and correctly discriminated as a list item. When an item is spontaneously recovered after recall failure, we know that it was retained despite recall failure, that its recall failure was due to retrieval failure, and that retrieval failure was due to difficulty in finding that item, not to difficulty in discriminating it from other items not on the list. Other studies also have shown that recall failures are retrieval failures due to difficulty in finding items rather than difficulty in discriminating list items. Ritter and Buschke (1974) found that retrieval of repeated items embedded in changing lists was increased by forced recall without significantly increasing intrusions, showing that additional items found during forced recall could be discriminated from items not on the list. Buschke (1975a) showed that adults can discriminate list items from intrusions without any feedback to confirm correct retrieval or delete intrusions. When adults were required to recall 20 animals on each trial of restricted reminding, intrusions decreased spontaneously as correct retrieval spontaneously increased without feedback. List items were correctly discriminated when found, and were reliably retrieved thereafter. In order to understand what happens during verbal learning, it is therefore necessary to do everything possible to obtain retrieval. This is especially important in developmental studies because they depend on maximum performance by all subjects to evaluate developmental differences. Since the only way to obtain maximum retrieval is through the use of extended recall, each subject should be given enough time and encouragment to maximize retrieval on each trial, even though this requires clinical judgment to decide when one trial ends and the next begins.

DIFFERENCES IN LEARNING BY CHILDREN, YOUNG ADULTS, AND OLDER ADULTS

We have seen how differences in recall can be analysed in terms of storage, retrieval, and stages of learning when subjects are allowed to show retrieval from long-term storage by recall without presentation. The general applicability of such analysis to developmental and age-related changes in learning is shown by the use of restricted reminding to account for differences in free recall learning by children, young adults, and older adults in terms of the components of such learning (Buscke, 1974b). Ten children (mean age 9 years, 4 months, $SD = 1.0$), 10 young adults (mean age 22 years, 9 months, $SD = 3.1$), and 10 older adults (mean age 42 years, 2 months, $SD = 7.7$) learned a list of 20 animals by restricted reminding. Figure 5 shows greater total recall by the young adults than by the older adults, and greater total recall by the older adults than by the children. This appears to be due principally to greater retrieval by young adults than by older adults or children, since storage by all three groups was similar. Although the children stored as many items as the older adults, the children's retrieval was substantially lower. The differences in consistent retrieval, which provides the most stringent measure of retrieval, were still greater.

Figure 6 shows an analysis of learning by these children, young adults, and older adults in terms of the two stages of item and list learning shown by random and consistent retrieval. This analysis is justified by the finding that the random retrieval of these subjects did not improve prior to the abrupt onset of consistent retrieval (Buschke, 1974b). The young adults showed great initial list learning, modest random storage and retrieval, and effective additional list learning. The children showed very much less initial list learning, more random

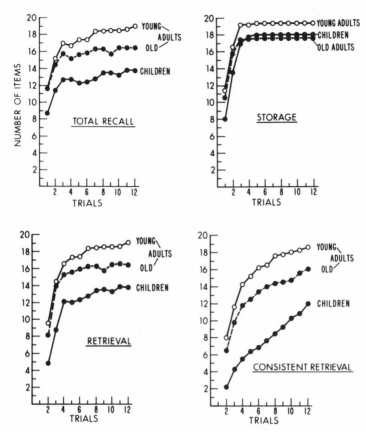

FIG. 5   Storage and retrieval in free-recall learning by children, young adults, and older adults, shown by spontaneous retrieval without further presentation of items recalled once. (From Buschke, 1974b.)

storage and retrieval, and similar additional list learning. The older adults showed slightly less initial list learning and slightly more random storage and retrieval than the young adults, and comparable list learning.

Figure 6 shows a striking difference between learning by the children and the adults. The children's recall was due to very different contributions by consistent retrieval and random retrieval than the adult's recall. While the adults had more consistent retrieval than random retrieval from initial recall on, the children had more random retrieval than consistent retrieval until late in learning. The young adults were able to retrieve 13.7 of the 20 items consistently from their first recall on (initial list learning). This is striking because it means that the young adults learned 68% of the items on or before their initial recall (which is the earliest observable indication that an item has been processed at all). Regardless of whether consistent retrieval is interpreted as list learning or

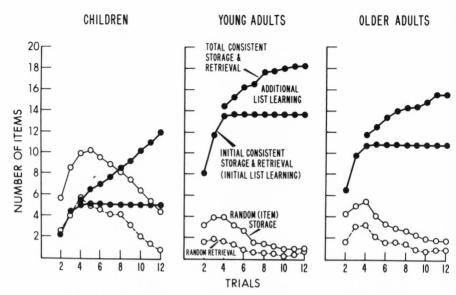

FIG. 6   Analysis of verbal learning in terms of stages of random retrieval (item learning) and consistent retrieval (list learning) from long-term storage, to show random (item) storage, nonincremental retrieval from random storage, initial consistent storage and retrieval (list learning), and transition from random to consistent retrieval (additional list learning). (From Buschke, 1974b.)

item learning, consistent retrieval of an item on all recall attempts without any further presentation clearly demonstrates complete learning of that item. This unexpected finding would not have been apparent without analysis of the consistent and random retrieval of individual items; conventional analysis of learning in terms of the total number of items recalled on each trial will not show that some items have already been learned when others have not.

The children stored nearly as many items as the adults; while they had less consistent retrieval than the adults, they also had more random retrieval. The lower total recall of the children apparently is due to retrieval difficulty, shown by less consistent retrieval. Their less consistent retrieval is due largely to less initial consistent retrieval from initial recall on. The reasons for their less consistent retrieval will require further investigation, which will probably involve consideration of what is retrieved and what children know about the items they are trying to recall. While some of the children's difficulties in retrieval may be related to their ability to organize storage and retrieval, some may also be related to the state of their knowledge about the items. The more a subject knows about an item and its relations to other items, the easier it may be to access that item and integrate its retrieval with that of other items. Since items may range from those with substantial cognitive and perceptual content to those that are just recognizable as English words, it may be necessary to evaluate the state of the items to be remembered for each subject.

Although we do not yet understand the factors responsible for consistent retrieval, it seems clear that consistent retrieval, rather than just total recall, should be analyzed in such verbal learning experiments. The main things that happen during such verbal learning are that more items reach the stage of consistent retrieval, and that the rate of retrieval increases (Buschke, 1976); neither of these has been thoroughly investigated yet. Regardless of how consistent retrieval without presentation is interpreted, it demonstrates learning more surely than total recall can, and should be analysed to account for the increase of recall during learning. This is not a new proposition; it can be regarded as an extention of Tulving's (1964) use of repeated recall from one trial to the next as a measure of inter-trial retention to evaluate learning. Consistent retrieval (on all subsequent trials, without any further presentation) is relevant because it clearly shows complete learning, while repeated recall just from one trial to the next does not, because it appears to be an integral stage of the learning process.

WHY DOES CHILDREN'S RECALL IMPROVE WITH AGE?

Restricted reminding is a special case of the more general paradigm of selective reminding, in which the subject is continuously reminded of any items that were not recalled on the immediately preceding trial (Buschke, 1973). Since those items that were recalled on the immediately preceding trial are not presented again unless the subject fails to recall them, such selective reminding allows the subject to show learning by recall without presentation, which identifies retrieval from long-term storage. Identification of true retrieval then permits analysis of learning in terms of storage, retention, retrieval, and the stages of learning shown by consistent and random retrieval. Such selective reminding allows the subject to learn all of the items eventually, so that maximum storage by children of different ages can be evaluated. Both selective reminding and restricted reminding are useful for developmental studies of learning (Buschke, 1974d), since selective reminding shows how much can be learned, while restricted reminding shows retention without confounding by any further presentations and provides the maximum estimate of storage because spontaneous retrieval on any trial will demonstrate storage on or before the last presentation of an item. Unlike conventional free recall learning, selective reminding and restricted reminding provide analysis of verbal learning based on direct demonstration of true retrieval from long-term storage. Since conventional free recall does not allow subjects to demonstrate retrieval from long-term storage by recall without presentation, any analysis of conventional free recall learning will depend on indirect identification of retrieval on the basis of some additional assumptions.

The first step toward explaining why children's recall improves with age is to analyse the components of verbal learning in children of different ages, so that the development of learning can be accounted for by changes in the components of learning. Therefore selective reminding and restricted reminding, as well as conventional free recall, were used by Dr. Elaine Daniels to analyze storage, retention, retrieval, and stages of learning in free recall learning by 180 5–9-year-old children from the same white, middle-class school (Daniels, 1975; Daniels, Buschke, & Voyat, 1976).

Two different lists of unrelated items were used. These items were chosen so that they might be as familiar to younger children as to older children. These lists probably are as appropriate as possible, since there is no satisfactory way to construct lists that are really equivalent for children of different ages. The items in one list were rope, apple, spoon, table, flower, clock, television, potato, nail, broom, bathtub, shoe, airplane, car, feather, drum, hill, lion, balloon, door. The items in the other list were bullet, banana, knife, chair, tree, lamp, book, corn, hammer, stove, church, doll, bus, eye, key, bell, wagon, elephant, cup, window. Each list was learned by half of the 6 girls and 6 boys in each age group for each paradigm. Each child was tested individually by Daniels, on one list with one paradigm. The testing sessions lasted about an hour because extended recall was used to obtain maximum retrieval on each trial, necessary for accurate evaluation of storage, retention, and retrieval.

The items were presented by reading them aloud to each subject at a 2-sec rate. On every trial the subjects tried to recall verbally all items in the list, in any order. In retricted reminding only those words not yet recalled at all were presented, in quasi-random order. In selective reminding only those words not recalled on the immediately preceding trial were presented, in quasi-random order. In conventional free recall all of the items were presented on every trial, in a different random order on each trial. The analysis of verbal learning by these three paradigms will be illustrated by typical individual learning protocols.

Restricted Reminding

Figure 7 shows a typical example of verbal learning by restricted reminding, in which each item was presented only until it was recalled just once. The stippling shows which items were presented on each trial and the numbers show the order in which items were recalled on each trial. Storage at the beginning of each trial is shown by the dashed and continuous underlining. The onset of consistent retrieval is shown by the arrows; the dots on the left mark those items that were consistently retrieved from their initial recall on. The dashed underlining indicates items in the first stage of learning prior to the onset of consistent retrieval and the continuous underlining indicates items in the second stage of list learning shown by consistent retrieval. The boxed circles show spontaneous recoveries after recall failures; 11 of the 12 recall failures were recovered spontaneously. It is apparent that a great many recall attempts may be required to achieve such spontaneous recovery. Note, for example, that the second item (apple) was not spontaneously retrieved until the 11th trial, long after its last presentation and initial recall on trial 2.

NAME: _V. R._____   DATE: _3/25/74_

AGE: _7:8_ SEX: _F_ TYPE TEST: _R.R._

TRIALS

		1	2	3	4	5	6	7	8	9	10	11	12
1.	BULLET •	7	10	5	8	1	9	5	5	8	6	10	
2.	APPLE	5										13	11
3.	SPOON •	3	7	12	9	7	3	2	9	11	10	9	
4.	TABLE •					7	9	5	1	10	4	14	4
5.	FLOWER	4		8	6	7	8	10	10	2	7	5	2
6.	CLOCK •	3	4	5	8	6	6	1	3	8	1	3	7
7.	TELEVISION			4									
8.	POTATO				4	5	4	7	8			8	3
9.	NAIL •					3	3	2	7	11	9	4	14
10.	BROOM				2								
11.	BATHTUB •				7	4	5	6	6	4	6	7	6
12.	SHOE	6		11				12	1	2	12	13	
13.	AIRPLANE			1									
14.	EAR	5						12	5	2	8		
15.	FEATHER			2									
16.	DRUM				3	10	4	9	3	12	9	12	
17.	HILL			10			11	6	3	11	5		
18.	LION •	2	6	7	2	2	8	4	7	10	1	1	
19.	BALLOON			3	9							15	
20.	DOOR			4						13			
TOTAL RECALL		6	7	10	12	9	10	10	12	12	13	14	15
INITIAL RECALL		6	9	14	18	20							
RETRIEVAL		4	5	8	7	10	10	12	12	13	14	15	
TOTAL STORAGE		6	9	11	14	16	16	16	16	16	16	16	
RANDOM RETRIEVAL		0	0	3	1	1	1	1	0	1	2	3	
RANDOM (ITEM) STORAGE		2	4	5	8	7	7	5	4	4	4	4	
ADDITIONAL LIST LEARNING		0	1	1	1	2	2	4	5	5	5	5	
INITIAL LIST LEARNING		4	4	4	5	7	7	7	7	7	7	7	
TOTAL LIST LEARNING		4	5	5	6	9	9	11	12	12	12	12	
CUMULATIVE RECALL FAILURES		2	5	6	10	10	10	10	11	11	12	12	
RECOVERED		-	1	3	3	4	4	6	7	8	10	11	

FIG. 7 Seven-year-old learning by *restricted reminding*: presenting each item only until recalled once. Stippling shows presentations. Numbers show recall order. (From Daniels, Buschke, & Voyat, 1976.)

Selective Reminding

Figure 8 shows a typical example of verbal learning by selective reminding, in which the subject was reminded only of those items not recalled on the immediately preceding trial. Selective reminding allows the subject to show learning by recall without presentation, and maximizes learning by presenting again those items that were not recalled on the immediately preceding trial (Buschke, 1973, 1974d). The stippled cells show which items were presented on

NAME: E. F.   DATE: 5/11/74

AGE: 7:11 SEX: M TYPE TEST: S.R.

	TRIALS	1	2	3	4	5	6	7	8	9	10	11	12
1.	BULLET ●	1	2	6	7	6	7	5	8	2	1	7	5
2.	APPLE ●	3	4	5	5	4	8	13	9	4	4	12	15
3.	SPOON ●	2	3	7	6	9	9	14	10	6	5	13	14
4.	TABLE ●	4	7	8	12	8	16	12	11	5	3	17	12
5.	FLOWER				4	10		2	13	15	6	11	
6.	CLOCK			3	1		2	4	10	3	10		
7.	TELEVISION ●			1	11	15	6	10	14	11	9	15	8
8.	POTATO		10	12		2	4	11	15	12		2	13
9.	NAIL		11	13		5		4	20	2		1	
10.	BROOM							1		3		1	2
11.	BATHTUB ●	5	6	10	8	10	14	15	12	7	7	14	13
12.	SHOE			2		7	18	13	15	11	4	11	
13.	AIRPLANE ●	7	6	9	10	11	13	7	7	8	6	9	4
14.	EAR			14	3		3	3	16	8	16	19	
15.	FEATHER			11	16	15	16		7	12	5		
16.	DRUM		8		2		3	2	16	18	17	18	9
17.	HILL ●			3	12	11	8	5	10	13	10	6	
18.	LION			2		13	12	17	6	9	14	11	7
19.	BALLOON	6	4		2		1	9	16	19	18		
20.	DOOR ●		3	11	9	7	6	6	4	13	18	8	3
	TOTAL RECALL	7	11	14	12	16	16	18	16	20	18	19	19
	INITIAL RECALL	7	12	16	18	19	19	20					
	RETRIEVAL		6	9	8	13	13	15	15	18	18	19	19
	TOTAL STORAGE		6	9	10	13	14	16	17	18	19	19	19
	RANDOM RETRIEVAL		0	2	0	3	3	3	1	3	2	2	2
	RANDOM (ITEM) STORAGE		0	2	2	3	4	4	3	3	3	3	3
	ADDITIONAL LIST LEARNING		0	0	1	1	3	4	6	7	7	7	7
	INITIAL LIST LEARNING		6	7	8	9	9	9	9	9	9	9	9
	TOTAL LIST LEARNING		6	7	9	10	12	13	15	16	16	16	16

FIG. 8 Seven-year-old learning by *selective reminding*: presenting only those items not recalled on the immediately preceding trial. Stippling shows presentations. Numbers show recall order. (From Daniels, Buschke, & Voyat, 1976.)

each trial, and the numbers show the order in which items were recalled on each trial. All 20 items were presented on the first trial. Since 7 items were recalled on the first trial, only the 13 items not recalled on Trial 1 were presented on Trial 2. On Trial 2, 11 items were recalled, so only the other 9 items were presented on trial 3, and so on throughout learning. The number of reminders (stippled cells) decreases as learning proceeds. Retrieval from long-term storage is demonstrated by recall without presentation, shown by numbers in cells without stippling. For example, recall of the first item (bullet) without presentation on Trial 2 demonstrates its initial retrieval from long-term storage, and shows storage of that item on Trial 1. Storage at the beginning of each trial is shown by dashed and continuous underlining from the first retrieval on, under the assumption that items remain in storage after initial encoding; the validity of this assumption has been shown by the spontaneous recovery of items after recall failure in restricted reminding. The arrows show the onset of consistent retrieval without any further presentation on all remaining trials; the dots on the left mark those items that were consistently retrieved from their initial recall on. Items in the first stage of learning shown by random retrieval are indicated by dashed underlining and items in the second stage of learning shown by consistent retrieval are indicated by continuous underlining. In scoring retrieval from long-term storage we assume that additional presentations after an item has been stored, such as the presentation of Item 5 (flower) on Trial 8, act as reminders; recall after such reminders is counted as retrieval from long-term storage. The assumption that presentations after an item has been stored act as reminders is supported by the observation that such reminders almost always result in retrieval, while presentations prior to storage are not nearly as effective. This can be seen in Fig. 8; many of the stippled cells prior to storage (i.e., those without underlining) do not contain numbers, indicating that those presentations failed to elicit recall, while all presentations after storage did elicit retrieval.

Conventional Free Recall

Figure 9 shows a typical example of conventional free-recall learning, when all 20 items in the list were presented in a different random order on each trial. Unlike most conventional free-recall studies, extended recall was used to obtain maximum retrieval on each trial, by providing as much time and encouragement as necessary. In contrast with restricted reminding and selective reminding, it is not obvious how conventional free recall is to be analyzed, since subjects are never allowed to show what they have learned by retrieval without presentation. Although it is possible to identify consistent *recall* in conventional free-recall learning, as indicated by the arrows in Fig. 9, it is consistent recall immediately after presentation of items on every trial, which is not the same as consistent *retrieval* without presentation. Tulving has suggested that retrieval from long-term storage can be identified in conventional free recall by the recall of an item after interference by presentation and/or recall of 7 or more other items since the last presentation or recall of that item (Tulving & Colotla, 1970; Craik & Birtwhistle, 1971; Ritter, Buschke & Gindes, 1974). Tulving's method was used to identify the first retrieval of items from long-term storage, which were then assumed to remain in storage, as indicated by the dashed and continuous underlining that shows the items in storage at the beginning of each trial. Using these assumptions, which apparently must be accepted if conventional free-recall learning is to be analyzed at all, the scoring of conventional free recall shown in Fig. 9 then was the same as in restricted reminding and selective reminding.

NAME: _H. H._   DATE: _3/25/74_

AGE: _7:3_   SEX: _F_   TYPE TEST: _CFR_

			TRIALS								
1	2	3	4	5	6	7	8	9	10	11	12

	1	2	3	4	5	6	7	8	9	10	11	12
1. BULLET			1	9	1			1		1	16	20
2. APPLE	5		5	11	14	13	17	16		2	9	3
3. SPOON	1	6	12	7	6	5	1	15		19	19	
4. TABLE ●	9	3	14	8	14	9	12	8	17	1	2	
5. FLOWER ●	10	11	8	17	8	16	18	12	11	8	11	
6. CLOCK	1	6		5	10	16	7	3	6	15	4	18
7. TELEVISION ●				13	6	15	10	8	7	16	5	8
8. POTATO ●	5	9	6	16	10	18	6	9	6	15	13	
9. NAIL	4	7					2		2	14	11	6
10. BROOM		2			2	14	15	16	18	17	1	
11. BATHTUB ●	2	4	8	7	4	11	19	7	10	7	14	16
12. SHOE	2	7		13	7	4	5	5	5	12	9	
13. AIRPLANE	3	3		9	11	5	13	13	3	3	7	12
14. EAR ●				1	15	12	20	4	14	12	6	17
15. FEATHER ●			12	4	18	9	15	17	11	10	2	4
16. DRUM ●					2	18	8	10	13	8	3	14
17. HILL ●					2	12	1	12	11	1	13	10	5
18. LION ●					3	13	17	11	9	18	9	20	15
19. BALLOON	6		4		1	13	13	14	17	19	18	1
20. DOOR ●	8	10	10	5	4	6	2	4	4	13	10	
TOTAL RECALL	6	10	12	14	18	18	20	18	18	19	20	20
INITIAL RECALL	6	12	15	19	20							
RETRIEVAL	4	7	10	16	18	20	18	18	19	20	20	
TOTAL STORAGE	5	10	14	18	20	20	20	20	20	20	20	
RANDOM RETRIEVAL	3	3	2	3	2	4	2	1	2	3	3	
RANDOM (ITEM) STORAGE	4	6	6	5	4	4	4	3	3	3	3	
ADDITIONAL LIST LEARNING	0	1	3	5	6	6	6	7	7	7	7	
INITIAL LIST LEARNING	1	4	5	9	10	10	10	10	10	10	10	
TOTAL LIST LEARNING	1	5	8	14	16	16	16	17	17	17	17	
SHORT-TERM RECALL	1	1	1	0	0	0	0	0	0	0	0	0

FIG. 9 Seven-year-old learning by *conventional free recall*: presenting all items in random order before every recall trial attempt. Numbers show recall order. (From Daniels, Buschke, & Voyat, 1976.)

Storage and Retrieval

Figure 10 shows an analysis of the total recall curves in terms of first recall, storage, retrieval, total and initial list learning. First recall shows the number of items that have been recalled at least once with presentation; this is the earliest indication of cognitive processing. First recall appears similar in conventional free recall and selective reminding for all ages except the 5-year-olds. The curve of first recall by 5-year-olds in conventional free recall shows that some 5-year-olds never recalled some items at all in 12 trials of conventional free

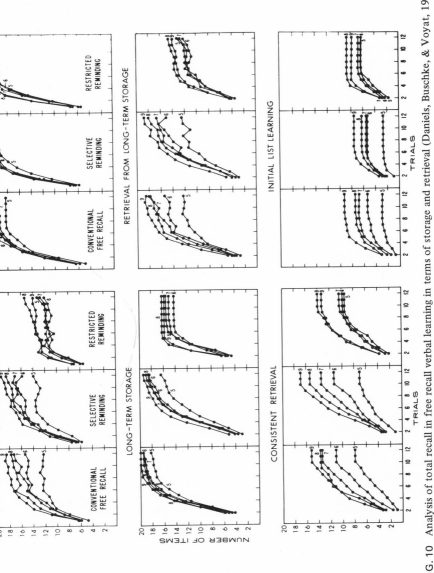

FIG. 10   Analysis of total recall in free recall verbal learning in terms of storage and retrieval (Daniels, Buschke, & Voyat, 1976).

recall. The continuing presentation of all items throughout conventional free-recall learning apparently made it difficult for some 5-year-olds to pick up some of the items, as they explicitly pointed out when they asked Dr. Daniels to "just tell me the ones I missed." The curves of long-term storage also show relatively little difference among age groups, except for somewhat lower storage by 5-year-olds in conventional free recall and selective reminding.

The retrieval curves seem to account for most of the differences in total recall in conventional free recall and selective reminding. In restricted reminding, greater total recall by 8- and 9-year-olds was associated with greater retrieval from long-term storage by the 8 and 9-year-olds than by the 5, 6, and 7-year-olds. These differences in retrieval from long-term storage are even more apparent in the curves of consistent retrieval or list learning, which also reflect the differences in initial list learning. It is interesting that initial list learning by 5-year-olds was less in conventional free recall and selective reminding than in restricted reminding. This suggests that continuing presentation of items in conventional free recall and selective reminding may intefere with consistent retrieval of items that were consistently retrieved from their initial recall in restricted reminding, in which there are no more presentations to disrupt retrieval after the first few trials. The data in Fig. 10 seems to indicate that greater total recall by older children is due more to greater retrieval than to greater storage, and that the greater retrieval by older children is due to more consistent retrieval.

Stages of Learning

Figure 11 accounts for total recall in terms of the two stages of item and list learning shown by random and consistent retrieval. The uppermost curve in each graph shows the total recall of each age group, while the lower four curves show the components of learning that together account for total recall on each trial. Similar changes in the composition of total recall were found by all three methods. The youngest children had the greatest random storage, slightly greater random retrieval, and the lowest initial and total list learning (consistent retrieval). Although the youngest children had the greatest random storage, their random retrieval was not much greater than that of older children, suggesting that the effectiveness of random retrieval may increase with age.

Initial list learning or consistent retrieval increased with age, as did total list learning. The most striking change is the progressive shift from more random storage and retrieval to more consistent storage and retrieval, a progressive shift from more item learning to more list learning as age increases. Even in restricted reminding, when items are never presented again after they have been recalled once, consistent retrieval increases with age. Both initial and additional consistent retrieval seem to increase with age. Greater recall in selective reminding than

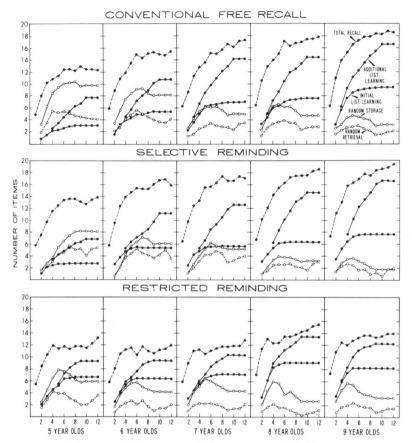

FIG. 11 Analysis of total recall in terms of two stages of item and list learning shown by random and consistent retrieval. (From Daniels, Buschke, & Voyat, 1976.)

in restricted reminding seems to be due largely to more additional list learning (consistent retrieval). The analysis in Fig. 11 illustrate how consistent retrieval can show further learning even when total recall does not. Since increasing consistent retrieval is the main thing that happens during such learning (in addition to increasing rate of recall), and since consistent retrieval without presentation clearly demonstrates learning, it seems reasonable to conclude that the development of verbal learning should be analyzed in terms of consistent retrieval as well as total recall, and that analysis of developmental changes in verbal learning should take into account factors affecting consistent retrieval. Since true consistent retrieval can be observed only when subjects are allowed to retrieve without continuing presentation, this will require the use of learning paradigms that permit recall without presentation.

PRESENTATIONS AS INSTRUCTIONS

Continuing to present all items in the list before every recall trial does not seem appropriate, since it confounds analysis, disrupts retrieval, and is not necessary to increase recall. While some presentation obviously is necessary, the use of restricted reminding shows that relatively little presentation may be sufficient for storage and retention. It is not yet clear just how much presentation is necessary for such learning or what form such presentation should take.

It may be useful to regard presentations as instructions that tell subjects what to retrieve, that is, which items to retrieve selectively from their permanent storage. The conventional kinds of verbal presentation are just one of several possible kinds of instruction. Presentation of pictures is another familiar way to let subjects know what to retrieve. In view of the apparent importance of the initial spontaneous retrieval, it is interesting that pictures are more likely to result in greater recall than words when pictures are presented without their labels (Davies, Milne, & Glennie, 1973), so that subjects must retrieve the name of each item for themselves. Other kinds of instructions also may be useful, since anything that leads subjects to retrieve the list items may be appropriate. In particular, definitions or descriptions are useful because they require cognitive processing by the subject in order to identify and retrieve the appropriate items.

Figure 12 shows the spontaneous retrieval of a 10-year-old girl after definitions of 40 unrelated items were presented just once. These definitions, which are illustrated at the top of Fig. 12, were those used in a study of the spontaneous retrieval of items presented as words, pictures, or definitions by Erdelyi, Buschke, & Finklestein, (1976). Each definition was read aloud to this subject, who responded with the appropriate item before the next definition was presented. After she had successfully identified all of the items at her own rate, she repeatedly tried to recall all of the items, in any order, without any further presentation at all. Extended recall was used on each of the six trials. She recalled 25 of the 40 items on the first trial and spontaneously recovered another 5 items on later trials, for a total retrieval of 30 items. The next day she retrieved 2 more new items, in addition to 29 of the 30 previously retrieved, without any further presentation. There were no intrusions in this unexpected final recall and only one item (candle) was omitted. All of the other items were consistently retrieved from their initial recall on. This fairly impressive spontaneous retrieval of 32 items after only a single presentation of 40 definitions makes one wonder just how much presentation really is necessary and whether the form of presentation may not be more important than the amount of presentation (Buschke, 1976).

Cognitive presentations that require subjects to identify each item are useful because they assure us that subjects have attended to each item, have thought about each item, know the item, and can retrieve it from their permanent memory. Although any analysis of learning and its development requires these

NAME: __J.V.__

DATE: __6/10/75__

AGE: __10 (April)__

SINGLE PRESENTATION OF WORD "DEFINITIONS"

FOLLOWED BY SPONTANEOUS, MULTIPLE RECALL TRIALS OF "WORDS"

- -

_____ SODA AND BEER CAN BE BOUGHT IN A CAN OR THIS. (BABIES OFTEN DRINK MILK FROM ONE.)

_____ USE THIS ITEM TWICE A DAY TO KEEP YOUR TEETH CLEAN.

_____ THE OLD FASHIONED WAY TO GET THE FLOOR CLEAN. THIS WAS SUPPOSED TO BE THE WITCH'S MODE OF TRANSPORTATION.

#	Item	1	2	3	4	5	6 (6/11/75)
1.	ARROW	3	1	2	28	2	19
2.	COMB						(30)
3.	BOOK	19	9	3	12	1	7
4.	GLASSES						
5.	FUNNEL	1	21	1	24	5	29
6.	HOOK	(23)	11	8	23		9
7.	IRON						
8.	FISH	(22)	4	1	24		8
9.	KEY	24	11	15	3	27	2
10.	SCISSORS	14	23	14	13	18	10
11.	TABLE	9	15	22	16	21	23
12.	OCTOPUS						
13.	TOASTER						
14.	UMBRELLA						
15.	CANDLE	(26)	2	9			
16.	WATCH	18	19	20	29	11	25
17.	BAT	6	7	7	4	10	6
18.	CHAIN	13	18	19	22	12	26
19.	DICE						
20.	FEATHER	5	3	28	25	30	20

#	Item	1	2	3	4	5	6 (6/11/75)
21.	HAT						
22.	BELL	20	8	13	26	28	21
23.	FLAG	25	12	16	20	15	15
24.	GUN	23	26	29	19	16	11
25.	LADDER	11	25	8	9	6	12
26.	PINEAPPLE	21	10	6	11	19	17
27.	SNAIL	17	2	10	7	22	4
28.	TELEVISION	22	13	17	18	14	14
29.	BOAT	(30)	21	4			16
30.	CHAIR	8	14	23	15	20	22
31.	BICYCLE	12	20	9	14	29	18
32.	XMAS TREE	(28)	12	10	8		5
33.	FOOTBALL	16	17	18	5	17	28
34.	HEART	2	5	27	27	3	24
35.	HOURGLASS	4	16	21	30	13	27
36.	SNAKE	16	4	5	6	25	3
37.	TELEPHONE						
38.	BOTTLE	7	6	25	23	26	1
39.	TOOTHBRUSH						(31)
40.	BROOM	10	24	24	17	7	13
	TOTAL	25	28	30	30	30	31

FIG. 12 Spontaneous retrieval after a single cognitive presentation that required the subject to identify each item from its description. Stippling shows the presentation of definitions. Numbers show recall order. Circles indicate additional items spontaneously retrieved on repeated recall attempts. The final recall occurred unexpectedly one day later.

assurances, they are not provided by conventional verbal presentations. Such cognitive presentations are of substantive as well as methodological interest. Instructions that require cognitive processing by the subject should be useful for investigating the effects of cognitive factors on learning and memory. There are several reasons why such presentations may be as effective as they seem to be. Such presentations may result in effective learning because they require the subject to retrieve each item spontaneously right from the outset, because they require cognitive processing, because they provide information about the item, or because they evoke imagery. These possibilities are not mutually exclusive and they are all interesting. For instance, we do not know how a subject's knowledge about an item may affect its encoding, retention, and selective retrieval; although we know that familiarity can affect learning, familiarity does not necessarily indicate knowledge about an item. A subject's knowledge about items to be recalled should be relevant for understanding what is retrieved during recall and what is learned that leads to increasingly accurate, reliable, and rapid retrieval in verbal learning. Greater understanding of the development of verbal learning will probably require more careful consideration of what is retrieved when an item is recalled, that is, more precise characterization of different kinds of "items" (Buschke, 1975b); such characterization will require information about the subjects knowledge about the items to be recalled.

CONCLUDING COMMENTS:
RETRIEVAL, PERFORMANCE, AND COMPETENCE

It is essential to obtain maximum retrieval if learning is to be analyzed accurately. The demonstration of storage and retention depends on retrieval. Successful retrieval shows storage and retention, shows that recall failures are due to retrieval failure, and shows that retrieval failures are due to difficulty in finding list items, not to difficulty in discriminating list items from items not on the list. When an item is successfully retrieved, we know that it was stored, retained, found, and correctly discriminated as a list item. When an item is not retrieved, we do not know whether it was not stored, was stored but not retained, was stored and retained but not found, or was stored, retained, and found but not discriminated. Since successful retrieval shows what happens during learning, while failure to retrieve is uninterpretable, it clearly seems necessary to do everything possible to obtain maximum retrieval from each subject. This means that testing conditions should be individualized for each subject to obtain that subject's maximum retrieval, rather than using some artificially standardized conditions that are supposedly equivalent for all subjects.

It is not really possible to establish equivalent testing conditions for different subjects unless the subjects are extremely homogenous with respect to relevant cognitive abilities. Perhaps such homogeneity may be assumed or demonstrated when the subjects in different experimental groups are all college sophomores. However, such homogeneity cannot be assumed in developmental studies, in which it is the differences between subjects at different stages of development that motivates such studies. There is no way to establish functionally equivalent testing conditions for 5- and 9-year-old children by formally identical conditions. The only kind of equivalent conditions that make sense in comparative investigation of learning by children at different stages of development are conditions that are equivalent in the sense of providing each child maximum opportunity to demonstrate storage and retention through maximum retrieval. For instance, there is no satisfactory way to obtain a list of words that is equivalent for children at different stages of development, since the items will mean something different to children at different stages of development. We can try to minimize this difficulty by using a list of items that is most appropriate for the youngest children, but that still does not solve the problem. Perhaps it might be resolved by using different lists of items for children at different stages of development, selecting items that are independently shown to be somehow equivalent for children in each stage of development. Similar considerations apply to other aspects of the experimental situation.

The critical role of retrieval in verbal learning is just one instance of the more general issue that the assessment of competence depends on performance. Since there are many reasons why performance may not reflect competence adequately, it is only when performance is successful that we can draw conclusions about competence. The proper assessment of competence, skills, and abilities requires that every effort be made to demonstrate those skills and abilities, just as every effort must be made to demonstrate storage and retention through retrieval. When younger children retrieve less than older children, we do not know whether it is due to lack of some essential abilities or to failure to use some essential abilities. Therefore, assessing some apparent lack of competence, skill, or ability would seem to require reevaluation after appropriate attempts have been made to train the child to use that ability.

If competence, rather than the use of competence, is the main issue in development, it seems necessary to make every attempt to demonstrate competence through successful performance, since evaluation of competence depends critically on performance. The implications of this view extend beyond the investigation of verbal learning: accurate and fair evaluation of those abilities and skills that may be considered important in school and job placements also may require evaluation after appropriate training under conditions that give each individual maximum opportunity to demonstrate competence, skill, and ability by successful performance. It is not logical, accurate, or fair to conclude that a child does not have certain essential skills or abilities at some stage of development simply because of poor performance in tasks that presumably require such skills or abilities. The only conclusions we can draw about competence, skill, or ability are the positive conclusions based on successful performance that demonstrates competence, skill, or ability.

ACKNOWLEDGMENTS

This work was supported by USPHS Grants MH-17733 from NIMH, NS-03356 from NIMS, and HT-01799 from NICHD. I thank Christine Sinclair-Prince for experimental and editorial assistance.

REFERENCES

Bower, G. H., & Theios, J. A learning model for discrete performance levels. In R. C. Atkinson (Ed.), *Studies in mathematical psychology*. Stanford, California: Stanford University Press, 1963.

Buschke, H. Selective reminding for analysis of memory and learning. *Journal of Verbal Learning and Verbal Behavior*, 1973, 12, 543–550.

Buschke, H. Spontaneous remembering after recall failure. *Science*, 1974, 184, 579–581. (a)

Buschke, H. Two stages of learning by children and adults. *Bulletin of the Psychonomic Society*, 1974, 4, 392–394. (b)

Buschke, H. Retrieval in verbal learning. *Transactions of the New York Academy of Sciences*, 1974, 36, 721–729. (c)

Buschke, H. Components of verbal learning in children: Analysis by selective reminding. *Journal of Experimental Psychology*, 1974, 18, 488–496. (d)

Buschke, H. Retrieval of categorized items increases without guessing. *Bulletin of the Psychonomic Society*, 1975, 5, 71–73. (a)

Buschke, H. Short-term retention, learning, and retrieval from long-term memory. In D. Deutsch & J. A. Deutsch (Eds.), *Short-term memory*. New York: Academic Press, 1975. (b)

Buschke, H. Learning is organized by chunking. *Journal of Verbal Learning and Verbal Behavior*, 1976, 15, 313–324.

Cole, M., Frankel, F., & Sharp, D. Development of free-recall learning in children. *Developmental Psychology*, 1971, 4, 109–123.

Craik, F. I. M. Two components in free recall. *Journal of Verbal Learning and Verbal Behavior*, 1968, 7, 996–1004.

Craik, F. I. M. The fate of primary memory items in free recall. *Journal of Verbal Learning and Verbal Behavior*, 1970, 9, 143–148.

Craik, F. I. M., & Birtwistle, J. Proactive inhibition in free recall. *Journal of Experimental Psychology*, 1971, 91, 120–123.

Daniels, E. M. Development of retrieval and storage in verbal learning. (Doctoral dissertation, Yeshiva University, 1975.). *Dissertation Abstracts International*, 1975.

Daniels, E. M., Buschke, H., & Voyat, G. Development of retrieval and storage in verbal learning. In preparation, 1976.

Davies, G. M., Milne, J. E., & Glennie, B. J. On the significance of "double encoding" for the superior recall of pictures to names. *Quarterly Journal of Experimental Psychology*, 1973, 25, 413–423.

Erdelyi, M. H., Buschke, H., & Finklestein, S. Hypermnesia for Socratic stimuli. *Memory and Cognition*, in press, 1976.

Erdelyi, M. H., & Becker, J. Hypermnesia for pictures: Incremental memory for pictures but not words in multiple recall trials. *Cognitive Psychology*, 1974, 6, 159–171.

Evans, R. B., & Dallenback, K. M. Single-trial learning: A stochastic model for the recall of individual words. *American Journal of Psychology*, 1965, 78, 545–556.

Frankel, F., & Cole, M. Measures of category clustering in free recall. *Psychological Bulletin*, 1971, 76, 39–44.

Fuld, P. A., & Buschke, H. Stages of retrieval in verbal learning. *Journal of Verbal Learning and Verbal Behavior*, 1976, 00, 000–000.

Glanzer, M. Storage mechanisms in recall. In G. H. Bower (Ed.), *Psychology of learning and motivation*. Vol. 5. New York: Academic Press, 1972.

Glanzer, M., & Cunitz, A. R. Two storage mechanisms in free recall. *Journal of Verbal Learning and Verbal Behavior*, 1966, 5, 351–360.

Jablonski, E. M. Free recall in children. *Psychological Bulletin*, 1974, 81, 522–539.

Kintsch, W., & Morris, C. J. Application of a Markov model to free recall and recognition. *Journal of Experimental Psychology*, 1965, 69, 200–206.

Laurence, M. V. A developmental look at the usefulness of list categorization as an aid to free recall. *Canadian Journal of Psychology*, 1967, 21, 153–165.

Pellegrino, J. & Battig, W. F. Relationships among higher order organizational measures and free recall. *Journal of Experimental Psychology*, 1974, 102, 463–472.

Restle, F. Significance of all-or-none learning. *Psychological Bulletin*, 1965, 64, 313–325.

Ritter, W., Buschke, H., & Gindes, M. Retrieval of repeated items embedded in changing lists. *Journal of Experimental Psychology*, 1974, 102, 726–728.

Ritter, W., & Buschke, H. Free, forced, and restricted recall in verbal learning. **Journal of Experimental Psychology**, 1974, 103, 1204–1207.

Roediger, H. L. Inhibiting effects of recall. *Memory and Cognition*, 1974, 2, 261–269.

Shapiro, S. R., & Erdelyi, M. H. Hypermnesia for pictures but not words. *Journal of Experimental Psychology*, 1974, 103, 1218–1219.

Shiffrin, R. M. Forgetting: Trace erosion or retrieval failure? *Science*, 1970, 168, 1601–1603.

Shiffrin, R. M., & Atkinson, R. C. Storage and retrieval processes in long-term memory. *Psychological Review*, 1969, 76, 179–193.

Tulving, E. Intratrial and intertrial retention: Notes toward a theory of free recall verbal learning. *Psychological Review*, 1964, 71, 219–237.

Tulving, E., & Pearlstone, Z. Availability versus accessibility of information in memory for words. *Journal of Verbal Learning and Verbal Behavior*, 1966, 5, 381–391.

Tulving, E., & Colotla, V. A. Free recall of trilingual lists. *Cognitive Psychology*, 1970, 1, 86–98.

Waugh, N. C., & Smith, J. E. K. A stochastic model for free recall. *Psychometrika*, 1962, 27, 141–152.

Waugh, N. C., & Norman, D. A. Primary memory. *Psychological Review*, 1965, 72, 89–104.

Part IV

READING

Within the last few years the study of reading has received a great deal of attention by cognitive psychologists. Reading was a topic of very great interest to the earliest psychologists working in the last nineteenth and early twentieth centuries, but seemingly fell into disrepute during the behaviorist period in American psychology. Some idea of this change in attitude toward complex processes such as reading is illustrated by the fact that the very interesting and now classic chapter on reading which appeared in Woodworth's 1938 edition of *Experimental Psychology* unfortunately was deleted in the 1954 revision of the book. The state of affairs has changed in the last ten years, and, along with the revival of other work on complex cognitive processes, research on the reading process has progressed at an enormous rate.

As in every field of inquiry, there are a number of central issues that define the problems to be studied and shape of the experimental questions to be pursued in the laboratory. The two chapters in this section are complementary in many ways, although as will become immediately apparent, the authors are by no means in complete agreement with each other. The first chapter by Gough and Cosky represents a sequel to Gough's well-known attempt several years ago to propose an explicit model which describes the processes that take place during one second of reading. In the present contribution, the authors review the progress that has been made over the five years since the original model was proposed. Even with the increase in research on reading by experimental psychologists, it is surprising to see how little progress has been made in understanding the complex processes in reading, particularly those aspects of the process that deal with the linguistic operations employed in sentence comprehension. However, a good deal of work has been carried out during the last few years on the word identification process. Gough and Cosky present one view of this process, a view that has been modified somewhat from Gough's original proposal that reading is carried out serially, letter by letter. However, Gough and Cosky continue to defend the view that some form of phonological mediation is involved in the reading process.

In the second chapter, Theios and Muise take issue with these views in their review of the word identification literature. It is interesting to note that many of the issues in reading studied originally by Cattell in the 1880s are still of central concern at the present time. Theios and Muise also attempt to formulate a tentative model for the word identification process in reading within the context of recent information processing models. It is very clear from the views presented in these chapters that a great deal of research still needs to be carried out on the reading process before we will be able to understand how a child acquires such a skill and how an adult uses it so effortlessly.

10
One Second of Reading Again

Philip B. Gough
Michael J. Cosky

University of Texas at Austin

Five years ago one of us had the opportunity to review the literature on the acquisition of reading for a conference on the relationships between reading and listening (Kavanagh & Mattingly, 1972). As he worked through these studies, he found himself trying to interpret their results in information-processing terms. Knowing no model of the inner workings of the reading process adequate to the task, he found himself inventing his own.

The result was an attempt to characterize the events which transpire in the head of the Reader (the moderately skilled adult) during one second of reading (Gough, 1972). Gough proposed that the printed word and sentence pass through a sequence of five stages enroute to their comprehension, and two more if they are to be read aloud (Fig. 1).

In brief, the model said this: As reading begins, the visual system produces an iconic representation of the material under fixation. Letters are read out of this icon serially, one every 10–20 msec, into a character register. The letters are then coded into phonological form by means of grapheme–phoneme correspondence rules. This form is used to locate the meaning of the word in the mental lexicon. The meaning of this and each subsequent word is deposited in primary memory, where a gifted homunculus applies his knowledge of syntax and semantics to discover the relations between the words, and places them in an abstract structure in The Place Where Sentences Go When They Are Understood. If the sentence is being read aloud, then this deep structure is handed to an editor who converts it into phonological form for execution by the vocal system.

When Gough proposed this model there was minimal evidence for its seven stages; the model could not measure up to standards like those exacted by Sternberg (1969). But the stages were not without justification, and he tried to

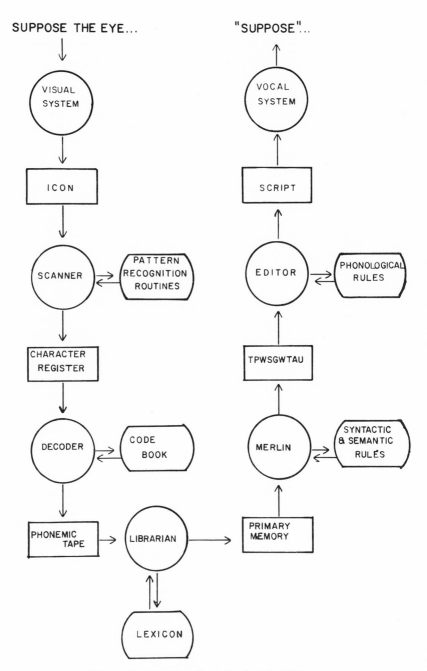

FIG. 1 A model of reading (after Gough, 1972).

adduce arguments for each of them. We propose now to ask what more can be said about them five years later.

We can say little new about the deeper stages of reading, about primary memory, and how the meanings deposited there are combined into propositions. Next to nothing has been learned about this problem (which we take to be the central question in psycholinguistics) in the past five years. Indeed, recent psycholinguistics seems to have turned its back on this problem in its haste to demonstrate new ones. Work on presupposition (e.g., Hornby, 1974) and implication (e.g., Just & Clark, 1973) indicates that more is (or at least can be) extracted from a sentence than the meaning of its words and their grammatical relations to one another. Work on context, both linguistic (e.g., Haviland & Clark, 1974) and extralinguistic (e.g., Bransford & Johnson, 1972) has demonstrated in a rigorous way what we felt we know all along, that context affects the comprehension of a sentence, sometimes to a surprising extent. But all this work has shed little light on the question of *how* context affects comprehension, and it has cast none whatsoever on the nature of the parsing process itself.

We can say little more about the most peripheral stage, the icon. The intent of this stage was to provide for the sensory registration of material being read, what might have been called, a century ago, the sensation of the printed page.

There is little that is controversial about this. Virtually every student of reading (save perhaps Geyer, 1970) would admit that reading is initially a parallel process. Everything under fixation falls on the retina at the same time, the receptors stimulated begin to function at the same time, and we must suppose that neural information about each of the resolvable letters in the fixation begins wending its way to the cortex at the same time. Moreover, it seems likely that for some time (i.e., some milliseconds) reading is just seeing, indistinguishable from any other visual activity. It stands to reason that there is some level of neural information processing at which an English word looks the same to a child, an etymologist, or an Eskimo.

The only novelty (if it was that) in this part of Gough's model was the suggestion that this "preperceptual" or "precategorical" stage should be equated with the activity in Brodmann's areas 17 and 18 of the visual cortex studied by neurophysiologists like Hubel and Wiesel (1962), *and* with the iconic memory studied by the likes of Sperling (1960). There was (and is) little evidence for these equations. But it would seem that the contents of 17 and 18 as revealed by Hubel and Wiesel's electrodes were like that needed, in a preperceptual stage, as input for character recognition. And it would seem parsimonious to assume that what *persists* in an iconic memory after a visual stimulus is gone is what was there when the stimulus was present. Moreover, it could be hoped that advances in our knowledge of these matters might then be extrapolated to elaborate our view of preperceptual processing in reading. For example, studies (reviewed by Turvey, 1973, p. 44) which seemed to show that poststimulus cueing was effective when based on some properties of the stimulus (e.g., size, location, color), but not when based on others (e.g., case, alphabet), suggested that the former, but not the latter, were present in the icon. It could be hoped that such techniques would reveal the nature of the icon's contents.

We have been disappointed in this hope. Neurophysiological studies of the visual cortex have not clarified our view of this hypothetical preperceptual stage; if anything, the picture has become less clear (see, e.g., Fishman & Michael, 1973). And studies of poststimulus cueing are, we can now see, susceptible of another, equally plausible, interpretation, namely, that *none* of the named properties are "present" in the icon, but rather that those which are effectively cued after the stimulus is gone are just those which can be "developed" rapidly from an iconic "film" before that film dissolves. (Note that it is easy to demonstrate that one can find and point to the large, or lowest, or red, items in a varied display faster than one can find the numerals, or the italics, etc.)

Thus we do not think we can say much more now about the contents of the icon than we could five years ago. The only thing we would now add is that we think there is better reason to believe the icon is at least as high as Area 17.

Our argument is this. We assume the icon to be precategorical, prelinguistic. We know that information from the two eyes is first integrated at Area 17. If we could show that linguistic information influenced the integration of the data from the two eyes at area 17, then we would have to infer that this level was not prelinguistic. If, on the other hand, linguistic information does not influence binocular interaction, then it seems fair to say that the information is still prelinguistic at that level.

We can find no evidence that linguistic information influences binocular (better, dichoptic) interaction. We have spent hours looking into a stereoscope at rival letter pairs (call them $L_1 L_2$ and $R_1 R_2$) presented at corresponding points to the two eyes. The usual result, seen 80–90% of the time, is the letter pair presented to one's dominant eye. But one sees, on occasion, each of the other combinations ($R_1 L_2$, $L_1 R_2$, and $R_1 R_2$).

Given this fact, one can ask a number of questions about linguistic influence. For example, if the letters presented to each eye ($L_1 L_2$ and $R_1 R_2$) form words, while the intereye combinations ($L_1 R_2$ and $R_1 L_2$) do not, is one more likely to see the intraeye combinations than if the opposite obtains? Or if the letters presented to one eye form a word, while those presented to the other do not, is one more apt to see the word? Or, if one intereye combination (say $L_1 R_2$) forms a word while the other ($R_1 L_2$) does not, is one more likely to see the word?

The answer in each case is no. In no circumstance have we found that a word has any advantage over a nonword. Regardless of the linguistic character of the resulting combinations, one sees the pair in the dominant eye most often, the pair in the nondominant eye next most often, and the intereye combinations least and equally.

These negative results are obviously not proof positive that information at Area 17 is still prelinguistic. But we know of no better evidence to the contrary, so we are prepared to conclude that that is the case.

We will continue to suppose, then, that there is an iconic (precategorical, preperceptual) stage, and that it is at least as high as the striate cortex. It is here that visual information begins to be transformed into linguistic, and it is here that the most controversial parts of Gough's model were located. Gough assumed that the stuff of the icon was read out letter by letter, and converted, in turn, into phonological form. Together these stages accomplish the heart of the reading process, word comprehension. There is more to be said about this.

WORD COMPREHENSION

Word comprehension can be viewed as a problem of memory search. We think it *should* be, if only to distinguish it from sentence comprehension, which cannot (cf. Gough, 1975).

Some of our colleagues object to viewing it in this way, perhaps because word comprehension seems so direct and immediate. To say one searches for the meaning of a printed word (say *table*) seems to connote that one has difficulty, as when one looks for the right word in speech production, and surely the reader seldom has any such problem. But formally the fact of the matter is that both *should* be viewed as searches; it is only that where one is remarkably efficient and (relatively) error-free, the other is (evidently) somewhat more fallible.

Word comprehension must involve memory search because the meaning of a word cannot be computed on the basis of its form. Excepting a possible minor role of phonetic symbolism (cf. Taylor, 1963), the relation between the form of a word and its meaning is arbitrary. It must be learned and stored in memory, and when we later perceive the word's form, we must take what Neisser (1967, p. 47) called the Höffding step and find its meaning in memory.

Conceived as a search task, what we accomplish when we understand a word is impressive. The memory we search is very large. The number of words in the *Oxford English Dictionary* known to educated Englishmen has been estimated at about 75,000 (Oldfield, 1963); we see no reason to suppose that Americans (or Chinese) know fewer. And this must underestimate the size of our lexicons, for the *Oxford English Dictionary* does not include the names of thousands of people known to each of us (celebrities, relatives, and friends), most geographical locations, movies, books, symphonies, songs, and laws, etc. Worst of all, the majority of words are ambiguous, so we must estimate the number of *meanings* stored in the lexicon as at least double that of the forms.

We search this vast lexicon very quickly. We do not know precisely how quickly we understand a word; there are serious problems in estimating this period. For one thing, there are difficulties in saying just *when* we understand a word. One seems to perceive that *badger* is a word before one knows that it names an animal, and that fact before one recognizes that it has still another meaning. Understanding some things about a word seems to take longer than others (cf. Collins & Quillian, 1969); recognizing ambiguity seems to take longer still (Forster & Bednall, 1976).

There are difficulties, too, with our measurements of the duration once we have decided how to define it. Whatever criterion we choose, the event we would like to time is central and we can only seek to estimate it by means of a mathematical model. And modeling is difficult, whatever the paradigm in which we seek an answer. We know, for example, that serial models can be mimicked by parallel (Townsend, 1974).

Still, to say that such efforts are difficult is not to say that they are useless; the attempt may at least inspire constructive criticism. Gough (1972) essayed the following: Rohrman and Gough (1967) found that if someone is asked to decide if a pair of words are synonymous, giving him one of the words in advance reduced his decision latency by about 160 msec. If we assume that giving the subject one of the words in advance has eliminated the time it takes to understand that word from the decision latency, then we can estimate the latency of word comprehension at this value.

We would now offer the same argument, with better data. We asked five subjects (the two of us, plus three dedicated undergraduates) to decide if 4000 pairs of words belonged to the same or different semantic categories, and measured their reaction times. The pairs constituted the Cartesian product of a set of 20 common names, half animal (e.g., *lion, horse*) and half vegetable (e.g., *pear, apple*). Each pair was presented 10 times, one word above the other, on a cathode ray tube, with the lower word delayed for 10 different intervals ranging from 0 to 900 msec. The results are presented in Fig. 2.

If we assume that the words are carried to the icon in parallel (in p msec) but are then understood one at a time (the upper in a msec, the lower in b msec), after which their meanings are compared and a decision indicated (in r msec), we can express decision latency (L) as a function of delay (d):

(1) $L(d) = p + \max(a - d, 0) + b + r$.

With $d = 0$, we see that

(2) $L(0) = p + a + b + r$.

With long delays, the function has an asymptote at

(3) $L(\infty) = p + b + r$.

The difference, $L(0) - L(\infty)$, provides an estimate of a, the time it takes to understand a word after it reaches the icon. For the five of us it averaged 220 msec. If we allowed as much as 100 msec for the formation of the icon (and a third of that seems more likely), then we must understand a word like *tiger* (at least to the point of knowing that it's an animal) in less than a third of a second.

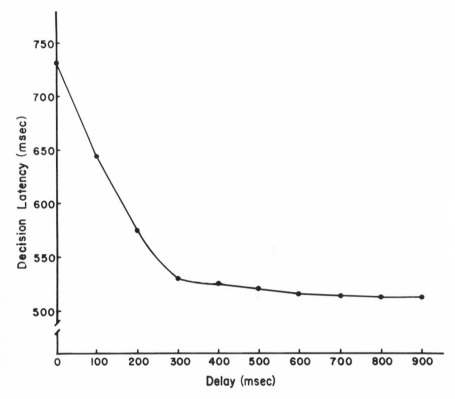

FIG. 2   Semantic decision latency as a function of delay interval.

Evidently we must have an efficient algorithm for lexical search. One of the most efficient is that which we use in searching for a word in an external dictionary like Webster's. Such a dictionary is organized on two principles. The most obvious principle is alphabetization: We arrange the words in an arbitrary but well-known order. But alphabetization is merely the superficial arrangement of the more basic organization, strict serial subcategorization. We sort the words into 26 categories according to first letter; within each of these categories we subcategorize according to second letter, and so on. Hence to locate a word within this dictionary, we need only note each of its letters in turn, and consult the appropriate space within the dictionary.

It is hard to imagine a more efficient system, and it is intriguing to imagine that our mental dictionaries are organized in similar fashion. A number of things would follow from such an assumption, and many of them hold true. For one thing, it correctly predicts that the difficulty of locating a word in the dictionary should be closely related to its length (cf. Gough, 1972). It also makes a number of accurate predictions about the difficulty of deciding whether a string of letters is in the mental dictionary or not.

It predicts that strings like SJIF or SIJF which violate the sequential constraints of the language (either orthographic or phonological), and which thus
correspond to no path through the search tree, will be rejected faster than
nonwords which do correspond to one (like SINT). Furthermore, only the first
such departure should matter (e.g., SJIF should be rejected as fast as SJMF). It
also predicts that pronounceable nonwords, since they must be traced to the
very end, will take at least as long as words.

We have repeatedly confirmed most of these predictions as a laboratory
exercise in experimental psychology (see also Snodgrass & Jarvella, 1972); some
typical data are presented in Table 1. (The exception is that a completely illegal
string like SJMF is often rejected faster than an early illegality like SJIF).

The majority of these results agree with the idea that we search our internal
lexicons the way we search external ones. They do not speak to the question of
whether the internal lexicon is organized and searched on the basis of orthography or phonology. One result obtained in the word–nonword decision task
does: It is the fact that nonwords which are homophonous with words are
rejected more slowly than nonwords which are not. This result was first reported
by Rubenstein, Lewis, and Rubenstein, (1971). We have replicated it a number of
times in our laboratory; one instance is reported in Table 1. It strongly suggests
that we search the mental lexicon with a phonological form.

The idea that we convert the printed word into phonological form is very
appealing (to us; not to Smith, 1971, or Kolers, 1970) on grounds of cognitive
economy. We have the machinery to understand the spoken word; if we could
simply convert print into speech, we would need to add nothing else to
understand the written. And it would be most efficient to convert print into
speech which has already been decoded, rather than converting it into articulatory *or* acoustic phonetic forms. That is, we know that the listener performs a
very complex analysis of the acoustic signal carrying a spoken message; he
converts a highly variable, context-dependent stream of sound into a string of
constant, commutable perceptual objects (Liberman, Cooper, Shankweiler, &
Studdert-Kennedy, 1967). Clearly, it would be inefficient to join the written
message to the spoken at the earlier level, only to subject it to this complex
analysis. Obviously, it would be far more sensible to map the printed word into
the spoken after, rather than before, the latter is processed.

TABLE 1
Word–Nonword Decision Latency as a Function of String Type

String type	Example	Mean decision latency (msec)
Word	DESK	708
"Full" unpronounceable nonword	SJMF	607
"Left" unpronounceable nonword	SJIF	644
"Right" unpronounceable nonword	SAJF	680
Pronounceable nonword	SARF	746
Nonword homophonic with word	SAIF	810

It was in service of this notion that Gough earlier proposed that the printed word was converted into the spoken at an abstract level, that a string of letters in the character register was converted (by means of grapheme-phoneme correspondence rules) into a string of systematic phonemes (Chomsky & Halle, 1968).

A systematic phoneme is an abstract entity; it cannot be operationally defined. We take it to correspond to the perceptual event which we hear as the initial segment of "pea" and "pa" (even though they are quite different acoustically), or the second segment of "split" (which, acoustically, may be *silence*). That is, we assume that the listener takes an acoustic speech signal and converts it into a succession of perceptual events. And it is these percepts into which the reader maps letters. Thus we assume that the reader, in effect, listens to print (but without speaking).

Five years ago little could be said in support of this conjecture. Now several lines of evidence can be adduced.

We have already noted that nonword strings which are homophonous with words are harder to reject than those which are not. With Lex McCusker, we have demonstrated an apparently related phenomenon: In proofreading, typographical errors which are homophonous with the intended word go undetected nearly twice as often as typos which are pronounced differently. We asked 162 students in an undergraduate methods course to proofread a 654 word passage (drawn from *Psychology Today*) which McCusker read aloud, circling any errors they identified. Two forms of the passage were prepared. Each form contained 24 errors, twelve homophonous (like *yeers* for *years*), twelve not (like *farst* for *first*); errors which were homophonous in one passage were not in the other, and vice versa. The forms were divided about equally among the subjects. On the average, our subjects failed to detect 2.08 homophonous errors and 1.30 nonhomophonous errors; the difference is highly significant. This result clearly indicates that phonology enters into proofreading (where it would seem to play no essential role).

In a similar vein, we have found that a string's phonological form can intrude upon another seemingly unrelated task. We asked 20 undergraduate subjects to name the color of ink in which 25 strings of letters were printed; four colors were used, and subject's time in seconds was recorded. We employed five different kinds of string: color words, ordinary (noncolor) words, nonwords (like *bloo* and *wredd*) homophonous with the color words, other pronounceable nonwords, and unpronounceable nonwords. The results are presented in Table 2. The most interesting result, in the present context, is that nonwords homophonous with color words produce interference as great as the color words themselves. That is, nonwords which sound like color words produce a Stroop effect as great as those words themselves (cf. Jensen & Rohwer, 1966).

We find these three effects impressive because they are *interference* effects. There is no question that the reader *can* convert print into phonological form, for he can readily read (and pronounce) any nonword which, like PHUNT or CLARMBOCK or MELSUNCERITY, violates no phonological rule. (Indeed, we

TABLE 2
Ink-Color Naming Time (sec) as a Function of String
Type

String type	Examples	Mean time (sec)
Stroop words	GREEN, BLUE	18.1
Stroop pseudowords	GRENE, BLOO	18.8
Control words	GRAIN, BLOT	14.6
Control pseudowords	GRAIF, BLOP	14.6
Consonant strings	GRJKF, BLSP	13.1

find that they can be read aloud virtually as quickly as common words.) But in these studies, the reader evidently does worse on the critical items because he converts them into phonological form, even when it would be to his advantage not to. Such results suggest that the reader has no choice in the matter, that he automatically and inevitably "hears" print.

Still, the astute skeptic will note that each of these results involves *nonwords*. He might well object that the reader has no choice, confronted with a novel letter string (which most nonwords must be), than to try to "sound it out", that is, to convert it to phonological form. But, so he might argue, words are a different matter; here the reader could, should, and does go straight from print to meaning.

We do not know how to convince the skeptic; it is hard to think of implications of the phonological assumption which involve words. One can cite the result of Meyer, Schvaneveldt, and Ruddy (1974), who found that subjects decide that a pair of orthographically similar words *are* words more rapidly if they sound alike (like MINT and HINT) than if they do not (like MINT and PINT). The result is readily explained if we assume that the recent use of certain grapheme-phoneme correspondence rules makes their application to a succeeding word more likely. Still, this result involves unlikely pairs of words in a somewhat artificial task, and it could be argued that it is spurious.

The most cogent test of the phonological hypothesis that we have yet seen was first proposed by David Fay; it was last conducted by J. D. Edgmon. Fay reasoned that if the printed word is converted into phonological form by means of grapheme-phoneme rules, then words which conform to regular rules should be converted (and understood) faster than words which constitute exceptions to such rules. Accordingly, Fay argued that we should compare the speed of comprehension of regularly and irregularly spelled (pronounced) English words. Edgmon was able to find 56 irregularly spelled words which met two criteria: that each word had a unique pronunciation (e.g., *bowl, gross*) which violates a grapheme-phoneme correspondence rule, and that there existed at least three words which examplify the rule (e.g., *cowl–fowl–howl, boss–loss–moss*). Each irregular word was yoked with a regular control word, matched in number of letters, syllables, form class, initial letter and phoneme, and frequency according to Kučera and Francis (1967). (To avoid any interactions, none of the examples of the rules which the irregular words violated were used.) The 112 items were presented in random order to each of 25 subjects (undergraduate and graduate students and faculty) who were asked to read them aloud as rapidly as possible. Each subject's median latency for regular and irregular words was computed. The means of these medians were 600 msec and 627 msec, respectively, and the difference is highly significant. Evidently regular words are recognized and named faster than irregular.

All of this evidence is easy to explain if one assumes a phonological stage in reading; indeed, it is difficult to explain in any other way. So while we cannot see how to show that the process is ubiquitous, we tentatively cling to the view that the reader automatically converts letters into phonological form, and then searches the lexicon for an entry headed by this form.

We must acknowledge, though, that there are difficulties with this view. While misspellings which are homophonous with their targets are harder to detect than others, they can be detected; we know that *sychology* is incorrect. If all we had in the lexicon was a word's phonological form, this could not be. But it is, so we must conclude that, in those cases where spelling and phonological form do not coincide, we store a word's spelling as well as its phonological form. And if that information is there, then it stands to reason that it could serve as the fundament of lexical search. What remains to be seen is whether it does; we cannot see how to settle the question.

An equally serious problem for the phonological hypothesis is that it is closely related to what may be a more controversial one. We submit that if you read phoneme by phoneme, than you must read letter by letter. The reason is simple: It is that our writing system—English orthography—maps letters onto phonemes. What this means is that if the reader is to use this mapping, he must recognize letters; grapheme—phoneme correspondence rules are useless without graphemes. So if we are to believe that there is a phonological stage in reading, we must be prepared to believe that we read letter by letter.

Few countenance the possibility that we do. The view that we read letter by letter has been in disrepute ever since Cattell (1886) found that short, familiar words are named as fast as single letters; if reading a word requires reading each of its letters, it would seem that it should take longer. The problem with this argument is that it identifies reading with naming. If reading is letter-by-letter, then reading a word must take longer than reading a letter; but naming a word must take longer than naming a letter only if the time it takes to produce a word (i.e., find and initiate its pronunciation) is comparable to that for a letter. There is good reason to doubt this; isolated letters are surely less familiar than common words. A sounder test of the same hypothesis would compare words of different lengths with identical frequencies. Cattell himself found that naming longer words takes longer than naming short, and we (Stewart, James, & Gough, 1968;

Cosky, in press) have found that word naming latency increases monotonically with word length from three to ten letters.

We find it somewhat curious that the letter-by-letter view should be so disreputable. Words are manifestly composed of letters. If one wished to build a device to recognize words, it would obviously be an enormous advantage to have available components which could recognize letters; indeed, it would make the task trivial. Moreover, to recognize words by means of letters would offer all the economy generally afforded by hierarchical recognition. If each letter can take m different physical forms, then an n-letter word can present itself in m^n different ways. A word recognition device which fails to recognize letters must thus take m^n different configurations, whereas one which mediates word recognition by letter recognition would require only mn. With m large (and it must be), the difference $(m^n - mn)$ is astronomical (save for one-letter words). We would argue that the letter-by-letter view of word recognition deserves a great deal of respect.

In one sense, it has received it. From Cattell to the present (e.g., Theios, Chapter 11 this volume), the majority of studies of word recognition have been dedicated to its refutation. The reason seems clear: the letter-by-letter hypothesis is the strongest (i.e., the clearest and richest) idea anyone has had about word recognition. In our view, it has not yet been done in, for most of its wounds have been superficial and easily treated. But it has recently suffered two severe blows.

One is that delivered by Reicher (1969) and Wheeler (1970). What they found is that a letter is more accurately recognized in a word than in isolation, with factors like redundancy perfectly controlled. Thus, if asked to decide whether a target letter was an A or an O, a subject who achieves 75% accuracy with the target (e.g., A) presented in isolation will achieve 85% accuracy if it is presented (for the same duration) within a word (like RAPE). No serial model can accomodate this result, for obvious reasons: If the reader is exposed to a stimulus for a duration which only enables him to recognize a given letter at 75% accuracy, then if there is *more* than one letter out there, he should do poorer on those letters (for in the interval they are available to him he would have no time to deal with the others).

For some time, we were reluctant to accept the Reicher–Wheeler results as fact, for Wheeler himself had difficulty replicating his own results in our laboratory (leading one to wonder how many other failures failed to reach the published literature.) But by now the result has been obtained by several investigators (and the serial model is embarrassed by even an equality between a letter in isolation and in a word, to say nothing of the word's superiority).

How the Reicher–Wheeler effect is to be explained remains, to our minds, a mystery. The most natural interpretation, that the perception of a given one of the letters in a word is facilitated (i.e., hastened) by the presence of the others, seems to be false. We asked 20 subjects to press one button if they saw an A, another if they saw an E; subjects were told that the critical letter would occur right on the fixation point whether the letter was alone or in a three-letter word. (Thus a subject stared at a point where an A or an E appeared, either alone or flanked by letters (P and T) which completed a three-letter word.) We found that subjects took 440 msec to categorize the letter standing alone, but 470 msec to categorize the same letter in a word. This result obviously provides no support for the idea that the target letter is perceived more rapidly when it is presented within a word.

However it is to be explained, the Reicher–Wheeler effect is clearly problematic for a serial, letter-by-letter view of word recognition. An advocate of the latter can only wave his hands and denigrate tachistoscopic presentation. But what may prove to be an even more embarrassing problem has been exposed by Cosky (in press).

Cosky reasoned that if words are recognized by means of their letters, then the difficulty of recognizing words should be related to the difficulty of recognizing their letters. Accordingly, he proposed to compare the speed of recognizing words composed of easy- and hard-to-recognize letters.

Cosky measured the relative legibility of the 26 letters created by the character generating routines of our computer, in three different tasks. In one, subjects were simply asked to name the letters. In a second, subjects were asked to discriminate the letters from the other nonalphanumeric symbols (e.g., #, ?, +). In a third, subjects were asked to discriminate the (normal) letters from rotated and inverted ones. In each case, the subject's response latency was measured.

With our font, the three measures showed substantial agreement. For example, E, R, and T were among the half dozen fastest in all three measures, C and J among the slowest five in each. Pooling them, Cosky divided the letters into the 13 easiest and 13 hardest to recognize. He then composed four words from the easy letters at each length from three to eight; corresponding to each easy word, he created one from the hard letters, yoking them on length, class, and frequency. Thus, there were 144 items, constructed factorially with two levels of letter difficulty and six of length. The 144 words were presented in random order to each of 15 subjects, who were asked to read them aloud; their response latencies were recorded. The results, presented in Fig. 3, were clear: Word recognition latency increased linearly with length, but was unaffected by letter difficult. Mean recognition latency for "easy" words was 576.6 msec, for "hard" words 575.5 msec.

The fact that recognition latency is virtually identical for words composed of easy and hard letters does not encourage one to believe that we read letter-by-letter, either serially or in parallel. But the fact that it increases with word length suggests that we do read in units smaller than the word.

We are confident that those units are neither spelling units nor syllables; neither of these bears any consistent relationship to word recognition latency. In his dissertation research, Cosky conducted three studies of word recognition

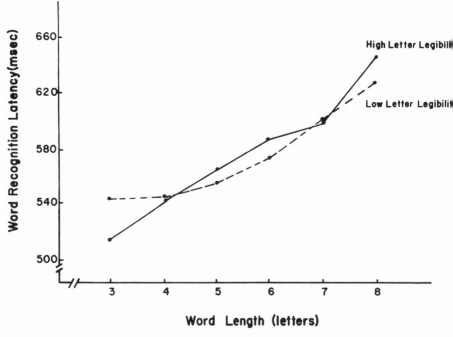

Word Length (letters)

FIG. 3   Word recognition latency as a function of length and letter legibility.

latency as a function of word length. In the first, he compared the recognition
latency of 100 four-letter and 100 five-letter words, with length in phonemes
(i.e., spelling units) and syllables (as well as frequency) controlled. In the second
experiment he made the same comparison, *mutatis mutandis*, for three- and
four-phoneme words; in the third, he compared one- and two-syllable words. As
Table 3 shows, only length in letters had any reliable effect.

The fact that word recognition latency increases with length argues that the
unit of word recognition is smaller than the word. Cosky's results would seem to
eliminate two conspicuous alternatives, the syllable and the spelling unit. If we
must reject the letter, we seem forced to contemplate that the word is recognized by units smaller than the letter, that is, features (cf. Smith, 1971).

We find this unpalatable, for we find the feature hypothesis virtually untest-
able. Trying to refute the feature notion is like trying to swat a swarm of gnats:
You cannot identify individuals, and whereever you strike, the collection turns
up somewhere else.

At one level, no one would try to refute the feature hypothesis. We all agree
that word recognition, however it proceeds, begins with some kind of "pre-
analysis" of the visual signal, perhaps into lines, angles, curves, junctures, etc.
That is, it seems that every student of word recognition assumes that it is
features, not retinal points, that serve as the input to the word recognition
device.

TABLE 3
Word Recognition Latency as a Function of Length in
Letters, Phonemes, and Syllables

Length	Mean recognition latency (msec)
Experiment I	
Four letters	581
Five letters	596
Experiment II	
Three phonemes	542
Four phonemes	540
Experiment III	
One syllable	551
Two syllables	554

What distinguishes the feature hypothesis is that it assumes that there are no intermediate levels of organization, no categorization of local collections of features into regular units, which mediate the perception of the word.

In particular, of course, it denies that there is any organizing of features into *letters*. This leads, we think, to the following prediction. Suppose we were to obliterate (by mask) a given area at successive half-letter serial positions along a word, and measure word recognition latency as a function of the mask's serial position. The feature hypothesis would surely hold that the mask would be more disruptive on the left than on the right, and more disruptive on the ends than in the middle, for it would hold that the features are richer (thicker, more important) in these regions. That is, it would predict a classic serial position curve, with maxima at the ends and a minimum somewhere in the middle. But, we contend, the feature hypothesis has no basis for predicting any other maxima or minima; it must predict that the function would be smooth between the extremes.

The facts are otherwise. We asked 12 subjects (faculty and graduate students to name 204 six-letter words, presented on a CRT, as rapidly as possible, and measured their reaction times. The words, like ARCTIC and VIOLIN, were selected such that if any one of its letter was masked, the word was still uniquely recoverable (i.e., only the deleted letter could be inserted to form a word). (Thus in these words, each single letter was completely redundant.)

For each subject, 17 words were presented intact, and 17 words were presented with a letter-wide rectangular mask centered at each of the 11 successive half-letter positions in a six-letter word. Thus, 17 words were presented with the mask covering the first letter, 17 with a mask covering the right half of the first letter and the left half of the second, and so forth. (The reason for the peculiar number is simple: words of this kind are hard to find.) The 12 word–mask combinations were rotated across the 12 subjects, such that each word was

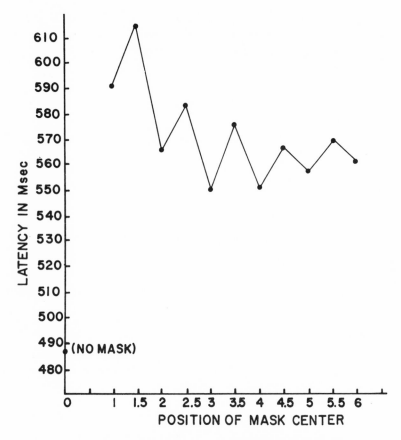

FIG. 4   Word recognition latency as a function of mask position.

masked at each position and each subject saw an equal number of words in each condition, but each word was presented to each subject only once.

The results are presented in Fig. 4. As a feature theory (or any other) would predict, there was a clear effect (averaging nearly 100 msec) of masking one-sixth of a word on the recognition of that word, and, on the whole, it varies in the classic manner with the serial position of the mask. But the effect also clearly depends on whether the mask covers one-half of two adjacent letters, or both halves of a single letter; on the average, masking parts of two letters retards word recognition by more than 20 msec more than masking one.

These data clearly indicate that, if features are involved in word recognition, their organization into letters is important. An obvious way to explain this is to assume that word recognition is mediated by letter recognition. The result is, we think, difficult to explain if one denies this; at least we will leave it to others to try.

Thus, while there is evidence that is difficult to reconcile with the view that we read words by reading their letters, there is evidence that is hard to explain otherwise. In the end, we are caught in the middle.

REFERENCES

Bransford, J., & Johnson, M. Contextual prerequisites for understanding: Some investigations of comprehension and recall. *Journal of Verbal Learning and Verbal Behavior*, 1972, **11**, 717–726.

Cattell, J. M. The time it takes to see and name objects. *Mind*, 1886, **11**, 63–65.

Chomsky, N., and Halle, M. *The sound pattern of english.* New York: Harper and Row, 1968.

Collins, A. M., & Quillian, M. R. Retrival time from semantic memory. *Journal of Verbal Learning and Verbal Behavior*, 1969, **8**, 240–247.

Cosky, M. J. The role of letter recognition in word recognition. *Memory and Cognition*, in press.

Fishman, M. C., & Michael, C. R. Integration of auditory information in the cat's visual cortex. *Vision Research*, 1973, **13**, 1415–1419.

Forster, K. N., & Bednall, E. S. Terminating and exhaustive search in lexial access. *Memory and Cognition*, 1976, **4**, 53–61.

Geyer, J. J. Models of perceptual processes in reading. In H. Singer and R. Ruddell (Eds.), *Theoretical models and processes of reading.* Newark, Delaware: International Reading Association, 1970. Pp. 47–94.

Gough, P. B. One second of reading. In J. F. Kavanagh and I. G. Mattingly (Eds.), *Language by ear and by eye.* Cambridge, Massachusetts: MIT Press, 1972.

Gough, P. B. Language and reading. In D. Duane & M. B. Rawson (Eds.), *Reading, perception and language.* Baltimore, Maryland: York Press, 1975. Pp. 15–38.

Haviland, S. E., & Clark, H. H. What's new? Acquiring new information as a process in comprehension. *Journal of Verbal Learning and Verbal Behavior*, 1974, **13**, 512–521.

Hornby, P. A. Surface structure and presupposition. *Journal of Verbal Learning and Verbal Behavior*, 1974, **13**, 530–538.

Hubel, D. H., & Wiesel, T. N. Receptive fields, binocular interaction, and functional architecture in the cat's visual cortex. *Journal of Physiology*, 1962, **160**, 106–154.

Jensen, A. R., & Rohwer, W. D. The Stroop Color-Word Test: A review. *Acta Psychologica*, 1966, **25**, 36–93.

Just, M. A., & Clark, H. H. Drawing inferences from the presuppositions and implications of affirmative and negative sentences. *Journal of Verbal Learning and Verbal Behavior*, 1973, **12**, 21–31.

Kavanagh, J. F., & Mattingly, I. G. *Language by ear and by eye.* Cambridge, Massachusetts: MIT Press, 1972.

Kolers, P. A. Three stages of reading. In H. Levin & J. P. Williams (Eds.), *Basic studies on reading.* New York: Basic Books, 1970.

Kučera, H., & Francis, W. N. *Computational analysis of present-day American English.* Providence, Rhode Island: Brown University Press, 1967.

Liberman, A. M., Cooper, F. S., Shankweiler, D. P., & Studdert-Kennedy, M. Perception of the speech code. *Psychological Review*, 1967, **74**, 431–461.

Meyer, D. E., Schvanereldt, R. W., & Ruddy, M. G. Functions of graphemic and phonemic codes in visual word recognition. *Memory and Cognition*, 1974, **2**, 309–321.

Neisser, U. *Cognitive psychology.* New York: Appleton-Century-Crofts, 1967.

Oldfield, R. C. Individual vocabulary and semantic currency. *British Journal of Social and Clinical Psychology*, 1963, 2, 122–130.

Reicher, G. M. Perceptual recognition as a function of meaningfulness of stimulus material. *Journal of Experimental Psychology*, 1969, 81, 275–280.

Rohrman, N. L., & Gough, P. B. Forewarning, meaning, and semantic decision latency. *Psychonomic Science*, 1967, 9, 217–218.

Rubenstein, H., Lewis, S. S., & Rubenstein, M. A. Evidence for phonemic recoding in visual word recognition. *Journal of Verbal Learning and Verbal Behavior*, 1971, 10, 645–657.

Smith, F. *Understanding reading.* New York: Holt, Rinehart, and Winston, 1971.

Snodgrass, J. G., & Jarvella, R. J. Some linguistic determinants of word classification times. *Psychonomic Science*, 1972, 27, 220–222.

Sperling, G. The information available in brief visual presentations. *Psychology Monograph*, 1960, 74, No. 11.

Sternberg, S. The discovery of processing stages: Extensions of Donder's method. *Acta Psychologica*, 1969, 30, 276–315.

Stewart, M. L., James, C. T., & Gough, P. B. Word recognition latency as a function of word length. Paper presented at a meeting of the Midwestern Psychological Association, 1968.

Taylor, L. K. Phonetic symbolism reexamined. *Psychological Bulletin*, 1963, 60, 200–209.

Townsend, J. T. Issues and models concerning the processing of a finite number of inputs. In B. H. Kantowitz (Ed.), *Human information processing: Tutorials in performance and cognition.* Hillsdale, N.J.: Lawrence Erlbaum Assoc., 1974. Pp. 133–186.

Turvey, M. T. On peripheral and central processes in vision: Inferences from an information-processing analysis of masking with patterned stimuli. *Psychological Review*, 1973, 80, 1–52.

Wheeler, D. D. Processes in word recognition. *Cognitive Psychology*, 1970, 1, 59–85.

11
The Word Identification
Process in Reading

John Theios
J. Gerard Muise[1]
University of Wisconsin

The task we consider is how literate humans identify words. We are concerned
with the process whereby visually displayed sequences of letters are transformed
into semantic units and phonetically rendered overt verbalizations. For purposes
of analysis we will consider only experimental situations in which a reader is
presented with an individual word and must either read it out loud or must
indicate whether it is the same as or different from a target word the reader is
holding in memory.

Most theorists would agree with an analysis of word identification similar to
that presented in Fig. 1. This is commonly referred to as the hierarchical
word-processing hypothesis. The process begins with stimulation by a visually
presented word. In the laboratory this would typically be via a chronoscope, a
tachistoscope, or a cathode-ray oscilloscope. In the normal reading of printed
text, stimulation would be initiated by a fixation of the eye after a saccadic
movement to a particular area in a line of text. From the research of McConkie
and Rayner (1975) and Rayner (1975) we know that the fixation would last
about 250 msec and that the visual system takes in approximately 20 characters
in the central foveal area of the eye (about 4° of visual angle). Thus, no more
than four or five complete words are ever seen at one time. The length of a
forward saccade is only about 8 or 9 characters. Thus, there presumably is about
50% overlap in what the eye sees in successive fixations. As a result it may be the
case that the visual system is processing only about 10 characters per saccade.

[1] On leave from the Université de Moncton, Nouveau Brunswick, Canada with support
from a Fellowship from the Canada Council.

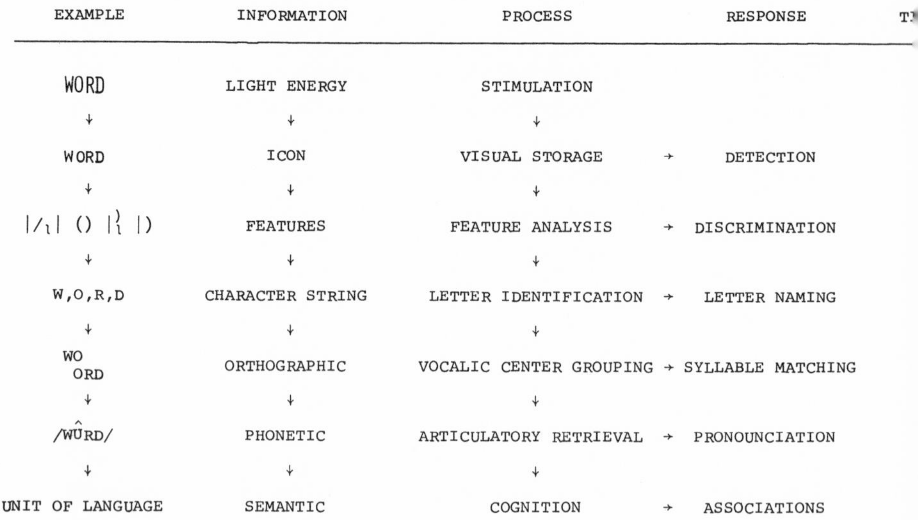

EXAMPLE	INFORMATION	PROCESS	RESPONSE	T.
WORD	LIGHT ENERGY	STIMULATION		
↓	↓	↓		
W O R D	ICON	VISUAL STORAGE	→ DETECTION	
↓	↓	↓		
I/ɪI ( ) I¦ I)	FEATURES	FEATURE ANALYSIS	→ DISCRIMINATION	
↓	↓	↓		
W,O,R,D	CHARACTER STRING	LETTER IDENTIFICATION	→ LETTER NAMING	
↓	↓	↓		
WO ORD	ORTHOGRAPHIC	VOCALIC CENTER GROUPING	→ SYLLABLE MATCHING	
↓	↓	↓		
/wÔRD/	PHONETIC	ARTICULATORY RETRIEVAL	→ PRONOUNCIATION	
↓	↓	↓		
UNIT OF LANGUAGE	SEMANTIC	COGNITION	→ ASSOCIATIONS	

FIG. 1   Representation of a serial, hierarchical model for the word identification process in reading.

Most investigators agree with Sperling (1963) that following a presentation of a visual stimulus, a two dimensional iconic representation of the stimulus pattern is maintained in what Massaro (1975) calls a preperceptual visual store. At this level of information processing, the observer presumably is in a position to make a detection response, that is, indicate that something visual has been presented. Much research indicates that the iconic representation is available in the visual store until another eye fixation or another stimulus presentation creates a new icon by writing over the previous one.

The next level of processing that occurs is feature analysis. Most theorists agree that the features of a visual display are processed in parallel with respect to type and position. Position in the visual field presents no problem, but no one as yet has delineated the specific visual features of letters which the visual system uses in word recognition. At this point in time, *features* are typically treated as theoretical primitives. An exception to this observation is the very serious research by Rumelhart and Siple (1974) on the identification of letters and words using a fixed feature set. Gough (1972) ignored the process of going from features to letters, but suggested that the information in the preperceptual visual store was read out letter-by-letter at a rate of 10–20 msec per character. In contrast to a serial read-out from iconic memory, most theorists assume that the feature analysis process going from features to letters is carried on in parallel, simultaneously for each character in the display. The icon is assumed to energize a set of feature detectors and the unique pattern of activated features is assumed to map onto or excite letter codes stored in long-term memory. During the feature analysis process the observer should be in a position to make quick discriminations on the basis of such cues as direction, length, angularity, and curvedness.

After the feature analysis process has finished, the reader is left with a string of characters in short-term memory. Presumably, the reader should now be in a position to name the letter or letters that were presented. The process of identifying and naming single characters presented in isolation has been detailed by Theios (1975). Naming latencies for individual characters are relatively fast (in the neighborhood of 400 msec) and independent of such variables as experimental character set size and character presentation probability. The data suggest that character identification is a largely perceptual process that operates essentially in parallel, at least not by a character-by-character internal scan of the experimental ensemble of characters stored in memory. It is generally assumed that after the memory codes for a string of characters have been activated in memory, the pattern of energized letter codes (along with relational information) excites a set of letter-grouping codes. Gough (1972) suggested that character strings map onto a set of systematic phonemes (in the sense of Chomsky & Halle, 1968) which are directly governed by the orthography of the language. Gibson (1971) and LaBerge and Samuels (1974) feel that letter strings activate spelling patterns. Hansen and Rogers (1968) and Smith and Spoehr (1974) proposed that character strings are decomposed into syllable-like units called vocalic center groups (VCG), which consist of a vowel and its preceding and following consonant clusters.

The activated codes for syllables, spelling patterns, or vocalic center groups energize memory codes for individual words. The memory code for a word might be a visual orthographic code, a phonetic name code, or a semantic meaning code. In any event, when the visual processing of a word has reached this "word" level, the reader should be able to recognize and name the word. Presumably, the processing of memory codes for words continues into semantic memory in such a way that the reader can give an association to or a definition of a word just shortly after the word can be named.

As we mentioned earlier, most theorists would not greatly disagree with the hierarchical analysis of reading which has just been given. A major problem, however, is the specification of the temporal relation of the levels of processing to each other. Some theorists seem to imply a serial, level-by-level processing progression (e.g., Gough, 1972; LaBerge & Samuels, 1974; Smith & Spoehr, 1974). Others imply a direct memory access or a strictly parallel processing system (e.g., Anderson, in press; Rumelhart & Siple, 1974; F. Smith, 1969, 1971). Turvey (1973) has suggested a mixed parallel-serial process for the visual system. A parallel net of receptors receives the stimulus information, and as the information proceeds through the nervous system the various levels of analysis overlap and operate concurrently with each other. The output of each level of analysis is fed forward to every higher level. A decision net receives information over time from all levels of analysis and interprets the continually growing matrix of information. Depending upon the requirements of the task (detection, discrimination, identification, transformation, classification, association, etc.) a response decision is contingent on a sufficient amount of information being aggregated. The word identification models of Estes (1975) and Massaro (1975) would seem to fit nicely into Turvey's (1973) concurrent–contingent representation.

If word identification is a serial hierarchical process as represented in Fig. 1, then with the right experimental arrangement, one ought to be able to infer the temporal course of processing from the ordering of the latencies of the required responses: detection, feature discrimination, character naming, syllable matching or vowel–consonant classification, word pronounciation, and finally word associations. On the other hand, with a parallel or a mixed-mode processor, this type of response ordering need not be necessary. In the literate human, processing might automatically proceed to a high cognitive level and then activate the phonetic code for the word. Answering orthographic questions like "Does the word contain the letter R or two vowels?" may take place by retrograde analysis of the word's components by reconstruction after processing has reached the cognitive level. In short, the system may operate more like that represented in Fig. 2, with phonetic, orthographic, and semantic information available at about the same time, *after* the entire word has been identified. Indeed, the output of the feature abstraction process may be the addresses of a number of memory files where phonetic, orthographic and semantic information about the word is stored. As such, reading may be an essentially direct-access memory retrieval process.

In this chapter we shall examine the results of a number of experimental studies which bear directly on the word identification process in reading. In turn, we will consider variables such as number of letters in a word, number of syllables in a word, vocabulary size, word frequency in the language, and phonologic, orthographic, and semantic properties of words. Following our previous work (Theios, 1973, 1975) our emphasis here will be on an analysis of the temporal course of information processing. Finally, a tentative model for the word identification process in reading will be suggested.

IS A WORD PROCESSED SERIALLY LETTER BY LETTER OR IN PARALLEL?

Gough (1972) suggests that the letters of a word are read out of iconic storage one at a time at a rate of about 15 msec per character. However, this question was addressed and answered by one of the first series of experiments ever conducted by an American psychologist. In 1873 Wilhelm Wundt founded the world's first laboratory of experimental psychology at the University of Leipzig, and in 1883 James McKeen Cattell became Wundt's first assistant. Cattell's (1886) dissertation directly addressed the question of the time course of processing in reading. Cattell's amazing series of experiments overwhelmingly indicated that word identification involves parallel feature processing as opposed to

PROCESS				RESPONSES	TIME
					‾‾‾‾
STIMULATION					↓
WORD					↓
↓					↓
ICONIC STORAGE		→		DETECTION	↓
WORD					↓
↓					↓
FEATURE ABSTRACTION		→		DISCRIMINATION	↓
|/₁| () |¦₁ |)					↓
↓					↓
MEMORY FILE ADDRESSES		→		(COGNITION)	↓
← word →					↓
↓	↓	↓			↓
SEMANTIC FILE	ORTHOGRAPHIC FILE	PHONETIC FILE			↓
unit of language	w,o,r,d	/wûrd/	→	PRONOUNCIATION	↓
↓	↓				↓
		→ → →		LETTER MATCHING	↓
↓					↓
→	→ → → →	→		ASSOCIATIONS	

FIG. 2   Representation of a mixed, serial-parallel model for the word identification process in reading.

sequential feature processing. In view of Cattell's very strong results, it is interesting to speculate why contemporary writers (e.g. Gough, 1972; LaBerge & Samuels, 1974; Smith & Spoehr, 1974) have ignored Cattell's historical results. The answer may lie in the fact that in the present state of science characterized by a virtual information explosion, only a very small part of the historical research literature has proved to be critically relevant to developing theory. Thus, contemporary investigators tend to discount old data or are not even aware of its existence. Cattell's (1886) research is an exception to this observation, and thus it is exceptionally relevant to current development of theories of reading. Since Cattell's classic results may not be widely known, we will summarize some of his data here, and relate it to contemporary theories of word identification.

Cattell's (1886) Experiment on Letter and Word Recognition

As a student at Leipzig, Cattell was greatly influenced by two events. The first was Donders' (1869) revolutionary paper on the use of reaction time to measure the speed of cognitive processing. The second was the invention by Mathias Hipp of the electric chronoscope in 1843. The chronoscope was a device for very quickly (to 1 msec) presenting a visual display to an observer and measuring

TABLE 1
Mean Recognition Latencies (msec) for Individually
Presented Stimuli[a]

Stimuli (26 each)	Single letters	Short words (4–5 letters)	Long words (9–12 letters)
Mean	318	346	354
Additional msec/letter		8	4

[a]Values calculated from data of Cattell, 1886

(again to 1 msec) a verbal or manual response to the visual display. In one series of experiments, Cattell used the Donders' Type c method and presented either single letters, short words (one-syllable with 4–5 letters) or long words (3–5 syllables with 9–12 letters). The observer was given a target stimulus verbally and instructed to lift his finger from a telegraph key only if the presented probe stimulus matched the target stimulus held in memory. On a random half of each series of 26 trials the probe matched the target and on the other half of the trials the probe was not the same as the target. The results of this experiment are shown in Table 1. Of the data, Cattell (1886) says "It will be noticed that the perception-time is only slightly longer for a word than for a single letter; we do not therefore perceive separately the letters of which a word is composed, but the word as a whole [pp. 387]." In contemporary metatheoretic language we would say that the data strongly suggest that the individual letters of a word are processed in parallel as opposed to serially, letter-by-letter. If we compute the additional time taken by a 4 or 5 letter word over a single letter it comes to about 8 msec per character. However, with a 9–12 letter word, the additional time over a single letter is only about 4 msec per character. Diminishing time estimates such as these are exactly what one would expect from a parallel processing system with some variance in the finishing times of the component channels.

Given that Cattell's (1886) study was one of the first experiments conducted in psychology, contemporary readers might raise questions about the soundness of his methodology. Is the data from two observers (one a native German reader) sufficient? Was there adequate balancing and randomization of the stimulus materials over trials and experimental sessions? Can we be sure that the observers were not using the initial or first two letters of the word to make a fast familiarity judgment rather than processing the entire word? Fortunately, Cattell's (1886) experiment has been replicated in essence by Johnson (1975) with appropriate controls, and the results are effectively equivalent.

Johnson's Replication of Cattell's Effect

In Johnson's (1975) Experiment II, 20 observers each received 200 trials in a target-probe experiment. The targets and probes consisted of either single letters

TABLE 2
Mean Recognition Latencies (msec) for Individual
Letters and Words[a]

Type of target and probe	Response type		
	Yes	No	Mean
Single letter	537	499	518
1-Syllable, 5-letter word	529	517	523
2-Syllable, 5-letter word	533	510	521
Mean	533	509	521

[a]Data from Johnson (1975).

or five letter words exposed for 300 msec. The probes were displayed visually in a tachistoscope. Half of the words were one-syllable words and half were two-syllable words. Half of the observers were tested on single letters first and half were tested on words first. On each block of 25 trials the observer was given a target stimulus and then a sequence of 25 probe stimuli with a 10 sec interstimulus interval. The task for the observer was to indicate, by pushing one of two buttons, whether or not the visually presented probe was or was not the same as the target. The probe stimulus was the same as the target on 20% of the trials and was different from the target on 80% of the trials. The pool of stimuli consisted of 20 letters, 20 one-syllable words, and 20 two-syllable words. The reaction time data from Johnson's (1975) experiment is given in Table 2. As can be seen, the observers were able to process one- and two-syllable five-letter words as fast as single letters. The data replicate the results of Cattell (1886) in all important respects. There is clearly no evidence whatsoever for the hypothesis that individual letters of a word are processed sequentially. Johnson's (1975) results also cast suspicion on Smith and Spoehr's (1974) hypothesis that a serial decoding of vocalic center groups takes place in word recognition. Johnson used both one- and two-syllable words in his experiment. The serial vocalic center group hypothesis would require that the two-syllable words take longer to be processed than the one-syllable words. This was simply not the case in Johnson's (1975) data.

Cattell's Experiment on the Reading of Individual Letters and Words

Cattell (1886) also performed an experiment in which the observer was to read out loud an individually presented letter or word. There were 26 letters, 26 short words (4–5 letters), and 26 long words (9–12 letters). Two bilingual readers were tested; one was American (Cattell) and one was German (Dr. G. O. Berger). The experiment was replicated twice, once using English letters and words in

TABLE 3
Mean Verbal Reading Latencies (msec) for Individually
Presented Stimuli[a]

Stimuli (26 each)	Single letters	Short words (4 –5 letters)	Long words (9–12 letters)
First Language[b]	410	388	431
Second Language[b]	478	414	464
Difference	68	26	32
Mean	444	401	448

[a]Values calculated from data of Cattell (1886).
[b]Languages: English and German.

Roman type font and once using German letters and words in Gothic type font. The stimuli were displayed visually on the Hipp chronoscope until the reader responded verbally. The latency of the verbal response was recorded by a voice relay to the nearest msec.

The results are given in Table 3. It can be seen that short words in both the readers' first and second language were read faster (401 msec) than either single letters (444 msec) or long words with 9–12 letters (448 msec). The data clearly reject the hypothesis (Gough, 1972) that words are read by a serial letter-by-letter decoding process. In this experiment, the readers were able to read a long 9–12 letter word as fast as they were able to read a single letter. Of his data, Cattell (1886) comments: "We find further that we named a word in less time than a letter. This is not surprising; we are constantly reading and using words, much more than letters; so the association between the concept and the name has become closer and takes place in less time [pp. 531–532]." In contemporary metatheoretic terms, we would simply say that the results strongly imply a parallel processing system for the decoding of individual letters of a word.

It is interesting to note that the processing time for short (common) and long (uncommon) words does not interact with whether the word is in the reader's first or second language. One might have expected that in a reader's second language, long (relatively uncommon) words might take much longer to process than short common words. The data, however, indicate that there is simply a constant difference of about 42 msec in processing first-language units as opposed to second-language units, which does not interact with word length.

EFFECT OF WORD UNCERTAINTY ON READING LATENCIES

It is often claimed that the redundancy in language is such that in many instances, the reader has a fairly accurate expectancy for a particular word before his eyes fixate on it. This has been alleged to be the basis for fast reading.

TABLE 4
Mean Silent Reading Time per Word (msec) as a Function of Vocabulary Size[a]

	Vocabulary size (Word uncertainty)								
	2	4	8	16	32	64	128	256	Mean
Reading Time:	259	286	288	299	295	291	291	286	287

[a]Values calculated from data of Pierce and Karlin (1957).

With an expectancy for a coming word or string of words, the reader does not need to process the expected word or string of words as fully as when the word was not expected (F. Smith, 1971; Venezky, 1974). Whether the presumed speed advantage for expected words is due to a response bias (e.g., inferential skipping of words) or due to faster identification of expected words is a completely open question. In this section we will consider laboratory reading experiments in which word uncertainty was systematically varied. The major question here is whether the speed of word identification is inversely related to word uncertainty, as some have claimed.

Pierce and Karlin (1957) conducted one of the first experiments on reading rate as a function of word uncertainty. They had three readers read pages containing a column of 60 unconnected common words per page. The number of different words encountered in a testing session (vocabulary size) was varied from 2 to 256. The mean reading time per word as a function of word uncertainty is given in Table 4. As is clearly obvious, ". . . reading rate is essentially independent of vocabulary sizes from 4 to 256 words when familiarity and word length are kept fairly constant" (Pierce & Karlin, 1957, pp. 499).

Since Pierce and Karlin's readers were reading from pages of words, the readers were most likely taking in more than just one word per eye fixation. The failure to find decreased reading speed with increasing word uncertainty may have been due to the readers parallel processing of several words per eye fixation.

Experiment I

Method. To eliminate the possibility of processing more than one word at once, we replicated in essence the Pierce and Karlin design, presenting words individually on a cathode-ray oscilloscope. The readers were 12 American college students whose first reading language was English and 12 foreign college students whose first reading language was something other than English.[2] All the readers were tested with vocabulary sizes of 2, 4, 6, and 24 English words and were

[2] The native reading languages of the 12 foreign readers were Chinese (2), French (1), French–Canadian (3), German (1), Hindi (2), Kannarese (1), Portuguese (1), and Spanish (1). The readers were all students at the University of Wisconsin who responded to a posted request for bilingual readers.

instructed to read the word out loud as soon as it appeared on the display. Reading latencies for individually presented words were recorded by a voice relay, and an audio taperecording was made of the reader's actual verbal response. A PDP-8 computer generated the words, recorded the data, and presented the words with a 500 msec response-stimulus interval with every word in a vocabulary set appearing 24 times.

Results and Discussion. The data are presented in Table 5, and it can be seen that we have replicated Pierce and Karlin (1957) in all important aspects. Reading latencies for individually presented words are constant and independent of vocabulary size.

It is interesting to note that our results on processing words in one's first or second language are similar to those obtained by Cattell in 1886. We had thought that there might be an interaction between word uncertainty and language such that word uncertainty would slow up the foreign readers, but not the American readers. This did not occur. As with Cattell's data, there was simply a constant difference of approximately 85 msec between American students reading English words and foreign students reading English words.

It is also interesting to note that in this study, number of letters in the word had no effect on reading latencies. The words varied from three to seven letters and the correlation with reading latency was −.01 for the American readers, +.10 (not significant) for the foreign readers, and +.04 (not significant) for both groups of readers combined. This lack of correlation is consistent with Cattell's

TABLE 5
Reading Latencies (msec) for Individually Presented Words in Experiment I

First language	Latencies (msec)					Correlations of Latency with:	
	Vocabulary size					Word frequency	Number of letters
	2	4	6	24	Mean	r_{LF}	r_{LN}
English							
Mean	493	519	509	507	507	−.41*	−.01
SD	64	82	67	73	72		
Foreign							
Mean	588	589	593	584	588	−.38*	.10
SD	75	80	64	79	72		
Pooled							
Mean	541	554	551	546	548	−.40*	.04
SD	84	88	79	95	82		

*$p < .05$.

TABLE 6
Mean Reading Latencies (msec) for Individually Presented Words as a Function of
Vocabulary Size[a]

	Number of words per condition (word uncertainty)								
	4	6	8	12	16	18	20	24	Mean
Experiment II (6 subjects, 192 trials/condition)		478		416		429			441
Experiment III (6 subjects, 200 trials/condition)					426		424	423	424
Experiment IV (12 subjects, 50 trials/condition)	424		420	422					422
Mean:	424	478	420	419	426	429	424	423	429

[a]Values computed from data of Perlmutter, Sorce, and Myers (1976).

(1886) results on the null effect of word length on reading times considered earlier.

Our results on reading latencies as a function of word uncertainty have been replicated by Perlmutter, Sorce, and Myers (1976). They included word reading sessions as controls in their experiments on associative reaction times. In three experiments they varied vocabulary size from 4 to 24, using 138 common nouns containing 4–6 letters. Words were presented on a video television monitor every 4 sec and a voice relay recorded the reading reaction times. The data are presented in Table 6. Again, reading latencies were effectively constant at approximately 429 msec as vocabulary size was varied as 4, 6, 8, 12, 16, 18, 20, and 24 words.

In Experiments III and IV Perlmutter et al. (1976) also varied the situational relative frequency with which a word came up in an experimental testing session. Twenty-five percent of the words were each presented with a high relative frequency and 75% of the words were each presented with a lower relative frequency. The relative frequency ratio was two to one over all vocabulary sizes. They found that over vocabulary sizes from 4 to 24, relative frequency of word occurrence did not have an effect on reading latencies. The data are presented in Table 7.

The Perlmutter et al. (1976) data on the reading of individual words is similar to that reviewed by Theios (1975) which indicates that the reaction times for naming single alphanumeric characters is independent of stimulus uncertainty. As such, the naming of individual alphanumeric characters may simply be reading of single element "words."

TABLE 7

Mean Reading Latencies (msec) of Individually Presented Words as a Function
of Situational Relative Frequency and Vocabulary Size[a]

	Number of words per condition (word uncertainty)						
Relative frequency of word	4	8	12	16	20	24	Mean
Frequent	418	416	422	430	421	424	422
Infrequent	429	424	421	423	428	422	425
Mean	424	420	422	426	424	423	423

[a]Values computed from data of Perlmutter, Sorce, and Myers (1976).

In summary, there is no evidence whatsoever to indicate that word uncertainty
has an effect on the speed at which words are perceptually identified. Taken
collectively, our results, together with those of Pierce and Karlin (1957) and
Perlmutter et al. (1976), are consistent with the hypothesis that word identification in reading is a parallel process which directly accesses that area in memory
where at least the articulatory code is stored.

If the observer in these experimental tasks involving the reading of individual
words, were to store the stimulus words in a short-term memory or buffer and
then scan the buffer in a serial fashion (either self-terminating or exhaustive)
then we would have expected the reading latencies to increase with experimental
ensemble (vocabulary) set size. Of course, the data were constant and independent of vocabulary set size. If responding in these experimental reading tasks
were a function of the strength of an association established *in the testing
situation* as a result of stimulus–response occurrences, we again would have
expected response latency to increase with vocabulary set size. Of course, it did
not. Thus, the data are consistent with a parallel processing model for word
identification and are inconsistent with serial processing and response strength
models based on situational frequency of occurrence of individual words.

EFFECT OF ORTHOGRAPHY, PHONOLOGY, AND SEMANTICS
ON WORD IDENTIFICATION

An important issue in understanding reading is the sequence in which orthographic, phonetic, and semantic variables have their effect on word processing.
Gough (1972) feels that meaning is mediated by phonology; a sequence of
recognized letters generates a sequence of phonemes dictated by the phonological rules of the language, and the reader understands the word through its
sound, which was learned in childhood. In a similar fashion, Hansen and Rogers
(1968) and Smith and Spoehr (1974) feel that the vocalic center group carries
the reader from a sequence of letters to speech sounds which mediate the

semantic characteristics of the word. On the other hand, Massaro (1975) feels that "the experienced reader is capable of going from features to letters to words to meaning without an intervening phonemic or phonological translation." LaBerge and Samuels (1974) also admit this possibility.

Still less clear are the constraints which orthography (relational properties of letters) places on word identification in reading. Smith (1971) feels that letter identification is bypassed in word recognition, with the reader going directly from features to meaning. This direct access view has also been suggested by Rumelhart and Siple (1974) and by Morton (1969) with his notion of the logogen, a template-like word memory in the lexical store. Venezky (1967, 1970) has made formal linguistic analyses of English orthography and letter-to-sound correspondences. Venezky (1974) has pointed out that letter-to-sound correspondences are necessary for the child who, early in the process of initially learning to read, sounds out letters to obtain a phonetic rendition from which meaning is derived. But for the competent reader, the use of letter-to-sound correspondence seems to occur only in determining the pronounciation and meaning of a new or unfamiliar word. In any event, very little definitive experimental research has been conducted on the contribution to the speed of word identification made by orthographic, phonetic, and semantic variables.

As a start on unraveling the question of the role of orthographic, phonetic, and semantic variables in reading, we analyzed the reading–pronounciation latencies collected by Nodine and Hardt (1969) on all 2100 consonant–vowel–consonant (CVC) trigrams in which the initial and final consonant differed. Nodine and Hardt (1969) were interested in the relationship between the judged meaningfulness of a CVC and its pronounciation latency. They found that the pronounciation latency correlated −.37 with Archer's (1960) judged meaningfulness values.

We, however, were interested in a different question, the effect of orthographic, phonetic, and semantic factors on the speed of reading CVCs. The population of CVCs can be partitioned into subsets according to semantic, phonetic, and orthographic properties. Some CVCs are in fact words, for example, *BAD, COG, DEN,* and thus have a high semantic value as well as conforming to the phonology and orthography of the language. Some CVCs are not words, but are valid English syllables which conform to the orthography and phonology of the language. The set of CVC syllables may be subpartitioned into two subsets: (a) CVCs that sound like real words (pseudohomophones) and thus have a high semantic value since they phonologically map onto real words, for example, *BAC, CED, FER,* and (b) CVC syllables which phonetically do not map onto real words and thus should have a lower semantic value, for example, *BAF, CEM, DIR.* Some CVCs are not syllables (they do not occur in English words and thus violate *empirical* orthography), and yet they are homophonic to English words, for example, *FAX, CEX, DOH.* In spite of their orthographic violations (or rareness) these CVCs presumably should have high semantic value since phonologically they map onto real English words. Other CVCs that do not

TABLE 8

An Analysis of Reading–Pronounciation Latencies and Association Value of CVCs as a Function of Semantic, Orthographic, and Phonetic Factors[a]

	Familiar English orthography			Unfamiliar English orthography			
Type of CVC: Example:	Word BAD	"Homophone" BAC	Syllable BAF	"Homophone" CEX	Pronounceable BEX	Not-Pronounceable XOL	All CVCs
Semantic component	Excellent	Good	Fair	Good	Poor	Poor	
Orthographic component	Good	Good	Good	Poor	Poor	Poor	
Phonetic component	Good	Good	Good	Good	Good	Poor	
Latency (L) (Nodine & Hardt, 1969)							
Mean (msec)	757	780	790	775	799	903	810
SD (msec)	102	99	119	94	110	160	133
Number of CVCs	488	201	290	132	470	519	2100
Association value (A) (Noble, 1961)							
Mean	96	92	84	78	59	38	70
SD	5	7	12	11	23	16	26
r_{LA}	$-.24^b$	$-.06$	$-.11$	$-.12$	$-.54^b$	$-.21$	$-.37^b$

[a]Values calculated from data of Nodine and Hardt (1969) and Noble (1961).
[b]Statistically significant at $p < .05$.

occur in English qualify neither as syllables nor pseudohomophones, and yet they are quite readable and pronounceable, for example, *BEP, CAX, DEZ*. These relatively meaningless, nonsyllable, pronounceable CVCs should be low on semantic and orthographic information but should be reasonably high on phonetic information since the letter-to-sound correspondence causes no problem for the reader. Finally there is the set of CVCs which most native English readers find difficult to pronounce or can be pronounced only by adding an implied vowel to one of the consonants, for example, *NAJ, XOL, ZOJ*. These CVCs should be low on orthography, phonology, and semantic meaningfulness.

We partitioned the set of 2100 CVCs into the 6 categories described above and considered the Nodine and Hardt (1969) reading–pronouncing latencies as a function of the semantic, phonetic, and orthographic information in the CVC.[3] The data are presented in Table 8. As can be seen, words were read fastest (757 msec), but there was no significant difference in reading latencies among the orthographically familiar pseudohomophones, valid syllables, and the orthographically unfamiliar pseudohomophones (pooled mean of 784 msec) which were significantly slower than the real words by 27 msec. Thus, both semantic meaning and orthographic familiarity significantly affect the speed of reading and pronouncing CVCs. The fact that there were no significant differences among the orthographically familiar and unfamiliar homophones and the syllables suggests that either good orthography and phonology or good phonology and meaning are equivalent in their contribution to reading and pronunciation speed. The nonword, nonsyllabic, nonhomophonic pronounceable CVCs had reading latencies of 799 msec, 15 msec slower than the previous trio of CVC categories. This significant difference suggests that good phonology (pronounceability) does not insure fast reading and pronouncing *unless* there is also a good orthographic or semantic component to the CVC. As expected, the "nonpronounceable" nonsense CVCs were 104 msec slower than the pronounceable

---

[3] In partitioning the CVCs, five judges (including the authors) who were native English readers were used. One was English, one was Canadian, and three were American. Of the Americans, one was from the West Coast, one was from the Midwest, and one was from the East Coast. A CVC was classified as a *word* if it was listed in the College Edition of the *Random House Dictionary of the English Language* (1969) or in *Webster's Seventh New Collegiate Dictionary* (1965) *and* appeared in the word frequency counts of Kučera and Francis (1970) or Carroll, Davies, and Richman (1971). Commonly used slang, abbreviations, nicknames, and foreign words (e.g. *LOS*) were classified as words since they occasionally do appear in print and have semantic meaning. A CVC was classified as a *pseudohomophone* if the judges agreed that it could be pronounced in a way equivalent to some English word. A CVC was classified as having an *unfamiliar orthographic structure* if it did not appear in any of the trigram counts given by Underwood and Schulz (1960). A CVC was classified as *pronounceable* if all the judges agreed that they experienced no difficulty in reading and pronouncing it. A CVC was classified as *"not pronounceable"* if at least one judge experienced difficulty pronouncing it. A pronounceable CVC which did not violate the *empirical* orthographic structure of English was classified as a *syllable*.

nonsense CVCs. Much of this 104 msec difference is presumably taken up by the reader searching for and inserting an extra vowel to render the CVC pronounceable.

It is interesting to note, that for the CVCs that were actual English words, there was no correlation between the reading–pronounciation latencies and the Kučera and Francis (1970) count of the frequency of the word in English text ($r = -.03$, $N = 488$ words). The frequency values ranged from 9,816 occurrences per million words to less than once per million, with a mean of 33 occurrences per million and a standard deviation of 82. The correlation between reading–pronounciation latency and the logarithm of word frequency[4] was also nonexistent ($r = -.05$). At least for three letter CVC words, there seems to be no effect of word frequency on speed of reading and pronouncing.

Several problems exist with the Nodine and Hardt (1969) data. Their pronounciation latencies are rather long compared to those recorded by other investigators. There are at least two reasons for this. First, since at least 500 of the CVCs are very difficult to pronounce (mean of 903 msec), the subjects may have adopted some nonreading processing strategy during runs of nonpronounceable CVCs. Thus, when a pronounceable CVC occurred, the subject may have continued to process in the nonreading mode, slowing the readers on some of the pronounceable CVCs (overall mean of 780 msec). Second, the instructions to the subjects stressed *pronounciation* and not *speed of reading* the CVC.

EFFECT OF WORD FREQUENCY ON READING LATENCIES

Experiment II

It is a commonly accepted hypothesis that the speed of identifying a word is directly related to the frequency with which the word occurs in the language. However, data regarding this hypothesis have typically come from nonreading experiments such as tachistoscopic word recognition tasks (e.g., Solomon & Postman, 1952) and lexical decision tasks (e.g., Rubenstein, Garfield, & Millikan, 1970). Forster and Chambers (1973) found that a small sample of 15 words having a mean Kučera–Francis count of 199 per million were read an average of 71 msec faster than a sample of 15 words having a mean frequency of only one per million. However, phonology and orthography were not controlled in their experiment. It is probable that word frequency is positively correlated with both the ease of letter-to-sound correspondence (phonology) and the degree to which orthography approximates some optimum. Thus, if the speed of word identification is in fact correlated with word frequency, the correlation may be fortuitous, with the critical variable being phonology or orthography.

---

[4] A transform of adding 1 to the frequency count for each word was performed in order to avoid the problem of taking the logarithm of values less than one in those cases in which the word frequency was less than one in a million.

In the present experiment we attempted to control for both phonology and goodness of orthography by using pairs of homophonic words and making within pair comparisons. This controls for phonology since the required response is identical for both members of the homophonic pair. With respect to orthography, the control is not as tight since the pair could differ on approximation to an optimal orthography. However, both members of each homophonic pair are real words, and thus by definition each has a legal orthography. It would be expected that in some instances, the lower frequency member of a homophonic pair would have a better orthographic structure than the higher frequency member. To the extent that this occurred, the correlation between word frequency and reading latency should be reduced, if indeed orthography has an effect on speed of word identification.

Method. There were 12 readers, all University of Wisconsin students. The word population consisted of nearly all (600) of the monosyllabic homophones listed in *A Dictionary of American Homophones and Homographs* (Whitford, 1966). Each reader received two sessions of 600 trials with a rest period after each block of 200 trials. In each session, a reader saw each word exactly once. During each session each reader received a different, completely random (without replacement) sequence of words. During one of the sessions, the words appeared in upper case letters, and in the other session the words appeared in lower case letters. Six of the readers received upper case words first and six of the readers received lower case words first. A PDP-8 computer generated and displayed the words on an oscilloscope and the readers were asked to read the words out loud as fast as they could without making any mistakes in reading or pronouncing. Reading response latencies were recorded by a voice relay and the reader's actual response was recorded by an audio taperecorder. Each word was displayed until the reader responded, and the response–stimulus interval was 1 sec.

Results and discussion. The 600 homophones yielded 304 pairs[5] in which one member of the pair had a higher Kučera–Francis (1970) frequency than the other. A completely within-comparison analysis of variance was performed on the latency data from these 304 pairs. The means are presented in Table 9. There

[5] The list of 600 homophones used is presented in Table A of the Appendix. The mean reading latency for each word is also given for those who wish to perform their own linguistic analyses.

The following 20 pairs of words were not included in the analysis of variance since our Midwestern readers did not respond to them as homophonic: adds, adze; air, heir; eye, aye; bard, barred; bow, beau; bowl, boll; corps, core; cue, queue; fain, fane; fur, fir; fold, foaled; lean, lien; moose, mousse; peak, pique; pique, peek; pie, pi; plate, plait; sweet, suite; tool, tulle; ward, warred.

The following 17 pairs of homophones were not included in the analysis of variance because they occurred with the same Kučera–Francis (1970) frequency in the language: braise, brays; brays, braze; braise, braze; cense, scents; coax, cokes; crews, cruise; fane, feign; hew, hue; knave, nave; leach, leech; moat, mote; prays, preys; quarts, quartz; retch, wretch; slay, sleigh; tucks, tux; wain, wane.

TABLE 9
Mean Reading Latency (msec) for Individually Presented
Homophonic Words as a Function of Word Frequency in
Experiment II

Session	304 Homophonic word pairs		
	Higher frequency	Lower frequency	Mean
First			
Mean	576	590	583
SD	113	123	119
Observations[a]	3532	3524	7056
Second			
Mean	557	563	560
SD	108	112	110
Observations[a]	3551	3540	7091
Pooled			
Mean	566	577	571
SD	111	118	115
Observations[a]	7083	7064	14147

[a]Data from trials on which mispronounciations occurred were not included in the analysis.

was no significant effect of type font case nor of order of case. Thus, these two variables will not be considered.

There was only a small difference of 11 msec between reading latencies for paired high-frequency and low-frequency words. This is true in spite of the fact that the higher frequency words occur an average of about 600 times per million and the low frequency words occur an average of about 32 times per million (Kučera & Francis, 1970). Because of the large number of observations (approximately 1200 per reader) the 11 msec difference is statistically significant [$F(1, 11) = 17.52, p < .005$]. Whether the small 11 msec difference is meaningful is open to question. It is quite possible that the difference is really due to differential orthographic structure or letter-to-sound correspondence and not due to word frequency.

Considering all 600 words, the correlation between reading latency and the logarithm (see Footnote 4) of the Kučera and Francis (1970) word frequency is low ($r = -.30$). Further, the log of word frequency also correlates $-.27$ with H_2, the second-order orthographic information in the word (Attneave, 1959; Shannon, 1951), which correlated $+.26$ with reading latency. If we consider the correlation between reading latency and the log of word frequency with the effects of second-order orthographic information partialed-out, the r is attenuated to $-.25$. Thus, word frequency alone is accounting for only about 6% of the variation in the reading latencies.

In the population of 600 monosyllabic homophones, the number of letters in a word varies from 2 to 7. The correlation between reading latency and number of letters in the word is also low ($r = +.30$). The linear regression equation is

$$L' = 525 \text{ msec} + (11.5 \text{ msec}) N, \tag{1}$$

where L' is the predicted latency in msec and N is the number of letters in a word. Rather than indicating serial processing of the letters of a word, the slope coefficient of 11.5 msec per letter probably is the result of lowered visual acuity as the additional letters moved away from the central fovea of the eye (Estes, Allmeyer, & Reder, 1976; Gough, Chapter 10, this volume). In our experiments there was an explicit fixation point, and the first letter of each word always appeared in this position. Thus, the final letter of a word varied from one to six character positions to the right of the fixation point.

EFFECT OF SPELLING ON READING LATENCIES

Experiment III

In controlling phonology by using paired homophonic words which differed in frequency of occurrence in the language, we found only a small 11 msec difference in reading latencies due to differential frequency. It could be argued that the observed frequency difference in the population of 304 monosyllabic homophonic pairs was not large enough to permit a sizeable difference in reading latencies. Thus, the question arises as to how large a reading latency difference could be obtained under extreme conditions when phonology is held constant. To answer this question we conducted an experiment in which readers were presented with a sequence of words and pseudowords, in which for each word, there was a yoked pseudoword which was homophonic to the word, but which was spelled differently and in fact was *not* a word in the English language. In this experiment the orthographic properties of the letter strings are varied, but the phonology is the same, and the letter-to-sound correspondence of the pseudoword mapped onto the semantic meaning of the real word. A critical feature of this experiment is that while the words will be familiar to the reader and have appreciable frequency counts, the pseudowords will be totally novel to the reader and by definition will have absolutely zero frequency of occurrence in the language. The important question for us to answer is, "How much can reading speed be slowed down by a totally incorrect spelling?"

Method. There were 12 readers, all college students, and 100 monosyllabic word–pseudoword pairs, each stimulus varying from 3 to 6 letters in length. Each reader received 800 trials in four blocks of 200 trials each. Each pseudoword was constructed such that its letter-to-sound correspondence resulted in a vocalization equivalent to that of its yoked real word. A PDP-8 computer generated and displayed the letter strings on an oscilloscope and the readers were asked to read the words or pseudowords out loud as fast as possible, without making any mistakes in reading or pronounciation. The reading response latencies were recorded by a voice relay and the reader's actual response was recorded by an audio taperecorder. The response–stimulus interval was 1 sec. Each word or pseudoword was displayed to the reader four times in the course of the experiment, twice in lower case letters and twice in upper case letters. For each reader the sequence of words and pseudowords was completely random (without replacement) on each block of 200 trials. Six of the readers received a session of two blocks of upper case letters followed by a session of two blocks of lower case letters. Six of the readers received a session of two blocks of lower case letters followed by a session of two blocks of upper case letters.

Results and Discussion. An information theory analysis of the homophonic word-pseudoword pairs based on their second-order orthographic structure (Attneave, 1959; Shannon, 1951) indicated that over all 100 words and 100 pseudowords, the average second-order orthographic information (H_2) is the same, 20 bits, for both the real words and the pseudowords. The words have a mean Kučera–Francis frequency count of 39 occurrences per million words and, of course, all the pseudowords have a frequency count of zero. A list of the homophonic word–pseudoword pairs and their associated reading latencies is given in Table B of the Appendix for those who wish to conduct their own linguistic analyses of these data.

An analysis of variance was performed on the latency data and the means are presented in Table 10. There was no significant effect of type font case nor of order of case. Thus, these two variables will not be considered further.

Holding phonology constant, there was an effect due to the orthography of the stimulus. Real words were read with a mean latency of 548 msec and pseudowords with a mean latency of 568 msec. The 20-msec difference is significant $[F(1, 11) = 88.44, p < .001]$. This 20-msec difference compares favorably with the 27-msec difference between pronouncing latencies for words and homophonic nonwords which we found earlier in our analysis of the data of Nodine and Hardt (1969). In fact, considering only the first session during which the readers were relatively unfamiliar with the pseudowords, the reading latency difference between words and homophonic pseudowords is exactly 27 msec. The effect apparently is real; nonstandard spelling slows down the reading of individual words by about 20–30 msec, even if phonology is held constant.

The overall session (practice) effect was not significant. However, there was a significant session by stimulus type interaction $[F(1, 11) = 13.70, p < .01]$. In the second session, the mean reading latency for the homophonic pseudowords decreased 26 msec from that during the first session, while the mean reading latencies for the real words decreased only 12 msec from the first session to the second session. Thus, familiarity with the experimental set of 100 pseudowords

TABLE 10
Mean Reading Latencies (msec), Word Frequency, and
Orthographic Information for Individually Presented
Homophonic Words and Pseudowords in Experiment III

	Stimuli		
Session	Words	Pseudowords	Mean
First			
Mean (msec)	554	581	567
SD	61	83	74
observations	1200	1200	2400
Second			
Mean (msec)	542	555	549
SD	64	70	67
observations	1200	1200	2400
Pooled			
Mean (msec)	548	568	558
SD	63	78	72
observations	2400	2400	4800
Kučera–Francis Word Frequency			
Mean	39	0	20
SD	69	0	49
observations	100	100	200
Second-order orthographic information			
Mean H_2	20 bits	20 bits	20 bits
SD	4 bits	4 bits	4 bits
observations	100	100	200

increased reading speed, but situational familiarity with the set of 100 real words did not have as much of an effect.

The results of the experiment are clear. The speed of articulation of a visually presented word is not mediated solely by phonology or letter-to-sound correspondence. An unfamiliar or nonstandard spelling slows down the articulation of words in reading.

The logarithm (see Footnote 4), of the Kučera–Francis (1970) frequency count of the real words correlated with reading latency −.38. However, the second-order orthographic information of the words (Attneave, 1959; Shannon, 1951) also correlated with both reading latency ($r = .35$) and word frequency ($r = −.37$). An attenuated correlation of only −.29 between latency and log frequency results when the effects attributable to orthographic information are partialed out. The attenuated correlation accounts for only 8% of the variance in the word reading latencies.

For the 100 words, reading latency correlates +.35 with number of letters in the word. The linear regression has a zero intercept of 480 msec and a slope of 15 msec per letter. For the 100 pseudowords, there is no significant correlation between reading latency and number of letters (r = +.06).

THE WORD IDENTIFICATION PROCESS IN READING

Our review of research on the speed of word identification has resulted in the following observations:

1. Words are not decoded letter by letter as is clearly demonstrated in the research of Cattell (1886) and Johnson (1975).

2. Holding number of letters constant at a reasonably small number, the number of syllables in a word does not affect its identification time, as demonstrated by the results of Johnson (1975).

3. Word predictability and uncertainty has no effect on the speed of identification of individually presented words, as was demonstrated by the results of our Experiment I and those of Pierce and Karlin (1957) and Perlmutter et al. (1976). This is in marked contrast to the data from choice reaction tasks involving manual responses in which response latency is an increasing function of stimulus uncertainty (e.g., Hyman, 1953; Merkel, 1885).

4. Good phonology or letter-to-sound correspondence is not sufficient to completely mediate the transformation from a visual representation of a word to its articulation. Both orthography and meaning have an effect on the speed of articulation. This was demonstrated by our Experiments II and III and by our analysis of the Nodine and Hardt (1969) data.

5. All three of our experiments indicated that word frequency seems to have a small but consistent effect on the speed of reading individually presented words.

What implications do these empirical observations have for theories of word identification in reading? First of all, Gough's (1972) conjecture of a serial letter-by-letter decoding of words may be dismissed as inconsistent with reality. The data overwhelmingly indicate parallel processing of the letters of a word. Secondly, Hansen and Rogers (1968) and Spoehr and Smith's (1973, 1975) suggestion of a serial decoding of vocalic center groups can be rejected on the basis of the multisyllabic data of Johnson (1975). A word containing two vowels should take longer to process than a word with a single vowel, other things constant. It simply does not. In our Experiment I, readers identified single voweled words in 545 msec and words with two vowels in 549 msec. The 4-msec difference is far from significant. Thirdly, we found that good phonology without either familiar orthography or meaning slows down articulation. This result can be taken as evidence for rejecting Gough's (1972) notion that the meaning of a word is mediated through its phonological memory code. Meaning seems to have an effect early in the reading process. Our Experiment III results on pseudohomophones shows that, holding phonology constant, spelling also contributes to the speed of word identification and articulation.

Other theories of word recognition (Estes, 1975; LaBerge & Samuels, 1974; Massaro, 1975; Morton, 1969; Rumelhart & Siple, 1974; and Smith, 1971) seem untouched by the experimental results we have reviewed. All six theories can permit parallel processing of the letters of a word and the nonnecessity of phonological mediation of meaning. The first three theories, however, make strong predictions regarding the sequential temporal order in which information about the stimulus should be available to the observer. Feature information should be available before letter information which should be available before orthographic (relational) information which should precede semantic informa- tion. The completely parallel or direct memory-access models of the last three theorists could permit all types of word information to be available at roughly the same time or in various other sequential arrangements. Future research should be carefully designed to precisely determine the temporal sequential order in which stimulus information is available to the observer.

For example, consider Johnson's (1975) Experiment I. Twelve observers were presented with either 4 letter or 6 letter words in eight blocks of 24 trials each. Prior to a block of trials the observer was instructed to look for a target stimulus, either a single letter or an entire word. On letter comparison blocks, the observer's task was to indicate with a manual response whether or not the target letter was contained anywhere in the presented probe word. On word comparison blocks, the observers were to manually indicate whether or not the target word was the same as the presented probe word. The probe matched or contained the target stimulus on half of the trials. The data are presented in Table 11. For word comparison, there was no significant difference in respond-

TABLE 11
Mean Search Latencies (msec) for Individual Letters and
Entire Word Targets[a]

Probe	Letter search latencies: Response type			Word search latencies: Response type		
	Yes	No	Mean	Mean	Yes	No
4-letter word	505	526	515	396	383	408
6-letter word	534	535	534	402	388	415
Mean	520	530	524	399	386	412

[a]Data from Johnson (1975).

ing yes or no. There was also no significant difference as a function of word length, and the word comparisons were relatively fast, 399 msec. For letter comparison blocks there was also no significant effect of either probe word length or yes-no response. However, the important result is the very large difference between comparing entire words and comparing single letters. The observers were 125 msec *faster* in comparing entire 4 or 6 letter words than in comparing a single target letter to the letters of a probe word. The data suggest two conclusions. First, target-probe word comparisons are performed in parallel with respect to the letters of the word and possibly other featural information. Second, letter comparison may be performed by a search of the letters of the probe word *after* the word has been encoded in memory and identified. It seems that the observers are mentally computing or visually scanning the individual letters of the probe word after the probe word has been semantically identified. This result causes difficulty for a *sequential* hierarchical processing model such as that proposed by LaBerge and Samuels (1974). In the hierarchical processing model, individual letter information should be available to the observer before whole word information. It seems not to be.

One could argue that lateral masking of the letters in the probe word could account for the suppression of reaction speed in the letter search conditions (cf. Townsend, Taylor, & Brown, 1971). However, on the surface, a 125 msec difference seems much too large to be attributable to lateral masking. To minimize the effects of lateral masking of letters in a word, Johnson (1975) ran a third experiment in which he instructed the observers to compare a target letter with only the *first* letter of a probe word. Control conditions included trials on which the target and probe stimuli were either both single letters or both entire words. Thus, there were three types of trials: those on which the observer was asked to look for, say, a B where the probe might be either BLOCK or CLOCK; trials on which, say, B was the target and the probe might be B or C; and trials on which, say, BLOCK might be the target with the probe being either BLOCK or CLOCK.

There were 72 observers in Johnson's (1975) Experiment III, and each received 72 trials per condition, 36 yes responses and 36 no responses. The data are presented in Table 12. There was no significant difference in the target-probe comparison speed between single letters and five letter words. The mean reaction times were 518 and 527, with a pooled average of 522 msec. On the other hand, comparing a single letter target to the first letter of a probe word took significantly longer, 564 msec. The 42-msec difference could be due to lateral masking from the letters to the right of the critical first letter. However, the 42-msec difference could also be a result of comparing the target to the probe display *after* the probe word has been read holistically by the observer. If this is in fact the case, the task of searching for a target letter in a probe word may tell us little about the process of word identification in reading since semantic and phonological information in the probe word may be extracted well before the letter matching process begins.

TABLE 12
Mean Recognition Latencies (msec) for Single Letter
and Word Targets and Probes[a]

Type of target and probe	Response type		
	Yes	No	Mean
First letter in word	539	590	564
Word	514	541	527
Single letter	493	543	518
Mean	515	558	537

[a]Data from Johnson (1975).

Lexical Decision and Word Identification

The lexical decision task has become a very popular paradigm for studying the processing of linguistic material by humans. For example, Rubenstein and his associates (Rubenstein, Garfield, & Millikan, 1970; Rubenstein, Lewis, & Rubenstein, 1971a, b) and Meyer, Schvaneveldt, and Ruddy (1974) have used the lexical decision task to study graphemic, phonemic, and semantic variables in word recognition. The observer is asked to classify a sequence of letter strings as to whether the presented string is a word or is not a word. Upon analysis, however, it may be argued that the lexical decision task may have little to do with the orthographic, phonetic, and semantic variables that are involved in *reading and understanding* a word. In reading, a person is not required to decide whether a letter string is a word or not. It is taken for granted that all letter strings encountered in reading are words. Only on the rare occasion when one chances to detect a typographical error, does a regressive eye movement focus on a letter string and the reader decides "No, that is not a word." Making a word–nonword lexical decision may be similar to the task of searching for a letter embedded in a word in the sense that the lexical decision process may occur *after* the observer has read, identified, and understood the word. A consideration of the overall mean reaction times from studies on the reading of individually presented words and the overall mean reaction time from studies on lexical decision lends support for this conjecture. In Table 13 are listed the mean reading latencies from studies of word identification (Cattell, 1886; North, Grant, & Fleming, 1967; Perlmutter et al. 1976) and the mean word classification times from studies of lexical decisions on individually presented words (Meyer & Ellis, 1970; Meyer, Schvaneveldt, & Ruddy, 1974, 1975; Rubenstein et al. 1970, 1971a, b). It should be noted that here we are not considering the lexical decision time to decide that a letter string is not a word, but only times for letter strings that actually are words. The average *reading* latency is in the neighborhood of 500 msec. The average *lexical decision* time is in the neighborhood of 700 msec. Humans seem to be able to read and articulate a word about

TABLE 13
Mean Reaction Time (msec) to Unassociated, Individually Presented Words
as a Function of Experimental Task

Reading–pronounciation		Lexical decision	
Cattell (1886)	425	Meyer and Ellis (1970)	640
North, Grant, and		Rubenstein, Garfield,	
Fleming (1967)	488	and Millikan (1970)	827
Perlmutter, Sorce,		Rubenstein, Lewis, and	
and Myers (1976)	429	Rubenstein (1971a)	836
Theios and Muise, Exp. I	507	Rubenstein, Lewis, and	
Exp. II	548	Rubenstein (1971b)	841
Exp. III	573	Meyer, Schvaneveldt, Exp. 1	566
Meyer, Schvaneveldt,		and Ruddy (1975) Exp. 2	606
and Ruddy (1975) Exp. 3	540[a]	Exp. 3	620[a]
Mean:	501		705
Standard error:	58		123
Number of samples:	7		7
Difference:		204	
		$t(12) = 3.96, p < .01$	

[a]Within-experiment, between subjects' comparison using a
vocal response for lexical decision.

200 msec faster than they manually indicate that it is a word. This is true in spite of the fact that the finger is as fast as or faster than the tongue in simple reaction time experiments (e.g., Cattell, 1886). We must, of course, be cautious in comparing the results of one experiment with those of a different experiment. However, given the general research literature, the observed 200 msec difference is appreciable as reaction time differences go. In point of fact, in a controlled within-subject, within-word experiment, Forster and Chambers (1973) found that word reading latencies (544 msec) were in fact 162 msec faster than positive lexical decisions (706 msec). A compelling interpretation of these results is that the information an observer needs in order to make a positive lexical decision is available only *after* he has read the word and understands its semantic meaning. The observation that verbal word identification is faster than lexical decision is consistent with the theoretical analysis of the time course of human information processing made by Theios (1975). He suggested that visually presented verbal–linguistic stimuli are processed in parallel and the name code (identification code or cognitive meaning) of the stimulus acts essentially as the address in memory of the "files" where other information, including possible response codes, are stored. The naming or reading response for verbal–linguistic stimuli (alphanumeric characters and words) is so fast, because only a small amount of further information translation need be done to arrive at the articulatory code for an alphanumeric character or a word. According to Theios' (1975) analysis, any

other response (except simple detection) to a visually presented verbal–linguistic stimulus (a response regarding its component features, its class memberships, its lexical status, etc.) should take longer than reading or naming because these other responses involve more complicated internal memory transformations than does reading, which is almost automatic.

It is interesting to note that this analysis easily accounts for the Stroop (1935) word-intereference color naming effect. The name of the intereferring color-name word is available to the observer before the name of the ink or background color. Thus, the word-reading response interferes with the color-naming response. In a similar manner, Theios' (1975) analysis also predicts that there should be a word-interference letter counting effect.[6] The experimental stimuli would be the words *zero, one, two, three, four, five, six, seven, eight, nine,* and *ten.* Controls would be nonword letter strings or other words with corresponding number of letters, word frequency, and discriminability. The observer's task would be to respond with the *number of letters* in the word or letter string. The prediction would be that the observer's performance would be poor on the number words, somewhat better on other words, and best of all on letter strings low on English orthography, for example, consonant clusters.

If further experimental research shows that the observer has the word name and meaning available before other types of information (such as featural, graphemic, phonemic, and categorical) then a severe theoretical strain would be placed on the serial hierarchical word recognition model of Gibson (1971) and LaBerge and Samuels (1974). At the moment, however, this remains an empirical question.

On the other hand, in the experiments considered in this chapter, the observers were asked to read individually presented words of unconnected text. A case could be made that in laboratory tasks using this procedure, the subjects may simply articulate the presented letter strings according to letter-to-sound correspondence before an understanding of the semantic content of the word is achieved. If this is the case, then orthographic and semantic as well as phonetic factors contribute to articulation. The articulation of observers in Nodine and Hardt's (1969) experiment and our Experiment II was slowed down by uncommon orthography. However, the deficit in articulatory speed caused by uncommon orthography was overcome somewhat if the phonology of the word mapped onto a real word. In the case of pseudohomophones, the deficit in articulatory speed was no larger than that suffered by real syllables of the language which presumably have a somewhat lower semantic content than pseudohomophones. If our observers were simply articulating the letter strings without really "reading" them, then both orthographic and semantic factors enter into the articulatory process.

[6] This experiment was suggested to us by Professor Donald Foss of the University of Texas at Austin.

Finally, it could be argued that we have been comparing different response systems, the vocal with the manual. Thus the differences in reaction times could be due not to cognitive processing differences, but simply due to response processes such as response determination, response selection, and response evocation. In future research, response processes hopefully could be controlled by careful experimentation. Either way, Theios' (1975) analysis predicts that, controlling for stimulus uncertainty, a reading response should generally be faster than other, more traditional "experimental psychology" manual responses, because typically a word can be read only one way, and thus in reading, response uncertainty is minimal, while practice and stimulus–response compatibility are maximal. However, with arbitrarily assigned responses, such as button pushes or other classification response, practice is minimal, response uncertainty is high, and stimulus–response compatibility is often low.

A TENTATIVE MODEL FOR WORD IDENTIFICATION IN READING

Our consideration of the research on word identification has led us to the following, tentative analysis of the word identification process in reading.

A saccadic movement of the eye focuses the fovea typically one one or two words (8–10 characters and spaces). An iconic representation of the word or words is set up in a sensory store in the central nervous system. The iconic image is processed in parallel and an analysis of the pattern of featural information (including orthographic structure) leads directly to various areas in long-term memory where information regarding the stimulus is stored. It is possible that the parallel identification process could be a holographic system (e.g. Pribram, Nuwer, & Baron, 1974) or a matched filter system (e.g., Anderson, 1973, in press). However, alternative parallel processing systems are just as viable (e.g., Spinelli, 1970). The locations in memory which are activated by the analysis of the iconic representation may be considered as the set of memory files from which other information associated with the stimuli may be retrieved. Owing to either primacy in acquisition or asymptotic practice, the articulatory name code of a word or alphanumeric character is so close in its informational form to the memory file codes of its processed visual representation, that the response of reading the character or word can be accessed, retrieved, and executed before most other associated response codes. Thus, in tasks requiring decisions regarding letters embedded in a word, lexicality of a letter string, categorization or classification of a word, or semantic associates of a word, the response should take longer than the almost automatic reading response. Indeed, a covert reading response may take place prior to all of these other types of responses. Cognition or the understanding of a word may come early in processing, at the name code level, or later, at a general semantic level. A rough diagram of the system for reading which we have in mind is represented in Fig. 2. Clearly our conjectures will have to be checked by further experimental research which is specifically designed to trace out the time course of the information available to the observer during reading.

SUMMARY AND CONCLUSIONS

We first reviewed current conceptions of the word identification process in reading. The dominant belief among current theorists is that of a sequential, hierarchical process. A visually displayed word is assumed to be first analyzed at a feature level, then a letter level, then an orthographic or syllabic level, followed by a phonological analysis which leads to semantic comprehension. The theorists disagree on how much of the word processing sequence is performed in parallel and how much is serial processing.

The hypothesis that visually displayed words are processed letter by letter can be rejected out of hand owing to the experimental research of Cattell (1886) and Johnson (1975). Similarly, there is little evidence that words are processed syllable by syllable (Johnson, 1975). The experimental evidence does suggest, however, that the letters and other features of a visually displayed word are operated on in parallel leading to the extraction of orthographic, phonetic, and semantic information. It is widely held that context and redundancy speed up the word identification process. However, experimental manipulation of word uncertainty has no effect on the speed of word identification (Perlmutter et al., 1976; Pierce & Karlin, 1957).

There is very little hard experimental data to support the consensus opinion that orthographic information is processed before phonetic information which is processed before semantic information. Our experiments with paired homophonic words and nonwords showed that good phonology or letter-to-sound correspondence is not sufficient to completely mediate the transformation from a visual representation of a word to its articulation. Familiar orthography and meaning do have a small effect on the speed of articulation of pronounceable strings of letters. Our experiments also showed that the frequency of the word in the English language has a very small, but consistent effect on the speed of articulating individually presented words.

Given a consideration of the sparse experimental data that exist on word identification in actual *reading* tasks, there is little evidence that favors a serial, sequential, hierarchical processing model over a parallel processing model. Specifically, the data are consistent with a theoretical process which assumes that the features of a visually displayed word represented in iconic memory map onto the addresses of a set of long-term memory files which contain information regarding the phonological, orthographic, and semantic properties of the word.

The articulatory memory code for a word is so close in its informational form to the memory code of its processed visual representation that the response of reading a word can be accessed, retrieved, and executed before most other, associative responses. Thus, in tasks requiring decisions regarding letters embedded in a word, lexicality of a letter string, categorization of a word, or semantic associates, the response should take longer than the almost automatic reading response. The question of whether cognition or the understanding of a word comes early in processing at the phonological level or later at a general semantic level will have to be decided by future research involving cleverly designed reading experiments.

ACKNOWLEDGMENTS

This research was supported in part by United States Public Health Service Grant MH-19006 from the National Institute of Mental Health and represents the collective efforts of a research team which included John Aeschlimann, Diane Flakas, Marie Kestol, Catherine Muise, Susan Nerlinger, Pam Sutherland, and the authors.

This research was conducted in part while John Theios was on research leave during the academic year 1974–1975 at the Rockefeller University. The research leave was made possible through awards from the James McKeen Cattell Fund, The Graduate School of the University of Wisconsin, and the Rockefeller University. Much thanks and appreciation is due to Professor William K. Estes of The Rockefeller University for his generous hospitality, use of his laboratory, and general research support provided through Public Health Service Research Grant MH-23878. Appreciation is also acknowledged to our colleague Dominic Massaro for the many hours of critical discussion of the issues addressed in this paper.

REFERENCES

Anderson, J. A. Neural models with cognitive implications. In D. LaBerge & S. J. Samuels (Eds.), *Perception and comprehension.* Hillsdale, New Jersey: Lawrence Erlbaum Assoc., in press.

Anderson, J. A. A theory for the recognition of items from short memorized lists. *Psychological Review*, 1973, 80, 417–438.

Archer, E. J. A reevaluation of the meaningfulness of all possible CVC trigrams. *Psychological Monographs*, 1960, 74, Whole No. 497.

Attneave, F. *Applications of information theory to psychology.* New York: Holt, 1959.

Carrol, J. B., Davies, P., & Richman, B. *Word frequency book,* New York: Houghton Mifflin, 1971.

Cattell, J. McK. The time taken up by cerebral operations. *Mind,* 1886, 11, 220–242, 377–392, and 524–538.

Chomsky, N. & Halle, M. *The sound pattern of English.* New York: Harper & Row, 1968.

Donders, F. C. Over de snelheid van psychische processen. Onderzoekingen gedaan in bet Physiologisch Loboratorium der Utrechtsche Hoogeschool, 1868–1869, Tweede reeks, II, 92–120. Translated by W. G. Koster in W. G. Koster (Ed.), *Attention and Performance II. Acta Psychologica,* 1969, 30, 412–431.

Estes, W. K. Memory, perception, and decision in letter identification. In R. L. Solso (Ed.), *Information processing and cognition: The Loyola Symposium.* Hillsdale, New Jersey: Lawrence Erlbaum Assoc., 1975.

Estes, W. K., Allmeyer, D. H., & Reder, S. Serial position functions for letter identification at brief and extended exposure durations. *Perception & Psychophysics,* 1976, **19,** 1–15.

Forster, K. I. & Chambers, S. M. Lexical access and naming time. *Journal of Verbal Learning and Verbal Behavior,* 1973, **12,** 627–635.

Gibson, E. J. Perceptual learning and the theory of word perception. *Cognitive Psychology,* 1971, **2,** 351–368.

Gough, P. B. One second of reading. *Visible Language,* 1972, **6,** 291–320.

Hansen, D. & Rogers, T. An exploration of psycholinguistic units in initial reading. In K. S. Goodman (Ed.) *The psycholinguistic nature of the reading process.* Detroit, Michigan: Wayne State University Press, 1968.

Hyman, R. Stimulus information as a determinant of reaction time. *Journal of Experimental Psychology,* 1953, **45,** 188–196.

Johnson, N. F. On the function of letters in word identification: Some data and a preliminary model. *Journal of Verbal Learning and Verbal Behavior,* 1975, **14,** 17–29.

Kučera, H. & Francis, W. N. *Computational analysis of present-day American English.* Providence, Rhode Island: Brown University Press, 1970.

LaBerge, D. & Samuels, S. J. Toward a theory of automatic information processing in reading. *Cognitive Psychology,* 1974, **6,** 293–323.

Massaro, D. W. Primary and Secondary Recognition in Reading. Chapter 7 in D. W. Massaro (Ed.) *Understanding language: An information processing analysis of speech perception, reading, and psycholinguistics.* New York: Academic Press, 1975. Pp. 241–289.

McConkie, G. W. & Rayner, K. The span of the effective stimulus during a fixation in reading. *Perception and Psychophysics,* 1975, **17,** 578–586.

Merkel, J. Die zeitlichen Verhältisse der Willensthätigkeit. *Philosophische Studien,* 1885, **2,** 73–127.

Meyer, D. E. & Ellis, G. B. Parallel processes in word-recognition. Paper presented at the Annual Psychonomic Society Meeting, San Antonio, Texas, November 5–7, 1970.

Meyer, D. E., Schvaneveldt, R. W., & Ruddy, M. Functions of graphemic and phonemic codes in visual word-recognition. *Memory & Cognition,* 1974, **2,** 309–321.

Meyer, D. E., Schvaneveldt, R. W., & Ruddy, M. Loci of contextual effects on visual word-recognition. In P. M. A. Rabbitt & S. Dornic (Eds.), *Attention and Performance.* Vol. V. London: Academic Press, 1975. Pp. 98–118.

Morton, J. Interaction of information in word recognition. *Psychological Review,* 1969, **76,** 165–178.

Noble, C. E. Measurements of association value (*a*), rated associations (*a'*), and scaled meaningfulness (*m'*) for the 2100 CVC combinations of the English alphabet. *Psychological Reports,* 1961, **8,** 487–521.

Nodine, C. F., & Hardt, J. V. A measure of pronounciability of CVC trigrams. *Behavioral Research Methods and Instrumentation,* 1969, **1,** 210–216.

North, J. A., Grant, D. A., & Fleming, R. A. Choice reaction times to single digits, spelled numbers, "right" and "wrong" arithmetic problems and short sentences. *Quarterly Journal of Experimental Psychology,* 1967, **19,** 73–77.

Perlmutter, J., Sorce, P., & Myers, J. L. Retrieval processes in recall. *Cognitive Psychology,* 1976, **8,** 32–63.

Pierce, J. R., & Karlin, J. E. Reading rates and the information rate of a human channel. *Bell Systems Technical Journal,* 1957, **36,** 497–516.

Pribram, K. H., Nuwer, M., & Baron, R. J. The holographic hypothesis of memory structure in brain function and perception. In D. H. Krantz, R. C. Atkinson, R. D. Luce, & P.

Suppes (Eds.), *Contemporary developments in mathematical psychology.* Vol. II. San Francisco: Freeman, 1974. Pp. 417–457.

Rayner, K. The perceptual span and peripheral cues in reading. *Cognitive Psychology*, 1975, 7, 65–81.

Rubenstein, H., Garfield, L., & Millikan, J. A. Homographic entries in the internal lexicon. *Journal of Verbal Learning and Verbal Behavior*, 1970, 9, 487–494.

Rubenstein, H., Lewis, S. S., & Rubenstein, M. A. Homographic entries in the internal lexicon: Effects of systematicity and relative frequency of meanings. *Journal of Verbal Learning and Verbal Behavior*, 1971, 10, 57–62. (a)

Rubenstein, H., Lewis, S. S., & Rubenstein, M. A. Evidence for phonemic recoding in visual word recognition. *Journal of Verbal Learning and Verbal Behavior*, 1971, 10, 645–657. (b)

Rumelhart, D. E., & Siple, P. Process of recognizing tachistoscopically presented words. *Psychological Review*, 1974, 81, 99–118.

Shannon, C. E. Prediction and entropy of printed English. *Bell Systems Technical Journal*, 1951, 30, 50–64.

Smith, E. E., & Spoehr, K. T. The perception of printed English: A theoretical perspective. In B. H. Kantowitz (Ed.) *Human information processing: Tutorials in performance and cognition.* Hillsdale, New Jersey: Lawrence Erlbaum Assoc., 1974.

Smith, F. The use of featural dependencies across letters in the visual identification of words. *Journal of Verbal Learning and Verbal Behavior*, 1969, 8, 215–218.

Smith, F. *Understanding reading.* New York: Holt, Rinehart & Winston, 1971.

Solomon, R. L., & Postman, L. Frequency of usage as a determinant of recognition thresholds for words. *Journal of Experimental Psychology*, 1952, 43, 195–201.

Sperling, G. A model for visual memory tasks. *Human Factors*, 1963, 5, 19–31.

Spinelli, D. N. OCCAM, a content addressable memory model for the brain. In K. H. Pribram & D. Broadbent (Eds.), *The biology of memory*, New York: Academic Press, 1970. Pp. 293–306.

Spoehr, K. T., & Smith, E. E. The role of syllables in perceptual processing. *Cognitive Psychology*, 1973, 5, 71–89.

Spoehr, K. T. & Smith, E. E. The role of orthographic and phonotactic rules in perceiving letter patterns. *Journal of Experimental Psychology: Human Perception and Performance.* 1975, 104, 21–34.

Stroop, J. R. Studies of interference in serial verbal reactions. *Journal of Experimental Psychology*, 1935, 38,.643–662.

Theios, J. Reaction time measurements in the study of memory processes: Theory and data. In G. H. Bower (Ed.) *The psychology of learning and motivation: Advances in research and theory.* Vol. 7. New York: Academic Press, 1973. Pp. 43–85.

Theios, J. The components of response latency in simple human information processing tasks. In P. M. A. Rabbitt & S. Dornic (Eds.) *Attention and Performance.* Vol. V. London: Academic Press, 1975. Pp. 418–440.

Townsend, J. T., Taylor, S. G., & Brown, D. R. Lateral masking for letters with unlimited viewing time. *Perception and Psychophysics*, 1971, 10, 375–378.

Turvey, M. T. On peripheral and central processes in vision: Inferences from an information-processing analysis of masking with patterned stimuli. *Psychological Review*, 1973, 80, 1–52.

Underwood, B. J. & Schulz, R. L. *Meaningfulness & Verbal Learning.* Philadelphia, Pennsylvania: Lippincott, 1960.

Urdany, L. & Flexner, S. B. (Eds.) *The Random House dictionary of the English language, College Edition*, New York: Random House, 1969.

Venezky, R. L. English orthography: Its graphical structure and its relation to sound. *Reading Research Quarterly*, 1967, 2, 75–106.

Venezky, R. L. *The structure of English orthography*. The Hague: Mouton, 1970.

Venezky, R. L. Language and cognition in reading. In B. Spolsky (Ed.), *Current trends in educational linguistics*, The Hague: Mouton, 1974.

Webster's Seventh New Collegiate Dictionary, Springfield, Massachusetts: Merriam, 1971.

Whitford, H. C. *A dictionary of American homophones and homographs*. New York: Teachers College Press, 1966.

APPENDIX TABLE A

Mean Reading Latencies (msec) for 600 Homophonic Words

Higher-frequency word	RT	Lower-frequency word	RT	Higher-frequency word	RT	Lower-frequency word	RT	Higher-frequency word	RT	Lower-frequency word	RT
ADDS	551	ADZE	693	BLONDE	575	BLOND	566	CORPS	656	CORE	575
AID	526	AIDE	564	BORE	557	BOAR	595	CREEK	580	CREAK	586
ALE	543	AIL	567	BOARD	565	BORED	573	CREWS	602	CRUISE	649
AIR	538	HEIR	757	BOWED	604	BODE	576	CUE	560	QUEUE	794
ALL	542	AWL	560	BOLD	570	BOWLED	612	DAMN	571	DAM	543
AUNT	571	ANT	540	BOWL	562	BOLL	595	DAYS	560	DAZE	542
ARC	551	ARK	519	BORN	578	BORNE	552	DEAR	552	DEER	551
EIGHT	553	ATE	542	BREAK	602	BRAKE	557	DENSE	564	DENTS	544
EYE	540	AYE	628	BREACH	633	BREECH	578	DIE	528	DYE	574
BE	541	BEE	559	BREAD	573	BRED	613	DOUGH	564	DOE	522
BAIL	572	BALE	573	BROOD	601	BREWED	582	DONE	559	DUN	566
BALD	560	BAWLED	655	BRUISE	588	BREWS	600	DUAL	601	DUEL	607
BALL	582	BAWL	572	BROWS	562	BROWSE	571	EARN	571	URN	578
BOMB	573	BALM	543	BUST	529	BUSSED	615	YOU	527	EWE	675
BAND	536	BANNED	572	BUT	533	BUTT	556	FAINT	568	FEINT	620
BARRED	634	BARD	632	SEAS	588	SEIZE	645	FAIR	583	FARE	569
BEAR	581	BARE	548	CAST	562	CASTE	564	PHASE	600	FAZE	569
BASED	538	BASTE	598	CAUSE	574	CAWS	622	FEET	558	FEAT	659
BEACH	538	BEECH	577	SEED	600	CEDE	631	FIND	555	FINED	575
BEAT	540	BEET	585	CELL	574	SELL	569	FUR	585	FIR	630
BOW	590	BEAU	593	CHEAP	522	CHEEP	542	FLAIR	613	FLARE	603
BEEN	551	BIN	604	CHOOSE	566	CHEWS	542	FLEA	612	FLEE	588
BELL	536	BELLE	608	SHOOT	511	CHUTE	598	FOLD	553	FOALED	589
BIRTH	563	BERTH	581	CLOSE	596	CLOTHES	592	FOUL	564	FOWL	568
BLUE	557	BLEW	561	COURSE	590	COARSE	585	PHRASE	609	FRAYS	610
BLOCK	559	BLOC	548	COAX	587	COKES	609	GATE	567	GAIT	568

Word		Word		Word		Word		Word		Word	
GUILD	615	GILD	618	OUR	529	HOUR	565	MAZE	571	MAIZE	543
GUILT	584	GILT	550	IN	527	INN	545	MALL	558	MAUL	553
GOURD	606	GORED	640	JAM	540	JAMB	539	MAST	543	MASSED	610
GRADE	554	GRAYED	605	JINX	570	JINKS	566	MEET	548	MEAT	540
GREAT	575	GRATE	563	KNAVE	654	NAVE	611	MIGHT	536	MITE	533
GRAZE	598	GRAYS	605	NEED	577	KNEAD	620	MINCE	578	MINTS	543
GRILL	574	GRILLE	645	NEW	549	KNEW	565	MIND	557	MINED	557
GRIP	556	GRIPPE	591	NIGHT	531	KNIGHT	547	MINKS	547	MINX	559
GROWN	583	GROAN	585	NOT	523	KNOT	534	MISSED	538	MIST	535
GUEST	549	GUESSED	545	NO	528	KNOW	549	MOAN	545	MOWN	592
GUYS	544	GUISE	603	LACKS	592	LAX	526	MOAT	528	MOTE	524
HAIL	530	HALE	547	LAID	554	LADE	567	MODE	549	MOWED	572
HAIR	551	HARE	582	LANE	554	LAIN	583	MOOSE	589	MOUSSE	696
HALL	538	HAUL	535	LEE	570	LEA	578	MUST	560	MUSSED	581
HAVE	542	HALVE	604	LEACH	553	LEECH	557	NONE	566	NUN	581
HAY	526	HEY	538	LEAF	573	LEIF	580	OH	564	OWE	536
HEART	550	HART	571	LEAK	524	LEEK	555	OWED	579	ODE	584
HAZE	574	HAYS	542	LEAN	564	LIEN	644	ONE	524	WON	545
HEEL	559	HEAL	562	LEAST	581	LEASED	577	PACED	550	PASTE	565
HERE	566	HEAR	579	LENS	554	LENDS	558	PACKED	551	PACT	574
HEARD	580	HERD	555	LIE	534	LYE	601	PALE	553	PAIL	595
HEW	600	HUE	576	LOW	550	LO	553	PAIN	549	PANE	567
HIGH	516	HI	545	LOAD	558	LODE	567	PALL	592	PAWL	592
HIM	537	HYMN	565	LOAN	538	LONE	557	PAST	560	PASSED	556
WHORE	590	HOAR	559	LOCKS	529	LOX	546	PAUSE	626	PAWS	556
HORDE	580	HOARD	576	LOOT	576	LUTE	606	PEACE	578	PIECE	587
HORSE	569	HOARSE	542	MADE	543	MAID	565	PEEL	573	PEAL	580
HOSE	596	HOES	546	MAIL	551	MALE	536	PEARL	659	PURL	589
WHOLE	541	HOLE	524	MAIN	565	MANE	588	PEER	549	PIER	600

(Continued)

323

APPENDIX TABLE A (Continued)

Higher-frequency word	RT	Lower-frequency word	RT	Higher-frequency word	RT	Lower-frequency word	RT	Higher-frequency word	RT	Lower-frequency word	RT
PENNED	611	PEND	591	ROSE	536	ROWS	549	SOUL	560	SOLE	552
PIE	605	PI	594	WROTE	536	ROTE	549	SOLD	535	SOLED	612
PLANE	646	PLAIN	618	RUSE	603	RUES	610	SOME	582	SUM	561
PLATE	592	PLAIT	613	RUNG	562	WRUNG	581	SON	557	SUN	563
PLEASE	579	PLEAS	623	WRY	556	RYE	562	STAYED	600	STAID	645
PLUMB	595	PLUM	596	SACK	569	SAC	566	STARE	620	STAIR	615
POLE	564	POLL	610	SALE	556	SAIL	604	STAKE	592	STEAK	606
POUR	577	PORE	572	SEEN	544	SCENE	592	STEEL	625	STEAL	630
PRAY	567	PREY	600	SKULL	615	SCULL	626	STEP	628	STEPPE	622
PRIDE	562	PRIED	624	SEEM	589	SEAM	560	STYLE	572	STILE	655
PRIZE	562	PRIES	612	SEAR	596	SEER	600	SWAYED	604	SUEDE	601
PRINCE	598	PRINTS	588	SURF	623	SERF	570	SWEET	570	SUITE	615
PROSE	581	PROS	612	SURGE	600	SERGE	596	TEA	604	TEE	562
QUARTS	612	QUARTZ	624	SO	544	SEW	585	TACT	582	TACKED	568
WRAP	552	RAP	584	SHEAR	524	SHEER	499	TAX	546	TACKS	572
REAL	592	REEL	581	SHOE	495	SHOO	503	TAIL	583	TALE	553
WRECK	552	RECK	609	SHOWN	506	SHONE	559	TAUGHT	584	TAUT	580
REST	548	WREST	594	SICK	574	SIC	579	TEAM	572	TEEM	556
RETCH	580	WRETCH	562	SIDE	586	SIGHED	577	TENSE	547	TENTS	552
RHYME	568	RIME	576	SIZE	566	SIGHS	592	THERE	562	THEIR	558
RING	532	WRING	576	SIGN	565	SINE	593	THROUGH	625	THREW	613
RISE	550	RYES	555	SLAY	603	SLEIGH	610	THROW	590	THROE	640
ROW	558	ROE	558	SLIGHT	634	SLEIGHT	599	THROWN	587	THRONE	594
ROLE	572	ROLL	544	SORE	580	SOAR	541	TICK	547	TIC	624
RUDE	570	RUED	577	SWORD	616	SOARED	609	TIED	564	TIDE	560

Word	Pg	Word	Pg	Word	Pg	Word	Pg	Word	Pg	Word	Pg
TOE	549	TOW	583	VEIL	617	VALE	585	WARD	576	WARRED	643
TOLD	541	TOLLED	584	VILE	576	VIAL	583	WEAR	586	WARE	571
TON	536	TUN	565	WEIGHED	557	WADE	562	WAY	557	WEIGH	586
TOOL	552	TULLE	854	WAIL	540	WALE	565	WE	550	WEE	576
TRACT	567	TRACKED	584	WAIN	583	WANE	559	WEEK	563	WEAK	570
TROOP	546	TROUPE	621	WASTE	542	WAIST	536	WELD	596	WELLED	546
TRUST	543	TRUSSED	623	WAIT	531	WEIGHT	565	WOULD	565	WOOD	563
TUCKS	554	TUX	545	WAVE	548	WAIVE	566				
BY	504	BUY	507	BYE	551	OR	550	ORE	610	OAR	543
BRAISE	620	BRAYS	583	BRAZE	581	PAIR	545	PEAR	553	PARE	603
CENT	569	SCENT	592	SENT	577	PEAK	560	PIQUE	610	PEEK	557
CHORD	623	CORD	582	CORED	624	PRAISE	611	PRAYS	566	PREYS	591
SIGHT	552	SITE	615	CITE	595	RAIN	588	REIGN	588	REIN	562
DO	541	DUE	552	DEW	583	RAISE	557	RAYS	571	RAZE	563
FAIN	593	FANE	574	FEIGN	564	ROAD	556	RODE	552	ROWED	589
FLEW	623	FLU	593	FLUE	612	TEASE	551	TEAS	584	TEES	570
FOR	561	FOUR	586	FORE	601	TO	546	TWO	530	TOO	565
FRIEZE	650	FREEZE	601	FREES	602	TOAD	564	TOWED	568	TOED	561
KNOWS	550	NOSE	576	NOES	553	VEIN	565	VAIN	581	VANE	584
SENSE	576			CENTS	556	CENSE	578	SCENTS	604		
RIGHT	536			WRITE	546	WRIGHT	585	RITE	544		

325

APPENDIX TABLE B

Mean Reading Latencies (msec) for 100 Homophonic Words and Pseudowords

Word	RT	Pseudoword	RT	Word	RT	Pseudoword	RT	Word	RT	Pseudoword	RT
BEAK	557	BEEK	541	FEEL	543	FEAL	566	PHONE	542	FONE	563
BEAR	550	BAIR	560	FIGHT	535	FITE	535	PHRASE	573	FRAZE	564
BEARD	547	BEERD	549	FIRST	523	FERST	577	PLAID	579	PLAD	608
BIRD	532	BURD	549	FLIGHT	560	FLITE	567	RAIN	532	RANE	553
BLADE	544	BLAID	582	FLOOD	561	FLUD	588	ROOM	545	RUME	594
BOARD	541	BORD	536	FOLKS	522	FOKES	531	SAID	567	SED	603
BOAT	515	BOTE	522	GEAR	576	GEER	596	SCALP	635	SKALP	650
BRAIN	529	BRANE	531	GLADE	565	GLAID	604	SCHEME	671	SKEME	659
BRIGHT	528	BRITE	518	GREASE	559	GREESE	555	SET	567	CET	717
BROOM	552	BRUME	577	GROAN	553	GRONE	546	SLACK	591	SLAC	627
CAKE	528	CAIK	633	GROW	526	GROE	575	SMALL	608	SMAUL	633
CALF	557	CAFF	556	HALF	524	HAFF	534	SNAIL	612	SNALE	611
CALL	534	CAUL	558	HEAD	524	HED	540	SNEER	639	SNEAR	650
CAN	534	KAN	569	HEALTH	525	HELTH	527	SOAK	578	SOKE	576
CAPE	553	CAIP	595	HEAR	531	HEER	556	STAIN	597	STANE	611

CARE	541	CAIR	604	HOME	511	HOAM	547	STALE	609	STAIL	616
CHANCE	533	CHANSE	570	KEEP	535	KEAP	571	STRAIT	605	STRATE	603
CHEAT	529	CHEET	534	KEY	563	KEE	624	STREAK	613	STREEK	613
CHEER	534	CHEAR	557	KNACK	563	NACK	549	SURE	476	SHURE	489
CHEF	577	SHEF	586	KNIFE	516	NIFE	534	TAPE	539	TAIP	590
CHIEF	557	CHEEF	625	KNOCK	513	NOCK	520	THIRD	533	THERD	560
CLIMB	548	CLIME	551	LAME	529	LAIM	552	TIGHT	533	TITE	556
CLOAK	564	CLOKE	579	LEAF	559	LEEF	564	TOUGH	546	TUFF	559
COME	523	KUM	576	LIGHT	535	LITE	515	TRAIN	538	TRANE	551
COURT	536	KORT	576	LORE	539	LOAR	568	TRAIT	551	TRATE	553
CRAWL	563	CRALL	581	MEAN	542	MEEN	555	TUNE	548	TOON	570
DANCE	512	DANSE	537	MEEK	518	MEAK	518	VOTE	531	VOAT	582
DARE	518	DAIR	555	MERE	534	MEER	544	WADE	532	WAID	554
DEAD	544	DED	535	MONK	540	MUNK	510	WAIT	519	WATE	534
DIME	505	DYME	535	MORE	534	MOAR	540	WEAVE	562	WEEVE	584
DOOR	521	DORE	538	NAIL	535	NALE	544	WEIRD	558	WEERD	570
FAIL	534	FALE	560	NEED	538	NEAD	585	WHITE	521	WITE	565
FAME	544	FAIM	553	NOTE	522	NOAT	539	WORE	550	WOR	578
FEAR	562	FEER	550								

Author Index

Subject Index